THE
INVISIBLE
SPY

THE INVISIBLE SPY

CHURCHILL'S ROCKEFELLER CENTER SPY RING AND AMERICA'S FIRST SECRET AGENT OF WORLD WAR II

THOMAS MAIER

HANOVER
SQUARE
PRESS

**HANOVER
SQUARE
PRESS**™

ISBN-13: 978-1-335-00060-6

The Invisible Spy

Hanover Square Press
22 Adelaide St. West, 41st Floor
Toronto, Ontario M5H 4E3, Canada
HanoverSqPress.com

Printed in U.S.A.

To Joyce and my family,

To Scott E. Schwimer, my entertainment attorney and friend.

And to the memory of Jonathan Cuneo, who shared so many of his insights for this book.

Also by Thomas Maier

Mafia Spies: The Inside Story of the CIA, Gangsters, JFK, and Castro

When Lions Roar: The Churchills and the Kennedys

The Kennedys: America's Emerald Kings

Masters of Sex: The Life and Times of William Masters and Virginia Johnson, the Couple Who Taught America How to Love

Dr. Spock: An American Life

Newhouse: All the Glitter, Power, and Glory of America's Richest Media Empire and the Secretive Man Behind It

All That Glitters: Anna Wintour, Tina Brown, and the Rivalry Inside America's Richest Media Empire

Montauk to Manhattan: An American Novel

THE
INVISIBLE
SPY

"I always liked to keep out of sight. Anonymity is freedom."
—**Ernest Cuneo**

TABLE OF CONTENTS

A NOTE TO THE READER

The world of *The Invisible Spy*—recounting the life and times of Ernest Cuneo—bears a remarkable resemblance to the headlines of today. Then, as now, America faced a daunting wartime challenge.

Looking back, Cuneo was the kind of "invisible" figure easily ignored by historians, especially those who focus on the "great" men and women of an age. Indeed, only in writing previous histories involving Winston Churchill and the Kennedys did I stumble upon obscure mentions of Cuneo and the British intelligence agency hidden in New York.

As a native New Yorker, I was amazed that hundreds of Churchill's spies, headquartered in a looming tower at Rockefeller Center, once worked on clandestine missions inside America without public notice. By actively helping the British as President Franklin D. Roosevelt's secret go-between, Cuneo became the first American spy of World War II.

Throughout his career, Cuneo avoided drawing attention to his actions. He rarely sought credit or public acclaim. Though once a National Football League player in New York, Cuneo eschewed fame the way that others crave it. His role as US "liaison" with Churchill's spies was deliberately vague, allowing him tremendous leeway. His work was top secret and hard to trace. His future wife, a Canadian spy whom he met and romanced at Rockefeller Center, also kept silent. And so did their friends and colleagues, as though they were invisible as well.

Cuneo was a spy in the broadest sense, with multiple duties and areas of influence. In some cases, he became involved in Sherlock Holmes–like sleuthing, calculating how to thwart the Nazis. More significantly, he worked closely with Churchill's intelligence agents in New York and Washington, placing numerous propaganda items in the American press or secretly influencing US elections. With the Office of Strategic Services (OSS), America's first spy agency, Cuneo had his greatest impact, serving as its official intermediary with British and Canadian spies, the FBI, the Justice Department and the White House. Later, during the Cold War, Cuneo was a willing source for the CIA, and so inspired his pal Ian Fleming that the former British secret agent dedicated one of his James Bond spy novels to him. While sifting through Cuneo's shadowy world, I even found documents suggesting that he received leaked information from former CIA director Allen Dulles during the Warren Commission's investigation into the 1963 death of President John F. Kennedy.

For all his efforts to become an insider—educated at an Ivy League school and as a savvy White House lawyer—Cuneo never lost his sense of being an outsider, borne of his Italian-American family's immigrant experience. As his son told me for this book, some critics might call Cuneo a traitor if they knew of all his clandestine actions for the president, but he always thought of himself as a true American patriot, unselfishly dedicated to his country by remaining anonymous.

Cuneo's vast, kaleidoscopic life reflected so much of America in the 20th century. It provides a unique window into the worlds of US presidential politics, undercover Nazi spies and Russian double agents, wartime strategizing between Churchill and Roosevelt, assassination attempts against Hitler and other enemies, "kompromat" sex, Hollywood, professional football, and the manipulation of American media, during both World War II and the ensuing Cold War.

The Invisible Spy slowly came into view, like an elaborate jig-saw puzzle, as I put together many pieces of information from once classified documents. Told through the dramatic stories of many spies and operatives involved directly and indirectly with Cuneo, this book details the origins of modern US intelligence, eventually leading to what is now the Central Intelligence Agency.

Like a real-life James Bond tale, this spy book is filled with extraordinary acts of heroism, violence, betrayal and seemingly endless intrigue. Ultimately, though, it examines what spying really means—on the deepest personal level—to one's sense of truth, love, loyalty and desire for lasting recognition.

—Thomas Maier, Long Island, New York

CAST OF CHARACTERS

ERNEST CUNEO—*Ex-NFL player, attorney, liaison between White House and Churchill's spies.*

WINSTON CHURCHILL—*Prime Minister of Great Britain, sanctioned US spy mission at Rockefeller Center.*

FRANKLIN D. ROOSEVELT—*President of the United States, used Cuneo as spy, propagandist and political fixer.*

WILLIAM "INTREPID" STEPHENSON—*Canadian war hero, oversaw Churchill's spies at Rockefeller Center.*

IAN FLEMING—*British spy, met Cuneo at Rockefeller Center, later author of James Bond spy novels.*

WILLIAM "WILD BILL" DONOVAN—*Headed first US spy agency, Office of Strategic Services (OSS).*

MARGARET WATSON—*Canadian secretary hired by Stephenson for spy work, married Cuneo in 1946.*

ZILPHA BENTLEY—*Columbia University student and first wife of Cuneo.*

WALTER WINCHELL—*Famous American radio and newspaper columnist, hired Cuneo as lawyer.*

DREW PEARSON—*Washington investigative columnist, teacher, friend and legal client of Cuneo.*

FIORELLO LAGUARDIA—*New York mayor and congressman who mentored Cuneo in politics.*

ADOLF BERLE—*Assistant US Secretary of State and friend of Cuneo at Columbia.*

J. EDGAR HOOVER—*Director of FBI and longtime contact with Cuneo.*

ALLEN DULLES—*OSS spy during World War II who later became CIA director.*

IVAR BRYCE—*British spy and childhood pal of Fleming who became Cuneo's business partner.*

H. MONTGOMERY HYDE—*Spy for Stephenson and later chronicler of British Security Coordination.*

STEWART MENZIES—*Known as "C," head of Churchill's spy agency in London.*

WILHELM CANARIS—*Hitler's spy chief, approved attack in US, became Allied double agent.*

KURT LUDWIG—*Nazi agent, headed US spy ring, involved in fatal Times Square incident.*

CHARLES LINDBERGH—*Aviation hero, promoted fascist America First movement.*

JOSEPH P. KENNEDY—*Father of JFK, wartime US ambassador in London, embarrassed by spy scandal.*

TYLER KENT—*American Nazi mole inside Ambassador Kennedy's London embassy, caught by Churchill's spies.*

AMY PACK—*British spy in America code-named "Cynthia," involved in sexual "kompromat" cases.*

ELIZABETH BENTLEY—*American who was a Soviet spy and recanted to the FBI as the Cold War began.*

JOSEPHINE BAKER—*Singer and French Resistance spy, disputed Winchell over Stork Club racial incident.*

ROALD DAHL—*British spy in Washington and future novelist, one of several writers in BSC.*

JOHN F. KENNEDY—*America's 35th President; FBI learned of Cuneo's inside source in Warren Commission probe of JFK's assassination.*

CHARLES HOWARD "DICK" ELLIS—*Stephenson's trusted deputy overseeing Churchill's spies at Rockefeller Center.*

PART I

Never Cease to Dare

"Today, Winston Churchill is the center of the British political arena... Mr. Churchill is audacity incarnate. He will dare, and never cease to dare."

—The American Monthly Review of Reviews, May 1905

"Never say 'no' to adventures. Always say 'yes.' Otherwise you'll lead a very dull life."

—Ian Fleming

Rockefeller Center,
Secret Headquarters of Churchill's Spies

Winston Churchill authorized a huge spy and propaganda operation inside America when he became British Prime Minister in May 1940 as Nazi bombs rained down on wartime London. Churchill's agents were stationed inside Rockefeller Center's International Building and worked with Ernest Cuneo, including a female Canadian agent who eventually became Cuneo's wife.

1

THE SPIES OF ROCKEFELLER CENTER

On the chilly Tuesday evening of March 18, 1941, two Nazi spies walked briskly through Manhattan's busy Times Square, carrying secret papers in a leather satchel. The blinding streetlights and nighttime shadows shrouded them like ghouls full of malice and murder.

Wary of being spotted, the two undercover agents dressed like other nondescript men in winter coats, wool scarves and fedora hats on the streets that night. Mundanity served as their disguise. One German agent, with horn-rimmed glasses, clutched his briefcase as he weaved through the crowd. The other spy, shorter and with blond hair, followed along diligently. They'd just come from a Midtown restaurant, where money and important papers from their homeland had been exchanged.

As the curtains fell at nearby Broadway theaters and movie palaces, departing audiences poured into the Midtown intersection known as "the Crossroads of the World." Flashing billboards and illuminated marquees cast a hazy glow above, as if protecting the city within a bubble.

There was little hint that the world was about to change, nor of the damage these two spies planned to inflict.

Most Americans were still isolationists. They didn't want the long Depression to be followed by an endless war in Europe similar to World War I. The nation seemed asleep to the dangers it faced, both from afar and in its own backyard.

During the past two years, the military machine of German dictator Adolf Hitler had advanced across Europe without mercy. It had crushed France, Belgium, Poland, Czechoslovakia and the Netherlands. Great Britain—at war against the Nazis since September 1939—now seemed Hitler's next target for invasion.

With bombs already falling on London, Prime Minister Winston Churchill gratefully accepted the American government's "lend-lease" of aircraft, tanks, battleships and other weaponry that same month of March 1941, in a desperate attempt to save his United Kingdom.

Steadily, the White House expressed concern about Hitler's aggression and talk of German spies infiltrating the United States. "Nazi forces…openly seek the destruction of all elective systems of government on every continent—including our own," warned President Franklin Roosevelt in a speech on March 15, 1941.

Yet in many ways, America—still officially neutral—averted its gaze as Europe went up in flames.

In Times Square that night, none of the theatergoers strolling by were aware of the two Nazi spies scheming to blow up New York City. Most headed home safely. Others sauntered over to eateries and bars like Sardi's for a nightcap.

However, the anonymity of the two German agents was shattered when they reached the intersection of Broadway, Seventh Avenue and 45th Street. The taller man with his briefcase suddenly crossed against a traffic light. His action—perhaps out of nervousness, perhaps in response to some perceived threat—proved catastrophic.

When the Nazi spy stepped off the sidewalk, a taxicab slammed into his body, knocking him unconscious. He collapsed onto the street along with his briefcase. An instant later, another oncoming car ran him over. The unforgiving vehicle cracked his skull like an egg.

The crash horrified onlookers. With broken bones and bloody clothes, the man remained on the pavement, unmoving. His flesh was exposed amid the cobblestones and cement. Nearly everyone in the crowd appeared transfixed by this tragedy—all except one.

Quickly, the other Nazi spy snatched the briefcase and fled the scene. He ignored his mortally injured companion. He left it to passersby to call for help.

When New York police arrived, detectives rifled through the dead man's clothes, searching for his identity. Papers in his pockets claimed he was "Senor Don Julio Lopez Lido," a message courier for Spain. Over the next few days, though, the Spanish embassy insisted there was no record of such a man. The stranger's corpse remained unclaimed.

Through their investigation, the New York police found the dead man kept a notebook with the names of American soldiers and strategic places in the New York area ripe for sabotage. There was even mention of a naval base in the Pacific, a place called Pearl Harbor. Oddly, all of these papers were written in German.

The baffled New York detectives called in the Federal Bureau of Investigation, then led by J. Edgar Hoover, its much-celebrated chief. But Hoover's "G-men," as his government agents were touted in the popular press, couldn't figure out the identity of the dead man from Times Square either. The answer wouldn't come until another set of foreign spies—already implanted in America—provided a crucial and ominous clue.

Around this time, at their secret headquarters high atop Rockefeller Center in Manhattan, spies sent by Winston Churchill gathered to share intelligence with a little-known White House insider named Ernest Cuneo. He was the sole representative of the United States government in the room.

Cuneo was an imposing man, heavyset and prematurely balding. He spoke energetically and with the snappy diction of a New York tabloid. Street-smart and media savvy, he was a gregarious, Ivy League–educated lawyer who'd once played professional football in the NFL before working for the president. At age thirty-five, Ernie embodied the stereotype of the big brash American. He was inclined to use gridiron phrases in conversation with the British and Canadian spies, as if they were all on the same team.

This group of intelligence agents met throughout 1941 to discuss many confidential concerns. Their latest mystery—the unknown spy killed in Times Square—would be added to the list. Cuneo and Churchill's secret agents, including the debonair Ian Fleming, future creator of the James Bond novels, talked discreetly about the Nazi threat inside America. They were determined to stop it—violently if necessary.

"The British are many things," Cuneo later observed, "but cowards they are not."

Rockefeller Center, with its Art Deco facades and stylish shops, seemed an unlikely setting for these secret meetings. From the skyscraper's thirty-sixth-floor windows, passersby below appeared like innocent pawns, oblivious to the ongoing chess match of international intrigue above. But for these two nations, the "great game" of spying had never seemed more urgent.

Although America had yet to declare war, Cuneo had already become the country's first spy of World War II. He knew how to keep secrets and a low profile, as if he were invisible.

"I always liked to keep out of sight," Cuneo explained about his espionage task, which was especially difficult given his ample girth and booming voice. "Anonymity is freedom."

For a while, virtually no one knew about this covert mission, set up by Churchill shortly after he became wartime leader of Great Britain in May 1940. This unprecedented foreign spy operation in the heart of New York City was unknown to virtually all Americans except Cuneo's boss, President Roosevelt.

The British agents impressed Cuneo with hard evidence that Nazi spies had infiltrated America, hatching plots for sabotage and destruction at an alarming scale. The explosions planned by the two Nazi spies in New York City were similar in scope to the successful 9/11 terror attacks decades later. Bombs from Hitler's planes had already killed thousands of civilians in London and throughout Europe, wrecking homes and lives and leaving cities in ruin. Yet the United States remained reluctant to join the conflict. Lending old battleships and weapons was one thing; sending troops to fight overseas was quite another.

Indeed, for many months before the Japanese attack on Pearl Harbor on December 7, 1941, the White House assured Americans that they would avoid getting into the fight against Hitler's regime.

During the November 1940 presidential campaign, FDR won an unprecedented third term with a promise of hands-off neutrality. "I have said this before, but I shall say it again and again—your boys are not going to be sent into any foreign wars," Roosevelt told a Boston crowd shortly before Election Day.

By then, however, the covert actions of Cuneo and Churchill's spies at Rockefeller Center belied FDR's public assurances. They were already at war.

As a spy, propagandist and secret fixer for the president, Cuneo served as an unseen middleman. He fed confidential tips and government propaganda—from both the White House and Great Britain—to the most famous newscasters of his time, Walter Winchell and Drew Pearson, and to the nation's top newspapers, reaching millions.

On numerous intelligence matters, Cuneo also acted as a key contact figure with the FBI, the Justice Department and the State Department. Eventually, he was appointed the official US "liaison" for the newly created Office of Strategic Services, headed by Colonel William "Wild Bill" Donovan—and the precursor of today's CIA.

No one quite compared to Cuneo. He often acted alone, as if a free agent. Yet like a good teammate, he regularly joined British and Canadian agents in carrying out a massive espionage campaign inside the United States—the biggest of its kind at that moment in history.

About a thousand spies, informers, tipsters and double agents would report to William Stephenson, mastermind of the British Security Coordination, as this clandestine outpost at Rockefeller Center was known. Stephenson, a wealthy Canadian businessman and former World War I flying ace, carried out his secret mission with a charismatic sense of adventure.

Using the cable address "Intrepid," which became his nickname, Stephenson executed Churchill's wishes with vigor and cunning. Fellow spy Fleming was inspired enough to use Stephenson as an exemplar for his fictional James Bond character. "He [Stephenson] is a man of few words and has a magnetic personality and the quality of making anyone ready to follow him to the ends of the earth," wrote Fleming.

As a spymaster, Stephenson understood the need to remain anonymous. Small and unremarkable in person, he could blend into a crowd without detection. As writer John le Carré later observed, "Few of the thousands who worked for him knew his name, let alone his face."

Over time and over drinks, Cuneo would become close friends with Stephenson and Fleming. He liked to share caviar, cocktails and confidential information with these undercover British agents while they sat beside the fireplace inside Stephenson's posh Midtown duplex.

Fleming, ever the wartime sophisticate, made sure the gin and dry vermouth he poured into his glass at their clubby meetings was prepared carefully, with what Cuneo described as the skill of a brain surgeon. Fleming preferred martinis—shaken, not stirred. He'd learned to smoke cigarettes with a holder held in place by his teeth. He was long and lean, certainly compared to Cuneo's broad physique. He mixed quips and bon mots among his puffs. The two became unlikely friends.

"Know what I'd like if I could have anything I wanted?" Fleming asked Cuneo on one tipsy occasion. "I'd like to be the absolute ruler of a country where everyone was crazy about me."

Both men burst out laughing, struck by the absurdity of the comment in a world dominated by an insane man—Hitler. Because they fancied themselves as writers, they enjoyed a good punch line or ironic twist to shield them from the ugliness of this reality.

After hours, Cuneo and Fleming liked to escort beautiful women—some of them spies as well—to various Manhattan hot spots, such as 21 and the Stork Club. One of them—Margaret Watson, an attractive Canadian staffer at Rockefeller Center—would become Cuneo's wartime lover and eventual wife.

Given the sensitivity of his role as a White House intermediary working clandestinely with Churchill's government, Cuneo had to be careful, and arguably the most discreet of all these spies. "Cuneo not only belonged to the President's Brains Trust, but was in a sense its coordinator as well as its link with Stephenson," recalled H. Montgomery Hyde, Stephenson's director of security.

This cadre of foreign agents inside New York had a three-fold mission. Most visibly, they protected Great Britain's shipping interests and vital supply lines needed for the ongoing war in Europe. As the Times Square incident revealed, they also conducted an undercover crusade against Nazis infiltrating the United States and the isolationist Americans who supported them.

But most important, Stephenson needed to convince America to join Britain's ongoing war in Europe. His carefully cultivated campaign—built on propaganda, political influence and dirty tricks—aimed to change the mood of public opinion. Given the strong opposition of US pacifists and prominent German sympathizers, this task would be the hardest of all.

Soon after becoming Great Britain's prime minister in May 1940, Winston Churchill dispatched a group of spies to New York's Rockefeller Center to keep an eye on pro-Nazi groups and help convince America to join the ongoing war against Hitler. Cuneo became their secret contact with the White House.

The undercover British spy operation in New York City, both audacious and likely illegal, was fundamentally a Churchillian idea. It was enacted with the unique daring and panache Winston exhibited his whole life. A prolific writer and historian (who later won a Nobel Prize in Literature), Churchill understood the power of words in determining a war's outcome. He also admired the mental tenacity and physical courage of men like Stephenson.

The enigma of spying appealed to Churchill throughout his career. During the First World War, known also as "the Great War," he reveled in the complexity of Britain's secret service missions. "Tangle within tangle, plot and counter-plot, ruse and treachery, cross and double-cross, true agent, false agent, double agent, gold and steel, the bomb, the dagger and the firing squad, were interwoven in many a texture so intricate as to be incredible and yet true," he described.

In this new war, espionage was even more complicated. The British couldn't take public credit for their intelligence successes in America, lest they arouse the ire and suspicions of an anti-war citizenry. From their Manhattan hideaway, Churchill's spies discreetly kept tabs on powerful isolationist Americans, such as Joseph P. Kennedy and Charles Lindbergh, and conspired against members of Congress and even those in FDR's administration who opposed them.

They were aided by prominent Brits in the United States—including Charlie Chaplin, Cary Grant, Alfred Hitchcock and Noël Coward—who passed along what they heard in Hollywood as well as Washington's social circles. "My celebrity value was a wonderful cover," explained Coward. Even Churchill's literary agent acted as an informer.

In this massive effort, no stone was left unturned, no spy tip ignored.

"For the British," Cuneo explained, "it was a life or death struggle."

That America lacked an adequate spy agency became brutally clear with the bloody Times Square incident in March 1941, a few months after Cuneo began his top secret work. While Hoover's FBI remained clueless about the dead man's identity, Stephenson's team at Rockefeller Center had a good idea who he was.

For months, British spies had been secretly opening mail from the United States involving suspected Nazi spies and their German-American sympathizers. They sifted through letters and packages in Bermuda—on their way to Europe—without detection. Any signs of impending danger were reported to Stephenson's staff in New York.

Some Nazi letters were written with invisible ink, as British chemists determined, made from a common drugstore powder given for headaches. Stephenson's team figured out the dead German spy's identity by reading one of these intercepted messages that contained a telltale clue.

The Nazi agent's real name was Captain Ulrich von der Osten, of the German military intelligence agency known as the Abwehr. Von der Osten, a chief aide to the Abwehr's legendary spymaster Wilhelm Canaris, had been sent to oversee Nazi covert operations within the United States. Hitler's generals anticipated America entering the war soon and dispatched teams of their own German spies to thwart that effort. Using an alias, von der Osten spent two nights in a Midtown Manhattan hotel before his fateful collision in Times Square.

With Stephenson's help, the FBI eventually caught up with the unknown companion who had fled the scene. His name was Kurt Frederick Ludwig, a German spy living in Queens, an outlying borough of New York, who used several aliases of his own.

If Ludwig thought he'd escaped successfully into the night, he was mistaken. In a remarkable stroke of luck, it was Ludwig's letter to his Nazi bosses—read by British censors working in the basement of a fancy hotel known as "the Pink Palace" in Bermuda—that described the Times Square crash. It even named the hospital where von der Osten's body had been taken.

Authorities quickly found Ludwig in New York but didn't arrest him. Instead, over the next five months, they kept Ludwig under surveillance, slowly collecting evidence of a Nazi spy ring, until the FBI finally apprehended him and several of his coconspirators.

The eye-opening twist of fate at Times Square led to the exposure of other instances of German espionage within the United States. That same year, the FBI arrested eight Nazi spies plotting to blow up power plants and other industrial targets. But unbeknownst to most Americans, the Nazis weren't the only ones with a foreign spy operation inside US borders.

★ ★ ★

As Cuneo began his secret mission in mid–1940, he realized that maintaining a good but hidden relationship with Churchill's spies would be essential. He had entered a high–stakes gambit with these British agents, with their headquarters hidden in the International Building, way above the skating rink and Christmas tree at Rockefeller Center. Outside the building stood a tall bronze statue of Atlas, the ancient Greek god, carrying the proverbial weight of the world on his shoulders. To Stephenson and his staff, the fate of Great Britain seemed no less a burden. Room 3603 was the center of undercover activity for the British Security Coordination office. As camouflage, a small sign carried the deceivingly innocuous name "British Passport Control" on its door.

By any measure, Churchill's undercover campaign in America was unprecedented, and far more extensive than the foreign spy efforts of either the Germans or the Soviet Union. Entrusting it to Stephenson, an inveterate risk–taker, was a calculated bet by Churchill that could blow up at any time.

Describing these risks, Cuneo later said Stephenson's BSC espionage agents "tampered with the mails, tapped telephones, smuggled propaganda into the country, disrupted public gatherings, covertly subsidized newspapers, radios, and organizations, perpetrated forgeries—even palming one off on the president of the United States (a map that outlined Nazi plans to dominate Latin America)—violated the aliens registrations act, shanghaied [sic] sailors numerous times, and possibly murdered one or more persons in this country."

This game of spying in the US had no rules, no assurances of safety. Cuneo's own part in sharing information with foreign spies might have been judged as treasonous by FDR's critics if they'd found out. But Cuneo believed Churchill's secret spy mission was vital to saving Western civilization from the looming threat of Hitler.

"My father…carried out things that Roosevelt wanted done, but Roosevelt needed deniability," recalled his son Jonathan Cuneo, a prominent Washington attorney. "He said if it ever came out what the British did, Roosevelt would be retroactively impeached. My father was a real idealist. If he thought it was the right thing, he did it."

Over time, Cuneo learned of a British "disposal squad," getting rid of those collaborating with the Nazis. He heard talk that the "accidental" Times Square killing may have been deliberate. In his unpublished memoir, Cuneo also made a fleeting reference to a British agent killed by a German spy near the intersection of Manhattan's 89th Street and East River Drive, not far from Gracie Mansion, the New York City mayor's residence.

This exchange of violence, no matter how discreet, was all part of the murky period before the US government formally went to war. As a go-between for the president, collaborating with a team of British spies, Cuneo made up his own rules of engagement as he went along. So did the man he referred to as "Intrepid."

"For security reasons, I can't tell you what sort of job it would be," Stephenson confided to Cuneo about his team's activities in the United States. "All I can say is that if you join us…you mustn't be afraid of murder."

2

ROAR OF THE CROWD

*After being a star football player at Columbia University, Cuneo went
on to play in the early days of the National Football League for the
Brooklyn Dodgers.*

JONATHAN CUNEO

*"Men have a solicitude about fame; and the greater share they
have of it, the more afraid they are of losing it."*

—Dr. Samuel Johnson

Covered in mud, sweat and blood, Ernest Cuneo marched off the field triumphantly, reveling in the game day violence of the fledgling National Football League. Being part of an underdog team was familiar to Cuneo. He'd been fighting against seemingly invincible opponents his whole life, starting with the same hardscrabble way he grew up.

On this late-September afternoon in 1929, his low-ranked team, the Orange Tornadoes, had wrestled its much stronger rival, the New York Giants, to a 0–0 tie.

"Both teams got inside the 10-yard line but neither was able to push the ball over," reported the *New York Times*. The home-town New Jersey crowd of nine thousand cheered for their rag-tag team after this dull, scoreless match as if it were a miraculous upset victory.

"Smash-mouth" football aptly described the NFL game in these early days. With little protection, combatants in the scrum like Cuneo wore minimal padding made of felt and wool. There were no face guards on their leather helmets. With abandon, they ran and hit each other at full speed. They were virtually defenseless compared to those wearing the hard plastic armor of today's NFL.

"It was a bruising game," Cuneo recalled. "We were playing because the game was in our blood, a compulsion that resulted from the spell of tremendous adrenaline-fueled exertion and excitement while under the influence of the crowd's applause."

At five feet nine inches tall, Cuneo carried 192 pounds on his stocky frame. With broad shoulders and a wide chest, he was built like a rounded Frigidaire, a human repository for food, with a healthy appetite and boundless energy. He needed every bit of his strength. He was expected to hit, block and tackle for all sixty minutes of each game, without substitution or a break.

Ernie, as his teammates called him, had expressive eyes that peered from beneath hooded lids and a gentle, ironic smirk that let friends know he was in on the joke. In his own way, Cuneo resembled another Depression-era player, Vince Lombardi, a fellow Italian American from New Jersey who played college ball at Fordham the same way Cuneo had played first for Penn State and later Columbia.

As professionals in a brand-new league, Cuneo and the other Tornadoes weren't paid much—between $50 to $75 per game—and sometimes not at all. Payment usually didn't arrive until the gate receipts of each game were collected. The most important compensation came in the reclaimed glory they once knew as college stars.

"We weren't playing for the money," Cuneo later explained. "Most of us as college athletes had gotten a good deal of 'fame,' as it is laughingly called, and, like many more important folk, we were the prisoners of that narcissistic narcosis currently referred to as our 'public image.'"

Wearing number 11 on his jersey, Cuneo served as a sort of jack of all trades lineman in the NFL. Depending on what was needed, he played either left or right guard—both offensively and defensively—as well as tackle and even center. He could usually be found in the thick of the gridiron action, knocking down opponents in between the hash lines.

Cuneo never appeared in the glory positions. He wasn't a quarterback throwing winning passes. Nor did he score touchdowns like the backfield runners and fleet-footed wide receivers. He wasn't a singular hero, as he'd sometimes been in college wrestling matches, but rather a faithful member of a struggling pro team, ready to enter the fray when called upon.

"For the addicted football player, the beautiful crisp autumn days bring an irresistible urge to spring down the sparkling green playing field and to set his fellow man flat on his derriere," he said.

The Tornadoes were a mediocre team, hovering above the Chicago Bears in the 1929 NFL standings, but well below the league-leading Green Bay Packers and Giants. Other squads from this primitive era included the Boston Bulldogs, Providence Steam Rollers and the Buffalo Bisons, all strapped for cash and fans.

The Tornadoes played on a scraggly grass field inside a make-shift stadium owned by the Knights of Columbus, a Roman Catholic fraternal group named for the famous explorer. The crowd for their scoreless season opener against the Giants proved to be their biggest of the year.

"Like the other teams, we weren't great, but we weren't slouches, either," Cuneo said. "We were, in the Damon Runyon vernacular, 'handy guys.'" In rowdy company outside of academe, Ernie enjoyed using slang like Runyon, New York's famous tabloid writer, whose stories later inspired the *Guys and Dolls* musical.

The Tornadoes team owner—a short, fat, wholesale meat salesman named Edwin "Piggy" Simandl—later sold his franchise, the remnants of which eventually became today's Washington Commanders. At the time, though, Ernie and his peers were amused by their pigskin impresario, hobnobbing with politicians and sponsors, trying to keep their team's finances afloat.

"Piggy was usually officious and bursting with his own importance," Cuneo recalled, "but he was flamboyantly agreeable, and everyone, including the team, liked him."

The same could be said of Cuneo himself. He had an outward affability that made him an easy teammate. But he also possessed a strong inner drive—an intellectual hunger and desire to make his own mark in other arenas—that eventually compelled him to reach for heights far beyond his humble origins.

The Cuneos were among the many Italian immigrant families who settled in the United States during the years surrounding Ernest's birth on May 27, 1905. Cuneo's father, John, had been a shopkeeper in Genoa, in the northern half of Italy; his mother, Louisa, came from the south. They both arrived in America shortly before the turn of the 20th century. They met and first lived in New York City before moving across the Hudson River to Carlstadt, New Jersey—a suburb about twelve miles from Manhattan—where their income improved steadily toward the middle class. The couple raised four children, including Ernest, the youngest.

As a youngster, Ernest became aware of anti-Italian bigotry and tried not to let it define him. His family avoided speaking Italian, even at home. Ernest fashioned himself as an all-American boy as much as he could, but faced difficulties attempting to climb the higher rungs of society. "Socially I think he was very insecure because he was Italian," recalled his daughter, Sandra Cuneo. "He was subject to a lot of discrimination as a child and young adult."

During the early 20th century, the steady influx of Italian immigrants, with their religious ties to Rome, stirred nativist resentments and not-so-subtle prejudices. These newcomers from the Mediterranean, like other minorities before and after, often found it difficult to blend into America's vision of a "melting pot."

Other first-generation Italian Americans in New Jersey shared similar feelings. "I saw myself always as an alien, an outsider," recalled writer Gay Talese, the son of Italian immigrants, in his memoir about growing up along the Jersey coast. "I was olive-skinned in a freckle-faced town, and I felt unrelated even to my parents, especially my father who was indeed a foreigner."

Though bright, curious and very verbal, Cuneo began as a lazy student with middling grades in public high school. However, his excellence in sports, as a champion wrestler and a standout in football, seemed to sharpen his attention in class, opening the door to greater possibilities.

While other family members toiled as local merchants, roofers and sheet metal handlers, Ernest relied on athletics to enter the very different realm of higher education. Going to college was still a rarity in most immigrant families. It gave Cuneo the chance to learn about a much wider world outside his New Jersey neighborhood.

At first, Cuneo went to Penn State, where he played on the freshman team. While Cuneo displayed talent on the field, he found the sprawling school's academics weak and unchallenging, with "a remarkable lack of intellectual effervescence." He had trouble fitting in. He endured numerous fistfights, and was stunned when the local Klu Klux Klan burned a cross near a Catholic Church.

The next semester, Cuneo left to enroll in Columbia University, the private Ivy League school in Manhattan. Sports again were a key to entrance. With the Lions, he eventually became a big man on campus—literally, if not figuratively—gaining recognition as a muscular wrestling and football star.

"*Columbia Matmen Top Harvard… Cuneo Gains Advantage,*" proclaimed the headline of a January 1929 *New York Times* story. It said "the [wrestling] meet, and especially the unlimited class bout between Ernest Cuneo and Captain Dike Howard of Harvard, was one of the best and most exciting ever held at Columbia."

On the gridiron, Cuneo attracted attention as an aggressive guard for the football team, earning all-Ivy, all-Eastern and all-American honors. He gained enough praise to land a professional job on the Orange Tornadoes, part of the emerging NFL, and became a local favorite.

Fame was alluring to young Cuneo. The roar of the crowd, the public acclaim, seeing his name in the newspaper, was a kind of validation for this immigrants' kid from Jersey. The rewards of playing football were worth the risk of bodily harm and injury. Like most gridiron gladiators, he felt invulnerable.

When Cuneo broke a bone during his amateur career, he wound up in the hospital. His psyche hurt most of all. "Recuperation and setting were painful," he recalled, "but nothing compared to the pain and humiliation of being merely human."

His hardworking father John—with his mix of old-world values and steadfast American practicality—condemned Ernest's foolhardy sport activities for which he was barely being compensated. Recovering in a hospital bed, Ernie asked when he might return to the field.

His father snapped, "Never." Cuneo had never witnessed his father's face so hard and stern. "Pay no attention to them," said the elder Cuneo. "They will destroy you."

"Destroy me?" Ernest repeated, dumbfounded by his father's reaction.

"Yes—destroy you," he insisted. "Look what they've done to you already."

Young Cuneo assured his father that the doctors expected his broken leg to heal quickly. He'd be back on the field in no time. "It's not so bad," Ernest insisted.

Cuneo's father realized his lesson wasn't getting through. His son didn't recognize the real malady that ailed him. The message he wanted to impart had to do with the lure of fame, the intoxicating applause his son thirsted for, the glory of the game at the cost of his body and soul.

"Oh, your leg is nothing. Nothing," his father repeated emphatically. "It's the plaudits of the mob. The plaudits of the mob that's gotten you."

Cuneo ignored his father's warning. Individual fame was only part of football's appeal to him. Being part of a team was also important, the sense of belonging to something bigger than oneself. He would always find great meaning through a joint cause, be it with sports or in other arenas. He seemed unable to resist the siren call of an energizing campaign.

"'The Team' was and is a special experience," he later explained. "Since the function of the whole is dependent upon the function of each, every team member has an electrical perception of the movement, strength and action pattern of his teammates. This becomes all but supersensory when the team is in action."

This rationale also seemed to inspire Cuneo's future actions on a team of spies where his code name was "Crusader."

Off the field, Columbia provided many other challenges for Cuneo, satisfying his abiding curiosity for the world around him. As a student, he befriended three liberal-minded teachers who would influence him greatly and affect his later career.

Drew Pearson taught an undergraduate course called "commercial geography" about geopolitics, before eventually moving to Washington, DC, where he became a nationally known syndicated newspaper columnist. At Columbia, Pearson encouraged Cuneo's interest in writing and Democratic politics. Cuneo also struck up a friendship with William O. Douglas, a Columbia law professor and future Supreme Court Justice. A fierce defender of civil rights and liberties, Douglas aligned politically with New York's then governor, Franklin D. Roosevelt, himself a Columbia Law School alumnus.

However, Adolf J. Berle Jr., a brilliant legal mind and foreign policy specialist, was the most influential Columbia teacher for Cuneo. After he obtained his undergraduate degree, Cuneo entered Columbia Law School and attended Berle's class. A critic of corporate power, Berle favored greater regulation of business. On his way to the presidency, FDR would rely on fellow Columbia alumni like Douglas, Berle and other Ivy League graduates. They advised him and eventually filled key positions in his administration.

But at Columbia, the person with the greatest impact on Cuneo was Zilpha Louise Bentley, a spritely young woman the same age as him. Despite their vastly different backgrounds, they soon became a couple, proving once again that in romance opposites often attract.

Born in March 1905, two months before Cuneo, Bentley's

early life in the Midwest was quaint and provincial, certainly compared to her boyfriend's rough-and-tumble existence. Following her birth in Missouri, Zilpha grew up in Richmond, Indiana, a tiny city along the Ohio border where the Wright Brothers once lived. She was the eldest child of the local schools' superintendent, Jerome Bentley, and his wife, also named Zilpha. A bucolic place founded by Quakers, Richmond prided itself on its literary arts clubs and cultural museum, home to two of Indiana's three Egyptian mummies.

The Bentleys were determined their bright daughter would go to college in New York City, the great metropolis. With its towering skyscrapers, New York seemed to offer the best of everything. By 1927, Wall Street was booming and the Yankees with Babe Ruth were baseball champs. That year, aviator Charles Lindbergh dazzled everyone with his solo flight across the Atlantic, from New York to Paris.

Uprooting themselves from their Indiana home, the Bentleys moved to Manhattan to oversee their daughter's success in education. At Columbia's Teachers College, Zilpha would win a national art design award, highlighting her talent with textiles and her promising future.

On the Morningside Heights campus, Ernie and Zilpha met and fell in love. As an athletic hero with an insider's knowledge of the big city, Cuneo surely impressed this small-town young woman. They married in June 1927 at the Riverside Drive home of Bentley's parents. The newlyweds moved to their own apartment on 113th Street near Columbia, and later to a downtown place in Greenwich Village.

While Zilpha worked on establishing her career, Cuneo tried to balance his demanding Columbia Law School studies with playing in the NFL—a seemingly impossible task for any man.

After the 1929 season with the Orange Tornadoes, Cuneo and some other teammates followed their coach to the Brooklyn Dodgers, a competing NFL franchise, for the next campaign.

These football Dodgers played at Ebbets Field, also the home of the more famous baseball team with the same name. The pigskin Dodgers were not quite as shaky financially as Piggy's money-losing team in New Jersey.

But the 1930 season didn't turn out well for Cuneo. He didn't play as often as he once did. He realized himself to be "sort of a run of the mill player among the pros," certainly not the star he had been at Columbia.

During one contest, Cuneo suffered "a deep forehead cut, an ugly gash just above my left eye which went down to the bone." His wound bled profusely. Afterward, it opened again every time he tried to play. Doctors feared he'd endanger his sight if he returned to his violent exchanges on the field.

Before the season ended, Cuneo's football days of fame and glory came to an ignominious finish. "I decided to quit before I lost the eye," he said.

Cuneo's law school career also suffered, forcing him to leave Columbia and finish his law degree through night classes at St. John's University. He managed to pay his bills by getting a part-time job at the *New York Daily News*, a scrappy tabloid. When the pro football season began again the following fall, Cuneo said he "nearly went mad." He missed the crowd's applause and the warm embrace he'd once experienced from fans.

Over the years, he'd witnessed other washed-up former players—addicted to the fame and glory of the game—who hung out at the stadium after their days were over, without any purpose. They seemed to have died a little when they handed in their jersey. For a year, Cuneo felt bad for himself, until finally it dawned on him that he too was addicted to fame.

"Cuneo, old boy, the trouble is with you," he thought to himself in an epiphany, recorded in his personal papers. "The people had sense enough to go home after the game and you're still in the stadium."

This realization loosened the chains on his imprisoned ego.

"I felt free, deliriously, incredibly free, like the Count of Monte Cristo let out of prison," he described. "Thereafter, I avoided, and indeed fought against any personal publicity, with the intensity of a member of Alcoholics Anonymous who knows that one drop is too much and thereafter an ocean isn't enough. This to me, an ex-addict, is the single greatest freedom of life—the Freedom of Anonymity."

Cuneo's newfound desire for anonymity—in effect, to become "invisible" in the eyes of the public—would eventually lead him to the greatest adventure of his life.

3

THE BRAIN TRUST

As a young lawyer, Cuneo worked for then congressman Fiorello LaGuardia and later President Franklin D. Roosevelt, first as a political aide and eventually as a spy.

The infamous 1932 Lindbergh baby kidnapping galvanized America's attention like few other crimes before or since— enough to be called "the Crime of the Century." Newspapers and radio stations followed each step of the lengthy police search for the curly-haired toddler, stolen from the New Jersey home of celebrated aviator Charles Lindbergh.

A ransom note left behind demanded a small fortune. When the twenty-month-old boy was found dead, the media covered the trial of his killer, German immigrant Bruno Hauptmann, with sensational daily dispatches.

For Cuneo, the Lindbergh case provided lasting lessons about the power of the press, politics and public opinion. Some leading characters in this drama—such as FBI director J. Edgar Hoover, who handled the federal investigation, and columnist Walter Winchell, who attended the trial—would later play prominent roles in Cuneo's life as a spy.

However, at the height of the Lindbergh crisis, Cuneo's new boss, then US Congressman Fiorello LaGuardia, made the most immediate impression on him with a reference to their shared ethnicity.

"We seldom discussed our common heritage of race, but when the Lindbergh baby was kidnapped, Fiorello said to me, 'I hope that bastard kidnapper doesn't turn out to be Italian,'" Cuneo recalled.

LaGuardia's newly hired aide, fresh out of law school, couldn't agree more.

Both men feared that if the Lindbergh culprit proved to be of Italian descent, another unfair slur on their shared heritage would further poison America's goodwill. They were sensitive to portrayals of Italian Americans as poorly educated, poverty ridden and violent criminals epitomized by mobsters like Chicago's Al Capone.

"It was embarrassing as well as galling, and there was no need for us to put our feelings into words—each understood how the other felt," Cuneo recalled. "The Italian immigration had taken place only three decades before, and its publicized effects upon the country were mostly lamentable, centering around tabloid headlines about the Capones, Fischettis, Costellos, and similar scum of the gangland."

Cuneo's political job—as a staffer for the hard-charging La-

Guardia—began a new chapter in his life after football. "Fiorello's office reminded me, upon arrival, far more of a locker room at game time than a mere place of business," he said. "If anything, the locker-room combat tempo was stepped up, and I never saw the tempo slacken."

His new position came at the recommendation of Cuneo's former editor at the *New York Daily News*, Lowell Limpus, who later authored a biography of the liberal Republican LaGuardia. Limpus praised Cuneo's affability in dealing with people as well as his streetwise writing style. As a rookie reporter, Cuneo had been weaned on the tabloid's diet of murders, fires and felonies.

He immediately hit it off with the congressman. "In the phraseology of Broadway's supreme accolade—this was one Hell of a Guy," Cuneo later said of LaGuardia.

The Little Flower—as LaGuardia became known publicly—first served as a local Manhattan congressman before being elected New York City's mayor in 1933. Squat, bold and always quotable, LaGuardia swiftly became an outsized political figure. By contrast, young Cuneo was learning to become more discreet in the circles of power.

With his legal degree and newspaper background, Cuneo was well armed as a political insider. He relished LaGuardia's reformist fight with the old corrupt Tammany Hall Democrats, a confrontation that threatened at times to become violent. Having Cuneo, a muscular former NFL pro football player, by his side appealed to LaGuardia.

When Tammany opponents once tried to disrupt a rally by pulling a fire alarm box, LaGuardia called on his beefy staffer to stop it. He even told Cuneo to confront a cop who wanted to intervene.

"We can protect ourselves, get tough with him," LaGuardia commanded. "And if you have to hit him don't hesitate… Punch him in the eye, if he tries to finagle us."

Another time, as a poll watcher on Election Day, Cuneo got

into a fistfight when he spotted Tammany hacks trying to stuff the ballot box with illegal extra votes. When he learned of the ruckus, LaGuardia hailed his fearless aide. "Attaboy, Ernest, give 'em hell!" he said.

Over time, Cuneo learned more subtle powers of persuasion. In 1932, Cuneo left LaGuardia's staff to handle international tax cases for private clients, but he never lost his taste for politics. The election of Governor Franklin Roosevelt to the American presidency—followed by LaGuardia's ascension to the city's mayoralty the following year—was a boon to Depression-era liberals like himself who recognized their opportunity to change government policies.

Several leading progressives devoted to FDR, often with ties to Columbia and Harvard, met frequently at a Manhattan restaurant, discussing how to make New Deal plans into reality. This "Brain Trust" included Columbia Law professor Adolf Berle and Harvard Law graduate Thomas Corcoran, who became prominent within the new Roosevelt administration. Often the youngest at these informal meetings, Cuneo became valued for his exceptional ability to communicate, both in person with his booming voice and eventually with his contacts in the media.

The Brain Trust connection provided opportunities Cuneo never imagined back in New Jersey. By 1936, Cuneo became associate counsel of the Democratic National Committee and a political operative for FDR, traveling back and forth between New York City and Washington, DC. During Roosevelt's reelection bid that year, Cuneo essentially served as an "advance man," a hidden hand in the background. He helped organize details and gather gossip and insider intelligence about their opponents. He made sure campaign appearances by FDR were a success.

At Roosevelt rallies, Cuneo was struck by the president's overwhelming appeal and personal inspiration to people down on their luck during the Depression. Disabled by polio, FDR managed to move his lifeless legs slowly toward the microphone stand—often with assistance—before he began his soaring orations in an Olympian tone. If Roosevelt could overcome his disabilities, his presence seemed to say, perhaps his crippled nation could succeed with economic recovery.

"The people turned out as if he were Gandhi," Cuneo recalled. "Forlorn people would line the sidewalks, or they'd press the car, quite moving, and saying 'You saved me.' I'd never seen anything like it, nothing like it. It was a vast tabernacle, it was a religious thing. The President took the stand, and no Hollywood man could have so picked a character. He picked up his magnificent head and spoke."

In Washington, Cuneo felt he could speak up for the concerns of immigrants like Italian Americans, a growing constituency group within FDR's big-tent coalition of liberals, minorities and Southern Democrats. Corcoran's Irish political instincts recognized the value of this young man from another important ethnic minority group.

"Ernie is wonderful to talk to—as I say, he'll talk your ear off," Corcoran recalled. "But Ernie has a sense of depth about this thing. Ernie understands urban politics—particularly the urban politics of New England and New York and Pennsylvania where his own people, the Italians, are so important—as nobody else in this town understands it."

After FDR's 1936 landslide victory, Corcoran assigned Cuneo to help Michigan Governor Frank Murphy in his 1938 reelection campaign. Murphy faced difficulty with labor unions because of violent auto strikes in his state. Cuneo quickly sized up the political situation. In a bold move, Cuneo recommended reaching out to nationally syndicated columnist Walter Winchell, to publish a sympathetic version of Murphy's views.

Winchell's column, published in dozens of newspapers, was delivered to twenty-seven million readers. His weekly radio broadcast on Sunday nights reached eighty-nine out of every one hundred adults in America, surveys showed. A good word from Winchell might help turn around Murphy's dismal political fortunes.

Cuneo first sought Winchell's favor earlier that year and soon became an important source of political news for the columnist. Their initial meeting took place at 21—an elegant Manhattan bar and restaurant, different and more sedate from Winchell's usual nightclub hangout, the Stork Club, with its loud and livelier entertainment. Cuneo's friend, Leonard Lyons, another Broadway newspaper columnist, arranged for this encounter.

As they sat down, Cuneo made reference to an old comedian known to Winchell from the days of vaudeville. But the columnist cut him off. As if conducting an audition, Winchell wanted to know if Cuneo could perform for him as a tipster. Ernest acted quickly to impress.

Surveying the crowd at 21, Cuneo recognized Lord Lothian, the British ambassador to the United States, and went over to introduce him to Winchell, whom he barely knew himself. As a syndicated columnist, Winchell wanted to expand his usual array of entertainment news to include the biggest political story of the moment. Winchell quickly took over from Cuneo.

"Lord Lothian, what is Great Britain going to do about Hitler?" asked Winchell, with his nasal, rapid-fire delivery.

Lothian answered slowly and cryptically. Unlike Winston Churchill, Lothian favored his British government's appeasement policy toward Hitler and the looming Nazi threat in Europe. "We shall try to fatten the tiger without strengthening him," he replied.

Winchell didn't think much of his answer. He was wary of appeasing Hitler, given the German leader's voracious appetite for conquest. Nevertheless, Winchell jumped on the "scoop" from the British diplomat that Cuneo's introduction had provided. His next day's column carried a loose translation of Lothian and Winchell's own warning to the American public:

"Britain will marry Hitler in the fall. The marriage will blow up into a World War."

Winchell's headlines and numerous loyal radio listeners impressed Cuneo tremendously. He urged Winchell to endorse President Roosevelt's political agenda, starting with favored candidates—like Murphy of Michigan—in pivotal Midwestern states.

Corcoran, then a top White House adviser overseeing much of FDR's domestic agenda, frowned on the Winchell idea. Seeking help from a gossip columnist—devoted to celebrities, gangsters and sports heroes—seemed beneath the noble aspirations of American politics.

"Tom bitched a bit about this," Cuneo recalled. "He said Winchell was notches below the dignity of the White House."

Despite Corcoran's reluctance, Cuneo prevailed. He argued Winchell's audience could be decisive at the polls. He even cited an ancient Greek proverb to make his point: "Necessity is above the gods themselves."

Murphy lost his 1938 election but was still headed upward. The following year, as a faithful FDR loyalist, Murphy was appointed US Attorney General and eventually landed on the US Supreme Court.

Cuneo also pushed for Winchell's intervention with another 1938 candidate—the little-known US Solicitor General Robert Jackson, whom FDR's Brain Trust wanted to become New York Governor. "There was only one person who could give instant recognition to a dark horse candidate—Walter Winchell," Cuneo argued. But Jackson's candidacy also failed to catch fire.

Lack of success in these 1938 campaigns didn't hurt Cuneo's standing. Rather, it cemented his relationship with Winchell and significantly increased his influence within the Roosevelt administration.

Over the next several months, Cuneo leaked to Winchell advance word of anticipated White House actions. He began to review Winchell's columns for any legal problems. And, without a byline or any credit, he wrote some of Winchell's column items and broadcast copy when they dealt with political news.

Eventually, Winchell, the nation's highest-paid media celebrity, hired Cuneo to be his private counsel. Cuneo was paid $10,000 a year (more than $200,000 in today's dollars) for providing various "legal services" to Winchell, at the same time he worked for FDR and the Democrats. As Winchell's biographer Neal Gabler noted, "Cuneo raised Walter's consciousness, framed his opinions, introduced him to insiders."

In return, Winchell expanded Cuneo's media influence exponentially and introduced him to New York's after-hours world. At the Stork Club, they exchanged laughs and drinks with Broadway's leading actors, visiting Hollywood stars and an array of chorus girls who frequented the nightclub. Each one made sure to stop by Winchell's table to pay their respects and maybe get a mention in his column.

Cuneo took note that even gangsters who visited the club—such as Frank Costello, the real-life prototype for *The Godfather* later in book and film—seemed to defer to Winchell's power of the press. "Winchell knew, of course, that the professional criminals would not shoot him," Cuneo recalled. "It was part of the laconic street wisdom of Broadway: never fight with a woman, a minister or a reporter because they will each have the last word."

FBI director J. Edgar Hoover, who frequented the Stork Club, was another friend and invaluable source for Winchell and Cuneo. The three men traded secrets the way jewelers exchanged gems, figuring out their worth. During the 1930s, Winchell's columns often lionized "the G-men" for their bravery, honesty and tenacity as hardworking sleuths. Winchell particularly singled out Hoover for hunting down notorious criminals such as John Dillinger and bringing them to justice. As Cuneo later said, Winchell portrayed Hoover as "an infallible combination of Sherlock Holmes, Dick Tracy and the Lone Ranger."

Winchell the newshound loved to make news himself. In a highly publicized 1939 case, with Cuneo counseling him, Winchell received a series of telephone calls at the Stork Club that led to the FBI arrest of wanted criminal Louis "Lepke" Buchalter, head of the Mafia hit squad called Murder Inc. After two years on the lam, fugitive Buchalter had decided to turn himself in to Winchell as "the one person I can trust."

In turn, Winchell trusted Cuneo to deal with the FBI. Although Cuneo maintained friendly contacts with Hoover, both realized the FBI director's personal ambition and investigative zeal should never be underestimated.

"John [J. Edgar Hoover] wouldn't tap *my* wires, would he?" Winchell asked Cuneo about his telephone calls with Buchalter.

"Perish the thought, Walter," replied Cuneo. But he too wondered how far Hoover's sleuthing extended beyond the law. "As usual," he later explained, "Hoover knew every card in the deck even as the game was being played."

After several years in the political arena, Cuneo had proved himself to be a master manipulator. He could act on commands and signals from the Brain Trust's leadership, the same way he once had as a pro football lineman. He remained unafraid to take on the toughest assignments, from Corcoran or the president himself. Indeed, he embraced the most daunting mission of all—convincing America that Roosevelt deserved an unprecedented third term.

With FDR's second term neared its ending, his advisers worried their New Deal reforms might all be lost if, after the 1940 election, the White House wound up in the hands of a Republican—or even a conservative Democrat. After much internal debate, they raised the idea of a third term for Roosevelt— something not tried in the nearly one hundred and fifty years of the Republic. All previous presidents had followed the example of George Washington, who gave up the reins of power after two terms, lest he be called a king.

As a trial balloon, Cuneo said, he floated the idea by inserting a call for a third term into a "short speech which I wrote" for Michigan's Frank Murphy during a July 1938 campaign stop in Traverse City. Initially, the press paid little attention to this "Draft FDR" movement, until Cuneo alerted his newfound columnist pal.

"I had Walter Winchell pick it up and he trumpeted it to 40 million people daily for the next two years," he recalled. "Winchell hurled himself into action."

Over national airwaves, Winchell cited unnamed White House sources for his scoop. "The President feels the nation needs him in the White House for another four-year term," Winchell inveighed, without official confirmation.

Over the next year, Winchell had buyer's remorse, covering his sure bet by suggesting Roosevelt might change his mind about seeking another term. But Cuneo urged on Winchell with certainty, afraid to tell him otherwise. "Look Walter," he wanted to tell him, "*you are* the Third Term campaign."

Winchell's constant crusade for the president, orchestrated by Cuneo and the Brain Trust starting in 1938, had its desired effect. FDR's Hamlet act—expressing interest and then denying it—extended the drama for many months. By early 1940, it became clear that FDR did indeed intend to run again. As Cuneo explained, "Walter [Winchell] smoked out the conservative opposition and gave Roosevelt's supporters two years to destroy it."

Cuneo had been right in his risk-taking. He enlisted Winchell's powerful media voice and other columnists like Drew Pearson to FDR's cause. "Walter Winchell was uniquely influential in developing popular sentiment" for Roosevelt's third term bid, concluded Richard Weiner in his 1979 history of syndicated columnists. Others in the president's circle took note of Cuneo's quiet effectiveness, feeding news items to the two famous columnists with radio shows. Cuneo had exercised the levers of power without leaving his fingerprints.

"There was a lawyer named Ernest Cuneo, used to be in this office, who was Winchell's lawyer, and he put in all the stuff pro-Roosevelt," recalled James Rowe Jr., a special adviser to FDR and part of the Brain Trust. "They were both very pro-Roosevelt, and had huge audiences and were listened to."

At age thirty-five, so much of Cuneo's life was now devoted to being a shadowy operative. He spent more time between Washington corridors and New York's nightclubs than at home. His marriage suffered. Cuneo's intense energy, his on-and-off personality, could make life difficult, far from tranquil. The roustabout lifestyle of Winchell—a mix of booze, women and many late nights—appealed to Cuneo, but not to his wife, Zilpha. When Winchell presided over "the Prettiest Girl" contest in the nation's capital, Cuneo tagged along, surely to his wife's chagrin.

This young couple of different backgrounds who'd met and married at Columbia found that their love for each other hadn't lasted. Full of his own ambitions, Ernie no longer shared Zilpha's dreams. By 1930, a few years after they wed, Zilpha was listed simply on census forms as "Wife-H" for housewife, with no mention of a career. Their lives had slowly drifted apart. After twelve years of marriage, the couple no longer lived together. There were no children, no lasting ties between them.

Eventually, Ernie and Zilpha agreed to a divorce, finalized in 1939. They parted ways a few months before Cuneo took on a new challenge—as a spy for the president.

4

"YOUR DUTY LIES THERE"

"Far away, happily protected by the Atlantic and Pacific Oceans, to you, the people of the United States, to whom I now have the chance to speak—you are the spectators, the increasingly involved spectators, of these tragedies and crimes."

—Winston Churchill, in a 1938 radio broadcast asking
America for help against Hitler's war in Europe

Prior to World War II, long before he met Ernest Cuneo, Canadian millionaire William Stephenson urged the assassination of Adolf Hitler. In 1938, Stephenson insisted that only Hitler's death would stop the Nazi leader's looming threat to the world, which would eventually result in millions of innocent people killed in global conflict.

As a private businessman familiar with the European steel industry, Stephenson was alarmed by Germany's buildup of weapons. Many in Great Britain still hoped for a lasting peace pact with Hitler. Stephenson offered a different plan—he would kill him.

Murdering Hitler, as a preemptive strike, seemed a tempting idea to UK secret intelligence officials. The head of MI6, Stewart Menzies, Great Britain's top spy, "displayed cautious interest" in Stephenson's proposal to shoot Hitler inside Germany with a high-powered rifle, according to Menzies's biographer Anthony Cave Brown. A similar claim that Stephenson "volunteered to assassinate Hitler" was made by H. Montgomery Hyde, who later worked as a top intelligence officer for Stephenson at Rockefeller Center.

A dashing man with boundless energy, Stephenson was already the stuff of legend as he approached his fortieth birthday. Adopted as a child, Stephenson grew up in Winnipeg and became a Canadian fighter pilot serving with British forces during World War I. He shot down several enemy planes, earning the United Kingdom's Distinguished Flying Cross medal for courage. Moving to London after the war, Stephenson married an American tobacco heiress but was, in every sense, a self-made man. He became rich as a highly successful inventor and entrepreneur, and was a millionaire before age thirty. His Sound City Films company produced many British movies at its Shepperton studios. His experience with aircraft and automobile manufacturing in Europe—especially through his industrial firm, Pressed Steel—convinced him of the need to confront Hitler.

Stephenson's substantial legacy of secret intelligence achievements during World War II was later obscured by the destruction of documents and his desire to keep matters secret. Nevertheless, there seems little doubt of other British discussions about assassinating Hitler, which extended beyond Stephenson.

Around the same time in 1938, Britain's military attaché to Germany, Noel Mason-MacFarlane, also proposed assassinating Hitler with a long-distance rifle as a preventative to all-out war. His plan called for killing Hitler at a huge Berlin rally being held for the Nazi leader's fiftieth birthday.

"Easy rifle shot," Mason-MacFarlane boasted. "I could pick the bastard off from here as easy as winking."

The Foreign Secretary, Lord Halifax, rejected this plan, just as he did Stephenson's purported offer. Top British officials viewed such actions as reckless and incendiary, especially after Prime Minister Neville Chamberlain agreed to a new peace pact in Munich with Hitler in September 1938.

"We have not reached that stage…when we have to use assassination as a substitution for diplomacy," Halifax said.

While others dismissed him, Stephenson's concern about the Nazi war machine did attract attention from Winston Churchill. Both shared the same alarm about Hitler's undeterred desire for conquest. Starting in 1936, Stephenson passed along information he learned about Germany's expanding supply of weapons and military equipment to those informing Churchill, who was then in the Parliament but out of favor within the Conservative Party. "That was my only training in espionage," Stephenson later said.

At the time, newspaper publisher Lord Beaverbrook (Max Aitken) advised Stephenson to reach out to his friend Churchill about Hitler rather than other, more appeasement-minded British officials.

Beaverbrook "could have sent [Stephenson] to Halifax or Chamberlain, but they were both idiots, and he wouldn't have got anywhere," explained writer Roald Dahl, who later worked as a spy for Stephenson during the war. "I think Max Beaverbrook advised him to do it too, because they were both Canadians. He was a close friend, a really genuinely close friend of Beaverbrook."

As much as anyone in England, the Churchills—both Winston and his journalist son, Randolph—sounded a clarion call against Hitler, early and often, starting in the early 1930s after their visits to Nazi Germany. By 1935, Winston condemned the "horrible bloodbath" by Hitler's henchmen, who murdered hundreds of political opponents in their march toward war.

Few in Great Britain listened at first. Many still suffered from their memories of dead loved ones killed in World War I and didn't want a repeat. They viewed Winston Churchill, seemingly past his prime, as an old chronic warmonger.

Events soon thrust Churchill from the backbench to center stage. In 1939, the year after the Munich Agreement, Hitler's armies trampled through Czechoslovakia and then invaded Poland, prompting Britain and France to declare war. Aware of its own military unpreparedness, Chamberlain's government asked Churchill to return as First Lord of the Admiralty, the position he held previously during the Great War. By May 1940, when Denmark and Norway fell to the Nazis, Chamberlain was forced to resign as prime minister. At age sixty-five, Churchill replaced him, and launched a desperate attempt to save the British Empire.

From the very outset, Churchill faced challenges that seemed insurmountable. With France and Belgium soon taken over by Hitler, Churchill hoped to convince the United States to enter the conflict, just as it eventually had in World War I. A Nazi invasion of England appeared imminent. Within a few months, the German Luftwaffe, with their "blitzkrieg" aerial attacks, would start bombing, killing some forty thousand people and forcing Londoners to seek shelter in the city's underground transit system.

Across the Atlantic, Americans remained reluctant to help Great Britain and become mired in an endless European war. Isolationists like Charles Lindbergh and several prominent members of Congress campaigned vigorously against any involvement.

Roosevelt's ambassador in London, Joseph P. Kennedy, privately labeled Churchill as a drunkard, always with a whiskey in his hand. Kennedy advised the president that the US shouldn't squander its precious blood and fortune in such a lost cause.

Nevertheless, against all odds, Churchill felt confident. A few days after taking office in May 1940, Winston confided in his son, Randolph, while shaving before a bathroom mirror.

"I think I see my way through," Churchill told his son.

Randolph wondered aloud if he meant the United Kingdom would "avoid defeat or beat the bastards?"

Churchill dropped his razor into the sink. He turned to his only son with great intensity.

"Of course we can beat them," he declared, as if addressing the whole nation. "I shall drag the United States in."

That same month, Churchill began his crusade. In public statements and diplomatic exchanges, the new prime minister lobbied for military aid from the US government. He personally beseeched Roosevelt to come to his rescue, a plea that went unheeded for many months. When or if the United States might join the Allied cause still remained anyone's guess.

In the meantime, Churchill took matters into his own hands. In May 1940, he secretly launched an unprecedented undercover campaign designed to get America into the war. It would rely on a foreign spying operation run out of Rockefeller Center, a large-scale propaganda effort to win favor with the US media, and underground actions against German agents and sympathizers already living in this country.

Stephenson, the kind of maverick with nerves of steel favored by Churchill, was selected to oversee this clandestine effort. "I was sent as a personal representative of Winston Churchill, an old friend, to cover the whole of the Western Hemisphere, and to do any job that he thought might be useful in the war effort in that whole area," Stephenson told a television interviewer years later.

As a man of considerable wealth, Stephenson could act independently. He didn't fear government bureaucrats inclined to blunt or avoid bold actions needed abroad. As a proven patriot to the Crown, Stephenson could be trusted with the most sensitive of state secrets. His covert actions in America would prove vital to Great Britain's success.

Stephenson's education as a spy began only two years earlier. While Churchill was still First Lord of the Admiralty, he endorsed Stephenson's secret 1939 mission to sabotage the Germans' supply of Swedish ore needed for weapons making. Although that plan didn't succeed, Stephenson was sent to Helsinki to help the Finns protect themselves through subversion and sabotage.

After Stephenson returned to London, British officials asked him in early 1940 to travel to the United States to establish a cooperative intelligence-sharing relationship with the Federal Bureau of Investigation run by Hoover. It was an audacious request, however, and would go nowhere without the approval of America's famous G-man.

"Churchill's vision was extralegal; no nation in the world openly allowed a foreign power to run an intelligence service on domestic soil," Hoover biographer Beverly Gage explained in 2022. "To make it happen, the British decided that they needed Hoover's assistance and permission."

Stephenson arranged a meeting with Hoover, set up by their mutual friend, the former boxing world champion Gene Tunney. Once an amateur pugilist, Stephenson first met Tunney during his days in the ring. Tunney later said Stephenson asked him to contact Hoover "quietly and with no fanfare."

The secret meeting with Hoover went well. Stephenson relayed his concern that in New York Harbor and along the East Coast, German saboteurs could disrupt the flow of ships carrying vital supplies from America to Britain. He proposed that British intelligence and the FBI work together to thwart any Nazi spy operations in the United States.

Hoover listened politely but told Stephenson he was constrained by the State Department and America's neutrality laws. "I cannot contravene this policy without direct presidential sanction," Hoover said.

"And if I get it?" asked Stephenson.

"Then we'll do business directly," Hoover said. "Just myself and you. Nobody else gets in the act. Not State, not anyone. You will be getting presidential sanction."

Before parting, Hoover said they must get a Roosevelt insider to act as a go-between for them, to help broker this most delicate espionage deal. As America's top lawman, Hoover had spent years building up the FBI. He didn't want this potentially illegal arrangement traced back to him.

The middleman was known to both of them. "Stephenson

agreed to this condition—indeed he had no alternative—and undertook to get one of the President's confidential advisers, with whom they were both acquainted, to put the matter before Mr. Roosevelt," recalled Stephenson's security aide, H. Montgomery Hyde. "The intermediary chosen for this purpose was Ernest Cuneo, a clever lawyer of Italian descent from New Jersey."

By this point in his White House career, Cuneo had learned how to operate under the radar, to remain essentially invisible, while he carried out the president's wishes. In recent months, Cuneo had proven himself with another sensitive political mission for the White House, promoting a third-term candidacy for Roosevelt, using his contacts with Winchell and other well-placed sources in the media. But now he was being asked to become engaged in spying, an even trickier endeavor.

After being approached by Hoover on Stephenson's behalf, Cuneo promised to see the president as soon as possible. Whether Cuneo pitched the idea directly to Roosevelt or—more likely—went through some other friendly higher-ranking aide like Thomas Corcoran isn't clear from the historical record. There was little chance such a potentially explosive directive from FDR would be written down on paper. It would have to be a stealth command created with what later presidents called "plausible deniability."

Within a day or two, according to Hyde and other accounts, Cuneo indicated the president "welcomed the idea enthusiastically." The White House's discreet message was that "there should be the closest possible marriage between the FBI and British Intelligence." Roosevelt repeated this same verbal approval to Lord Lothian, then the British ambassador in Washington.

Stephenson left New York triumphantly, pulling off an international coup with the skill of a diplomat. On the way home to embattled England, he came up with an even bigger and more audacious plan.

With the tacit cooperation of FDR already secured, Stephenson suggested the British expand their espionage in America beyond traditional intelligence gathering and include "counter-espionage, political warfare and 'special operations.'" He realized this aggressive approach would be more provocative than the one discussed with Hoover, but necessary if British interests abroad were to be protected.

By the time Stephenson returned home to London, Churchill had even bigger demands for him. The prime minister's top spymaster, Menzies, directed that Stephenson go back to the United States again to establish the secret espionage headquarters eventually housed at Rockefeller Center. As "cover" for his spy role, Menzies said, Stephenson should list his job as "Passport Control Officer."

Despite his considerable self-confidence, Stephenson wasn't sure he wanted the spy job in New York. He spoke to a number of friends in London, including Lord Beaverbrook, the longtime friend of Churchill. Beaverbrook had recently been recruited to pump up British aircraft production, desperately needed to fight off the Nazi assaults in the skies. Eventually, Stephenson asked to speak to Churchill.

The prime minister agreed to meet at his old Admiralty offices because he had yet to move into his new official home at Downing Street, according to Hyde's published account. During this meeting with Stephenson, Churchill reprised what he previously told his son, Randolph, about the need to drag America into the war. He agreed with Stephenson that virtually everything in the spy bag of tricks could be used, including "special operations," a euphemism for drastic and deadly actions.

Then, with his bulldog face, Churchill stared Stephenson in the eye and implored him to be his top spy in America.

"Your duty lies there," Churchill commanded. "You must go."

There was no further debate in Stephenson's mind. On June 21, 1940, he and his wife, Mary, arrived in New York Harbor aboard an ocean liner and checked into the Waldorf Astoria hotel. They eventually moved to the St. Regis Hotel, owned by Vincent Astor, an old millionaire friend of FDR who liked Stephenson.

After a few days in New York, Stephenson visited Lord Lo-thian at the British embassy in Washington. Waiting for him was a cable from Churchill. It urged him to remind Roosevelt "if we do go down, Hitler has a very good chance of conquer-ing the world."

Over the next several months, Stephenson began to assemble what would become the largest foreign espionage operation ever conducted inside the United States. And his constant source of contact with the American government would be another ci-vilian turned spy—Ernest Cuneo.

5

WHAT THEY DIDN'T KNOW

From their very first Rockefeller Center meeting together, Ernest Cuneo was impressed by William Stephenson's investigative skills. While checking into the secret British headquarters at 630 Fifth Avenue, he noticed a list with his full name spelled out completely, including his two little-used middle initials—Ernest L.T. Cuneo. This small detail surprised him and left a lasting impression.

"Since the only time that this [middle initials] has ever been used was on my baptismal certificate, I concluded, and correctly, that Stephenson knew a hell of a lot more about me than I did about him," Cuneo observed.

Stephenson bounded out of his office. He greeted Cuneo with a friendly handshake, like some long-lost relative. Known as "Little Bill," he appeared different than Cuneo had expected.

At five feet seven inches tall, with wavy brown hair and chestnut eyes, Stephenson seemed bigger and more impressive than his nickname suggested. He spoke and presented himself with a sophisticated, slightly aristocratic air. There were no scars on his ruddy face from his days as a lightweight boxer. He was carefully groomed and tailored. As Cuneo described, "His manners were Chesterfieldian English but he moved with the quickness of a Canadian cougar."

Within a few short months, it became evident that Churchill's spymaster in Manhattan knew far more about Nazi whereabouts and covert actions than any US agency. At that time, no single government entity in America kept track of foreign espionage. Various parts of that responsibility were shared by intelligence agents assigned to the US Army, the US Navy and J. Edgar Hoover's FBI.

Cuneo's sizable task was to work cooperatively with Stephenson, in total secrecy, and report back to the White House. Similarly, Stephenson "had instant communication with Churchill" through Menzies and others. Over the next few years, Cuneo said, they had "almost daily meetings or discreet conversations, setting up exploration trial balloons on matters of major policies, including not only the conduct of the war but the shape of the peace."

Cuneo recognized immediately that Stephenson was far better equipped for being a spy than he. For them, Rockefeller Center became "a curious no-man's land in British American relations," helping to determine the fate of both their nations with their undercover actions.

From the outset, Hoover seemed impressed with Stephenson and the spy-catching ability of British intelligence. He'd been the first to suggest the name "British Security Coordination (BSC)" used by Stephenson's covert operation in New York. During their second confidential meeting about working together, Stephenson shared a major disclosure with Hoover.

Shortly after Churchill became prime minister in May 1940, British agents arrested Tyler Kent, an employee in US Ambassador Joseph Kennedy's embassy in London, and charged him with espionage. The deeply embarrassing Kent spy case was full of the kind of juicy details the FBI chief kept in his own private files.

Kent was caught stealing top secret exchanges between Churchill and President Roosevelt, which wound up in the hands of the Hitler's Germany. He worked as a clerk with access to the embassy's cipher machines translating messages. With knobs, key wheels and dials, these mechanical devices looked like elaborate typewriters. With the flick of a switch, the ciphers could encrypt messages sent to friendly spies and embassies, or decode those from enemies.

Kent's stolen documents threatened to become a political firestorm. They clearly showed a greater level of wartime planning and cooperation between Great Britain and the still-neutral United States than was known publicly. After an intense investigation, British agents quietly arrested Kent for sharing the documents with Nazi collaborators. They kept him in jail for the remainder of the war.

But at that time, in May 1940, the secret arrest raised disturbing questions about Kennedy, a leading isolationist, and whether he might secretly favor Germany. British intelligence clearly had their doubts about the US representative in London and had been tracking him prior to Kent's arrest. "We had reached the point of bugging potential traitors and enemies," Churchill's son, Randolph, later wrote. "Joe Kennedy, the American ambassador, came under electronics surveillance."

Cuneo recalled his own dealings with the outspoken ambassador. While relaxing with Walter Winchell at a Florida resort in early 1939, they spotted Kennedy, home temporarily from his London embassy. The Kennedy family often spent winter holidays at their oceanfront Palm Beach mansion. The ambassador, dressed in sports clothes, seemed "jaunty with confidence, vibrant with energy," Cuneo noted. "As the ambassador approached, I thought I had never seen a more handsome man… the picture of a man in his prime."

Winchell instead saw red meat for his nationally syndicated column. He immediately asked Kennedy about the Munich pact, agreed upon a few months earlier by Hitler and Britain's then prime minister, Neville Chamberlain. The agreement permitted the German takeover of western Czechoslovakia in exchange for a dubious promise of peace from Hitler. Very animatedly, Kennedy claimed he played a "big part" in the Munich Agreement, by providing Chamberlain with written estimates of Nazi air power provided by Charles Lindbergh after a recent visit to Germany.

"Lindbergh dropped in at the embassy," Kennedy told them. "He had just inspected the Luftwaffe. What he told me was so important that I had him sit down at a typewriter and type it out himself. It was so important I, myself, brought it over to Chamberlain."

"What did Lindbergh say?" Winchell asked further, smelling his next scoop.

"He said the Luftwaffe was by far the most powerful air-force in the world, absolute tops."

When Winchell asked if the Lindbergh memo about Germany's air superiority had anything to do with Chamberlain's decision, Kennedy emphatically claimed "it was the decisive factor...absolutely."

Winchell's headline-grabber with Kennedy caused a furor in London. It was one of the ill-timed and defeatist comments by the millionaire ambassador that soon forced FDR to replace him. For all of Joe Kennedy's previous wizardry with Wall Street moneymaking and Hollywood movies, he never mastered the world of diplomacy. To the British, Kennedy appeared self-centered and naive, never fully grasping the Nazis' evil intent with their military buildup.

For Cuneo, this encounter in Florida made it easier to believe that Kennedy's embassy was so slipshod, so poorly run, that a spy in their midst like Tyler Kent would go undetected until stopped by Churchill's agents. Kennedy's comments were bad enough, but the gross violation of security exposed by the Kent case was intolerable.

During the summer of 1940, Stephenson's revelations to Hoover about this matter when he arrived in New York underlined the weakness of US intelligence abroad, especially when it came to sophisticated counterespionage methods to protect against double agents like Kent.

But Cuneo's discussion with Stephenson and other British spies at Rockefeller Center also showed him how little America knew about Nazi espionage activities in their own backyard.

Previously, the British had tipped off American authorities about German infiltration. An early example was Gunther Gustav Rumrich, a naturalized citizen who lived in New York City. He was known to his Nazi spy collaborators by his code name, "the Crown."

In 1938, Rumrich was arrested and revealed to be at the heart of a German espionage ring in Manhattan, run by the Abwehr, Hitler's intelligence agency. Along with several other Nazi sympathizers in the United States, Rumrich sought out compromising secrets at navy bases, industrial shipyards and defense aircraft manufacturing facilities.

Despite his dangerous assignment, Rumrich was hardly an ace spy. A ne'er-do-well who had deserted from the US Army, Rumrich proved neither smart nor adept at espionage. Nevertheless, the Abwehr agreed to take him on as an undercover agent in America, an arrangement that began by placing an obscure ad in the *New York Times*.

For nearly two years, Rumrich failed to produce much value for his Nazi bosses. Eventually, he concocted an ambitious plan to steal blueprints for two US Navy carriers. American authorities were clueless about his activities until British intelligence learned of "the Crown" by intercepting and steaming open his letters to a Nazi go-between located in Scotland.

Rumrich was finally arrested when New York police caught him attempting to obtain thirty-five blank passports and posing as a top State Department official. The resulting investigation revealed several others arrested in Rumrich's Nazi spy ring, including those planning sabotage to create bottlenecks in America's supply chains to Great Britain and stealing documents about US weaponry. Unlike the unlucky Rumrich, some of his fellow Nazi spies managed to evade arrest and fled back to Germany.

The overall response by Hoover's FBI was slow and disorganized. To Hoover's angry chagrin, his top agent on the case, Leon Turrou, published his own 1938 book portraying America as awash in Nazi espionage. Turrou's account inspired a thinly veiled dramatic movie called *Confessions of a Nazi Spy*, starring Edward G. Robinson, which drew widespread publicity. The Warner Bros. film was the first major Hollywood studio production aimed directly at Hitler's Nazi threat. Angered by Turrou's headline-grabbing, Hoover tried to stop the film, but his ham-handed attempt backfired. Hoover looked more concerned about his public image than any foreign threat to national security.

"It was hardly a roaring success for the FBI," the agency's historians acknowledged about the "Rumrich Nazi Spy Case" decades later. "Four times as many spies had escaped, including the biggest fishes. The Bureau was roundly criticized in the press, and for good reason, as it was simply unprepared at that point in history to investigate such cases of espionage."

Worries about Nazi espionage in America were compounded by concerns about the German American Bund, a pro-Hitler group. In February 1939, they held a giant rally at Madison Square Garden, ostensibly in honor of George Washington's birthday. Wearing swastikas and saluting with Nazi jabs, more than twenty thousand heard German American Bund leader Fritz Kuhn extol the Führer, condemn President Roosevelt, and spew anti-Semitic hatred.

Cuneo feared the Bund followers, with their "Free America!" chants, were "utterly reckless of life, limb or rules." They seemed as bad as the Ku Klux Klan, American fascists and other right-wing extremists like the Silver Shirts, who were enamored of Hitler's rhetoric.

"The Ratzis are going to celebrate George Washington's

birthday at Madison Square Garden, claiming G.W. to be the nation's first Fritz Kuhn," an appalled Walter Winchell told his nationwide radio audience. "The symbols of America and the symbols of Nazism sit side by side." Undoubtedly, his words were applauded by his associate Cuneo, if not written by him outright.

Cuneo now felt himself in a high-stakes game unlike anything he'd experienced before. As he began working secretly with Stephenson in 1940, Cuneo believed much was at "mortal stake," especially with the country's isolationist mood so prevalent. The battle over America's soul was like "one of those lethal chariot races of ancient Rome," he wrote. On one side were "the black chariot of the German American Bund, supported by the sinister camouflaged chariot of German Intelligence and Propaganda, of limitless resource and financial power." The other side featured the "quick, anxious, ingenious and limitlessly resourced British intelligence and diplomatic services." Cuneo believed a third term for FDR in the White House would provide the sure-handed captain needed to steady the ship. Like others in the president's Brain Trust, he foresaw a great clash among rival civilizations. "A world at war was the stadium," Cuneo observed, "the life or death of mighty nations was the wager, already posted by huge armies in the field and vast fleets at sea, and the prize, the only prize, was the Presidency of the United States."

Increasingly, Roosevelt rang the alarm bell about a "Fifth Column" of Nazi spies and sympathizers hidden inside America. (The term "Fifth Column," popularized during the 1930s Spanish Civil War and adopted by Churchill, referred to any group within a country at war who secretly favored the enemy.) During a "fireside chat" radio broadcast on May 26, 1940—a few days after Churchill became prime minister and Stephenson moved to Rockefeller Center—FDR used the phrase to issue a stiff warning.

"Today's threat to our national security is not a matter of military weapons alone," Roosevelt told the nation. "We know of new methods of attack. The Trojan Horse. The Fifth Column that betrays a nation unprepared for treachery. Spies, saboteurs and traitors are the actors in this new strategy. With all of these, we must and will deal vigorously."

Even Joe Kennedy, before leaving his ambassador post in London, warned about these home front dangers. "Those with whom I have talked here are of the opinion that the United States has more to fear from Fifth Column activities than any other nation," he warned in a note to Secretary of State Cordell Hull in August 1940.

Toward ending that threat, Roosevelt provided Hoover's FBI with more money to combat Nazi espionage and sabotage. Hoover, a careful empire-builder, avoided being blamed or replaced for the FBI's early foul-ups. He created a foreign intelligence unit within his own agency. Roosevelt gave him wide permission to use wiretaps, open diplomatic mail and bend other rules to stop this foreign-sponsored subversion.

To Cuneo, Hoover was "the master bureaucrat" with whom he always stayed friendly but formal in conversation. "When it came to protecting his realm, he [Hoover] had the Richelieu touch of nuance and a Jefferson avidity for gossip," Cuneo described. Most of all, Hoover knew how to survive.

However, Roosevelt had a person other than Hoover in mind to oversee this clandestine fight against Hitler. He would choose an American war hero to carry out espionage tasks similar to Stephenson's. And in this first-time effort to create a US intelligence agency, FDR's new spymaster would be joined by Cuneo, once again acting as an anonymous middleman.

6

THE PRESIDENT'S "SECRET LEGS"

Out of the clouds, a giant seaplane from England circled twice against the Manhattan skyline on the Sunday evening of August 4, 1940. It touched down gently along the water basin at the municipal airport in Queens, later named for Mayor Fiorello LaGuardia. Because of the Nazi threat, this flight had been long and harrowing.

Camouflaged with patches of green and blue paint, the amphibious aircraft dubbed "the Clare" had traveled with its radio off part of the time to avoid detection. A convoy of British fighter planes accompanied it. With four motor propellers, a 114-foot wingspan and Union Jack insignia on its side, the Clare was an easy target. This trip was its first mission in months because of the war.

At the New York marine terminal, reporters waited for the plane's sole civilian passenger to emerge—William J. Donovan, a fifty-seven-year-old lawyer and World War I hero known to some as "Wild Bill." They wanted to pepper him with questions about his trip and whether America might enter the European conflict.

Donovan appeared energetic and friendly despite his exhausting journey. He mentioned nothing of substance to the press, except to say he was headed to Washington to report his find-

ings. Donovan seemed amused when one questioner asked if he
had violated US passport and neutrality laws by traveling aboard
a belligerent vessel. "He laughed and replied that he was traveling on a special passport," reported the *New York Times*.

Donovan's top secret White House assignment had begun
three weeks earlier. At President Roosevelt's request, he left on
July 14, 1940 to see the newly installed Prime Minister Winston
Churchill in London and evaluate Great Britain's seemingly slim
chances of defeating Hitler. From an intelligence perspective,
he'd also investigate how the infiltration of German subversives
and double agents in Europe might affect American security,
including the recent arrest of Nazi spy Tyler Kent at Joe Kennedy's London embassy.

Over time, Donovan became what Roosevelt, crippled by
polio, called "my secret legs."

Donovan, a conservative Republican, seemed an odd choice
to become a Roosevelt confidant. Until this point, his remarkable life had often run a parallel course to the president's, though
in different ways.

As ambitious young men, both attended Columbia Law School
as classmates. Roosevelt studied there for three years, from fall
1904 to spring 1907, though he didn't get his degree. (His 1932
presidential campaign publicity sometimes listed him errone-
ously as a graduate.) Instead, FDR passed the state bar exam
and immediately began practicing admiralty law in Manhattan,
entering politics soon after. As an undergrad, Donovan played
quarterback on the 1905 Columbia Lions football team before
graduating from Columbia's law school in 1907 and joining a
law firm in his native Buffalo.

During World War I, both men burnished their reputations
by serving in the nation's military. Roosevelt became Assistant
Secretary of the Navy, overseeing a buildup of navy ships and
personnel and meeting with various French and British officials
(including briefly with Churchill, then First Lord of the Admi-

ralty). FDR's impressive success during wartime catapulted him into the upper echelons of national politics, running for vice president on the unsuccessful 1920 Democratic ticket headed by James Cox.

Donovan's troops nicknamed him "Wild Bill" for his unwavering personal courage and brave leadership. As a major, he was wounded while fighting in France with his New York battalion called "the Fighting 69th," later the subject of a 1940 movie starring James Cagney. (Actor George Brent played Wild Bill.) Donovan became the most honored military member of his time, the only American to win the nation's four highest awards, including the Medal of Honor and the Distinguished Service Cross.

In 1932, the two men's fortunes intertwined once again. Bolstered by his recent prominence as a top US Justice Department official, Donovan ran unsuccessfully to replace New York's then governor, Franklin D. Roosevelt, who was elected that same year to the presidency. Viewed as a possible Republican presidential contender for much of the decade, Donovan criticized FDR's domestic policies as being too liberal and too expensive. But as a private lawyer and businessman, Donovan's travels to Germany and elsewhere in Europe convinced him that Roosevelt's foreign policy was right—Hitler had to be stopped.

By 1940, the two men put away their differences when Frank Knox, a Republican newspaper publisher from Chicago, joined Roosevelt's cabinet as Secretary of the Navy. Knox recruited Donovan for the delicate and still undefined espionage position. One of those pushing his appointment was Churchill's spymaster in New York. William Stephenson suggested Donovan visit London and judge things for himself.

When FDR sent Donovan abroad in July 1940 as his confidential envoy, the British recognized it as a golden opportunity to reset their frayed relationship with the United States. "I arranged that he [Donovan] should be afforded every opportunity to conduct his inquiries," Stephenson recalled about his message to superiors in London. "I endeavoured to marshal my friends in high places to bare their breasts."

During his visit, Donovan enjoyed an audience with King George VI and met with Churchill, who, in the midst of a bloody war, found time to debrief him about British military needs and strategy. Churchill particularly appealed for more destroyers, reflected in his urgent cable to FDR during Donovan's visit: "Mr. President, with great respect, I must tell you that in the long history of the world this is a thing to do *now...*"

British intelligence officials shared information about "Fifth Column" spies—including a list of thousands of suspected foreign subversives. The presentation, orchestrated by Churchill, MI6's Stewart Menzies and Admiral John Godfrey (Director of Naval Intelligence and boss of Ian Fleming), convinced Donovan that they should work together until the Nazi threat was vanquished.

These Brits didn't act defensively with Donovan as they did with Kennedy. The isolationist American ambassador wasn't notified about Donovan's visit until he arrived. Kennedy resented the snub. "Frankly and honestly, I do not enjoy being a dummy," he fumed in a message back to Washington.

When Donovan returned home, he gave a hopeful assessment of Churchill's wartime chances. He shared his insights with Knox and others in the administration, including Roosevelt during a long train ride to New England. No longer was America's choice simply between loaning ships and money to Great Britain or writing the country off completely as a certain loser to Hitler. Now, Donovan argued, America must inevitably be prepared to enter the war and learn from the British example.

Stephenson was overjoyed. He cabled back to London that Donovan, his new partner in spying, was "doing much to combat defeatist attitude in Washington by stating positively and convincingly that we shall win."

During his London trip, Donovan had worked with US journalist Edgar Ansel Mowrer on preparing a report about Nazi espionage as an internal threat to America's security. Shortly afterward, their warning about a growing number of "Fifth Column" Nazi supporters appeared in newspapers and radio broadcasts around the nation.

"In the United States, an organization of Nazis is being trained in arms," Donovan proclaimed. "As matters now stand, it is conceivable that the United States possesses the finest Nazi-schooled fifth column in the world, one which, in case of war with Germany, could be our undoing."

Around that same time, a New York City bombing injured nine people at a travel and foreign exchange agency, which the FBI said was run as a front by the Gestapo as a way of disseminating Nazi propaganda. Donovan claimed Hitler was spending $200 million for spying and propaganda around the globe. "Nazi Germany is a conspiracy," he said. "Its scope is universal and its aims worldwide domination."

In December 1940, Donovan returned again to London—traveling together with Stephenson under the aliases "Donald Williams" and "Mr. O'Connell"—to meet with Churchill more extensively.

They discussed how to ensure that vital shipping lanes across the Atlantic would be protected from Nazi submarine attack. More importantly, Churchill outlined his offensive strategy for winning the war. Rather than lead a direct assault through France, Britain would first attack German outposts in the Mediterranean and support resistance guerilla fighters. The plan outlined by Churchill made sense to Donovan, who promised to lobby for it back in Washington.

Like a roving ambassador, Donovan then went on a long tour of the Balkans and Middle East to see British efforts for himself and report back to Roosevelt. When Donovan returned home in March 1941, Churchill thanked FDR for sending the envoy who'd served as Roosevelt's eyes and ears. "He [Donovan] has carried with him throughout an animating heart-warming flame," Churchill said.

A few months later, Roosevelt created a new job for Donovan as Coordinator of Information, inspired by Stephenson's spy operation at Rockefeller Center. Never before had the American government had such a clandestine post, answerable only to the president. As CIA historian Thomas Troy later described, Donovan's new unit was "a novel attempt in American history to organize research, intelligence, propaganda, subversion, and commando operations as a unified and essential feature of modern warfare."

Without an existing staff of his own, Donovan had to start from scratch. While Donovan could be disorganized, he had a keen eye for talent. He recruited Allen Dulles, a savvy New York lawyer who would eventually shape American intelligence. Dulles quit his high-paying legal job and moved into the small office set up by Donovan at Rockefeller Center, close to Stephenson's secret headquarters in the same building.

As a spy, Dulles had an uncanny ability to anticipate crises, as if he could see around corners. Dulles appeared like an avuncular pipe-smoking professor, wise about the ways of the world. With aplomb, he traded in suspicions and lies, careful never to be outfoxed by adversaries. He distrusted the Russian Communists almost as much as the Nazis. He detected the hidden hand of other foreign intelligence services in acts of violence, like the February 1941 gunshot death of a Soviet defector, Walter Krivitsky, in a Washington hotel room.

As a former head of Russian military intelligence, Krivitsky had provided important secrets to both British and American officials. Publicly, he detailed the abuses of Russian leader Joseph Stalin. Privately, he passed along information about a Soviet spy ring in Washington, DC. For these disclosures, Krivitsky knew he was a dead man. "If they ever try to prove I took my own life, don't believe it," he warned congressional investigators.

Local authorities, who examined Krivitsky's dead body at the Bellevue Hotel, ruled he had killed himself with a bullet to the head. Dulles thought otherwise. Assassination was more likely. "I shall never accept the story that he committed suicide," Dulles insisted.

In one of his first official actions, Donovan asked Ernest Cuneo, with his unique set of skills and contacts, to join his staff. Cuneo's unofficial status as a spy for the president was now formalized. Trusted because of his loyalty to FDR and friendship with Stephenson, Cuneo became a "liaison" for Donovan, dealing with competing agencies, such as the military, the Justice Department and Hoover's FBI, as well as with Congress and the press.

"Since I had been a friend and protagonist of all the departments involved, I anticipated little trouble," said Cuneo, who "plunged in" as soon as he learned of the president's approval.

The two energetic OSS men bonded by talking about their glory days playing football at Columbia. Donovan still seemed "a magnificent warhorse, heavily reined in under control but surging at the bit," recalled Cuneo. He was under no illusion about his own "liaison" position. "If things went wholly awry, the OSS could disavow me," Cuneo said. "The State department needn't even do that; diplomatically, I did not exist."

Prior to Donovan's travel to London, Cuneo and others in the Roosevelt administration were careful to bend, but not break, existing neutrality laws while secretly helping the British. With FDR seeking another term on the promise not to go to war, they didn't want to do anything that would inadvertently lead to conflict with Germany—like the sinking of the *Lusitania* did with World War I. Or what nearly happened in August 1939 with the SS *Bremen*.

Parked in New York Harbor, the *Bremen*, one of the finest

passenger liners in the world, was ordered by its German government to return home immediately, a few days before Hitler entered into war with Great Britain. But US Customs officials unexpectedly detained the *Bremen* at the dock along the Hudson River, claiming they needed to search for weapons and contraband.

Everyone involved, especially the *Bremen*'s captain, recognized the two extensive searches by Custom agents as a stalling tactic. Secretly, American officials had provided information about the location of Nazi ships to the British, who asked for the delay. In this case, Cuneo met with US Attorney General Frank Murphy to discuss how they could legally drag out the *Bremen*'s departure so a British warship, far off in Bermuda, could catch up and attack the German liner after it left New York's harbor.

"Murphy was visibly nervous as he wracked the Law to find every possible pretext for holding the great German superliner, the Bremen, until the British Atlantic Squadron could sink her as she cleared," recalled Cuneo. They used the media as part of their game plan. "We broadcast bulletins, ostensibly news" about the *Bremen*'s impending departure, Cuneo said, a clear tipoff to the Royal Navy about when to expect the *Bremen* to appear in international waters as a sitting duck.

As the exhaustive Customs inspections were nearly finalized, Cuneo suggested New York State health inspectors be summoned to the ship to check the crew for venereal disease. "Legal excuses were running out," he recalled. "As a last resort, I suggested [the health checkups] to give the Royal Navy a few more hours for the kill."

As the ship sailed out of New York Harbor, the *Bremen*'s captain gathered his sailors on deck to sing patriotic songs. Defiantly, they stuck out their arms in a Nazi salute as they passed under the Statue of Liberty. Out in the Atlantic, the *Bremen* managed to get away. In rough weather and traveling at top speed, it evaded the oncoming Royal Navy cruisers and landed safely back in Germany.

In retrospect, Cuneo realized, the sinking of the *Bremen* by the British would have been a political disaster for the president.

"FDR had reached the limit of the help he could offer," Cuneo said. "He could have had a fast US destroyer tail the Bremen, reporting her location. But it was far too dangerous in terms of American public opinion to shadow German ships at that time. Actually, Great Britain was none too popular west of the Alleghenies, to say nothing of the Irish Catholic big cities. And the Far West was much more concerned about Tokyo than Berlin."

Roosevelt's victory for a third term in November 1940 in effect allowed America's fledgling spy operation to expand. Pearl Harbor and the president's declaration of war against the Axis powers was still a year away. Yet his reelection meant that FDR could give a green light to men like Donovan and Cuneo to work undercover against Hitler.

In his own discreet way, Cuneo had shown a remarkable ability to move adeptly between the bruising egos of Washington politics and New York media. And now as a spy, he dealt with Stephenson's secret agents at Rockefeller Center, who ultimately answered to Churchill in London. From this point forward, they would share secrets against a common enemy. They were now partners in espionage.

7

SETTING UP SHOP

Cuneo first met this British spy Ian Fleming at Rockefeller Center during the war, and they became friends and later business associates. Fleming dedicated his James Bond novel Thunderball *to Cuneo, whom he called his "muse."*

Whether fact or fiction, Ian Fleming could always spin a good spy tale. The charming, inventive British Naval Intelligence officer first met Cuneo in 1941, and they soon began a long-term friendship. Though discreet about their top secret assignments, the two men liked to converse candidly on a vast array of top-ics, including sex, fame and adventure.

A favorite shared story was how Fleming and William Ste-phenson broke into the Japanese Consul General's office, lo-cated below the British Security Coordination headquarters in Rockefeller Center, and fleeced them of their secrets.

In espionage terms, it was a perfect crime. As Fleming's bi-ographer John Pearson later described, "Stephenson knew that coded messages were being transmitted from this office back to Tokyo by short-wave radio and he decided that the time had come to find out more."

During their daring 3:00 a.m. break-in, Stephenson, Fleming and two other spies entered the closed Japanese offices without being detected. Duplicate keys had been made. Fleming acted as a lookout for any security guards. They picked the locks to a safe and "borrowed" the Japanese code book and other confi-dential documents. They ran upstairs to their own offices and microfilmed all the important Japanese material.

Then downstairs again, they put the code book and top se-cret papers back into the safe. Meticulously, they left the pilfered material in the same order as they originally found it. Before departing, Fleming and Stephenson made sure nothing in the consul general's office appeared disturbed. And then, without a trace, they escaped into the night.

"To Stephenson, it was a straightforward operation," Pear-son recounted in *Life* magazine, "to Fleming a great and glee-ful adventure."

Years later, Fleming took this real-life experience and upped the ante through his fictional James Bond character (a literary effort that Cuneo would eventually help his friend translate to the movies). Instead of thievery, this time it was portrayed as murder.

In Fleming's first novel, *Casino Royale*, Bond killed a Japanese cipher expert who was cracking British coded messages inside Rockefeller Center. As an assassin, Bond shot the Japanese agent from a distance. He aimed from another building with a Remington rifle, equipped with telescopic sights and silencer.

"It was a pretty sound job," Bond summarized. "Nice and clean too. Three hundred yards away. No personal contact."

While far more violent than what actually happened, Fleming's fictional depiction also sounded vaguely like the proposed real-life hit job on Hitler that Stephenson wanted before the war.

Cuneo's friendship with Fleming began before America entered the war. In June 1941, Fleming accompanied Admiral John Godfrey of British Naval Intelligence to New York and Washington. They met several Americans, including Cuneo, to organize mutual spy plans. (Godfrey was a prototype for Bond's boss "M," the head of MI6, in Fleming's novel.)

Like Cuneo, Fleming grew to admire Stephenson, with his cool ingenuity and steely demeanor. Gleefully, Fleming told Godfrey about the successful Japanese break-in, hoping the spirited story would reach Churchill's appreciative ears. Winston's approval mattered to Ian on a personal level. Churchill had been friendly with Fleming's father, Valentine, a fellow Conservative in Parliament, who had been killed by German shellfire in World War I when Ian was only nine.

In Washington, Fleming conferred with America's new spymaster, William Donovan, who was already working hard to replicate a version of Stephenson's BSC for America. Impressed by the British agent's help, Donovan later gave Fleming a gift—a Colt Police Positive .38 revolver, engraved with the inscription "For Special Services."

New York was exciting for Fleming. While in town, he spent much of his time with Cuneo and Stephenson. The three very different spies—an American, a Canadian and a Brit—would share large dry martinis in quart glasses at Stephenson's palatial penthouse suite at the nearby Hotel Dorset, gossiping and plotting out strategy.

Stephenson could down several drinks without showing any apparent effect. Cuneo's description of how he got to know Fleming sounds like a scene from a Bond movie as well.

"There was a huge fireplace in which logs always glowed," Cuneo recalled. "It was an elegant and spacious room of warm shadows. Here, as the lights of the metropolis blinked on, visiting great and near-great of the British High Command gathered. It was here I met Ian Fleming."

At first glance, Cuneo seemed to have little in common with the British agent, with different backgrounds and sensibilities. Certainly they didn't look the same.

At age thirty-six, Cuneo appeared older and far heavier than his NFL football days, with thinning hair and drooping eyes. Fleming was taller and thinner, almost gaunt, from endless cigarettes, up to eighty a day. He had a high forehead with thick, curly brown hair neatly combed and parted, piercing blue eyes and a prominent jaw. Fleming possessed a poker face with a broken nose unrepaired. His stance suggested he once might have been a lightweight fighter.

With a slightly aloof air, Fleming, thirty-three years old, displayed a worldly knowledge. His creativity for espionage allowed him to come up later with Operation Mincemeat—the spectacular ruse that, with Churchill's blessing, used a corpse carrying phony war plans to trick the Germans prior to the Allied invasion of Sicily.

Friendship between the two young spies began with a rocky start when Cuneo noted Fleming's junior status among the other Brits in the room. Ian immediately objected.

"Do you question my bona fides?" asked Fleming, as if crossing swords.

"No, just your patently limited judgment," recalled Cuneo, with his gruff New Yorkese.

Both laughed at the exchange and dropped their defenses. Often, their meetings with Stephenson would migrate over to 21—one of Cuneo's favorite places in Manhattan—where he spent more hours trading insights and drinks with Fleming. As intelligence agents, they preferred a table off to the left from the entrance so they could keep an eye on everyone in the room.

"All but tirelessly, we taxed and challenged each other over the years, each accusing each other for what he himself was," Cuneo recalled. "He fancied me as the romanticist and he the realist." Fleming, like Stephenson, was a heroic, almost quixotic character, in Cuneo's estimate. When considering the state of the world, Fleming could "lapse into a melancholy pensiveness."

Cuneo was impressed that Fleming, a sophisticate with a discerning eye, held Stephenson in such unabashed high regard. It was "all but blind adoration," Cuneo described. "William [Stephenson] was one of the very few firm and brilliant stars in the heavens of Ian Fleming."

The British carried a seriousness of purpose to their spycraft—even the most potentially violent of their covert operations—that reflected their constant awareness of the life-and-death realities back in England. Their willingness to do whatever was necessary, even if it broke American law, was vital to saving their beloved United Kingdom. Because of his close involvement with Churchill's team at Rockefeller Center, Cuneo remained sympathetic to their cause.

"Recalling the Battle of Britain and the frightful losses of the R.A.F. pilots, I told my good friends that if New York City was bombed and burning and 868 West Point cadets had been killed in the air over Sandy Hook [the New Jersey oceanfront site of Fort Hancock military base] defending the city, extreme and perhaps illegal measures on the part of Americans would be understandable and even forgivable," Cuneo explained.

★ ★ ★

The British spies were new tenants at Rockefeller Center, as were nearly all those inhabiting the huge complex in the middle of Manhattan. The historic landmark known to millions of visitors today took more than a decade to build during the Depression.

Along Fifth Avenue, one of the complex's first structures, the British Empire Building with its limestone facade, went up in 1933. A radial sun symbol on its wall lionized the United Kingdom's global empire on which "the sun never sets."

Next door, the high-rise International Building—where Stephenson's spy headquarters would be located—opened two years later. From its thirty-sixth-floor windows, one could easily see the nearby Empire State Building, a towering skyscraper built in 1931 that became the bustling city's trademark. The entire sprawling Rockefeller site, on twelve acres leased from Columbia University, was finally completed in 1940, the same year Stephenson's spies moved in.

The sleek, urbane beauty of the International Building, like some secular cathedral across from St. Patrick's, seemed to enhance its mysteries. Inside, the subtle lighting and defining Art Deco touches captured the swank mood and style of Manhattan. Young spies who toiled for the BSC entered each day from Fifth Avenue. They walked through revolving doors into a majestic four-story lobby with marble walls and Greek columns, then were whisked away in elevators, ascending to their secret headquarters high above on the thirty-sixth floor.

Before the war, Rockefeller Center was a beehive of foreign intrigue humming beneath the surface. Several nations and international groups kept offices there, including those involved with the French Resistance. (Eventually, the FBI caught a Nazi, a Japanese and several Soviet Russian spies operating in the complex, apprehended with help from Rockefeller officials.)

As a special favor to Churchill's government, the Rockefellers, one of America's richest families, allowed British intelligence
to use two floors virtually rent-free as their secret headquarters. Ironically, the Germans wanted the same space in the mid-
1930s, but the Rockefellers, concerned about Hitler's hateful
Nazis, declined to lease it.

Churchill, whose mother was a Brooklyn-born American,
had his own special relationship with the Rockefellers. Some
genealogists claim Winston was a distant cousin to John D.
Rockefeller, the immensely wealthy founder of the Standard
Oil Company and fountainhead of the family fortune. In the
early 1930s, the family requested that Churchill, a well-known
writer as well as a politician, put together a fulsome biography
of the senior Rockefeller, portraying him as a great man. To
complete such an endeavor, Winston requested a huge advance.
The book project never got off the ground.

By mid-1940, the most important Rockefeller for the British was Nelson, the oil magnate's ambitious thirty-two-year-
old grandson. (A moderate Republican, Nelson later became
Governor of New York, and then Vice President of the United
States under Gerald Ford in the 1970s.)

Young Rockefeller voiced concern about growing Nazi influence in Latin America, where the family had sizable oil interests.
He warned about security risks as Hitler's foreign business interests, sometimes mingled with US companies, affected wartime
supply lines to Great Britain. In August 1940, President Roosevelt appointed Rockefeller as Coordinator of Inter-American
Affairs, a goodwill job that included keeping an eye surreptitiously on the Germans. Nelson soon began trading spy secrets
with Stephenson's staff located in his family's building.

In setting up shop, Stephenson relied on an eclectic group
of talented young people who, like Ian Fleming, added to the
intrigue surrounding the BSC. One recruit was successful

screenwriter Benn Levy, who received a taste of this clandestine behavior when he was sent over from London.

British officials refused in advance to tell Levy the address of Stephenson's headquarters. Instead, they instructed him to memorize a specific telephone number. When he arrived in Manhattan, according to his marching orders, Levy was told to call that number and say, *This is Mortimer.* Once he uttered those magical words, he would receive further directions over the phone.

For Levy, who'd already written and directed various suspense and horror films (including one produced by Alfred Hitchcock), these directions sounded like a Hollywood melodrama, a two-reel thriller.

But like a bad actor, Levy fumbled his line when he arrived in Midtown New York. He dialed the correct telephone number—but then froze while trying to remember the cover name.

"This is...this is..." Levy repeated, unable to recall the code "Mortimer."

Levy stumbled over and over. Finally, he cried out in frustration, "This is Benn Levy!"

Stephenson's telephone operator on the other end didn't seem fazed at all.

"That's quite all right," said the operator. "We've been expecting you. Come right up."

The operator told Levy to report to Room 3603 at 630 Fifth Avenue.

Stephenson often entrusted his Rockefeller Center spy operation to his top deputy, Charles Howard "Dick" Ellis, its most seasoned intelligence agent. A diminutive man, Ellis was known to be both amiable and knowledgable, interested in all aspects of espionage and everything going on in the office.

When Stephenson traveled back and forth between London and other destinations, he relied on Ellis to deal with dozens of in-house staffers, visiting intelligence agents and outsider friends like Cuneo.

"Stephenson insisted I meet Colonel Ellis...a really little man, blonde, almost petite," recalled Cuneo. "What was most striking about him was his delicate hands. He was a magnificent pianist, of concert stature." Ellis struck him as a well-traveled, cosmopolitan man, far more conversant about spying than Stephenson, a relative newcomer to the game.

Born in Australia to British parents, Ellis became a decorated war hero in World War I, shot three times in battle. Afterward, he studied at Oxford and the Sorbonne and became fluent in Russian and German. He served as a career officer in British intelligence for several years, building a reputation as smart and reliable. Ellis also spent time as the British vice-consul in Berlin and as a newspaper correspondent in Vienna, cultivating undercover sources with Russian agents also working with the German Abwehr.

Ellis's dedication to the Crown seemed unquestioned when his London superiors dispatched him from the Foreign Office to Rockefeller Center in 1940. "I had been 20 years in the professional intelligence service when in 1940 London sent me to Intrepid's headquarters in New York to help maintain secrecy," Ellis later recalled.

At that time, Stewart Menzies, the fabled "C" of MI6, considered it a good fit. Wary of Stephenson's impulsiveness, Menzies installed Ellis into the BSC as a steadying influence. Menzies hadn't liked Churchill's selection of Stephenson for the risky assignment in Manhattan. He sent along Ellis as a way of mitigating any possible damage. To seal the deal, it was arranged that Ellis's wife would get a job in the coding department.

Ellis expressed unwavering loyalty to his new boss, Stephenson, and the leadership at 10 Downing Street. "With the outbreak of war," Ellis later said, "Churchill turned to those who stood by him in the prewar years, among whom Stephenson had been...a close friend, whose mature judgment and energy had already been manifested."

In New York and Washington, Ellis shared secrets with the FBI's Hoover and assisted William Donovan as he created the fledgling US spy operation. Cuneo was impressed and so was his American intelligence boss. According to Cuneo, Ellis instructed the OSS on "the technique of clandestine communications of which he was a foremost expert." He came to Washington to help oversee the installation of the new US spy agency's methods of reaching all its agents and sources of top secret information.

"Donovan told me how desperately [the US spy agency] needed him," Cuneo recalled about Ellis, "and I now could see why."

On a personal level, Cuneo was impressed by "Dickie," as he called him, with his remarkable wartime experiences and command of history. Cuneo learned Ellis was a "tremendous scholar, a master of the Arabic tongues" who had journeyed to Afghanistan, Iraq and the Russian border. With a knowing tone in his voice, Ellis praised one particular Soviet contact for his valuable information. He claimed this double agent was "no fool, and like most Russians of his type, played both ends against the middle."

Ellis seemed a character right out of Rudyard Kipling's Kim—the beloved novel about the conflict between Russia and Great Britain in Central Asia—and its description of spying as "the Great Game," a phrase used commonly ever since.

"Colonel Ellis, a most active player in 'The Great Game,' was particularly equipped to play it," said Cuneo, who imbibed the "romantic" war tales Ellis told him. "He was a close friend of H.G. Wells at the time he was writing his classic, 'Outline of History.' Ellis recounted to me some of their conversations of the ancient Egyptian, Babylonian and Persian Empires. It occurred to me that Ellis' knowledge of these ancient civilizations and Islam was even more encyclopedic than that of Wells himself."

To a remarkable degree, Donovan took Ellis into his confidence, probably more than he should with a foreign agent. They discussed the selection and training of new US spies, money spent on covert operations, and counterespionage efforts designed to catch traitors in their midst. Ellis learned about special American weapons being developed and Donovan's secret contacts with enemy intelligence services.

"Ellis was at the center of Donovan affairs," Menzies's biographer Anthony Cave Brown explained. "He consulted and assisted in all phases of the development of Donovan's organization."

Donovan either didn't realize Ellis was reporting all his confidences back to London or simply didn't care. Counterintelligence—searching for security leaks and double agents—was still a relatively new concept in the OSS. What Ellis may have said to other intelligence agents would remain hidden throughout the war. But certainly Menzies was happy with Ellis's cultivation of America's top spy. As Brown concluded, "Thus 'C' could expect to be well informed about what was happening inside Donovan's offices."

With his seasoned professionalism, Ellis seemed to put everyone's mind at ease, both in London and the United States. No one questioned his loyalty, nor his willingness to always be accommodating. In his own words, Stephenson relied on his deputy director as "one of the very few you could be certain about."

In this menagerie of talent, Cuneo also met H. Montgomery Hyde, who, like other key BSC staffers, became a spy after spending time in the world of letters. Originally from Belfast in what is now Northern Ireland, Hyde was trained in the law as a barrister but worked most notably as a historian and writer. He published two books before joining British intelligence in 1939, the year Great Britain went to war against the Nazis.

Dapper and erudite, Hyde was among the most valued of "Stephenson's boys," as Cuneo remembered, because of his unique spy skills. "In addition to being a barrister, [Hyde] was used as a highly expert individual in opening safes and letters to such an extent that he instructed [Donovan's US spies] and the FBI in their daring acts," Cuneo said.

Hyde's job at Rockefeller Center was a most delicate assignment—security and counterespionage. In New York, with so many German sympathizers, his task demanded constant vigilance. Done correctly, it would protect the BSC from any breaches of confidential information, from without or within. And Hyde would do so inimitably, in his own raconteur style.

"With such a large organization as BSC, there was always the danger of leakages, particularly among the junior staff," Hyde later conceded. "Of course, it was sometimes difficult for the senior members of Stephenson's staff to conceal the true nature of their activities, particularly when they encountered friends from former civilian life."

From his own experience, Hyde learned how hard it was to keep masked his spy identity. He bumped into an old friend, Irish poet Oliver St. John Gogarty of Dublin, after both had moved to New York. During a few more friendly meetings, Hyde still kept up the charade. "Gogarty never showed the slightest hint that he was aware of what I was doing," Hyde recalled.

But Hyde found out otherwise when he invited Gogarty to a small dinner party in his apartment. All the other guests were women and men from the BSC. As the night proceeded, the Irish poet asked for a blank sheet of paper and began scribbling some verse on it. When finished, he gave the paper to Hyde.

"I think you will all like this," Gogarty said to the gathering of spies.

Then Hyde read the naughty limerick:

A lady of doubtful nativity
Had a fanny of great sensitivity
When she sat on the lap
Of a Nazi or Jap
She could detect Fifth Column activity.

Hyde and his guests all laughed. They gave the limerick manuscript to their boss, Stephenson. "He in turn passed it onto the President's adviser, Ernest Cuneo, and no doubt it caused some hilarity when it was recited in the White House," Hyde later wrote.

Over time, Hyde would become Stephenson's Boswell, writing admirably about the Rockefeller Center spymaster's actions, just like Fleming and Cuneo.

8

DOUBLE AGENTS

"It is essential to seek out enemy agents who have come to conduct espionage against you and to bribe them to serve you. Give them instructions and care for them. Thus double agents are recruited and used."

—Sun Tzu, *The Art of War*

The Norden bombsight was touted in intelligence circles as America's secret weapon. No one was supposed to know about it, especially the Nazis.

From twenty thousand feet up in the sky, a warplane pilot using the special device could hit targets on the ground with uncanny accuracy, like a flying Annie Oakley. Its whiz-bang potential was spoken of with the same awe as drones flown by later generations.

The US government poured more than $1 billion in today's dollars into building the Norden bombsight. A crude analog computer, it resembled a lawn mower engine, with gyros, mirrors, gears and ball bearings inside.

Though its accuracy proved less pinpoint than predicted, military leaders placed such faith in the Norden bombsight that it was later used on massive air raids on Germany and when the Enola Gay dropped an atomic bomb on Hiroshima, Japan.

Utmost secrecy shrouded the development of the Norden bombsight. At a heavily guarded manufacturing plant in Manhattan, FBI agents checked each employee before they left to make sure the secret plans were safe. Yet somehow in 1938, an assembly inspector named Hermann Lang managed to get his hands on its blueprint plans. At a secret meeting, Lang gave copies of them to a top Nazi spy hiding in New York.

"Is it really the Norden Bombsight?" asked Nikolaus Ritter, Chief of Air Intelligence for the Abwehr, as if he'd found the Holy Grail of aviation.

Lang, a naturalized US citizen who considered himself "a good German," explained the blueprints detailed only part of the Norden bombsight. He promised to get the rest.

"The Americans are so secretive about this device," explained Lang, who was given "Paul" as his Nazi code name. "But I have no doubt that your engineers will be able to reconstruct the missing sections from the prints I'm able to give you."

Admiral Wilhelm Canaris, the head of the Abwehr, had already authorized German spies and their informers in the United States to keep track of shipping routes and military installations. Now, Canaris sent Ritter to New York on this special assignment, telling him that Hitler's fleet of planes must have this top secret device developed by the Americans.

"My message to you to expand our coverage of the United States stemmed from a request of the Luftwaffe to procure for them the design of the Norden bombsight," Canaris explained to Ritter, identified as "Dr. Rantzau," his secret code name. "This is a very important assignment and the mission is fraught with considerable risk."

Ritter sent Lang's purloined bombardier plans to Germany, hidden in the hollow of an umbrella. A different German agent, employed at another US defense plant in Brooklyn, provided the plans for other sophisticated warplane devices, including radio instruments and gun mountings. These plans also were sent to Germany and used by the Luftwaffe.

The Nazi espionage inside America seemed to be going on underneath the nose of FBI watchdog J. Edgar Hoover, traditionally more concerned with homegrown gangsters and bank robbers than foreign agents. The lack of an organized US intelligence system was quite apparent to William Stephenson when he took on his Rockefeller Center assignment in mid-1940. He felt America was ripe for Nazi sabotage and infiltration, especially at its major ports, and was handcuffed by existing neutrality laws.

"It was comparatively easy for the Germans to recruit dock labourers and stevedores from the local German, Italian and Irish communities, who hated Britain," recalled Hyde, the BSC security official, "while the F.B.I. agents were unable to intervene so long as German subversive activities did not directly threaten American interests."

America's vulnerability was highlighted by the fatal Times Square incident in March 1941. The truth about the dead man's alias and real identity seemed unsolvable to the FBI without the BSC stepping in. "It was Stephenson's organization which provided the missing link in the chain of investigation," recalled Hyde.

A few months later, in June 1941, Hoover's fortune changed dramatically when a large group of spies assembled by Ritter were arrested, including Hermann Lang.

"The greatest spy roundup in U.S. history," Hoover proclaimed about the arrests on Walter Winchell's Sunday-night radio show. Hoover doubled down on the publicity. "One of the most active, extensive and vicious groups we have ever had to deal with," he declared.

In all, thirty-three spies and coconspirators were eventually convicted. Alarming details from these prosecutions fueled American fears about a hidden Nazi threat within their own borders. "The secret of the Norden Bombsight, this country's most jealously guarded air defense weapon, has been in the hands of the Germans since 1938," charged the federal prosecutor at Lang's trial.

Ironically, the big break for Hoover's FBI with this case occurred when Ritter made the mistake of recruiting William

Sebold, another German immigrant to New York, as a spy. The Nazis threatened to harm Sebold's family in the homeland if he didn't cooperate. Instead, in early 1940, Sebold informed the American authorities of Ritter's offer. He became a double agent for his adopted country. The FBI paid him $50 a week.

In his low-key manner, for several months Sebold sought out secret information from other Nazi spies, most notably Frederick Duquesne, a veteran spy who acted as a leader of the group arrested by the FBI. The FBI set up a phony Manhattan office for Sebold, who posed as a diesel engineer sympathetic to the Nazis. When Duquesne visited his office, Hoover's G-men operated hidden microphones and a camera through a peephole.

Although Hoover generally disdained reliance on double agents, Sebold proved invaluable. FBI agents used a Long Island radio transmitter set up by the Abwehr and impersonated Sebold over the air, sending dozens of messages containing false information back to Germany.

Sebold helped the FBI snare many other German spies and informers in the New York region, all part of the so-called "Duquesne spy ring," whose activities involved everything from sabotage to sexual favors. The arrest lineup included those linked to the German American Bund movement, along with such characters as Lily Stein, a sultry artist's model "whose tiptoe trail zigzagged from Vienna to New York, through embassies and drawing rooms," according to *Time* magazine.

The story of Sebold and the Duquesne spy ring later inspired a Hollywood film—this one made with Hoover's blessing—*The House on 92nd Street*, which won an Oscar for best original story.

The increased public attention on Nazi infiltration, encouraged by the White House, became a media obsession directed at America's still largely isolationist audience. Newspapers, radio, movies and even comic books featuring Superman, Batman and Wonder Woman portrayed this threat.

"Captain America," the original superhero character (and eventual cornerstone of Marvel Comics) was created in 1941 and often seen fighting against Hitler and his spies. This popular comic reflected the views of its writers Joe Simon and Jack Kirby, both American Jews, expressing their outrage at the Nazi assault on Western civilization.

"Gentlemen, the time has come when the democracies must stand together," proclaimed Steve Rogers (aka "Captain America") dressed in his red, white and blue garb on the illustrated cover of an early 1941 issue. "The fate of the world depends on Britain's victory."

Sensing the changing national mood, Roosevelt directed the FBI to step up its surveillance of German sympathizers, and even isolationists. In the name of national defense, the president allowed wiretapping, which had been banned previously, to avoid "sabotage, assassination, and 'Fifth Column' activities."

Aviation hero Charles Lindbergh, a prominent isolationist and leading figure in the America First Committee, suspected his phones were tapped. By 1941, America First had seven hundred chapters and nearly one million members across the country. Many of them were friendly to Nazi Germany and openly anti-Semitic.

Lindbergh's FBI file, released decades after his 1974 death, shows how Hoover's G-men treated him more like a foreign spy than a national hero. Partly through electronic surveillance, they detailed both Lindbergh's critical statements of American policy in public and his private comments filled with racist remarks. (In a 1939 article in the isolationist *Reader's Digest*, Lindbergh hailed the technology of aviation as "one of those priceless possessions which permit the White race to live at all in a pressing sea of Yellow, Black and Brown.") One lengthy memo summarized all of Lindbergh's speeches around the country in 1941 and said he was paid $700 by the America First Committee for each appearance.

At Rockefeller Center, Stephenson also focused on America First, a major obstacle to US entry into the war. His British spies attended America First meetings throughout the States, keeping track of members, what they said, and figuring out "new and effective ways of instigating counter-propaganda." One British agent convinced the group's lecture bureau chief to provide information about its propaganda plans, its financial backers and any possible ties to the Nazis.

The BSC's biggest attempt to undermine Lindbergh took place at an October 1941 America First rally inside Madison Square Garden. British spies issued phony duplicate tickets for the event to pro-British disruptors, hoping to upset Lindbergh's speech to his rabid followers. The move backfired, however, creating a larger crowd for its featured speaker Lindbergh than would have ordinarily been the case.

The BSC's secret efforts to disrupt the event remained unknown to the American public. But in his speech that night, Lindbergh complained about how his opponents made "constant use of undercover methods" and "smearing campaigns" to stop him.

In New York, Duško Popov was another double agent, working undercover simultaneously for both the Nazi Abwehr and Churchill's spies. Keeping Popov's existence secret, however, seemed an impossible task. Eventually, Cuneo would learn of his story too.

A handsome, smooth-talking playboy from Serbia, Popov drew attention in Walter Winchell's newspaper column for dating French actress Simone Simon. Popov's fondness for women—especially frolicking with two in a bed, prompted his British keepers to give him the jocular code name "Tricycle."

Popov's wartime espionage in America—like other parts of the Rockefeller Center spy saga—began with the fatal Times Square car crash in March 1941. Following the taxicab death of Ulrich von der Osten, Germany's top spy in the States, the Abwehr decided to send Popov to Manhattan as his replacement.

By that time, Popov had established himself as a reliable provider of confidential information to the Nazis in Europe, drawing upon his wealthy connections in café society. But secretly, Popov's contempt for Hitler's henchmen compelled him to become a double agent for the British. When the Nazis sent him to New York as the new head of their spy ring, the British intelligence service told Popov to report to William Stephenson and make the most of this opportunity.

In a book-lined study with a fireplace, British spymaster Stewart Menzies gave Popov some advice before he left London. "You are a double agent and, as such, more vulnerable than an ordinary one. Your activity calls for the use of deception and the penetration of the Abwehr," Menzies instructed. "You and your usefulness may live and last only if thoroughly protected and managed."

Menzies warned the twenty-eight-year-old Popov that his reputation for risky living could bring unfortunate consequences. "You have the makings of a very good spy, except that you don't like to obey orders," Menzies said, as Popov later recalled in a memoir. "You had better learn or you will be a very dead spy."

Before departing for New York, Popov visited a swank hotel casino in neutral Portugal, a favorite location of spies from both sides to relax and outfox one another. Popov later claimed he spotted British Naval Intelligence officer Ian Fleming "skulking around," following him throughout the resort's lobby and restaurant. Presumably Fleming was there checking on this new double agent. (Fleming would soon be in New York himself, answering to Stephenson.)

But at the elegant Estoril Casino, Fleming watched anxiously as Popov made a huge bet at a baccarat table—using British intelligence money meant for his spy efforts in New York—and called another player's bluff.

"I don't know what devil was behind me, perhaps Fleming or the knowledge that he was there," recalled Popov, who grabbed the large bills from his evening jacket and placed them on the table's green felt covering. "Somehow the wager communicated itself to the other tables in the room, and all became silent. I glanced at Fleming. His face was the green of bile."

For Popov, it was high noon at the casino. At the last minute, the other player sitting across from him folded. Embarrassed before the crowd of onlookers, his baccarat opponent said he didn't have the cash to match Popov's wager.

With a flourish, Popov made a big stink about this sudden dropout. He grabbed back his cash, and loudly complained that the management needed to weed out those who were not serious players. The bravura spy performance, undoubtedly, stuck with Fleming. "He had a smile of amusement on his face," Popov recalled. "I'm sure he had seen through and enjoyed my comedy."

That dramatic scene was also imitated in Fleming's first novel, *Casino Royale*. "I'm told that Ian Fleming said he based his character James Bond to some degree on me and my experiences," mused Popov. "Could be. More to the point, I rather doubt that a Bond in the flesh could have survived more than forty-eight hours as an espionage agent."

When he arrived in New York, Popov carried along special instructions from his Nazi handlers. A telegram he received contained a microdot message—roughly the size of a printed period that could be enlarged—asking about US aviation defenses. But it also contained questions about security details surrounding the US naval base at Pearl Harbor, the home of America's Pacific Fleet. During a debriefing with FBI agents in New York, Popov made clear his belief that the questions in the German telegram were forwarded by the Japanese and that they intended to attack.

But when the microdot documents reached Hoover's desk, the FBI chief focused on Popov's lifestyle rather than his warning.

Hoover condemned Popov for taking an underage girlfriend to Miami for a fling. He threatened to prosecute him under the Mann Act unless he left the United States immediately.

"You're like all double agents," Hoover yelled at Popov during their meeting. "You're begging for information to sell to your German friends so you can make a lot of money and be a playboy."

Certainly Popov's womanizing and lavish spending may not have been to Hoover's liking, but it made for excellent cover in duping the Germans. "I don't think a choir boy could perform my job," Popov argued, "but if I've caused trouble, I pray you, forgive me." The FBI director, who wanted to become America's top spy as well, wasn't in a forgiving mood. He soon ended the meeting.

Stunned by Hoover's incredible response to his warning, Popov complained to the Brits at Rockefeller Center, in particular Stephenson's deputy, Dick Ellis, who'd been given access to Popov's secret documents. Ellis said there was little the BSC could do with the headstrong Hoover.

"America is still uncommitted, and Hoover probably thought you were warmongering," Ellis said with a sympathetic look. "Any intervention from us would do more harm than good. Hoover is very jealous about any interference with his organization, especially from the British."

Eventually, Hoover summarized the Pearl Harbor inquiry into a memo for naval intelligence—emphasizing the microdot technology and not the Japanese interest in the US naval base. But neither they nor the White House heeded the implicit warning in the Pearl Harbor questions.

Some historians have blamed Hoover's hubris for this gross oversight. Still others have suggested the British, desperate for the US to enter the war, were content to have the playboy spy's warnings ignored. Years later, Popov claimed to be haunted by the fact he'd tried in August 1941 to warn the US of an impending Japanese attack, four months before it happened. "How, I asked myself, how?" Popov recalled. "We knew they were coming."

By this point in the summer of 1941, the cooperation that Stephenson had once enjoyed with Hoover's FBI—based on the deal that Cuneo had helped broker a year earlier with FDR's approval—was drying up. Increasingly, Hoover resented the incursion into his turf and, at Stephenson's urging, the growing influence of Donovan as FDR's new intelligence chief.

The mishandling of double agent Popov would anger Churchill's spies in New York and fill them with regret. As Stephenson later claimed, "I had no doubt that Pearl Harbor was *a* target and perhaps *the* target."

9

INCOGNITO CUNEO

"An invisible man can rule the world! Nobody will see him come, nobody will see him go. He can hear every secret."

—actor Claude Rains in *The Invisible Man*, a film adapted from the H.G. Wells novel of the same name.

The grand Mayflower Hotel in the heart of Washington, DC, was a favorite of the Roosevelt administration from its very start. On the eve of his presidential inauguration in 1933, FDR wrote his famous "The only thing we have to fear is fear itself" speech in Room 776.

On this particular day, Ernest Cuneo rushed through the Mayflower's elegant lobby on his way to meet a top FDR aide, Thomas "Tommy the Cork" Corcoran, about some pressing confidential matters.

Cuneo was hard to miss. Although bulky since his days playing football, Cuneo's weight had grown to nearly three hundred pounds. With his hair nearly gone, he looked older than his years. But he still carried tremendous energy in his stride and had not lost his quick wit.

Evie Walker Robert, the vivacious wife of the Democratic Party's treasurer, recognized Cuneo in the lobby and stopped him. She asked what had brought him to Washington.

"Sh-h-h—don't tell anyone I'm in town!" Cuneo said, pretending to be horrified. "I'm here incognito."

This amusing anecdote later appeared in Drew Pearson's nationally syndicated newspaper column called "Washington Merry-Go-Round," with a small item under the headline "Incognito Cuneo." It was a rare mention of him in print.

Pearson had been Cuneo's college instructor and he lauded his former student as "the brilliant New York attorney and ex-Columbia football star." When in Washington, Cuneo sometimes gossiped over lunch at the Mayflower with Pearson and Harold Ickes, an FDR aide. But the source of this merry little item was likely Evie Robert—who lived at the Mayflower and wrote her own local newspaper column—rather than Cuneo, who viewed invisibility as essential to his influence and power.

Pearson eventually retained Cuneo as a private attorney, just like Walter Winchell. The two top columnists both relied on Cuneo for an endless flow of confidential news tips and deep background leaks from the Roosevelt administration. But Cuneo's name never appeared as the source for those items.

He preferred to remain incognito.

Knowing how to manipulate the press was crucial in politics, as Cuneo learned in working for the White House. Over the past decade, he had received a master class in the art of political messaging that would prove invaluable as a spy. These lessons—in what Cuneo called "combat journalism"—were taught by his old boss LaGuardia and by White House insiders like Corcoran, Adolf Berle and James Farley, FDR's campaign manager (and later Postmaster General) who appointed him associate general counsel of the Democratic National Committee.

"My experience in combat journalism was extremely valuable," Cuneo said of his pragmatic training, which went far beyond what he'd learned in law school.

Cuneo absorbed the most by watching Roosevelt—the greatest politician of their age. Cuneo's full-time devotion to FDR, his Brain Trust pals and the thrill of politics probably cost him his first marriage. But he felt proud to be working for the White House, especially given his minority background.

Cuneo was "one of the first Italian Americans to advise a US president [and] served a variety of important, if often unseen, roles in FDR's administration," historian Salvatore J. LaGumina noted. For his secret but effective lobbying with Winchell for another term in 1940, Roosevelt "gratefully acknowledged Cuneo's role by inviting him to sit in the presidential box for the inauguration—an offer Cuneo refused, in keeping with his preference for anonymity."

Cuneo viewed Roosevelt as a force of nature. As an administrator, FDR regularly pit one faction against another, hoping to draw the best out of both. "Having served with that other hurricane, Fiorello H. LaGuardia, it took me no time at all to realize that the man who was operating the ship in the maelstrom, in this Cave of Winds, was FDR," he explained. "In simplest terms, his method was to assign the same job and the same jurisdiction to two different men, both powerful and ambitious."

Roosevelt could outmaneuver, scramble and score big points in the public arena—just like "Galloping" Red Grange, the human marvel from the NFL's early days, whom Cuneo compared to the president. Cuneo marveled at Roosevelt's sleight-of-hand ability, his thoroughbred political talent. Famously, FDR said, "I am a juggler—I never let my right hand know what my left hand does." Cuneo was inspired and acted like a sports fan around him. "I saw many champions in many fields, but I never saw any one who approached the stature of FDR," he attested.

Despite the dizzying effects of White House power, Cuneo learned to do his job with as little notice as possible. To be a successful operative, silence and rectitude were required. In particular, Corcoran taught him that lesson. "He was FDR's Field Marshal with that quality which FDR most insisted upon—'the passion for anonymity,'" Cuneo wrote. "'The Passion for Anonymity' was regarded as the standing order of the day by the Commander-In-Chief."

Tommy the Cork was a stickler for this stealth approach in politics. "The security of Corcoran's Palace Guard was so close and intense" that Cuneo joked he "suffered from a feeling of agoraphobia."

Though nothing was written down anywhere, Corcoran's methods followed the same tight rules and discipline as a spy manual.

"The Palace Guard kept very few records, if any," Cuneo explained. "Its principal—perhaps exclusive—means of communication was the telephone. Corcoran called it *The* Weapon. He told me, 'A bullet moves at 750 miles an hour, but a telephone moves at 186,000 miles a second and leaves no trace.'"

Cuneo believed one of Corcoran's best White House achievements was the creation of an "invisible" team of White House lawyers who fought behind the scenes to enact FDR's programs during his first two terms. "It is little less than amazing that the genesis of those institutions which governed the daily life of the country has received scarcely the notice, much less the evaluations, of the professional historians," he contended.

However, as America turned increasingly toward war, the 1930s domestic agenda that Corcoran championed as a virtual "deputy president" was now pushed aside. Other trusted FDR aides like Harry Hopkins—a chief liaison dealing with Churchill and Stalin—became more important. Corcoran's power was now ebbing away. Rather than fight over White House priorities, he decided to leave.

"I'm too Irish to wholeheartedly support the British and I'm too Catholic to wholeheartedly support Russia," Corcoran explained.

By the time Cuneo began working as a spy with Stephenson and the BSC, he scarcely saw Corcoran anymore. He had learned to survive politically. Cuneo developed a considerable set of skills as an intermediary, a go-between, an effective fixer between foreign allies and domestic agencies. "My own lines of communication remained strong with Justice, the FBI and State," he said after Corcoran's departure.

For all his many inroads to White House power, Cuneo still acted like a free agent, very much his own man. On certain matters, he even acted independent of the Roosevelt administration.

Behind the scenes in 1939, for example, Cuneo assisted liberal Americans who volunteered as doctors, nurses and ambulance drivers in the ongoing Spanish Civil War. The bloody conflict in Barcelona, between the leftist Republican government and General Francisco Franco's rebel forces supported by Hitler and Mussolini, became a precursor to the world war that soon followed. But because of America's neutrality law, Secretary of State Cordell Hull refused to give out any passports to Spain. The volunteers enlisted Cuneo to oppose Hull, one of FDR's most powerful cabinet members.

Citing the Bill of Rights, Cuneo threatened court action if Hull didn't grant passports to the volunteers and allow shippers to send medical supplies to Spain. American Civil Liberties Union attorney Morris Ernst—best known for successfully defending Random House against obscenity charges with James Joyce's novel *Ulysses*—joined him in this fight.

In a remarkable turnaround, Hull backed down. Cuneo's supporters said the death toll in Barcelona, as bad as it was with thousands of casualties, would have been even worse if not for the American medical personnel and supplies freed up by his legal intervention.

"Almost no one knows it, but the one man responsible for their presence is Ernest Cuneo, an unobtrusive New Deal adviser who forced the State Department to issue American passports for Spain," wrote Pearson in his Washington column in February 1939. "Cuneo kept in the background, said nothing about his efforts. But his long legal brain probably was responsible for many lives being saved before and after Barcelona."

For most White House aides, running the risk of embarrassing a Secretary of State and opposing the administration's position in public would be grounds for a quick exit. Cuneo learned he could stand his ground privately with stars of the administration if his words sounded like good advice from a wise lawyer. Unafraid and tough by nature, Cuneo was increasingly sure of his instincts and not afraid of confrontation.

During the Lend-Lease Act controversy in March 1941, Attorney General Robert Jackson told Cuneo that sending ships and other military equipment to Britain under the legislation was unconstitutional. Before day's end, Jackson confided, he planned to send his written opinion to the president.

"Bob, you can send the memorandum if you want, but I wouldn't go home if I were you because it's coming right back," Cuneo replied, in a frank assessment. "The president is going to send the destroyers no matter what his Attorney General thinks."

Cuneo was well aware how private lobbying by Britain had convinced FDR about that much-needed help. As Cuneo later recalled, "I told him [Jackson] not to feel too badly: that by one o'clock that day, he would either reverse himself or he'd be asked for his resignation."

Around this time, Cuneo decided he needed a residence in Washington as a political pied-à-terre. With his marriage broken, he no longer spent every night in Manhattan at his home on Sutton Place. He rented a large apartment at the Anchorage, a hotel on Connecticut Avenue that became a clubhouse for those working with William Donovan's growing spy operation. "I needed little: five telephones, paper and pencils," he explained.

Cuneo could pay for his expensive back-and-forth commuting lifestyle because he was flush with money as Winchell's legal adviser and occasional ghostwriter in New York. In the District of Columbia, his Anchorage neighbors included fellow lawyer Arthur Goldberg, an intelligence officer for Donovan who later became a US Supreme Court Justice.

"I have a very great fondness for it," Cuneo said years later about the Anchorage, in an oral history for the LBJ Presidential Library, "because in the years subsequent my apartment was more or less used as a headquarters, off-scene, for General Donovan's Strategic Services, and through it passed various people like Arthur."

As a newfound bachelor, Cuneo enjoyed the social life of Washington as well as the nightclubs of Manhattan. To women, Ernie could be fun and lively, a well-connected lawyer who didn't reveal much about his daytime work but seemed to know plenty of celebrities and politicians. His various girlfriends and female acquaintances later wound up answering questions about him when Cuneo tried briefly to sign up for the US Navy in a swell of patriotic fervor after Pearl Harbor. Cuneo's background check—performed by four Navy officers who "went over every detail of my life like ferrets"—quickly became too personal.

"When they started thoroughly investigating some young ladies I knew, thereby frightening the wits out of them, I told them [the Navy officials] to get the hell out of my life and stay out," Cuneo recalled. "I later learned the recommendation from the New Deal White House, believe it or not, made me unacceptable from the start. A great red 'PI' was marked on my file— Political Influence—a code designating 'get rid of this guy.'"

His White House–related recommendations for the Navy job also included letters from two US Supreme Court justices then on the bench. Though Cuneo doesn't reveal their names in his memoir, it was likely Justice Frank Murphy and Justice William O. Douglas, whom he'd considered friends when they served previously in FDR's administration.

After Cuneo read their words about him, though, he was struck and hurt by their ethnic reference.

"I was annoyed somewhat in that two of them referred to me as an Italian-American," he recalled, a reminder of the prejudice he'd felt so many times before in a still largely white Anglo-Saxon Protestant society. "Up until this time, it hadn't even occurred to me that they thought of me other than as American as they."

10

THE PROPAGANDA WARS

"All propaganda is lies, even when one is telling the truth."

—George Orwell

By early 1941, Ernest Cuneo realized that both British secret intelligence and their Nazi nemesis, the Abwehr, were far better at propagating disinformation in America than US officials were at stopping or even detecting it.

"That phenomena peculiar to the Twentieth Century, the propaganda war, reached new heights," Cuneo recalled. "The full power of the modern state was put behind the communication apparatus—newspapers, radio, magazines, wire services—to advertise, conceal, convert and mislead, establish and discredit."

Spycraft, as Cuneo would learn, was full of covert weapons hard to discern. There were seemingly harmless pens containing deadly knives, "lipstick" guns loaded with a single bullet, plastic explosives masquerading as tropical fruit, and other sabotage devices hidden from view.

But only one weapon was truly invisible—propaganda.

In the world of espionage, propaganda was powerful and pervasive. Like a windstorm, it was carried along the airwaves, slipped into publications and spread widely through pamphlets and via word of mouth. This potent mix of handpicked "news," rumors, lies, and half-truths sprinkled with facts was used by governments to manipulate public opinion and influence the minds of millions. Few people recognized these dissembling morsels in their daily news diet for what they were.

Nazi Minister of Propaganda Joseph Goebbels was a master of misinforming and inciting the German masses through film and the press. To the world, his propaganda lionized Hitler's early military victories in Europe and North Africa. He portrayed Churchill as a certain loser. Influenced by his lies, most Americans were still reluctant to back Great Britain.

Journalist William L. Shirer recalled that vulnerable moment in his classic book about the Third Reich. "The predicament of Britain, which now held out alone, battered at home by nightly Luftwaffe bombing...seemed darker and more hopeless than ever before," wrote Shirer. "Its prestige, so important in a life-and-death struggle where propaganda was so potent a weapon, especially in influencing the United States and Russia, had sunk to a new low point."

Cuneo quickly realized the intensity of this conflict, as though he were entering a new world. While Hitler openly pushed propaganda in the US to divide and conquer, Churchill's spies, mindful of America's isolationist mood, preferred more subtle yet equally determined methods of convincing.

"The propaganda war," as Cuneo called it, "was fought with deadly ferocity, like a battle with thousands of tanks on each side locked in fierce, lethal combat, firing at point blank range. The moral hatred hung over the field like poison gas. No chivalry, no Geneva Convention, no code of military honor governed the war of words."

Domestically, Cuneo had handled the press before as an "incognito" White House political operative, but he learned his true lessons about propaganda by working secretly with the foreign spy William Stephenson. Together, they dispensed wartime leaks to the press in measured doses without a trace. Cuneo now had a front-row seat as the main liaison between the BSC and

Donovan's fledgling spy effort. Rockefeller Center became a key site in this propaganda war, where the grand prize, the ultimate objective for Stephenson and his bosses in London, was America's long-awaited entry into the war.

"Since the might of the United States was the decisive factor, and the center of the American press and publicity was New York, Manhattan became the decisive battleground," said Cuneo.

Thrust into the middle of this propaganda war, Cuneo still seemed unaware how risky his espionage assignment could be. He would soon find out.

America's top WWII spy, William "Wild Bill" Donovan, pins a medal on William "Intrepid" Stephenson, who oversaw Churchill's spies at Rockefeller Center and greatly influenced the creation of America's intelligence services. Cuneo was often an intermediary between both men.

LIBRARY OF CONGRESS, PRINTS AND PHOTOGRAPHS DIVISION, NYWT&S COLLECTION

Churchill's spies increasingly depended on Cuneo for crucial confidential information. A secret history of the BSC, not published until a half century later in 1999, described Cuneo's role as "an excellent intermediary" without identifying him by name.

"He was an American lawyer," described the secret history about this mystery man. "He was considerably prominent in the political world and had direct access to President Roosevelt. Since he was a sincere admirer of Great Britain and was convinced of the necessity of Anglo-American cooperation, his acquaintance with WS [William Stephenson] and certain members of the staff of BSC soon became a close working partnership."

As an informer, Cuneo provided plenty of inside information to Stephenson, gleaned from his many sources. In return, the BSC prepared their own propaganda package for Cuneo to present as news to Walter Winchell, the man with the biggest microphone in America. "As the alliance grew closer," the history said, "BSC found itself able not only to place items in Winchell's column but, on occasion, to write a part or even the whole of the column itself."

In Cuneo's propaganda stronghold, Winchell and Drew Pearson remained his most potent allies, the two biggest guns. While celebrity columnist Winchell in New York had the largest national audience, the political focus of Pearson's "Washington Merry-Go-Round" column became a favorite for BSC leaks. Winchell would allow some propaganda into his columns directly, virtually unedited, while Pearson usually filtered leaks through his own point of view, aimed at national decision-makers. With his spy material, Cuneo made sure the two columnists didn't bump into each other.

"The principal difficulty was to prevent Winchell and the 'Merry Go Round' from covering the same stories, since there was no collaboration in the ordinary sense of the term," Cuneo said. "But both, without mercy, continued to bombard the Nazis with everything in their arsenal."

While Cuneo treated Pearson as a college friend from Columbia, Stephenson recognized him as a prime strategic asset. The American columnist "should be cultivated as a potential source of important intelligence," he ordered. One BSC officer spent months gaining Pearson's confidence and identifying his sources.

Eventually, Pearson shared his insider information with Stephenson about "political changes, The President's intentions, and the views of high naval and military officials," according to the BSC history. When he could get his hands on them, Pearson also published "eyes-only" intelligence memos to the president.

Similar behavior in Britain would have landed Pearson in jail under the Official Secrets Act, but in the US, Pearson was able to avoid legal problems. He counted the FBI's chief Hoover as a top source and protector. He also had Cuneo as his lawyer.

The BSC history said Winchell and his "excellent intermediary" Cuneo consistently exchanged information with the spies at Rockefeller Center. One of several give-and-take examples involved Stephenson's concern about Argentina secretly helping the German submarine fleet. Winchell published the BSC's strategy memo in its entirety, handed to him by Cuneo. The Argentine scoop made a big splash in Winchell's column and Sunday-evening radio show, pleasing him greatly.

"This is terrific," Winchell told Cuneo. "For God's sake don't make me a flash in the pan. Keep going."

Several months later, while talking with Stephenson, Cuneo recalled Winchell's enthusiasm for more scoops of that same kind. It's not clear if Cuneo knew that Stephenson had arranged for all their important conversations to be recorded. An extract of their taped conversation transcript read as follows:

Cuneo: "Got any more stuff on Argentina? Walter is still after me for more stuff about this. He was crazy about that first batch that you gave him."

Stephenson: "I think we should leave that alone for the time being. The public has had about as much as it can stand of that at the moment."

Cuneo: "I'm inclined to agree with you."

Stephenson: "But there's something here which might interest you. Some details about the V-2s [rockets] and how tough they make it for the British people. Don't you think it's time they realized over here that London is still being bombed quite heavily?"

(PAUSE)

Cuneo: "Goddam it, Bill, I never realized that it was as bad as this. I'll take this along with me if I may..."

Along with cultivating journalists as informers, the BSC propaganda machine kept a constant focus on American politics. One way of influencing US public opinion was to finance polls that appeared scientific and objective but were deliberately misleading. They steered the results in favor of Great Britain's interests, and then convinced US news outlets to write or broadcast about them as truth.

For FDR's 1940 reelection, the BSC and Cuneo collaborated with Sanford Griffith, a former newspaperman, who ran a polling company called Market Analysts Inc. One of its surveys said Americans overwhelmingly favored a military draft of civilians if America joined Britain in the war—even though most constituent mail to Congress ran strongly against the idea of conscription. With another report from Market Analysts, Stephenson acknowledged privately, "Great care was taken beforehand to make certain the poll results would turn out as desired."

During that presidential campaign, Market Analysts concocted a poll of delegates at both the Democratic and Republican national conventions. Both surveys claimed surprising delegate support for providing more "help to the Allies short of war." The firm's research, cited prominently in the *New York Herald Tribune*, helped clear the path for the unlikely GOP nominee

Wendell Willkie, an interventionist, over Thomas Dewey and other isolationist rivals.

By the time of the later Democratic gathering, more aid to Britain seemed like a bipartisan position, thanks to BSC-funded polling cited in news stories. In its July 15 edition, the *New York Times* featured a story with the headline, "Big Majority of Delegates Favor Help to the British" and cited Market Analysts Inc. as the source of the polling research. The BSC and their American go-between were delighted.

"Dear Ernie: Enclosed are the final results of our opinion poll," Griffith reported to Cuneo in July 1940. "We got good play throughout in the Chicago Daily News, the New York Times, and a couple of the agencies... Sandy." Griffith even talked to Cuneo about having Market Analysts become the Democratic Party's own pollster.

Advocacy front groups created with BSC support, such as Friends of Democracy and the Irish American Defense Association, also provided "news" events and pronouncements that slanted coverage repeatedly in American media. Griffith and Cuneo worked together on another such group, forming France Forever, supporting Charles de Gaulle and the French Resistance.

"I have been asked to head up a committee of Americans who are in sympathy with the best of old French ideals and want no traffic with the Vichy France," Griffith wrote to Cuneo in August 1940. "This committee will include prominent Harvard and Columbia people and will be militant. Have you any candidates?"

In April 1941, Stephenson authorized BSC agent Sydney "Bill" Morrell, a newspaper friend of Lord Beaverbrook, to work with William Donovan and his deputy at Rockefeller Center, Allen Dulles, to form Fight for Freedom, Inc., designed to fight Nazi propaganda in the States. Though a British front group, members of Fight for Freedom (FFF) included several US journalists, including Joseph Alsop, Chicago newspaper publisher Marshall Field and *Time* magazine owner Henry Luce.

The FFF, housed rent-free at Rockefeller Center, pushed hard for America to enter the war. "The most effective of all propaganda toward the US would be through a unified organization which could be used to attack the isolationists, such as America First, on the one hand, and to create a Nation-wide campaign for an American declaration of war upon the other," wrote the BSC's Morrell.

Throughout it all, Cuneo remained well positioned to know about British undercover work in America and reported to the White House constantly. "Hope that you can talk to Ernest Cuneo today," wrote a FFF official in a telegram to White House staffer David Niles, also friendly with BSC. "He is at the Anchorage for the day and is anxious to talk to you."

The initial efforts by British intelligence to influence America before Pearl Harbor were in part a response to Hitler's publicity in the US and his American sympathizers. From the very outset, the Nazis understood the power of propaganda—words and images meant to incite rather than enlighten.

"Propaganda is a truly terrible weapon in the hands of an expert," Hitler wrote in his *Mein Kampf*, long before he seized the reins of government. In true Orwellian terms, he called his propaganda agency the "Ministry of Public Enlightenment."

Nazi propaganda fueled the raging anti-Semitism of Hitler's Third Reich, influencing films, literature, music, art and even schoolbooks read by children. This ministry censored the press, dehumanized its enemies and provided a twisted motivation for the Holocaust. As Donovan warned, the Nazis were spending a huge amount to spread their propaganda abroad, including the United States.

The British worried that the American public, with pressure from groups like the German American Bund, might never support a war against Hitler. The isolationists still seemed to be winning the national debate. As historian Thomas E. Mahl later noted, "the British were desperate to stem the flow of German propaganda and improperly interpreted news."

In the days ahead, the British effort at Rockefeller Center would become more intense as the conflict in Europe expanded into a full worldwide conflict—and involved Ernest Cuneo even more.

PART II

Prelude To War

Alarmed by "Fifth Column" Nazi sympathizers within America, President Roosevelt railed against this insurgent domestic threat in public and encouraged propaganda against them, which included information Cuneo provided to Walter Winchell for his broadcasts.

"War ought to be the only study of a prince. He ought to consider peace only as a breathing-time, which gives him leisure to contrive, and furnished ability to execute military plans."

—Niccolo Machiavelli, as quoted in the *Congressional Record* in 1939

"We knew almost nothing about the tens of thousands of things we were going to have to learn about in a hurry. As emergencies developed we found ourselves all too reliant upon British intelligence."

—Sherman Kent, Yale history professor and former Office of Strategic Services analyst, summarizing US intelligence in 1941

11

FOREIGN ENTANGLEMENTS

"Why, by interweaving our destiny with that of any part of Europe, entangle our peace and prosperity in the toils of European ambition, rivalship, interest, humor or caprice? It is our true policy to steer clear of permanent alliances with any portion of the foreign world."

—George Washington, "Farewell Address," 1796

On a warm summer afternoon in August 1940, US Senator Ernest P. Lundeen climbed into a plane for a long flight home, so he could appear at a state picnic in Minnesota. He planned to give a speech, shake hands and explain his opposition to joining the war in Europe.

An outspoken isolationist, Lundeen had recently voted against selective service draft legislation as an unwanted step toward joining Britain in its battle against Hitler. Many years earlier, as a Republican congressman, he'd opposed US entry into World War I. The slogan on the posters for his 1936 Senate campaign—when Lundeen ran under the progressive Farmer-Labor Party's banner—encapsulated his worldview: "No Foreign Entanglements."

With a thunderstorm in the distance, the plane carrying the sixty-one-year-old senator and twenty-four other passengers took off from Washington, DC. It didn't get far. Within minutes, the packed aircraft crashed at a farm field in Virginia, killing everyone aboard.

"It sounded like the plane exploded when it hit the ground," said Lester Mason, a gas station operator. His home was closest to the wreckage. "The plane was broken to bits and so were the bodies of the people in it."

The nosedive crash of the "Trip 19" flight with Lundeen aboard was the worst commercial aviation disaster in US history to date. Congressional colleagues mourned Lundeen's death with a stirring memorial at the Capitol.

"As a member of the Senate Military Affairs Committee, he opposed involvement of the United States in the intrigues and entanglements which would take this country into war," Rep. Joseph P. O'Hara said in praise of Lundeen. "The cause of peace had in him its staunchest advocate."

But there was more than tragedy to the Lundeen air crash. Two weeks afterward, newspaper columnist Drew Pearson dropped a shocking revelation about Trip 19. Instead of foul weather as the cause, he suggested a mystery plot far more ominous.

"If federal authorities probe deep enough into the crash... which carried Senator Lundeen to his death in Virginia, they may find some highly interesting facts regarding Nazi activities in the United States," began Pearson's "Washington Merry-Go-Round" column.

Pearson said Lundeen, "a rabid pro-German isolationist," was under investigation at the time of his death. Aboard the wrecked aircraft with him was a "G-man, a Department of Justice attorney and an FBI secretary," he reported, and "at least one of them" was shadowing the senator when their plane went down.

Most significant was the Nazi connection. Pearson said the "German propagandist" George Sylvester Viereck, a self-avowed "friend of Adolf Hitler's Germany," had been previously seen visiting Lundeen several times, prompting the federal probe.

"Lundeen was one of the isolationist bloc in the United States

Senate, and his speeches followed the line of the fifth columnists in the sense that they were bitterly anti-British and vigorously against American preparation," said Pearson. "Justice department agents were attempting to find out the extent to which Berlin was definitely hooked up with any members of this congressional bloc when Lundeen's plane went down."

Eventually, Pearson reported that Lundeen had delivered a speech on the Senate floor on June 19, 1940, ghostwritten by Viereck, who was paid by Germany. The headline-grabbing disclosure—linking a dead senator to a Nazi spy—caused an uproar in Washington. It also put a spotlight on Viereck and fueled the deep suspicions surrounding Hitler's infiltration plans in America.

At first, both the FBI and the US Attorney General denied investigating the senator, just as Pearson had predicted they would. Acknowledging such a nasty inquiry so soon after Lundeen's death would have been politically awkward—and would likely start an unnecessary firestorm among other isolationists in Congress.

Yet court testimony in the months to come would show that government investigators had indeed been aware of Lundeen's connections.

As Cuneo later explained, when Lundeen's plane went down, "a tremendous break came" for the truth to emerge. "Pearson forced it" into the public spotlight with his stunning revelations. Along with his own sources, the columnist relied on Cuneo's network of foreign spies and federal investigators. Despite his skeptical instincts, Cuneo agreed with Pearson's doubts about the plane crash.

"Pearson had hundreds of informants outside of the government," recalled Cuneo, who was convinced that Viereck, the experienced German spy, had "corrupted" Lundeen. "The Nazi apparatus was panic stricken. Senator Lundeen was killed in a plane crash in a thunderstorm, quite a coincidence. A vast mess resulted, which was later handed to me to straighten out."

George Sylvester Viereck proudly displayed three photographs of people he admired on the wall of his Riverside Drive apartment in New York, not far from the Columbia University campus. One was Dr. Joseph Goebbels, Nazi Germany's propaganda chief. The second was Kaiser Wilhelm, whom Viereck once served as an intelligence agent. The third photo portrayed Adolf Hitler, about whom Viereck predicted in 1929, "This man, if he lives, will make history."

How Viereck became the focal point of Nazi Germany's spy effort in America is itself a mystery, but his eventual arrest provided an alarming glimpse at the extent of Germany's spy network in New York and elsewhere prior to the US entry into the war. It also revealed fateful weaknesses in the Abwehr run by Admiral Wilhelm Canaris and the poor, chaotic decision-making of Hitler himself.

Born in Munich, Viereck came to the United States at the age of eleven and went on to graduate from City College of New York. Slim with blond hair, Viereck dressed as a bit of a dandy, with what one observer called "meticulous neatness— suit, shirt, tie, shoes and pocket handkerchief all in harmonizing shades." He showed talent in writing and exuded grandiosity. He claimed friendship with Freud and Einstein and predicted an illustrious destiny for himself.

"In any other age, I would have been a great poet," he insisted. "My three ideals were Christ, Napoleon and Oscar Wilde."

During World War I, Viereck first gained notoriety as a top propagandist for Germany. He ran a magazine called *Fatherland* in New York and tried unsuccessfully to buy a newspaper in Boston. Federal authorities said Viereck collected more than $100,000 ($2.3 million in today's dollars) for pro-German propaganda in America, even after the US joined World War I in

1917. Viereck duped contributors into giving money to a front group called the Agricultural Farm Labor League, ostensibly for the relief of unemployed farm workers.

"Viereck started this organization when his supply of money furnished by the German Government ran out and he could not get any more because we were at war with Germany," explained Deputy Attorney General Alfred L. Becker. Viereck avoided criminal prosecution, but public anger lingered. He even drew condemnation from young Franklin Roosevelt.

As a vice presidential candidate in 1920, FDR criticized Viereck as part of a "small but dangerous element which was not loyal during the war." In a reply that appeared prominently in the *New York Times*, Viereck rebuked Roosevelt, saying "it is clear that you accept at par the brass checks of British propagandists."

Over the next several years, Viereck remained in New York, where he revived his writing career with successful novels and other work. By 1940, the *New York Post* described him as "a man with two loves—American dollars and German ideologies." His enchantment with Hitler led to a $500 monthly retainer ($120,000 a year in today's currency) from a Nazi newspaper.

Given Viereck's previous notoriety, he seemed an odd choice by the German high command to oversee their undercover spy network in America. But apparently no alternative seemed better.

Generally, the Abwehr's leader, Wilhelm Canaris, encouraged his operatives in America to aggressively seek out any secrets about US military, technology and economic developments. Despite his own misgivings about Hitler, Canaris turned German diplomatic missions, including the Washington embassy, into espionage centers.

Back in Berlin, however, Hitler's aides urged caution about spying in the US, worried about provoking the still-neutral American government into joining the European conflict. Dr. Hans Thomsen, the head of the German embassy in Washington, also warned Berlin about the poor quality of their spies in the States.

"The agents who are known to this Embassy do not seem to be suited for such activities," Thomsen complained to Berlin. "Lacking in expert knowledge and savvy, we doubt that these agents could ever make a contribution valuable enough to compensate for the risk of jeopardizing German-American relations."

Unhappy with the ineffective spies in New York, Thomsen bumped into Viereck while vacationing at a German spa and signed him up. Viereck's cover was writing for a Munich newspaper, paid for with secret funding by the Foreign Ministry. Viereck quickly began courting isolationist congressional members and their staff. He gathered as much secret intelligence as he could through paid informants and forwarded it to Berlin.

"Viereck succeeded in spinning a web of confidential informants in key and strategic places in Washington, especially on Capitol Hill," said intelligence expert and military historian Ladislas Farago. "He developed close relations with a number of lawmakers whose isolationism and anti-Roosevelt bias made them easy prey."

The 1940 national political conventions were an inviting target for Viereck. Through another German front group, Viereck paid for ads in the *New York Times* and other newspapers saying "Stop the war machine! Stop the interventionists and warmongers!" He organized and helped pay travel expenses for a meeting of isolationist GOP senators and other delegates at their Philadelphia convention. In secret messages to Berlin, Viereck claimed he sneaked several planks favorable to Germany into the Republican Party's platform.

At the Democratic convention, Viereck and his coconspirators also rallied support among isolationist Democrats. He ran a similar ad in the *Chicago Tribune*, claiming 93 percent of Americans wanted to avoid the war. On July 18, Viereck's spies sent another report to Berlin about GOP senator Gerald P. Nye. "After lengthy negotiations," he said, Nye agreed to distribute one hundred thousand copies of an anti-war speech, considered by the

Germans to be a very effective piece of propaganda. While it's not clear if Viereck wrote Nye's speech, there was little doubt he did so for Lundeen.

In Pearson's follow-up columns, he detailed how Viereck's ghostwritten speeches for Lundeen were entered into the Congressional Record. They were reprinted and sent out at taxpayer expense to Nazi sympathizers around the nation. Bundles of copies were mailed for free, using envelopes marked with the congressional franking privilege.

As a well-known senator, Lundeen didn't hide his opposition to the British. But no one seemed aware he was secretly backing the Nazis.

"I have never heard a German, or a German born American, with the gall to ask that we help Germany, but red, yellow, brown, black and white races all are expected to die for the British Empire," Lundeen argued. "I warn the American people that we cannot defend America by defending old, decadent, and dying empires."

After his crash, Lundeen's ghostwritten words lived on even in death. The same speech written for Lundeen later appeared in a book written under Viereck's pen name, "James Burr Hamilton," and published by Flanders Hall, an imprint subsidized by Viereck. The anti-Semitic "radio priest" Charles Coughlin plugged the book on his hate-filled national show. The same publisher agreed to distribute books by other isolationists in Congress, and translations of those were financed by the German Information Bureau, a Nazi propaganda agency.

Months earlier, Stephenson's spies at Rockefeller Center had alerted the FBI to Viereck's pro-Nazi activities. In October 1941, federal authorities arrested Viereck at his Manhattan home, intent on making their accusations stick, unlike two decades earlier. They charged him with failing to disclose his propaganda activities fully to the State Department. Always media savvy, Viereck cast himself as an anti-war martyr.

"My real crime...is that I am an American of German blood and I oppose the desperate and despicable attempt to catapult our country into Europe's war," Viereck claimed. "I do not hate the English people, but I resent British machinations and the British meddling in the affairs of the United States."

Winchell jumped on the anti-Viereck bandwagon started by Pearson. In his own column, he mocked this Nazi posing as a journalist, and made light of any threats of a Viereck libel suit. "He had his lawyer write a letter demanding reasons," Winchell snapped. "The reply will be a hunk of literature." It was the kind of Winchell trademark quip that, if his lawyer Cuneo hadn't written it himself, would surely make Cuneo laugh.

At Viereck's criminal trial, the Lundeen spy mystery unraveled further. The senator's secretary testified the Nazi propagandist had written three separate speeches for her deceased boss. She also said Lundeen's widow "stripped" any mention of Viereck from her husband's office files right after the plane crash. Under oath, Lundeen's widow disputed that account. She claimed her house was burglarized and that her husband's files stored in the attic were disturbed by unnamed intruders.

Eventually, a jury convicted Viereck of violating the Foreign Agents Registration Act, but the US Supreme Court overturned that conviction and ordered a new trial. On its second try in 1943, the government managed to send Viereck away to prison. A congressional aide, who received payments from Viereck, was also sent to prison on perjury charges for lying about Nazi propaganda efforts.

Cuneo's role in Pearson's scoop about the dead senator is hard to trace. BSC's Hyde later said "Stephenson's liaison officer with the Justice Department" was involved in the Viereck case, the same person who had helped in the Times Square crash investigation leading to the arrest of the spy Ludwig. But Hyde didn't mention Cuneo by name. Not so discreetly, Cuneo's other client, Walter Winchell, led the loud chorus praising Viereck's conviction, even taking credit for his arrest.

"Smear was the word George Sylvester Viereck used when I exposed him," Winchell told his radio listeners in December 1943. "Smear is easier to prove than proving me wrong."

Viereck became part of the largest US sedition trial of its kind in history. In all, he was among twenty-nine defendants—mostly anti-Semitic right-wing extremists—charged with conspiring to distribute publications urging disloyalty in the armed services and causing an insurrection at the behest of the Nazis. But those charges in 1944 ultimately resulted in a mistrial—after a long, circus-like proceeding that culminated in the judge suffering from a heart attack—and were later dropped.

To prewar America, Viereck's defiant words and public bombast created a worrisome impression of widespread Nazi infiltration in America. Stephenson's spies at Rockefeller Center had seized on the Viereck case and scored a major propaganda victory. They'd alerted not only Pearson's and Winchell's audiences, but had also delivered a wake-up call to the White House about the internal Nazi threat. The BSC secret history later revealed that Churchill's spies had targeted Viereck long before the FBI—and had undoubtedly been aware of his ties to the Minnesota senator. British agents "watched him [Viereck] from the very beginning," it said. "One of them knew him personally and spent much time with him and his friends."

Before Viereck's arrest, British censors in Bermuda had unsealed all of his letters, which he had addressed to a Nazi propaganda office in Munich. The letters were opened inside British spy offices located underneath the luxury Hamilton Princess Hotel, a favorite of honeymooners.

Stephenson passed along this top secret information about Viereck to the FBI, and to American intelligence coordinator William Donovan to give to the Attorney General. When the Viereck spy ring investigation was completed, the federal prosecutor thanked the BSC for allowing one of its Bermuda agents to provide key testimony against Viereck.

To drive home its point, the BSC highlighted the German

spy actions in a report called "Fifth Column Propaganda of the Axis in the US." Donovan decided to share it with his staff and the White House. "It made a considerable impression" on President Roosevelt, the BSC history said. "He [FDR] had not hitherto realized how widespread and how purposeful this propaganda was, for at the time no US agency had been engaged in studying it."

In his own quiet, determined way, Stephenson achieved a major objective with his underground campaign. FDR became convinced of the need for an American foreign intelligence agency, but was still unsure who should run it. Hoover, by expanding the FBI's domain? Or Donovan, the BSC's choice? It still appeared to be an open question in mid-1941.

The Viereck case proved foreign espionage inside America could be a very risky business. Whether spying had anything to do with Senator Lundeen's fatal crash would remain a riddle. As Rachel Maddow observed on a 2022 MSNBC podcast, "Just as the journalist Drew Pearson predicted, the cause of the crash of 'Trip 19' has remained a mystery, indefinitely. We still don't know."

In informing the American public, Cuneo's friends, Pearson and Winchell, had relied on the BSC for inside information, as if playing a sure bet. But soon Cuneo would learn that not every piece of information from Stephenson could be trusted, nor given to the president without checking if it were true.

12

THE PRESIDENT'S FAKE NEWS

"Oh, how the ghost of you clings!
These foolish things remind me of you"

—lyrics to "These Foolish Things (Remind Me of You),"
a popular song standard cowritten by Eric Maschwitz under the
pseudonym "Holt Marvell"

While at Rockefeller Center, Ernest Cuneo was introduced to
Ivar Bryce, a British spy and childhood friend of Ian Fleming.
Like his pal, Bryce possessed a lively mind and clever sense of
humor. "The tremendous bond of lifelong friendship united
them," Cuneo observed of the two.

A lad of privilege and wealth in England, Bryce first met
Fleming at age eleven, building sand castles along the beach in
northeast Cornwall. Ian invited him to join in the fun along
with his brothers. The two friends later attended Eton together
and edited the school magazine, *The Wyvern*, where Fleming's
first short story appeared.

Angular and handsome, with a full head of hair, Bryce made
for good company in New York. Cuneo socialized with Ivar and
Ian in Manhattan's nightlife, drinking with abandon as young
men in wartime are wont to do. Among his many gifts, Bryce
could make a mean "Vesper" martini, a trait surely appreciated
by Fleming in writing his 1953 novel *Casino Royale*. (His char-

acter James Bond instructed, "Three measures of Gordon's, one of vodka, half a measure of Kina Lillet. Shake it very well until it's ice-cold, then add a large thin slice of lemon-peel. Got it?")

By day, Bryce answered directly to Richard Coit, head of BSC's Latin American intelligence operation (humorously nicknamed "Coitus Interruptus"). Though fun to be with, Cuneo and Fleming didn't think much of Bryce's spying ability.

Early on, Bryce fouled up a meeting with a British undercover agent at Delmonico's bar in downtown Manhattan. As arranged, the other agent was identifiable by the *Daily Express* newspaper he was holding. Ivar gave him the wrong code word. Luckily, the agent turned out to be a cousin of Bryce's family and corrected him. It made for a good laugh with his pals later on but damaged his reputation for subterfuge.

Not everything was a bloody mess with Bryce, though. During the summer of 1941, Bryce dreamed up a fanciful stunt that would eventually gain the unwitting attention of President Roosevelt and the rest of the world. Like the corpse that Fleming later used to fool the Nazis in "Operation Mincemeat," Bryce concocted a phony Nazi map designed to throw off German sympathizers and bring the United States one step closer to war.

It began simply enough. While sketching out existing maps at his BSC desk, Bryce wondered how the Nazis might realign Latin America if they could control it.

"Of the possible changes, on my blotter, I came up with one showing the probable reallocation of territories that would appeal to Berlin," Bryce recalled in a memoir. "It was very convincing: the more I studied it the more sense it made."

Staring at his imagined map, Bryce realized it could have tremendous political potential. If somehow the doctored document looked convincing enough, perhaps the BSC might fool people into thinking Germany's invasion plans included the Western Hemisphere, not just Europe.

This fakery would undermine the isolationists and German

sympathizers by convincing Americans that the Nazis planned to be at their doorstep on the southern border. Somehow, if the phony map was discovered and publicly declared to be real, Bryce realized, "what a commotion would be caused."

Bryce pitched the idea to William Stephenson and, quite remarkably, the BSC chief approved and embraced it. This covert action would be only a hint of Stephenson's many secret maneuvers that would go far beyond usual intelligence collecting.

While most US officials, including the FBI's Hoover, viewed the BSC as a gatherer of facts and figures, Stephenson quickly showed a willingness to take matters into his own hands and slyly manipulated outcomes favorable to the UK's interests.

Offering a phony map to the world was an audacious act, one that virtually any responsible diplomat would avoid. But for a spy like Stephenson, willing to control events rather than merely observe them, the idea of a counterfeit map designed to undermine the Nazis, Britain's sworn enemy, was irresistible.

Such a stunt, though not officially sanctioned by the prime minister, had a certain Churchillian cheek to it. Stephenson's BSC was not a rogue operation but rather an American extension of Churchill's Special Operations Executive (SOE) in London, an underground army set up shortly after he took office to conduct secret guerilla warfare against the Axis powers in occupied territories.

"And now, go and set Europe ablaze!" Churchill commanded. Sabotage and even assassination were in their arsenal. Bomb-makers and secret gadgets meant to kill were part of "Churchill's Toyshop," with machine guns inspired in part by those of American mobster Al Capone. "Churchill felt this was no time for niceties," said biographer Andrew Roberts. "Unorthodox warfare appealed to Churchill, who believed that Britain should take direct, full-scale, expensive continental military engagements only once the Germans were severely weakened."

Stephenson would rely on other phony documents, including

a fabricated letter that insulted Brazilian leaders and resulted in them breaking off relations with the Axis powers. Up until that point, Brazil had been an important part of the supply chain for the Nazis. The phony letter, dated October 30, 1941, was put together meticulously at Station M, a Canadian lab specializing in forgeries with impressive authenticity. In that ruse, American embassy officials were kept in the dark about the real BSC source of the letter.

Bryce's bogus South American map—gleaned from other actual existing documents—followed this same pathway of deception but enjoyed even greater success.

The fake map contained geopolitical dynamite. It divided the southern continent into five large regions, generally ignoring traditional national boundaries. Some countries, like Ecuador, Uruguay and Panama, would lose ground or disappear altogether into a larger neighbor. The document's realignment also suggested that if Argentina, Brazil, Colombia, Chile and Venezuela went along with the Nazi war plans, they could count on getting even bigger.

The phony map, according to Bryce, landed in American hands through another BSC ruse. He said Stephenson arranged for the map to be planted in a German safe house in Cuba targeted by the FBI. J. Edgar Hoover, looking to expand his powers, had recently received presidential permission to investigate Nazi influence in Latin America.

When the G-men raided the Cuban safe house, they discovered the document written in German, Bryce said, and believed it to be genuine. Soon after, Hoover gave the recovered map to William Donovan, America's newly appointed Coordinator of Information. Its weather-beaten appearance—another trick of the Station M forgery experts—was convincing enough to Donovan. As soon as Stephenson forwarded him the map, Donovan quickly passed it along to the president.

It's not clear if Cuneo was involved in this handoff to the

White House, but it's likely he may have, at the very least, known of its existence based on his closeness to the British spies. (Bryce later described Cuneo as a "lone wolf lawyer on the edge of the Democratic Party," friendly with both Stephenson and Fleming.)

Regardless of its authenticity, Bryce's map fit the political narrative of the Roosevelt administration at that time. As historians John F. Bratzel and Leslie B. Rout Jr. concluded in their own analysis of the map controversy: "When Donovan informed the President that the secret map had been made available by the British, it would have been immediately obvious to FDR that the map could bolster his position while undermining that of his isolationist foes."

Some in the administration worried about a forgery. It wouldn't be the first. Previously, a fabricated letter put together at Station M falsely portrayed the Nazis as attempting to take over Bolivia. The British concocted a cover story—known as a "paper clip" in spy lingo. It claimed a friendly agent had stolen the Bolivia document from a German courier inside a crowded elevator.

Behind this fantasy-making was Station M's mastermind, Eric Maschwitz, a talented civilian spy married to actress Hermione Gingold. A few years earlier, Maschwitz cowrote the Oscar-nominated screenplay for *Goodbye, Mr. Chips* and composed lyrics for the song "These Foolish Things (Remind Me of You)" under the pseudonym "Holt Marvell." He coauthored another standard, "A Nightingale Sang in Berkeley Square," supposedly written while in the BSC.

In his new role, Maschwitz had a genius for faked documents and inventive "paper clips" that could pass forensic inspection. As a result, numerous newspapers repeated this Bolivian falsity. Eventually so did the president.

One of Cuneo's longtime friends—Adolf Berle, Assistant Secretary of State and Cuneo's former Columbia professor—was deeply suspicious. Stephenson's agents were "manufacturing documents detailing Nazi conspiracies in South America," warned

Berle in a memo to his boss, Cordell Hull. "I think we have to be a little on our guard against false scares." The prospect of going to war, spurred on by a fake document, was alarming to him.

Nevertheless, Bryce's phony map surfaced at a Navy Day dinner held at the Mayflower Hotel, where talk of imminent war consumed the ballroom. A few days earlier in the Atlantic, an exchange of fire took place between German U-boats and US ships.

Introduced at the Mayflower's podium by Donovan, President Roosevelt told the crowd that the "shooting has started" and he referred to a "secret map" showing how Hitler planned to gain control of South America.

"Hitler has often protested that his plans for conquest do not extend across the Atlantic ocean," Roosevelt said. "I have in my possession a secret map made in Germany by Hitler's government."

Just as Bryce had planned, the president described how fourteen separate countries would be turned by the Nazis into five "vassal states, bringing the whole continent under their domination." Roosevelt said the secret map showed that "one of these new puppet states" would be Panama's republic and include "our great lifeline—the Panama Canal." He vowed that plan "will never go into effect."

In the same speech, Roosevelt warned about isolationists who minimized Hitler's threat and loudly protested his attempts to provide aid to Allied nations like Great Britain. "The fact is that Nazi propaganda continues in desperation to seize on such isolated statements as proof of American disunity."

With great moral outrage, FDR said the Third Reich intended to get rid of all religions and replace the Bible, with Hitler's *Mein Kampf* "imposed and enforced as Holy Writ. And in the place of the cross of Christ will be put two symbols—the swastika and the naked sword."

Any hope of peace with Germany now appeared gone. The president said he had proof positive of Hitler's intent.

"The map makes clear, my friends, the Nazi design, not only against South America but against the United States as well," he said. The stirring address was beamed to fifty million Americans listening on radios at home.

Almost immediately, Germany cried foul. They insisted Roosevelt's secret map was a fraud and blamed the British for instigating it. The following day, the press asked Roosevelt for a copy. He declined, saying written notations on the map would give away its source.

"What would you say to the charge of the suspicion that that map was—had been foisted on you in some way?" asked a reporter during the contentious press conference. "That it was also a forgery or a fake of some sort?"

After some back-and-forth, Roosevelt said he received the map "from a source which is undoubtedly reliable. There is no question about that." The president made no mention of Churchill's spies at Rockefeller Center or any anonymous figures in the US government working with them.

When told that the Nazis called him a "liar" and "faker," FDR laughed it off.

The press seemed to go along with the joke. *"Nazi Ire over 'Secret Map' Is a 'Scream' to Roosevelt,"* reported the front-page *New York Times* story. Even if the Roosevelt administration now harbored doubts about the map's authenticity, not much skepticism was shown prior to its mention by the president.

Donovan's executive assistant, James R. Murphy, who delivered the map to the White House, insisted later that neither he nor Donovan suspected the map to be a fake. "If Donovan had been told, or knew that it was not authentic," Murphy said, "he would not have given it to the President."

Some historians suggest FDR might have wondered if the secret map was a phony. Like the secret source who gave it to him, though, Roosevelt viewed the map as a tool for a bigger purpose. "It was Roosevelt's policy to wage war without declaring it," explained FDR biographer Joseph Lash. "And this map seemed to fit the new approach."

Once again, Cuneo was the man in the middle—as liaison for Donovan, loyalist to Roosevelt and increasingly sympathetic to the British cause, which now included a map concocted by Fleming's best friend Ivar Bryce. Though in the nexus of this spy case, Cuneo made sure nothing was traceable to him directly.

The secret map and other fakeries were just the beginning, however, of Stephenson's covert actions in America brought to Cuneo's attention. The list would be long: targeting congressional members and administration officials for their isolationist views; sexual compromise by women linked to the BSC; nighttime break-ins for secrets from foreign diplomats; British informants in Hollywood and Broadway, confidentially reporting what they heard to Stephenson; violence, when necessary, against other foreign spies and double agents; and politically manipulating allies, particularly the United States, through propaganda and the media.

Yet to Cuneo, it all seemed justifiable in the name of stopping Hitler. "Given the time, the situation, and the mood," he later explained, "it is not surprising the BSC also went beyond the legal, the ethical and the proper."

13

THE INFORMANTS

Winston Churchill's literary agent, Emery Reves, possessed all the ingredients of an excellent informant. Smart, intuitive and world-wise, Reves despised the Nazis as much as Churchill, perhaps even more so, for personal reasons.

Born in Hungary as "Imre Revesz" to Jewish parents, Reves had been forced to leave his successful literary agency jobs first in Berlin and later in Paris because of Hitler's anti-Semitic persecution. "All my possessions were taken away by the Gestapo," recalled Reves, who fled to England. "I was not allowed to take with me more than a toothbrush and my pyjamas [sic]." Eventually, his mother and other family members would perish in the Holocaust.

In February 1941, Reves joined Churchill's fight. The thirty-six-year-old literary agent traveled to New York to help the British propaganda effort at Rockefeller Center. He had begun representing Churchill's literary interests in 1937, and would later earn a sizable fortune for his famous client with writing contracts after the war. But at this moment, Churchill wanted a place for Reves in his cast of talented informants.

"I strongly hope some use may be made of him," Churchill wrote to the Ministry of Information about Reves. "I can speak from personal experience of his all together exceptional abilities and connections."

Informants like Reves might be more colorful than conventional spies but could be equally effective. A debonair man with a taste for beautiful women and fine art, Reves kept his eyes and ears open in America and secretly reported what he learned to Stephenson and other UK authorities.

"There is a large field and great opportunity of extending influence," Reves advised Churchill in private memos. "There is much to be done in the American film and press in order to avoid that most dangerous of all American attitudes: boredom and apathy toward the European struggle."

Reves set up his own separate office inside Rockefeller Center, like any other private businessman. He believed the British effort to counteract the corrosive impact of isolationists like Charles Lindbergh on US public opinion must be done subtly, executed quietly, with the help of other discreet Americans.

The lineup of Brits willing to serve as secret agents in America impressed Cuneo, charged with helping to coordinate all the players in this real-life drama.

"The principal sources of anti-Nazi propaganda…[included] virtually the united front of Britain's best in all fields," Cuneo observed, citing playwright Noël Coward, actress Beatrice Lillie and film producer Sir Alexander Korda, to name a few. "As far as I knew then, there was nothing official about the deep rapport between the American press and the beleaguered British. Fleet Street, Mayfair, Hollywood and Broadway had been, for all practical purposes, one community for years."

Before leaving for New York, Reves shared some secret information with Churchill. In a "strictly confidential" May 1940 memo, Reves alerted the newly installed prime minister to what he'd learned from another of his literary clients—former Nazi supporter Fritz Thyssen.

A wealthy German iron-and-steel baron, Thyssen had favored

Hitler's rise to power in the early 1930s before repudiating him after Kristallnacht, the bloody Jewish pogroms of 1938. Using Thyssen's memoir-like notes, Reves put together a new book called *I Paid Hitler*, eventually published in 1941. Reves had managed to interview his client in Monte Carlo before Thyssen landed in jail in Germany.

"This was a private conversation which he [Thyssen] did not authorize me to publish," Reves told Churchill, "but I am communicating to you his observations believing that Thyssen belongs to those few people who know exactly [the extent] of German armaments and industrial production."

Thyssen thought the German war machine was much weaker than portrayed by the likes of Lindbergh, due to a lack of supplies and poorly trained soldiers.

But most intriguingly, Thyssen told Reves that the German generals had "wished to do all in [their] power to avoid war on the Western front, including the overthrow of the regime." When Hitler managed to stay in power, another path was pursued by the generals to get rid of him.

Thyssen said "that a certain person 'whose name if known would come as a surprise' had been accredited by the General Staff to enter into contact with British circles," according to the Reves memo. "He does not know to what extent it has been possible to carry out this scheme."

Perhaps Churchill already knew the name of this German double agent, but Reves certainly didn't. Like some Sherlock Holmes mystery, all he had was one tantalizing clue.

"Who is the mysterious intermediary to whom Thyssen refers? Dr. Schacht? Not impossible," Reves said. "An interesting detail in connection with the anonymous go-between is that he carries with him on his person a poison which causes instant death and never leaves him."

Reves's guess about "Dr. Schacht" probably wasn't far off. Hjalmar Schacht, a proud banker, didn't like Hitler and surely wanted to see him go. In 1939, Schacht differed with Hitler about the economic costs of the war and was pushed out as president of Germany's Reichsbank. The Gestapo later arrested Schacht, linking him to those involved in a 1944 assassination attempt against Hitler. He landed in the Dachau concentration camp and barely managed to survive the war.

Schacht was not the rumored mole, but Reves never learned the man's identity.

Not every British volunteer in the entertainment world was trained or personally well-suited to be a spy. But many were capable of being informants, including Noël Coward, the playwright and bon vivant of musical theater.

"Celebrity was a wonderful cover," explained Coward, thrilled by the noirish melodrama surrounding the BSC. "My disguise would be my own reputation as a bit of an idiot…a merry playboy." Coward's London office had been destroyed in the Blitz while he was putting together his best-known play, *Blithe Spirit*.

Entertaining at the White House in mid-1940, Coward merrily sang "Mad Dogs and Englishmen" for the president. Afterward, over a nightcap, a delighted Roosevelt explained efforts to get more aid to Great Britain as if Coward were a diplomat. Stephenson recognized Coward's value and, urged on by his friend Ian Fleming, he signed Coward up as an informant. At various soirees, Coward kept an eye on the abdicated Duke of Windsor and his wife, both considered pro-Nazi.

Stephenson also dispatched Coward to Hollywood, where— guided by actor Cary Grant, another British informant/spy— he reported back to London about the number of isolationists and the pro-Nazi sentiment in Tinseltown. (Around that time, Grant began making a film with Ginger Rogers in which he played a foreign correspondent who warns an American socialite that she's engaged to a secret Nazi sympathizer. In real life, biographers claim Grant spied on actor Errol Flynn and his Nazi connections, and provided advice to Stephenson's BSC about propaganda in America.)

Generally, British celebrities received simple assignments from the BSC, enough to feel they were part of the action, as if one big ear for Stephenson. "Bill [Stephenson] would ask him to do the tiny little things, because he passed through New York, and Noël Coward would go all over the place saying 'I'm working for Bill Stephenson,'" recalled Roald Dahl, then a genuine BSC spy before becoming a famous author. "Any celebrity that passed through, Bill would try to see. And he gave them some little piddly thing."

When Coward offered to take on more dangerous assignments for Stephenson, Churchill disapproved. "I had a gnawing suspicion that there was something about me that he didn't like," wrote Coward, a closeted gay man. "He kept saying, 'No use, you'd be no good—too well known.' I said, 'That's the whole point.'"

Some accounts say the usually flippant Coward made a "sliding remark" at a dinner party about Churchill's randy son, Randolph, and sparked the old man's ire. Or perhaps Churchill was right in claiming Coward, so great onstage, would be poor at undercover work.

After making some silly but disparaging remarks about US soldiers from Brooklyn, Coward was forced to issue his regrets through the biggest megaphone of all—Walter Winchell. According to the columnist, British officials "contacted friends of mine" to see if Winchell "would accept a written apology for all Americans" from Coward the entertainer. Though Winchell didn't say whom the British contacted, this media deal was clearly the kind his friend Cuneo loved to broker.

The power of film employed by British moviemakers in Hollywood, most notably Alfred Hitchcock, helped awaken Americans to the Nazi threat. London critics were upset by Hitchcock's departure in 1939, with the nation at war against the Nazis. But the director left for Hollywood with the British government's blessing, recognizing his propaganda impact abroad.

In Hitchcock's 1940 thriller, *Foreign Correspondent*, the lead character is a naive American newspaper reporter, thrust into the ongoing European conflict, who nearly gets killed by Nazi spies. Hitchcock's 1942 film, *Saboteur*, made before the Pearl Harbor attack, reflected the isolationist mood in America that the British found so dangerous.

"We were in 1941 and there were pro-German elements who called themselves America Firsters and who were, in fact, American Fascists," Hitchcock later explained.

Local movie theaters provided a window to what was going on across the Atlantic. Starting in 1938, *The March of Time* documentary series from Henry Luce's Time Inc. gave an up-close glimpse of Nazism's ugly grip on the German populace. "It tells the truth about Germany in a highly effective way," said William E. Dodd, United States ambassador to Germany. Luce and his wife, writer-politician Clare Boothe Luce, were strongly pro-British interventionists.

The BSC had more direct influence on Alexander Korda and his films. Korda was best known for his 1933 smash hit, *The Private Lives of Henry VIII*, which won an Oscar for its star Charles Laughton. Cuneo later described Korda as part of Stephenson's inner circle of intelligence agents called "the Club." Korda's moviemaking business served partly as a cover for British intelligence, with his own New York office based at Rockefeller Center. He later hired H. Montgomery Hyde, a top Stephenson aide, as his legal adviser.

Korda and Churchill had a long history together. In London, the Hungarian-born filmmaker kept a penthouse apartment at Claridge's, where Winston and Lord Beaverbrook would share a brandy or two with him. In 1935, Korda hired Churchill as an assistant producer and adviser for a new film about King

George V. It should be "an imperial film embodying the sentiments, anxieties and achievements of the British people all over the world," Churchill enthused.

Though that film never got off the ground, Churchill recognized the power of the cinema. "The pictures are among the most powerful instruments of propaganda the world has ever known," he wrote.

When Churchill became prime minister in May 1940, Korda met with Minister of Information Duff Cooper and strategized about American propaganda. Korda moved to Hollywood, where he rallied other top producers—like Jack Warner of Warner Brothers, Harry Cohn of Columbia and Sam Goldwyn of MGM—to the British cause.

As a talented director, Korda quickly made *That Hamilton Woman*, a 1941 historical film about facing down dictators, starring Laurence Olivier and Vivien Leigh, fresh from her star-making role in *Gone with the Wind*. A grateful Churchill watched the film repeatedly. He pushed for Korda to be knighted the following year, the first time for any moviemaker.

The America First group and other isolationists sharply criticized Korda's films as British propaganda. The FBI later investigated Korda's film company, London Films Inc., for paying British agents in Latin America. At its Rockefeller Center office, nearly a dozen Korda employees, including the secretaries, were British intelligence agents.

One of Korda's close associates in this cause was Grant, the movie star and spy. "I strongly suspect that Cary Grant was involved, because that would explain the friendship," later said the author Michael Korda, the director's nephew. "Cary would have known what was taking place in the film studios, and the whole purpose of the operation was to have people you could use."

For Ernest Cuneo, the buzz of propaganda in America rose to a crescendo by 1941, with a chorus of voices urging intervention.

No voice was louder than Walter Winchell's. But he wasn't the only interventionist in Cuneo's array of media contacts. Cuneo kept a delicate balance with his actions, if not his loyalties. In effect, Cuneo had become a British intelligence asset as well as a White House confidant.

"On the one hand, Cuneo was feeding Walter [Winchell] information at the behest of the White House, which was coming to believe in the inevitability of America's entrance into the war," observed Winchell's biographer Neal Gabler. "On the other hand, he was secretly feeding Walter British propaganda and top-level intelligence through Stephenson."

The British cast a favorable light on American journalists who extolled their cause. These ranks included CBS's Edward R. Murrow (with his stirring broadcasts from London), columnist Walter Lippmann (who advised surreptitious operations against isolationists), and Arthur Hays Sulzberger, publisher of the *New York Times* (who financially supported pro-interventionist groups).

Cuneo realized journalists, both foreign and domestic, made good informants. Some lesser lights had their hand out, trading information for money, regardless of its source. "Newspapers, always focal points of information, converted the crack reporters into virtual intelligence men," Cuneo recalled. "From the nations in struggle came all sorts of 'inside' information. Ugly rumors circulated that certain writers were on foreign payrolls. Had they so desired, the money, big money was there."

Without being detected, the BSC sought ways to combat the influence of isolationist publishers, such as William Randolph Hearst and "Colonel" Robert R. McCormick of the *Chicago Tribune*. One Stephenson plan, meant to drive Hearst out of business, called for buying up his $10.5 million debt to a Canadian paper mill and then demanding payment.

Some publishers, right-wing or rigidly isolationist, were "beyond hope of conversion and the possible advantage to be gained from contacting them would clearly not have discounted the danger of doing so," explained the secret BSC history. "Yet during a critical period before Pearl Harbor, they represented such a great menace to the British cause that serious consideration was given to the possibility of putting them out of business."

Headlines and radio airtime turned into battlegrounds for arousing American public opinion. Just putting a spotlight on a Nazi menace inside America could be an effective weapon. The BSC's secret history later described how Stephenson leaked "through an intermediary" information about lawyer Gerhard Westrick, a registered diplomat and suspected Nazi spy doing business with US companies. The *New York Herald Tribune* and other media ran prominent stories about Westrick, including his home address in the New York suburbs. Westrick soon fled back to Germany.

The unnamed "intermediary" was likely Cuneo, particularly given the story's wide-scale play in American media, including the Winchell and Drew Pearson columns. Using a media go-between like Cuneo became "one of the principal methods which BSC employed in disseminating subversive propaganda" in America, the secret history described. "All that was necessary was contact through a reliable intermediary with one influential newspaper."

Churchill's spies learned what the Roosevelt Brain Trusters had discovered years before—there was no one more reliable in planting news stories than Ernest Cuneo.

14

DANGEROUS LIAISONS

Margaret Watson was one of several young Canadian women who worked for the British Security Co-ordination at Rockefeller Center in highly confidential roles with the organization's chief, Bill "Intrepid" Stephenson. There, Watson met Cuneo and later married him after the war.

JONATHAN CUNEO

In her dark dormitory room, Margaret Watson fell asleep after another long day of work for the British Security Coordination at Rockefeller Center. Sometimes on nights like this, Watson dreamed of Winnipeg, the provincial capital where she was recruited—along with dozens of other young Canadian women—to join Winston Churchill's spy operation in New York.

Curling up in bed, Watson didn't let the constant honk of taxi horns outside, the cacophony of Midtown Manhattan, disturb her. In this deep slumber, she didn't hear the intruder who entered her room with the intent to kill her.

The move to New York had been a bold decision for Watson, a woman of Scots Presbyterian descent with long wavy brunette hair, attentive brown eyes, and a reserved manner. At age twenty-six and having never married, she decided in mid-1941 on a dramatic, life-altering plan. She would leave her parents' safe and tranquil home for a new life of intrigue in a foreign city during a time of war.

Although listed as a "secretary" on her American immigration papers, Watson's tremendous memory and ability to keep a secret soon landed her in the ranks of intelligence agents. She was assigned various tasks, part of the effort to root out Nazi spies and German sympathizers hidden in America. Her mental acuity with complex numbers made her a natural fit for encryption and deciphering. She was given a code number, like all the other active agents.

Despite her long hours and fatiguing chores, Watson remained unflaggingly dedicated to the British spy mission in New York.

"She had top secret clearance and was one of the people who knew what was really happening," explained her daughter, Sandra, years later. "If you told my mother a secret, and told her not to tell anybody, it went into a lockbox, never to be heard from again. She never betrayed a secret. She was utterly trustworthy and had a tremendous amount of integrity. If she said she was going to do something, she'd do it. You could rely on it."

Initially, Watson considered her tasks challenging but not personally dangerous. She was soon proven wrong.

On that night, with her head resting on a pillow, Watson suddenly awoke in a panic. She felt the overwhelming force of a strong man's weight against her body. The intruder grabbed the pillow and stuffed it into her face. The terrifying blackness, with no air to breathe, made her frantic.

At first she couldn't move, pinned against the mattress. With no escape, she'd soon be smothered to death. There seemed nothing she could do.

Eventually, Watson wriggled free, resisting with every ounce of strength in her arms and legs. Her muted screams now turned into loud cries for help. She fought off her attacker until a dormitory guard ran into her room. He pulled the assailant off her.

In her darkened bedroom, Watson could see only shadows of her would-be killer, struggling with the guard. Soon, other security officers arrived. They wrestled him to the floor.

The intruder spoke only a few garbled words—perhaps in defiance or seeking mercy, but clearly with a German accent—before being whisked away by British security.

New York police were never called, and the German agent was never seen again. He was "dispatched," to use the lethal euphemism of the time.

The intruder specifically wanted "to kill her, not rape her— *kill her*," recalled Watson's son, Jonathan, who heard the story directly from his mother years later. "It didn't end well for him [the German agent]. I don't think he was let go that night, let's put it that way."

Watson was singled out for attack in the secure British-run dormitory, her son theorized, because she was by then involved in tracing the flow of Nazi banking funds abroad.

"Her role in British intelligence dealt with South America, and it dealt in a large part with banking operations," recalled Jonathan. "She could memorize bank information and numbers and accounts. She had a nearly photographic ability to remember numbers and cards. If you played bridge with her, she would say, 'the Seven of Hearts went in the third hand' without any difficulty."

On the night of Watson's attack, British guards alerted William Stephenson, the forty-four-year-old spymaster, of their top secret mission. Within a few minutes, Stephenson arrived from his nearby residence, responding to the emergency call.

As Stephenson learned what had happened to Watson, how she'd nearly lost her life, he undoubtedly showed grave concern. He knew her personally. In mid-1940, Stephenson had recruited Watson—along with several young Canadian women from his hometown of Winnipeg—to work at the BSC's headquarters at Rockefeller Center. Some eight hundred Canadian women would serve in his spy corps during the war.

This initial band of energetic, conscientious women were selected on the recommendations of Winnipeg business owners who knew and respected Stephenson. Watson had been picked specifically because she'd become an impressive top aide at a local company, even though she didn't have a college education.

"When British Security Coordination was set up in New York, Stephenson brought five women with him from Winnipeg to New York—he went back to his roots," recalled Jonathan about the initial group, which included his mother. "They were simple prairie types who had lived through the Depression and understood hardship. They lived in a disciplined way and could be trusted. They all lived together and were escorted everywhere. They carried around secrets of British intelligence."

Stephenson felt an almost paternal responsibility for these young Canadian women and their safety. They looked to him for leadership and moral strength. But he couldn't deny the perils they faced being spies for the Crown.

As the threat of foreign espionage within America intensified, the risks became more treacherous. This night's attempt by an assassin to suffocate Watson was a stark example.

Circumspect by nature, Watson tried not to admit her fear to Stephenson. "She admired him enormously, she had enormous respect for him," recalled her daughter, Sandra. "She was sort of in awe of him."

Each morning in Rockefeller Center's mammoth International

Building, Watson and her colleagues ascended the elevators to their skyscraper offices, where they followed Stephenson's commands faithfully. Outside their thirty-sixth-floor window, they could see St. Patrick's Cathedral from across Fifth Avenue, with its neo-Gothic-style spires reaching toward the sky. Among his staff, Stephenson was known as "God," his secretary as "Gabriel," and his doorkeeper as "Peter," a heavenly joke somewhat grounded in reality.

Yet Stephenson barely seemed noticeable in a crowd, even when spotted getting on the elevator. "The first time I saw him, I said, 'Who is that?' And the answer came loud and clear, 'That was God,'" recalled Dorothy (Dunlevie) Culter, a BSC secretary on the communications desk for three years. "Stephenson appeared at the door of the elevator and got in and said, 'Good Evening Miss Dunlevie.' And I was astounded that he would know me and know my name. It left me speechless and he just sort of stood there. Nobody else was in the elevator and we went down the thirty-six floors very silently."

In know-it-all Manhattan, whose denizens boast of seeing through phonies and facades, Stephenson pulled off an extraordinary charade. Under the guise of a "passport office," the BSC grew into a state-of-the-art espionage center, with complicated machines buzzing all the time and hundreds of employees working intensely in three shifts around the clock.

On the thirty-sixth floor, inside the main offices called the "Registry," women staffers sat working away at a cluster of desks. They handed out decoded confidential messages from London and around the world to Stephenson and other top BSC officers, like Dick Ellis and H. Montgomery Hyde. Another room, devoted to propaganda for the American audience, was called the "Office of War Information," with file cabinets stuffed with news clips and information about isolationist groups like America First. The south-facing windows provided a picturesque view of the Empire State Building and other skyscrapers against the horizon. The clocks on the wall—set to Greenwich Mean Time—were a constant reminder of the war raging back in England.

On a mezzanine floor below, the communications department became an inner sanctum of secrets. Big clattering "Telekrypton" machines received and sent out decrypted messages in a steady hum. Heavy pads placed below each cipher machine kept their shaking and vibrations from being felt elsewhere in the building. Incoming coded messages were printed out on long paper tapes. They were cut up and pasted together, like Western Union telegrams, by the teams of women assemblers. Each exchange of coded messages was on a "need to know" basis only.

Pneumatic tubes, with their swooshing sound, carried messages in hard plastic capsules from one BSC office to another. Once, a capsule flying out from a tube nearly hit visiting OSS spymaster William Donovan in the head.

"I didn't think I was too popular, but I didn't think anybody wanted to kill me," Donovan joked, easing tensions in the room.

Great effort was made to keep their headquarters a secret. No one was allowed to give out the BSC's telephone for personal calls. If asked by a stranger, those working the late shift were instructed to say they were nurses. Somehow this veil of secrecy surrounding their location remained in place.

"Thousands of our agents and experts passed under the statue of Atlas on Fifth Avenue, yet their identities and activities remained effectively masked," recalled Ellis. "But as an increasing number of Americans also passed Atlas and entered the crammed BSC offices, the probability of exposure increased substantially. To our astonishment, the secret endured."

Despite the "Passport Control" nameplate on the door as cover, few travelers came by. Helen Woolley, a secretary in the filing department, later recalled, "No one thought to ask me, 'Who was getting a British passport in 1941 in the middle of a war?'"

As neighbors to the north, Canadian women like Woolley and Margaret Watson seemed a better fit for this highly classified assignment in New York than those with British accents. "The staff was mainly Canadian because Canadians had a special facility for getting on with Americans and could be recruited nearer at hand," *Maclean's* magazine described years later.

The Canadians, despite their proximity to the United States, were even closer in spirit to the British as royal subjects in the United Kingdom. They too had been at war since September 1939. In the first significant attack of World War II, many Canadians were killed and wounded when torpedoes from a Nazi U-boat sank the SS *Athenia*, an unarmed passenger ship in the Atlantic.

"Canada left no doubt of where it stood," recalled Ernest Cuneo. "It declared war and called for volunteers. A million men answered the call, marching down to the station to 'Auld Lang Syne' and 'The Maple Leaf Forever.' In the meantime, into Halifax harbor came the survivors and the coffins of the *Athenia's* passengers."

Many volunteers who answered Canada's call to action were young women like Watson. She never forgot the jarring impact of the *Athenia* disaster. Neither did Cuneo. "For reasons deep in my subconscious and unknown to me," he later said, "the torpedoing of the *Athenia* was a blasting emotional event in my life."

The prospect of Margaret Watson or any other staffer being killed was just one risk in Stephenson's clandestine world. Extreme measures for most people—like assassination and sexual "kompromat"—were not out-of-the-question weapons in this underground war with the Nazis.

Within a few months of his arrival, Stephenson had put together a remarkable espionage organization—a secret kept not only from Manhattan passersby but congressional members who opposed US entry into the ongoing war in Europe. In June 1941, Desmond Morton, Churchill's top aide for spycraft, summarized the delicate situation in New York.

"Another most secret fact of which the Prime Minister is aware...is that to all intents and purposes US security is being run for them at the President's request by the British," Morton wrote in a confidential letter. "It is of course essential that this fact should not be known in view of the furious uproar it would cause if known to the isolationists."

Under this veil of secrecy, an atmosphere charged with excitement and danger prevailed at Rockefeller Center. Several BSC secretaries who became female spies, like Watson, faced unprecedented challenges. There was no telling what Stephenson might ask of them, what new German threat might be detected.

"We were aware it was as secret as you could get—as far as the organization was concerned, 'Don't ask any questions,'" recalled Mary Patricia "Patsy" Sullivan, who worked on codes and ciphers from 1940 to 1945, in the inner office on the thirty-sixth floor. "I never regretted going to New York and working at BSC. It was being on the fringe of big events."

Sullivan had graduated from the University of Saskatchewan and was working in Toronto for the Oxford University Press when she got the call to go to New York. "I didn't want to be a teacher and there wasn't much for women in those days," she recalled. Becoming a spy was undoubtedly more exciting. The BSC fingerprinted her before she started. She also signed an Official Secrets Acts document, promising to remain quiet about whatever she witnessed.

One of Margaret's closest friends—Merle Cameron, another Canadian from Winnipeg—headed Stephenson's filing section and had access to all his secrets. Early in the war, Cameron's boyfriend, the man she intended to marry, was killed in combat. Grieving and seeking to avenge his death by the Nazis, Cameron eventually gave up her desk job in New York and volunteered for a perilous undercover assignment in occupied France.

Another close friend, Grace Garner, was Stephenson's top secretary and had a fierce sense of loyalty to the boss. She kept track of the whereabouts of various informants, along with their code names and aliases. To her, Stephenson was the ultimate spy.

"He had that quality of blending into a crowd," Garner said. "He had very dark, piercing eyes and the uncanny stillness of the man. When he walked he was very quiet and still. He walked like a black panther."

At Rockefeller Center, many staffers endured a constant unspoken tension in their private lives. Several had loved ones overseas serving in combat. Some had spouses who were spies like themselves. "All the men simply vanished—so it was a female world," recalled Pat Spendlove Thomas, a "mail interceptor" from Ottawa, who spent hours each day carefully inspecting other people's mail without detection.

Iris Montagu—the wife of Ian Fleming's Naval Intelligence colleague Ewen Montagu—was another female spy who joined Stephenson's group in New York. She helped create so-called "black propaganda," designed to look authentic and fool the Nazis.

Heartfelt letters between Iris and Ewen, a couple apart for much of the war, reflected the fateful life-or-death drama in their secret spy world.

"If I am killed there are four or five people who will be able after the war to tell you the sort of things I have been doing," wrote Ewen, many miles away from Rockefeller Center. He expressed pride that his wife, who grew up in the London art scene, served as a spy.

Iris was now, as Ewen said, "in the racket."

15

INDISCRETIONS

"She was learning to spy, guess, and reason. She saw everything and everybody in a new light."

—Guy de Maupassant

For Churchill's spies in America, sex could be a double-edged sword. The moral complexities of modern covert operations seemed to clash with the Edwardian niceties of their upbringing.

Both female and male agents found themselves caught in this dilemma of undercover work. Intimacy, as they soon discovered, could be as useful as any other weapon in the defense of England and the greater glory of the Crown.

Whitehall seemed to understand this duplicity. While government ministers didn't sanction sexual intrigue officially, they certainly didn't get in the way. They seemed to understand implicitly the human factor in spying. As Churchill once acknowledged, "In the higher ranges of secret service work, the actual facts of many cases were in every respect equal to the most fantastic inventions of romance and melodrama."

At Rockefeller Center, the British spy headquarters usually upheld the highest standards of decorum. When Sir John Foster, the genial British embassy counsel, used some "very earthy language" to describe his excitement about a spying operation,

Ernest Cuneo remembered it "caused some consternation among the young ladies in the code room."

Cuneo didn't associate the solemn, hardworking women inside the BSC's offices with curse words. These female spies handled ciphers, intercepts, code-breaking and electronic transmission devices with the utmost seriousness. He couldn't envision them trading sexual favors like the legendary Mata Hari, the convicted spy temptress of the First World War. By mastering the technology of this new conflict, Cuneo said, these female agents "indicated that not only Mata Hari, but the era of that kind of intelligence died before her firing squad."

However, ever so discreetly, the British did welcome raw intelligence from both men and women, those who relied on physical attraction and sexual wiles to loosen the lips of enemy diplomats, soldiers and sympathizers. The Russian secret police under Stalin came up with a word for it—"kompromat." Such compromising sexual information, gleaned from pillow talk or perhaps intimate photographs, could be turned into blackmail. Targets of kompromat faced an agonizing choice: either reveal state secrets or have their sexual affair or proclivities revealed.

Quite unofficially, the BSC used those willing to act as human lures in an "all is fair in love and war" battle with the enemy. Relying on these volunteers was certainly less risky than bribes, brothels or bloodshed. As Stephenson's security aide, H. Montgomery Hyde, later described, "In the penetration of enemy and unfriendly missions in the Western Hemisphere and the discovery of their secret codes and ciphers, BSC was particularly adept...in the delicate operation of discrediting their staff members through their individual indiscretions."

The most celebrated player in this game of indiscretions was a British spy, Amy Elizabeth Thorpe Pack, known by the code name "Cynthia."

Cynthia provided top secret information about the Axis powers through a sexual affair she initiated with a Vichy French embassy official in Washington, DC. She also conquered other diplomats in Washington and gained information through a reputed love affair with an Italian naval officer.

Top secret documents obtained by Cynthia were claimed to have helped crack enemy naval codes, providing a winning advantage during the 1942 Allied invasion of North Africa. As the BSC's secret history later judged, "it would be difficult to over-emphasize the importance of her work."

Cynthia was regularly debriefed by Marion De Chastelain, a Stephenson spy based at Rockefeller Center, who spoke seven languages, including French. The middle-aged De Chastelain was both confessor and counselor to Cynthia, keeping her special agent steady and focused during the most challenging spy experiences.

"I commuted back and forth to Washington," recalled De Chastelain, who conferred with her highly sensitive agent on a weekly basis. "I met her [Cynthia] in odd places. Sometimes in her hotel. Told her what we needed. Cheered her up if she was blue."

Unhappily wed to a former British embassy official named Arthur Pack, Cynthia became a Mata Hari–like spy for the BSC, committed to the cause, body and soul. She used her sex appeal as a tool to compromise various male officials, often married, and pry away tightly held state secrets needed in war.

"Ashamed? Not in the least," she later explained of her deeds. "My superiors told me that the results of my work saved thousands of British and American lives... It involved me in situations from which 'respectable' women draw back—but mine was total commitment. Wars are not won by respectable methods."

While De Chastelain didn't consider Cynthia a great beauty, she recognized her effectiveness with men. Hyde, Stephenson's security aide, was more appreciative of Cynthia's allure, with her light hair and deep green eyes.

"Unusually beautiful, she had an exquisite, narrow-boned figure; a light quick-silver wit, a sharp intelligence and a soft and soothing voice that somehow inspired trust and confidence," Hyde later described in a biography about her. "It was by a combination of these formidable qualities that she was able to extract secrets of the highest political and military importance from the men of influence and position she cultivated for that purpose."

Even the BSC's secret history (written by men and overseen by Stephenson) couldn't help describing Cynthia's physical attributes. "That she was physically very attractive cannot be doubted," it said, "for the powerful hold she exercised over the worldly wise men whose secrets she sought to obtain was clearly based on sex."

Perhaps Cynthia's most remarkable conquest was the middle-aged Vichy French press attaché who helped her steal documents from his own embassy in Washington, where cipher books and other classified information were kept in a locked safe in the code room.

At Cynthia's prompting, the agreeable Vichy official paid the night watchman to look the other way while they conducted an illicit affair in his office. Their real purpose was to break into the safe, remove and photograph secret documents, and return them without a trace of having being disturbed.

After a few failed attempts, they finally succeeded one night—but only after the suspicious night watchman appeared without warning at their door.

Cynthia heard his advancing footsteps and reacted swiftly. She took off all her clothes and urgently ordered her Vichy lover to do the same.

"Get undressed quickly!" she whispered.

When the door slowly opened, the night watchman shone his flashlight around. He was shocked to discover a naked Cynthia on a sofa with the embassy official. A beam of light revealed she was wearing only a string of pearls around her neck. As she scampered to put on a slip, the embarrassed night watchman excused himself and wasn't seen again.

Quickly redressing, Cynthia signaled to the BSC's ace lock-smith, who'd been waiting outside the embassy. He came in, broke into the safe and soon the cipher documents were copied.

The legendary stories about Cynthia were only part of the atmosphere of sexual intrigue surrounding spying at Rocke-feller Center.

While the BSC neither trained nor directly encouraged their agents to partake in "dirty work"—the phrase used in their office—officials were grateful for any intelligence obtained through pillow talk, said another Cynthia biographer, Mary S. Lovell. She cited one French Resistance female agent known as "Amniarix" who, after seducing a German officer, provided an "outstanding" report about the Nazi Flying Bomb organi-zation, which built the V-1 "buzz bombs" terrorizing London from the sky. Lovell also said there were "several well-known agents who employed the same methods," including a "beauti-ful young blonde from His Majesty's consulate in Tangiers who kept an open bed for notable Spanish and Axis officers."

Male spies seduced female targets as well. For a time, Hyde was in charge of another highly successful double agent, code-named "Springbok"—a handsome German businessman of "noble descent"—who helped the BSC break up Nazi espio-nage in South America. As Hyde later described, Springbok was "a man of powerful attraction to women," a seeming asset for their cause.

But Springbok's charm offensive boomeranged for Hyde per-sonally. As another analyst later wrote, Hyde was "particularly irritated" to learn that one of the women "seduced" by this charismatic double agent during the war was Hyde's first wife. Other male spies also used their sexual powers of persuasion, though not quite so close to home.

For President Roosevelt, the boudoir tales of spies giving their all for the Allied cause provided racy reading in otherwise dull classified dossiers reviewed by him at night. He liked them "as a bedtime story," and declared it "the most fascinating reading I have had for a long time."

In dealing with so many female staffers, Stephenson remained courteous without a hint of impropriety. He was faithful to his wife, Mary, unlike other well-known, powerful married men who would brag about how many women they had slept with. "In a lot of ways, Stephenson wasn't one of the boys as they say," said Dahl. "In a lot of ways he was a man apart."

Sexual compromise in spying was a constant security concern, particularly among young and naive female staffers who had no intention of behaving like nuns in a monastery. To avoid giving up secrets, BSC women were instructed not to interact with Americans unless it was part of their overall espionage and intelligence duties.

"I was dating a young man very briefly who was an American, and should have been in the forces according to them [BSC]," said Dorothy Sewell Evenson, who worked in Stephenson's communications department. During the austere wartime years, Evenson said this wealthy American, of seemingly independent means, came under British suspicions for the reason that "he also owned a car, which was unheard of in Manhattan, because private cars were very few and gas restrictions were on."

At the BSC's instruction, Evenson became an undercover spy while out on a date. "I was told to find out exactly what he did, and that night we went to Long Island to a country club for a dinner dance," she recalled. "And on Monday morning, I was told it was probably a good idea to stop going out with him. Which was fine that that happened. I just didn't go out with him anymore."

For the young women at Rockefeller Center, the demands of spying provided a certain mystique to their otherwise humdrum jobs. Most were stuck behind desks rather than given intriguing undercover assignments. They were reminded constantly to keep their mouths shut with strangers.

Not everyone was content with having their social lives monitored. Two Canadian women broke the BSC's rules by giving "an air of intrigue" about themselves and their work, inviting potential compromise. Stephenson promptly sent them home.

Nevertheless, the allure of sexuality—with young people engaged in dangerous liaisons and risky pursuits—made romance inevitable, regardless of the rules. Rockefeller Center seemed a natural setting for one spy to meet another—as Margaret Watson of Winnipeg eventually learned.

16

"OUR MAN"

"If Bill Donovan had been a Democrat, he'd be in my place today."

—President Franklin Roosevelt

At the German consulate in New York, secret Nazi paperwork that was no longer needed was burned as trash in the basement furnace. An extra effort ensured its destruction without a shred of security problems.

Each time a big pile of waste arrived from offices upstairs, a German consulate employee first sifted through it, looking for possible explosives. Then, after ruling out any sabotage, the employee signaled to the furnaceman to toss the trash into the blaze and soon left the dingy room. In the roaring fire, classified orders from Berlin—and communiqués referring to undercover agents inside the United States—went up in smoke, gone without a trace.

On one occasion, however, the furnaceman, an American, decided to check out these papers for himself. He deliberately heaved the secret papers into the furnace in a way that would cause them to choke off the draft. Eventually, the furnaceman grabbed the papers out of the fire and began to read them. Recognizing their importance, he called federal authorities.

At that time, in early 1941, J. Edgar Hoover's FBI was still working agreeably with William Stephenson's BSC, drawing upon British expertise in investigating cases of Nazi espionage in America. Several months earlier, Hoover had agreed to this arrangement with the blessing of President Roosevelt—relayed by Ernest Cuneo.

One of the documents recovered from the furnace mentioned Paul T. Borchardt, a German spy. The secret paper was part of a decoded radio message from Nazi headquarters. It directed the German consulate to find Borchardt at his stated address in New York and tell him to "heat" (burn) a previous order he'd received from his superiors.

The FBI alerted Stephenson's spies about Borchardt. The BSC quickly provided a wealth of background information about the fifty-six-year-old former German Army officer, who'd immigrated from England the year before as a "refugee" from the Nazis.

After his arrest later that year, the two agencies tied Borchardt to other members of the Kurt Ludwig spy ring, including the German spy killed in the Times Square car crash and identified by Stephenson's sleuths. Eventually at trial, two intelligence officers of the BSC testified to help convict Borchardt, who was given a twenty-year jail sentence.

"Although the Federal Bureau of Investigation did not really get on the trail of the alleged spies until one of them was accidentally killed by a taxi in Times Square last March, the letters turned over by the British dovetailed neatly with what the FBI uncovered here," summarized the *New York Herald Tribune*.

By that point, however, the once amiable relationship between Hoover's FBI and Stephenson's spy agency had deteriorated.

Hoover didn't like sharing credit for headline-grabbing investigations of Nazi spies, especially not with a foreign entity like the BSC that outshone his own agents. Despite their earlier cooperation agreement, the FBI chief resented how Stephenson increasingly favored William Donovan, FDR's Coordinator of Information, with a branch office at Rockefeller Center.

According to his own appeal to President Roosevelt, Hoover wanted the FBI's spy dragnet to extend worldwide, as the federal agency with the most investigative experience and best capable of handling intelligence operations. Some top FDR aides—like Assistant Secretary of State Adolf Berle, who oversaw national security—agreed with Hoover.

"We likewise decided that the time had come when we would have to consider setting up a secret intelligence service—which I suppose every great foreign office in the world has, but we have never touched," Berle wrote in his diary after a meeting with the FBI chief.

Historically, the United States avoided the idea of spying, particularly any type of covert intelligence operations like the kind Churchill had set up at Rockefeller Center. For a decade after World War I, the US Army ran a cipher bureau, commonly called "the Black Chamber," with cryptanalysts deciphering secret codes and messages from other nations. In 1929, however, Secretary of State Henry L. Stimson ended the practice. He famously declared, "Gentlemen do not read each other's mail."

The folly of America's weak approach to espionage became abundantly clear with the rise of Hitler, especially when compared to the sophisticated, long-established spy services of Great Britain and the Soviet Union. Cuneo believed the 1938 Munich Agreement was the "trip wire" that convinced President Roosevelt "to put the U.S. on a war footing," though America was far from prepared with spies.

"At that time, the U.S. had no actual intelligence service," Cuneo recalled. "Neither was there a propaganda department. It was perfectly apparent, however, that Hitler was waging vigorous if undeclared war through both an intelligence and propaganda service adding up to an effective psychological war by enlisting, engendering and distributing anti-democratic, pro-fascist and pro-Nazi dogma."

Cuneo said this potent propaganda effort by Hitler's spies was aimed at "uniting the isolationist, pro-German and anti-Semitic lunatic fringe in the U.S. into a formidable opposition."

However, Hoover's bid to become the czar of spying failed. Eventually, Roosevelt created the Office of Strategic Services (OSS) in June 1942, fashioned very much like the BSC, and he appointed COI director Donovan as its head. Hoover resented the snub, but the British were delighted by FDR's choice.

Donovan's selection had been urged by Stephenson and Ian Fleming's boss, Rear Admiral John Godfrey of British Naval Intelligence, with the backing of MI6 chief Stewart Menzies and Churchill himself. Instead of widening the scope of Hoover's FBI, Roosevelt heeded their advice to create a whole new agency with the OSS.

"You can imagine how relieved I am after three months of battle and jockeying for position in Washington that our man is in a position of such importance to our effort," Stephenson cabled to London about Donovan's initial appointment.

Stephenson and "our man" Donovan talked several times about how the new American agency would be designed and come to life with the BSC's help and advice. Among others, the short-hand names for the two became "Big Bill" for Donovan and "Little Bill" for Stephenson, though the BSC chief's views clearly dominated their early discussions.

By the time Borchardt's New York arrest was announced in December 1941, Donovan had begun filling up the OSS with his own talented staff of amateurs, often with little background in espionage or law enforcement. Eventually an OSS staff of more than ten thousand would be spread far and wide in Europe, Africa and Asia, with a headquarters based in Washington.

Women made up nearly a third of the OSS's staff, with many sent overseas as shadow warriors vital to the overall effort. Their various tasks ranged from acting as saboteurs, undercover agents and message couriers, to creating fake news stories that undermined enemy morale, to analyzing aerial photographs for missions behind enemy lines. "Women spies parachuting into Southern France had to depend, not on glamour and seductiveness, but, as with their male counterparts, on their courage, steel nerves and resourcefulness," described author William B. Breuer in his 1997 study of American women at war.

The OSS staff became an American mirror version of British intelligence. While Stephenson's BSC members included such eclectic choices as entertainer Eric Maschwitz and advertising guru David Ogilvy, Donovan's crew was even more diverse. The OSS roster included gourmet chef Julia Child, future Nobel Peace Prize winner Ralph Bunche (one of the few Black members), future Supreme Court judge Arthur Goldberg, baseball catcher Moe Berg, historian Arthur M. Schlesinger Jr. and filmmaker John Ford. This ensemble also included a few members with criminal backgrounds.

"In Donovan's rush to build up, early applicants were hired with no more security check than someone vouching for their family connections," described Donovan biographer Douglas Waller. "It resulted in Nazi sympathizers slipping in, who had to be weeded out later when they were more carefully screened. Communists were a dilemma. Donovan wanted them to work with him but not necessarily for him."

As an example of these tensions, Waller pointed to a false item in Walter Winchell's column, apparently leaked by Hoover, that claimed G-men discovered a Hungarian American with fascist ties in Donovan's OSS. Undoubtedly, Cuneo, as the OSS's official liaison, wasn't thrilled by this squabble. Waller described Cuneo as "a Democratic Party operative" whose job was "cajoling cooperation out of the FBI and other agencies."

In his new job, Donovan discussed with Cuneo how to handle Stephenson and other BSC spies. Cuneo impressed upon him the intensity the British brought to their cause. He advised that "England was not a country but a religion, and that where England was concerned, every Englishman was a Jesuit who believed the end justifies the means."

As a spy capable of writing a speech, Cuneo wasn't afraid of being a "ghost" for Donovan, as he'd done for FDR's administration at the White House. "Ghosting is the reverse of playwriting; a ghost must fit the play to the actor," Cuneo explained. "Tom Corcoran and I wrote a lot of scripts together."

Unlike Stephenson, Donovan wasn't publicity shy. His new spy agency became the talk of Washington. Many top officers came from elite colleges and privileged backgrounds. With such a heady atmosphere, some quipped that "OSS" stood for "Oh So Social."

As the nation's new top spymaster, Donovan didn't like bureaucracy. He favored a loose, intuitive style that upset other government officials but became the stuff of "Wild Bill" legend among his OSS admirers. To them, Donovan was, as filmmaker Ford described, "the sort of guy who thought nothing of parachuting into France, blowing up a bridge, pissing in *Luftwaffe* gas tanks, then dancing on the roof of the St. Regis hotel with a German spy."

Years later, Stephenson said Donovan had been too proud to lobby for the job, and that he'd convinced FDR to appoint Donovan. He even had a witness to attest to it. "And you can ask Ernest Cuneo about that," Stephenson insisted.

As the OSS grew, Donovan's staff increasingly worked with Stephenson on joint ventures in the United States. American code breakers communicated by radio and cable with British intelligence, usually routed through Rockefeller Center.

The most remarkable communications project involved a fifty-thousand-watt shortwave radio station in Boston called WRUL, which had been sponsored in part by the Rockefeller family. By mid-1941, the BSC had surreptitiously taken over the radio station's programming. They used its powerful broad-casting abilities to spread pro-British propaganda around the world. As soon as Donovan's spies joined them, more money was provided for this radio station as part of the "Political War-fare" department.

While Cuneo and others had been helpful in planting stories on the Walter Winchell and Drew Pearson radio shows, as well as with numerous print journalists reaching millions of Ameri-cans, WRUL's international audience, broadcasted in different languages, was even bigger and more impressive. WRUL was heard in such varied places as New Zealand, Egypt and Tur-key, as well as much of Western Europe. In occupied France alone, there were an estimated four hundred thousand listeners. One specially aimed program for neutral Spain was designed to convince its dictator, General Francisco Franco, not to join the Nazis in the war.

"Running a radio programme was a far more complicated business than placing an occasional article in a newspaper," the BSC's secret history later described.

WRUL offered listeners their London-approved information in the guise of "neutral" American news shows, with some US broadcasters hired as announcers. No one in the radio audience seemed to know the difference. WRUL had a policy against broadcasting anything that had not appeared in the American press.

"But BSC got around this by inserting its own material in friendly newspapers, and then quoting it" on WRUL, said the spy agency's secret history. To those listening in, the news pro-grams, subtly manipulated, sounded believable.

America was ripe for propaganda. Only a few years earlier, Orson Welles's 1938 "War of the Worlds" broadcast jolted the nation with a fake radio show claiming Martians were invading Earth. It caused an outcry when believers realized it was a hoax. The on-air manipulations at WRUL went undetected, just as intended. When *Washington Post* columnist David Ignatius got his hands on the secret history in 1989 and published details of WRUL's radio broadcasts, he said it portrayed the United States as "a society almost laughably easy to manipulate."

Cuneo helped orchestrate one of WRUL's most extraordinary ruses—quoting a phony astrologer who predicted Hitler's death. Spreading such on-air rumors about the Führer proved remarkably powerful when beamed around the world. At the request of Stephenson's BSC, Cuneo orchestrated a New York press conference for astrologer Louis de Wohl when he arrived in June 1941 from London.

With his bow tie, lengthy hair and scholarly glasses, de Wohl presented himself as a "Astro-Philosopher" of international repute. He looked like the "Wizard of Oz" character in the recent MGM movie. He called himself "the Modern Nostradamus." In fact, de Wohl was a novelist and overall fabulist employed by Churchill's spies.

When he first began, the British Special Operations Executive set de Wohl up in a posh London apartment, with the rent supposedly paid by a wealthy female patron of this soothsayer. De Wohl named his one-man effort "the Psychological Research Bureau." He filed a secret report entitled "The Astrological Tendencies of Herr Hitler's Horoscope," kept classified until the UK's National Archives released it in 2008.

The British believed Hitler was superstitious about the occult and inclined to listen to those predicting his astrological future when making key strategic decisions. De Wohl tried to calculate a possible Nazi invasion of Britain in 1940 by studying Hitler's birth under the zodiac sign of Taurus.

"Checking up on the events of the past, I found that all major enterprises of Hitler since he came to power have been undertaken under 'good aspects,'" de Wohl advised. "Hitler's famous 'divine intuition' is in reality simply knowledge about planetary tendencies."

De Wohl's magical appearance in Manhattan was one more

step by the BSC to push America toward entering the war. He told reporters the planet Neptune was "in the house of death" and would align soon with Uranus in a way that spelled doom for Hitler. It was contrary to German propaganda quoting other stargazers predicting success for the Nazi dictator.

News about de Wohl's predictions traveled around the globe, first in print and then on the air. WRUL's broadcast about Hitler's astrological bad fortune, for example, reached the Middle East. A French-speaking radio station—purportedly owned by the Vatican but in actuality run by Churchill's SOE—gave it the same coverage.

With Cuneo's help, the BSC arranged for de Wohl to go on tour around the United States, with his proverbial crystal ball foreseeing future problems for the Nazi leader. The phony astrologer was assigned "not only to convince the public but to alarm that great believer in astrology, Hitler himself," the BSC said, leaving "little doubt that his [de Wohl's] work had a considerable effect."

Although plenty were dubious of de Wohl, British Naval Intelligence chief John Godfrey also became convinced that Hitler's key military actions were indeed based upon the Zodiac. "The significance of Hitler's astrological researches is not therefore whether or not we believe in them or if they represent the truth," Godfrey explained, "but that Hitler believes them."

Shortly before de Wohl arrived in New York, the Federal Communications Commission dropped its ban against astrologers on the air. Increasingly, Donovan's staff took over the WRUL programming and later expanded its radio propaganda to stations in California beaming across the Pacific.

Eventually, de Wohl would go back to England, later writing several bestselling works of fiction once his horoscope days ended in America. But Stephenson was pleased by the phony astrologer's impact in the States. As the BSC chief reported, "an ever-growing audience [is] becoming convinced of his supernatural powers."

★ ★ ★

Donovan's reliance on Stephenson for guidance increasingly irked Hoover. The cooperation between British and American spies was still hampered at times by the FBI director's bruised ego and insistence they follow the existing neutrality laws. By late 1941, there was "a period of embitterment in the relationship between the FBI and the BSC," said Stephenson's secret agency history, which cited repeated examples of Hoover's obstructionism.

The FBI director often complained, sometimes rightfully so, that the BSC was holding back information from him, especially regarding Latin America, where the FBI was allowed to conduct investigations. Invariably, Donovan and others, including Cuneo, were dragged into these disputes. Perhaps the most obvious showdown took place during the Cynthia spy operation in Washington.

Around the same time as Cythia's rendezvous at the Vichy French embassy, the BSC and Donovan planned other break-ins at the Spanish embassy, similarly designed to steal, photograph and return their code books without detection.

Donovan's top spy for this mission, Donald Downes, a quirky college professor, had also spied for the British under Stephenson's savvy deputy, Dick Ellis. At a restaurant near the Rockefeller Center skating rink, Ellis directed Downes to keep an eye on isolationist Americans and see if Nazi money was making its way to America First groups. As part of his training, Downes said he learned "silent killing" methods—which included swinging a sock with a rock inside it to crack a man's skull.

In the OSS's Spanish embassy case, Downes recruited a young Spanish-speaking woman, code-named "Ella," to get a secretarial job there. She eased the way for an after-hours break-in by Donovan's undercover agents.

One night, while the Spanish embassy staff was entertained at a party in suburban Maryland secretly arranged by the BSC,

Donovan's spies entered their foreign embassy. The agents photographed thousands of Spanish documents unlocked from a safe. The OSS chief was "practically delirious with joy" over the successful operation, Cuneo said, though the happiness was short-lived.

Hoover's G-men were also conducting their own spying operations on foreign embassies in Washington with the president's approval. The FBI director argued that neither BSC nor the OSS were authorized to conduct domestic spying. Rumors about the Cynthia operation annoyed Hoover, particularly because he was kept in the dark about it.

When Donovan's crew attempted another break-in at the Spanish embassy, sirens went off. The OSS safe-cracking team fled and barely avoided being caught. But they spotted FBI agents outside and complained to Donovan that the G-men were at fault for this failure.

Both Donovan and Hoover went directly to the White House with this bitter dispute. Hoover said his agents had already been conducting black bag jobs at the Spanish embassy and that Donovan's spies had been warned not to interfere. Roosevelt eventually sided with Hoover in this dispute, instructing Donovan to focus on the OSS's spy missions abroad.

But the bitter internecine quarrels between Hoover and Donovan would continue. Each kept secret files on the other. Agents learned about Donovan's extramarital affairs and that Hoover was likely homosexual, compromising personal information kept in their respective files like a weapon. Throughout the war, the two agency leaders waited for the other to slip up and lose their influence with the president—which would eventually happen with one.

In the meantime, FDR remained wary of giving Donovan, the FBI or Stephenson's BSC too much power. As historian John Ranelagh observed, "It was typical of Roosevelt to play people and agencies against each other in this way."

Cuneo was no stranger to Roosevelt's political dexterity, his uncanny ability to scramble and avoid being trapped in one position. He had watched the master during the 1930s, as top counsel for the Democratic Party. In his own way, Cuneo learned to work all sides without making enemies. He remained on friendly terms with Hoover (partly due to his connection with Winchell), and while he also worked as official liaison for Donovan, he was probably most loyal in heart and spirit to Stephenson.

In preparing his reluctant nation for war, Roosevelt could only go so far. Illegal spycraft actions were kept from public view, no matter how necessary. Cuneo trusted the president's judgment, though Roosevelt probably had little idea of the risks taken. If those in isolationist America found out what Cuneo'd been up to with a foreign power, they'd surely condemn his actions as traitorous, something akin to being a "Fifth Column" conspirator.

"He [FDR] himself had said he was a quarterback," Cuneo recalled, "and I saw him as a quarterback who was constantly searching to move the ball as far upfield as public opinion would allow him."

FDR's modest football career, playing on a Harvard scrub team, couldn't compare with Cuneo's own glorious days at Columbia and in the NFL. But Ernie understood and followed the president's instructions like a good teammate. Anticipating his next move, Cuneo positioned himself on the front lines of a war that America was about to enter.

17

THE SINISTER TOUCH

"There is required for composition of the great commander not only imagination but an element of legerdemain, an original and sinister touch, which leaves the enemy puzzled as well as beaten."

—Winston Churchill, *The World Crisis*

The best ways to kill, sabotage and subvert the enemy were lessons taught at "Camp X."

It was the code name for Churchill's authorized school for spies in the Western Hemisphere, hidden in an isolated stretch of land along Lake Ontario, east of Toronto, Canada. Camp X's ability to turn a neophyte into a well-trained undercover agent was reflected in its syllabus of mayhem and murder instruction.

For instance, "Unarmed Combat" and "Sabotage by Fire" dealt with inflicting mortal injury on the enemy. Other sessions featured jumping from a plane, launching nighttime assaults, and diving headlong into "underwater explosive training."

Camp X opened on December 6, 1941—the day before Pearl Harbor. There, trainees learned that sudden violence was the calling card of covert operations. The camp served as an offshoot of Churchill's Special Operations Executive underground fighting unit in Europe and Asia, and it was overseen by William Stephenson's British Security Coordination in New York.

Here in the Canadian hinterlands, Stephenson said, Churchill wanted to turn Camp X into "the clenched fist that would provide the knockout blow" to Hitler and the Axis threat.

Once a farm, the 275-acre facility, with its hazards and bombs, resembled the movie set from *The Dirty Dozen*.

Each trainee "was taught how to shadow a man and how to escape surveillance himself, how to creep up behind an armed sentry and kill him instantly without noise," said the BSC secret history. "In the unarmed combat course, he learned many holds whose use would enable him to break an adversary's arm or leg, knock him unconscious or kill him outright. He learned to handle a tommy-gun and to use several different types of revolvers and automatic pistols, as well as the use of a knife."

American intelligence chief William Donovan was delighted to learn from Stephenson about this secret site for teaching spies. He eventually sent four hundred Americans to study and practice all facets of espionage before being dispatched by OSS into the field of unconventional warfare.

"We have to admit this [OSS group] was a bunch of amateurs," recalled William J. Casey, himself an OSS staffer long before becoming CIA director in the 1980s. "It was Sir William [Stephenson] who provided the know-how and the training which made it possible for them to develop into an effective intelligence service."

According to Casey, Donovan told FDR that "intelligence, psychological warfare and irregular forces drawn from the great ethnic melting pot which is America would be the spearhead to liberate occupied Europe. General Donovan said it after the war—'Bill Stephenson taught us everything we ever knew about foreign intelligence.'"

Donovan couldn't be more pleased that this spy camp was in Canada, far beyond the critical gaze of the FBI's Hoover or an isolationist Congress. Next to Camp X's training facilities, the BSC operated a tall radio tower and high-speed transmitter called Hydra, sending and receiving encrypted messages from around the world.

In time, Camp X's reputation became legendary, both as a place for coldhearted warriors and for inspiring imaginations. A visit to Camp X supposedly sparked Ian Fleming's love of the spy gadgets and fiery explosions found in his James Bond fiction. Paul Dehn, who later cowrote the screenplays for Fleming's *Goldfinger* and John le Carré's *The Spy Who Came in from the Cold*, was one of Camp X's top instructors. Understanding murder techniques helped Dehn portray them on the silver screen.

"Paul [Dehn] actually had been in our Special Operations Executive during the war, and he had been, among other things, a professional assassin," le Carré—himself a British spy in the late 1950s—claimed years later. "It was a gruesome fact. Paul was a very gentle guy, lovely to work with."

In overseeing this spy school, Stephenson carried out Churchill's vision of "ungentlemanly warfare"—an aggressive approach to covert action as well as intelligence gathering. Although his own SOE was slow to unleash its underground agents in Europe, Churchill encouraged Stephenson to boldly but secretively assert the BSC inside the United States—and bring along Donovan and his agency with him if possible.

To the British, the moral imperatives and sense of urgency couldn't be more clear. This wasn't a time for niceties, but for action. "Churchill's support for SOE and his faith in European resistance provided a beacon of hope, not a mirror of self-delusion, for those who lived in the darkness of Hitler's rule," wrote historian David Stafford. "SOE was a new and unorthodox secret service wedded to a doctrine of subversion whose job was to cause mayhem and disorder."

Stephenson relied on the element of surprise. And just how much his BSC had extended this "mayhem and disorder" within US borders was a surprise to Ernest Cuneo, along with a handful of others who found out about these covert actions.

★ ★ ★

Inside his office, US Attorney General Francis Biddle burst into anger at the idea of British kidnappings on American soil during a meeting with Cuneo. From behind his desk, Biddle leaped to his feet, his face livid.

"God damn it, they have British Shore Patrols operating on the American waterfront," Biddle snarled at Cuneo. "Down in Miami, they konked some British deserters on the head, handcuffed them, put 'em in a Pullman car drawing room and delivered them to a British ship just as she sailed. It's been going on for some time."

Cuneo sat listening quietly as the nation's top law enforcement officer vented. He knew Biddle from their days together in FDR's White House and considered him a friend. He'd never seen Biddle get so angry—Cuneo later recalled it was "one of the most towering rages I had ever witnessed."

Kidnapping was one of several covert actions performed in the United States by Stephenson's BSC, part of an aggressive underground campaign not known publicly.

Starting several months before this Biddle meeting, the BSC had been rounding up as many as one hundred seamen a week. They had deserted British merchant vessels while in US ports, hoping to avoid the war and get jobs in high-paying American factories. Deserters were also a security risk for Stephenson, lest they become German spies or informants.

Cuneo tried to settle Biddle down. Biddle was a Harvard and Groton graduate, whose family harkened back to the American Revolution—his great-great-grandfather Edmund Randolph had been the first US Attorney General, and a distant cousin, President James Madison, was a framer of the Constitution.

A tall elegant man with a high forehead and a pencil mustache, Biddle wasn't inclined to tolerate law-breaking, even by an ally like the British. Biddle often sniffed as he talked. During this rant, the sniff was in high gear. As he cooled down,

Biddle explained the situation to Cuneo, the proverbial man in the middle between the BSC and US agencies.

After Biddle found out about the kidnappings, he complained to the British ambassador in Washington, Lord Halifax. But the British diplomat rebuffed him.

"When I told Halifax what was going on, he said that he had it on highest authority that it was permissible," Biddle explained to Cuneo, reenacting the scene. The clear implication was that Stephenson had some legal clearance from President Roosevelt to do this kidnapping, and that Halifax had been so instructed by Churchill's government in London.

"Highest authority, Lord Halifax? *I* am the highest authority," Biddle informed Halifax. "I am the Attorney General of the United States—and as this nation's highest law enforcement authority, I tell you that if it happens again I will have you indicted by a federal grand jury."

Cuneo knew that wasn't going to happen. By the time of this meeting, the British kidnappings had been largely curtailed. Cuneo realized the biggest struggle was a political one. It involved US agencies upset by the overall actions of the BSC and William Donovan's OSS.

"I perceived at once the basic cause of the hostility towards Stephenson," Cuneo said. "The FBI and sundry other US Departmental agencies were out to cut Stephenson down not because the British were violating the laws of the United States, but because the British were furthering the Office of Strategic Services, which almost certainly would intrude on their bureaucratic territory which was bad enough, but would have superior access to President FDR."

On sensitive matters of espionage and statecraft, top officials like Biddle and Halifax always staged a circuitous back-and-forth. "It is SOP [standard operating procedure] for diplomats to deny that they have any knowledge of a bungled intelligence action, and it is compulsory for the diplomats of the offended nation to accept the denial," Cuneo said.

This Washington game became more intense during wartime. Each side had their own competing rules and reality, regardless of the truth. "This is an important formality, and a most necessary one, the diplomatic counterpart of what is called in jurisprudence a 'fiction of the law,'" Cuneo explained. Kidnappings on American soil were the pretext for a bigger dispute, Cuneo said. "The charges of illegal British activities were the excuses; the reason was that Edgar [Hoover] wanted to protect his turf," he concluded.

In his conversations with White House officials, Cuneo essentially became the lawyer for Churchill's spies. "I was thus posited in the position of *de facto* counsel for the defense of British Security," he said. Cuneo argued how vital Stephenson's sophisticated spy agency was to the rapid development of Donovan's OSS.

But privately, Cuneo also asked presidential aides—especially those fellow intermediates with "a passion for anonymity" like himself—if Roosevelt really wanted to keep the OSS. The question reeked of an ultimatum, though he felt it worth the risk to get the president's commitment.

"The answer was that the President indeed wanted OSS to continue, but also, and emphatically, he wanted no horsing around inside the United States by either the OSS or the BSC," Cuneo recalled. "It was conveyed to me and unmistakably, that the President knew the nature of the terrible instrument he had authorized, that it was a wartime measure against foreign enemies, even to his remark that 'God help the country if such an agency was ever unleashed against the American people.'"

While FDR feared creating such a Frankenstein's monster, the real creature Cuneo found himself defending was far more complex. He knew about darker aspects of BSC's activities in America—a list that included violent exchanges and "disposal squads"—which definitely gave him pause.

In his unpublished memoir, Cuneo mentioned confrontations between Nazi spies and the British on American soil, including one death on Manhattan's Upper East Side. "Both they [Stephenson's BSC] and the Germans had agents in the US, and the Germans, in fact, killed a British agent at 89th Street and East River Drive," Cuneo wrote, without further explanation.

Stephenson avoided detailing sensitive operations to his American middleman, Cuneo, especially those involving lethal intent. But years later, he apparently claimed to an interviewer that the BSC had its "own disposal squads to handle such disagreeable duties."

Cuneo told family and friends that he didn't know of any assassination attempts on American soil. While working for the OSS, though, he did hear some discussion about killing someone in Portugal. He left the room, unwilling to be part of it. Nevertheless, Stephenson's previous words of warning remained seared in Cuneo's memory: "All I can say is that if you join us... you mustn't be afraid of murder."

Getting rid of enemy spies was rarely spoken about with specifics at Rockefeller Center. "I remember things like—could this man not be eliminated?—and things like that," recalled Grace Garner, Stephenson's top secretary, without adding details.

The BSC's H. Montgomery Hyde, who chronicled the agency in a 1963 book, disclosed even more in a 1988 television interview.

When asked if Stephenson's BSC "knocked off any people in America," Hyde replied: "One on a ship, as far as I know, only one, who was bringing information to the enemy. To my knowledge, in the United States, the British Security Coordination, which was under the direction of William Stephenson, there was one seaman on a neutral ship—I think it was a Portuguese ship—who was detected giving information to the Germans. And as far as I know, he was liquidated. But I only know that one case. The United States hadn't come into the war then."

Before America entered the war, Britain also investigated a different spy case coming out of New York and Boston. Stephenson's secret agents gathered evidence about a traitorous British merchant seaman, George Johnson Armstrong, who offered to sell information about ship convoy movements to the Nazis. For his disloyalty, Armstrong would pay the highest price.

At first, Armstrong approached German spies in neutral Spain, but they refused, suspecting he was a counterespionage agent. When Armstrong's ship landed in New York, however, BSC agents were tipped off and waiting. They followed him to the German consul's office in Boston, where a Nazi official purchased the shipping information from Armstrong.

With America still neutral, Stephenson's agents busily collected damning evidence in the States against Armstrong, but refrained from arresting him. However, when Armstrong came home to England, authorities charged him under the Treachery Act. After being found guilty, Armstrong was hanged in a London jail in July 1941, the first executed traitor of the war.

Undeterred, German spies in America kept up their skullduggery. One notorious example involved top British scientist Sir Henry Tizard, who'd arrived in Washington carrying many British secrets for nuclear fission, radar and even penicillin. Two men, seemingly FBI agents, offered to escort him around. Tizard checked them out with Stephenson, who quickly learned they weren't G-men but rather Nazi spies.

Rumors of Nazi assassins and sabotage conspiracies eventually reached Capitol Hill. The death of American oil businessman William Rhodes Davis aroused many suspicions. Davis was suspected of being a Nazi sympathizer and providing Mexican petroleum supplies to the Nazi regime during their bombing of Britain. Davis also donated a huge amount of money—secretly given to him by the German government—in a failed attempt to swing Pennsylvania voters away from reelecting FDR in 1940.

While the US Senate was investigating him, Davis dropped dead of a heart attack in August 1941.

Voicing America's fear and paranoia as it prepared for war, Oklahoma Senator Joshua Lee, a Democrat, claimed Davis's death was part of a pattern of Nazi covert actions in the United States. He suggested Davis wasn't the only victim of this sinister touch.

"They reached their long arm into the United States and rubbed out a man who used to be a newspaperman in Germany," Lee claimed in November 1941. Before the Senate could investigate Davis "and where he was getting his money, and where it was going, he suddenly died," Lee said. "A man who had never had heart disease suddenly died of heart disease. You say 'Oh you have a good imagination.' The Nazis do stranger things than that."

As he delved further into this netherworld of spies, Cuneo realized how true those Churchillian words about a "sinister touch" might be.

18
POLITICAL HEADHUNTING

As US ambassador in London, Joseph Kennedy (seen here with sons Joe Jr. and future president John F. Kennedy) offered news tips to Walter Winchell and Cuneo but upset Churchill with his isolationist views. A Nazi spy scandal at Kennedy's embassy in London, exposed by Churchill's spies, helped seal Kennedy's ouster.

As a pal of Walter Winchell, Ernest Cuneo had met Joseph P. Kennedy before in places like Florida's sunny resorts. The multimillionaire Kennedy, with his shoot-from-the-hip style, was always a quotable source who provided grist for the columnist's gossip mill.

But by early 1941, as an American liaison working surreptitiously with British spies, Cuneo realized how troublesome Kennedy could be.

After being pushed out of his job as US ambassador in London, Kennedy continued to cast doubt on Great Britain's ability to fight Hitler, and warned that America should not enter another European war. Like many parents, Kennedy's isolationism seemed rooted in a fear of losing his sons in combat.

However, at the BSC's headquarters inside Rockefeller Center, Kennedy was viewed as an evil doppelgänger of that much more friendly Irish Catholic, William Donovan, who was unflaggingly helpful to the British.

"Kennedy is doing a great deal of harm to our cause," Stephenson cabled to London, referring to Kennedy's controversial visit in Hollywood, telling movie producers to prepare for a German victory. "He tells them that they will eventually have to look to Hitler for their market... Undoing Donovan's good work."

The British intelligence dossier described Kennedy as "embittered and in a vicious state of mind" with "no loyalties except to his own pocket." In a 1941 memo, British consul Eric Cleugh warned about Kennedy's ability to damage future British propaganda efforts in America. Cleugh suggested "it would probably be advisable for some countermeasures to be taken by an unofficial visitor here." Presumably that "unofficial visitor here" meant Stephenson, without specifically mentioning him.

British agents kept an eye on Kennedy when he returned home to America in November 1940, just as they had during the Tyler Kent spy fiasco in London several months earlier. But the BSC wasn't the only agency keeping an eye on the Kennedys. Before the end of 1941, an FBI investigation of Kennedy's second-oldest son, John F. Kennedy, revealed his romantic relationship with Inga Arvad, a beautiful married journalist believed by the FBI to be a Nazi spy. She'd previously interviewed

Hitler twice and was the Führer's guest at the 1936 Summer Olympics in Berlin.

Ironically, news of the affair broke in Walter Winchell's column, the favorite megaphone for Stephenson, Cuneo and, at one point, Joe Kennedy himself.

"One of ex-ambassador Kennedy's eligible sons is the target of a Washington gal columnist's affections," Winchell reported. "So much so she has consulted a barrister about divorcing her exploring groom. Pa Kennedy no like."

Indeed, the embarrassing episode infuriated the elder Kennedy and eventually led to his son, a naval intelligence officer in Washington, being shipped off to the Pacific for battle aboard a PT boat. Arvad, who denied the spy claims, later married an American actor best known for B-movie Westerns.

Besides former Ambassador Kennedy, there were other Americans on Stephenson's watch list. With far more success than the German spies, British intelligence secretly battled and undermined several major US politicians who didn't agree with them. Churchill's agents particularly targeted isolationists in Congress, including Representative Hamilton Fish of upstate New York, a favorite bête noire of FDR, as well as several more on Capitol Hill.

During the 1940 election, British agents traveled to Fish's home district in an effort to defeat him. Their front group promised to "put the fear of God into every isolationist senator and congressman." They pushed literature and spread rumors asking "Is Hamilton Fish Pro-Nazi?" They kept Cuneo informed of their progress.

"I suggest you call this campaign to the attention of friends in Washington," wrote British agent Francis Henson to Cuneo. In fall 1940, Fish was staked out by Henson, along with his BSC superior Sandy Griffith, who consulted with Cuneo on polling and fed propaganda to news sources like Walter Winchell.

"I also hope that you will suggest to Walter that he put something into his column about the matter and give us a plug over the radio Saturday night," Griffith wrote in a note.

It was a remarkable request by a foreign government. Two weeks before Election Day 1940, the British tried to get nationwide publicity to oust Fish by showing an old photo of him with a notorious Nazi sympathizer during a state government meeting. In it, Fish could be seen standing next to Fritz Kuhn, the leader of the German American Bund who had organized the 1939 Nazi rally at Madison Square Garden.

However, smearing Fish as someone unpatriotic seemed a stretch. Fish had been in Congress for twenty years, having graduating from Harvard, where he'd been a star football player. His family's domestic roots dated back to before the founding of the Republic. His grandfather had been Secretary of State under President Ulysses S. Grant, and his cousin had fought with Teddy Roosevelt's "Rough Riders," becoming the first US soldier killed in the Spanish-American War.

Undoubtedly Fish was a determined, if not naive, isolationist, reflecting the mood of his conservative district. But he was hardly a fan of Hitler. He'd offered a congressional bill denouncing the brutal German treatment of Jews. Nevertheless, his persistent opposition to America's entry into the war made Fish a target for Stephenson's spies.

"I enclose some very interesting material issued in connection with the 'Stop Fish' campaign," the British agent Henson informed Cuneo. "Sandy and I are working on the matter and will probably be here until election day."

Shortly afterward, Drew Pearson's nationally syndicated column published an explosive but untrue item. It claimed the Nazis were subsidizing Fish by overpaying on his rental properties. Fish survived his 1940 reelection by only a few votes. (He would lose his seat four years later.) In a postmortem to Cuneo about "the Hamilton Fish fight," BSC friend Sandy Griffith complained that a little more money could have carried the day against Fish but that "the local Democratic machine was of practically no help."

After the election, BSC kept up its quiet monitoring of Fish's office. One investigator figured out that mail from a Nazi front group was being delivered for free using the congressional franking privilege. (This was the same case in which top Nazi spy George Sylvester Viereck was convicted.) When Fish's top aide George Hill was quizzed about it before a grand jury, he lied. The slight, nervous and bespectacled Hill denied knowing about delivery of the propaganda mail to Fish's office or knowing Viereck, and was eventually charged with perjury

Hill's federal indictment appalled Fish. He had first met Hill while fighting in France during World War I and he defended his aide. "George Hill is 100% O.K., and I'll back George Hill to the limit on anything," he insisted. Fish testified for his old buddy, but a jury convicted Hill.

Fish's once sterling reputation was never the same again. Years later, documents showed that Hans Thomsen of the German embassy secretly funneled money to Fish to help influence other isolationist congressional members. But at the time, the influence of foreign nations in US political campaigns was largely unknown to the American public.

Disloyalty became a frequent charge hurled at other isolationist American politicians, like Senator Gerald Nye of North Dakota, a Republican who favored the "America First" movement.

In September 1941, Nye held a Senate hearing criticizing films he considered pro-British propaganda, including Charlie Chaplin's *The Great Dictator* and Churchill's favorite, *That Hamilton Woman*.

To a *Variety* reporter, Nye condemned Hollywood as a place "where selfish, scheming, foreign-born Nazi-haters are doing their utmost to plunge the United States into the European war to protect their pocketbooks." In classic demagogue style, Nye later admitted he hadn't seen most of the films on his watch list.

Nye wound up being targeted secretly by the BSC. Before a 1941 speech in Boston, more than twenty-five thousand hand-bills calling Nye a "Nazi lover and appeaser" were distributed by the BSC-funded front group Fight for Freedom. When iso-lationists like Nye would appear at a public event, British agents were instructed to "do all that they could to disrupt it and dis-credit the speakers."

Compromising sexual allegations were another secret weapon to be deployed. During the crucial lend-lease debate in the Sen-ate, the BSC spy known as Cynthia aimed her charms at iso-lationist Senator Arthur Vandenberg of Michigan. Not to be outdone, Vandenberg's other mistress—Mitzi Sims, the wife of a British embassy attaché—also worked as an undercover Brit-ish intelligence agent.

Homosexuality, then a socially taboo subject kept under wraps, could be used by spies for blackmail and intimidation. Another longtime senator, David I. Walsh—a Massachusetts Democrat and closeted gay man who opposed US entry into the war—was linked falsely to a Brooklyn male brothel suppos-edly infiltrated by Nazi spies. In truth, Walsh was the victim of false identification and exonerated only after a US Senate in-vestigation.

The *New York Post* started the Walsh controversy with a spuri-ous exposé aimed at ruining the isolationist senator. "Senator X Visited Spy Nest During Wartime," blasted the *Post*'s headline, with stories that eventually identified Walsh by name. Started by Alexander Hamilton, the *Post* was then owned by Dorothy Schiff, a strong Roosevelt supporter. The BSC later said the *New York Post*, among other newspapers, "rendered service of par-ticular value" to their US propaganda campaign.

Winchell joined in taunting Walsh with a gay slur. "The ad

libbers are having fun with the yarn about Brooklyn's spy nest," said the columnist, "also known as the swastika swishery."

Other isolationists like Nye objected to the smear campaign against Walsh. The right-wing *Chicago Tribune* called it "one of the most despicable attempts at character assassination that could be conceived."

Walsh, arguably the first major US politician outed publicly for homosexuality, was later defeated for Senate reelection in 1946 by Republican Henry Cabot Lodge Jr. He joined the list of isolationists whose political careers had been disrupted by anonymous attacks.

"All this and much more was handed out by devious means to the great, impartial newspapers of the country," the BSC secret history stated, by planting stories against isolationists. "Personalities were discredited, their unsavory pasts were dug up, their utterances were printed and reprinted... Little by little, a sense of guilt crept through the cities and out across the states. The campaign took hold."

Critics of FDR's foreign policy complained bitterly of unfair influence by Churchill's supporters in the US media. Unfortunately for these critics, Stephenson made sure his hidden hand didn't leave any fingerprints. As the American middleman with the BSC, Cuneo carefully guarded his sources of information, especially when dealing with journalists like Pearson and Winchell. "Actually, the British, wise in these matters, came nowhere near Winchell," recalled Cuneo.

A sharp opponent of Roosevelt's war policy, Senator Burton Wheeler, an isolationist Democrat from Montana, didn't have any qualms about lambasting Winchell for his unstinting support of the White House. On the Senate floor, Wheeler charged that Winchell was on the payroll of the British.

The feud quickly escalated. On the air, Winchell called Wheeler and others like him "dunderheads, dupes, utter babes in the woods," recalled Cuneo, and that "they were stupid fronts for Hitler's abattoirs," oblivious to the slaughter taking place in Europe. In this exchange, Cuneo said, "Wheeler neither flinched nor did he abate, but mounted his attack."

Wheeler "drew blood," Cuneo said, when he claimed Roosevelt's policy planned for "ploughing under every fourth American boy on foreign battlefields for the benefit of a decayed British empire." The comment infuriated FDR and caused Winchell to bear down on the outspoken senator even more.

On a visit to Washington, Winchell complained to Roosevelt about Wheeler's charge that he was secretly beholden to the White House.

"Imagine it, Mr. President! Imagine!" Winchell said, who adored the president and acted as though he were in the school principal's office. "He says I'm on the payroll of the New Deal!"

Rather than get upset, Roosevelt quizzed Winchell humorously. "How much did you pay in income tax last year, Walter?" he asked.

When Winchell mentioned the huge tax bill he'd paid to the government, Roosevelt replied, "Sit down, Walter, you're a partner."

Winchell's army of listeners were incited by his angry political rhetoric aimed at Wheeler. It spilled over at the senator's public appearances. On one occasion in Arizona, Winchell's angry supporters pelted Wheeler with garbage. Eggs, vegetables and harder objects hit Wheeler. Winchell delighted in it. As his lawyer, Cuneo demanded that Winchell denounce the mob.

"If Wheeler gets killed, you'll be held responsible for it," Cuneo chastised.

Winchell went ahead with a condemnation of the violent mob. "But he was a man of mixed emotion when he did it," Cuneo recalled. "I had a hell of a time getting him to do it."

Cuneo's ethical conflicts during this time are reflected in his private papers, especially in discussing cases like Senator

Wheeler. Undoubtedly, Cuneo knew that acts of sabotage, slander and violence by the BSC's agents in America were questionable, if not outright illegal.

But as a lawyer, spy and political fixer for the president, his job was to make things happen. The moral imperative to fight against Hitler—such a malevolent force for evil in the world—made virtually all actions justifiable, even if Cuneo did not participate directly. He could always clean up the untidy mess afterward.

In his unpublished memoir, Cuneo's concerns about political violence against Senator Wheeler are explicit. Cuneo said he remained "extremely careful for fear that Wheeler would be assassinated, in which case Winchell would be in the same soup in which [newspaper publisher William Randolph] Hearst found himself when, by his provocative editorials, he was blamed for the assassination of [President William] McKinley."

Yet when he later repeated this anecdote publicly in a book about Winchell, Cuneo never mentioned the word *assassination* with respect to Wheeler. Instead, he made a joke about Winchell's reluctance to apologize.

As the Wheeler case implies, privately, Cuneo thought of himself as a man of more character than Winchell. He viewed the columnist as an amoral, poorly educated newshound, unthinkingly satisfied with scoops like a shark with meat. Yet Cuneo, with his Ivy League degree from Columbia, was a font of slanted information gleaned from foreign spies, served up to millions of Americans as gospel truth. Though he'd fought against discrimination against Black people—and felt the sting of ethnic prejudice as an Italian American himself—there's no evidence Cuneo distanced himself from Winchell's homophobic comment about Walsh. Perhaps he even laughed at that "swastikas of swishery" line himself.

As America moved inexorably toward war, Cuneo found himself at a crossroads in this invisible espionage arrangement. To varying degrees, he was answerable to Donovan at the OSS, Stephenson's BSC, Hoover's FBI and various White House officials like Adolf Berle. He also acted on behalf of private clients, like Winchell and Pearson, whom he fed insider tips and legal advice. This moral quandary for Cuneo was often conflicting and remarkably complex.

Yet Cuneo was very much alone, relying on his wits. He wasn't a man without a country, but rather an intermediary agent beholden to at least three—England, Canada and his own. Though he portrayed himself as a former newspaperman, he'd become a skilled propagandist, leaking provocative items to the media, strategically placed for intended political effects.

For those in Washington, the drumbeats of impending war were rising, drowning out any objections by the isolationists. Each day's headlines or radio news program brought America closer to this precipice. Seeking moral clarity in the grayness of espionage no longer seemed possible. In service to his president, Cuneo had become a deeply committed partisan for Churchill's spies. And he would become even more emotionally involved with them in the days ahead.

PART III

Wartime Underground

Margaret Watson and Ernest Cuneo, the Stork Club, circa 1945.

JONATHAN CUNEO

"They say the best men are moulded out of faults;
And, for the most, become much more the better
For being a little bad."

—William Shakespeare, *Measure for Measure*, 1604

"I'd put Stalin on the OSS payroll if I thought it would help
us defeat Hitler."

—OSS Director William "Wild Bill" Donovan

19

PEARL HARBOR

On Sunday December 7, 1941, Ernie Cuneo's former gridiron team, the Brooklyn Dodgers of the National Football League, pulled off an upset victory against their crosstown rival, the New York Giants. It would prove to be a day of many surprises.

The two teams played at the Polo Grounds stadium, in an Upper Manhattan locale called Coogan's Bluff—a perfect place to forget about the cares of the world and enjoy an athletic contest. Only bragging rights in the city were at stake.

Seated in the stands, among fifty-five thousand cheering spectators, was the nation's top spy—William J. Donovan—enjoying himself many years after his own glory days as a Columbia quarterback.

Suddenly, an urgent call for Donovan rang out on the stadium loudspeaker.

"An ominous buzzing was heard around Coogan's Bluff after an announcement over the public address system informed Colonel William J. Donovan that he was being paged by Washington," described the *New York Times*. "Immediately after the game came the announcement that all officers and men of the Army and Navy were to report to their stations."

Taking the call over a private telephone, Donovan learned of the day's biggest, most devastating surprise—the Japanese bombing of Pearl Harbor in Hawaii. The attack killed twenty-four hundred Americans and destroyed much of the US Navy's Pacific Fleet.

Donovan left swiftly for Washington. Within hours, he arrived at the White House, where he spoke to the president around midnight. Roosevelt bristled at how the Japanese had managed a staggering raid without any prior detection by American authorities.

"To think that all of our planes were *caught on the ground*," the president said disgustedly. Donovan talked about America's preparedness for war and the resources needed for intelligence abroad. Unlike the British or the Germans, America was still without a full-fledged spy agency of its own.

"It's a good thing you got me started on this," Roosevelt told Donovan, then the Coordinator of Information. Wild Bill was soon elevated to director of the newly created Office of Strategic Services.

The following day, Roosevelt appeared before Congress asking for a declaration of war against Japan because of this sneak attack on December 7—"a date which will live in infamy." Within the week, the United States was at war against all the Axis powers, including Hitler's Germany and Mussolini's Italy.

Stephenson informed London about the sheer number of casualties and the extent of military losses at Pearl Harbor. He based his report on confidential information he'd received from Donovan and Cuneo. They understood it would be shared with Churchill and his top advisers. The prime minister had already called the White House, shortly after he heard of the attack. The president told Churchill, "We are all in the same boat now."

For more than two years, Great Britain had been at war with Germany, in a desperate struggle that it often appeared Hitler would win. Repeatedly, Churchill pleaded with the United States for "the tools" to fight back—more armaments, more supplies, more financing. Each show of support by America was hard-won, barely enough and resisted by the isolationists.

But now, in the aftermath of this American declaration of war, isolationists like Senator Gerald Nye could not afford to look disloyal or treasonous. They would have to muzzle their complaints. "It is just what the British planned for us," Nye bristled.

Before the Pearl Harbor attack, as historical documents suggest, British spies in America had some clues that the Japanese were planning some sort of an unspecified action. Certainly Duško Popov, the playboy double agent, claimed he warned the FBI about a violent Japanese surprise. And according to the BSC's historical account, one of Stephenson's agents—a British subject who spoke Japanese fluently—learned about Japan's serious intent after meeting with a Japanese official at its embassy in Washington. Ten days before Pearl Harbor, Stephenson sent a telegram to London: "Japanese negotiations off. Services expect action within two weeks."

Speculation about such advance warnings soon faded underneath the weight of war. Following Pearl Harbor, Churchill rushed to the United States for strategic planning with FDR. He was grateful to have a full partner after waiting so long. He spent the Christmas holidays at the White House, where the two leaders decided their main focus would be first on Europe, rather than the defensive fight in the Pacific.

Before Churchill left town in January 1942, Roosevelt invited Donovan to a private dinner with the prime minister. But Donovan remained a secondary character in Roosevelt's planning, not a key strategist. Both he and Stephenson, his British intelligence counterpart, would remain behind-the-scenes figures, unknown to the public despite their important contributions. Recalling Churchill's grand gestures during his White House visit, Donovan remarked, "Very few get their names into history who don't see to it that their names are included."

★ ★ ★

No one seemed more surprised than Cuneo by the reaction to Pearl Harbor. For a year and a half, he'd been an American spy working against the Nazis, trading confidential information with Stephenson and reporting to the White House. But after so many months had gone by, he didn't think America would enter the war.

"Drew Pearson was absolute in his conviction that there would be war, and in spite of heavy confirming information coming into Winchell, I disagreed," Cuneo recounted.

The reason wasn't a lack of insight or knowledge on Cuneo's part, but rather too much of both. In a sense, he had a better idea of America's fighting potential than any of Hitler's informants. As a legal liaison for the auto and aircraft workers union, Cuneo understood the capability of manufacturing plants in Detroit and other Midwest cities to turn their civilian production into military weaponry.

"I knew what they could do—bury Hitler," he said. "Run over him in an avalanche of production which would build a tidal wave of hardened steel on wheels."

During factory visits, Cuneo had met many strong, tough workers—"extraordinarily burly men"—who reminded him of the old NFL. "They seemed like a thousand giant linemen coming at me," he wrote. "I felt like dropping to my knees in a goal-line, last ditch defense. They were big-biceped men, solid in their trade, confident of getting the job done."

According to Cuneo's streetwise New York way of thinking, the Nazis would be crazy to get into a fight with such an opponent, an industrial giant. It was clear to him that the German Abwehr mostly wanted industrial espionage information from their agents hiding throughout America. Many Nazi spy cases handled by Stephenson and Hoover involved surveillance inside aircraft manufacturers and defense factories, figuring out the reality of America's might. Surely, he felt, Hitler was listening to his own spies.

"It was inconceivable to me that Hitler didn't know this," Cuneo recalled, "and I therefore believed that he was bluffing— and that obviously, his bluff should be called."

In conversations with columnist Drew Pearson, his old Columbia teacher, Cuneo resisted Pearson's view that the Nazis were so maniacal that they'd ignore their own spy intelligence.

"Look, Drew," Cuneo argued. "Hitler is crazy as a fox, not crazy. Czechoslovakia he can overrun but Detroit he can't."

History proved Pearson's view correct: Hitler wanted war all along. Cuneo realized his error in judgment when he heard top presidential aides Harry Hopkins and Harold Ickes were "switching public works programs to military support installations."

On that fateful Sunday at the Polo Grounds, it's not clear if Cuneo, the old Brooklyn Dodger, accompanied his boss Donovan to the game. But later that evening, Cuneo was likely in a Manhattan studio with his other boss, Walter Winchell, excited by the news of war.

"Good evening, Mr. and Mrs. America, and all ships at sea!" Winchell began his broadcast. "The American population is electrified tonight with the knowledge that every quarter of the globe will be at war tomorrow night..."

20

DIRTY TRICKS

During America's prelude to war, Ernest Cuneo felt honored when his longtime friend Adolf Berle asked for a favor—to help in rearming the US Navy fleet. Once again, Cuneo would be the middleman, making things happen, always out of sight.

"Assistant Secretary of State Berle called me, urgently, to request Walter's assistance," seeking Winchell's public support for more Navy ships in the Atlantic, Cuneo said. Berle said his request was vital, to "help prepare the country for war." Berle wondered if Winchell would do this favor for the president.

There was no doubt in Cuneo's mind.

"Adolf, the guy thinks he has been doing this since 1930," Cuneo replied about Winchell, a constant drum-beater for Roosevelt. "I'll answer for him now—yes."

Berle's plea came several months before the Pearl Harbor attack, around the same time Churchill became prime minister in May 1940, amid the Nazi bombing of London. At a secret White House meeting, FDR met with Berle, Secretary of State Cordell Hull and others to gauge the nation's vulnerability.

"The President said we desperately needed a two-ocean Navy—we had no Atlantic Fleet," Cuneo recalled about Berle's summary. "Congress was balking about providing one.

Fifty billions were needed. Berle asked me to ask Walter's assistance."

Winchell was only too happy to oblige. In his nationwide broadcast and syndicated column, Winchell urged Americans to write Congress "without fail" to support the Navy program. More than 1.2 million letters, cards and messages came pouring into the congressional post office. Eventually, FDR got his naval fleet rebuilt—dozens of new battleships, carriers and cruisers; hundreds of destroyers and submarines; and fifteen thousand warplanes.

Berle listened to Winchell's Sunday-night broadcast from his home. "An hour later, Cuneo telephoned to say that the radio station had been jammed with favorable response," Berle noted in his diary.

As thanks from the Navy, Cuneo recalled, Winchell was later invited to enjoy the trial run of a newly rebuilt ship. "With his childlike wonder he said, 'Ernie you have no idea of the noise!'"

Cuneo's longtime friendship with Berle meant much to him. At Columbia, Berle had been his teacher, introducing him to the world of corporate governance. For years, Berle served as a major adviser both for Mayor LaGuardia and in President Roosevelt's administration, where Cuneo's career flourished.

In his memoir, Cuneo described Berle as "an original Brainstruster for FDR," "a great mind" and "a disciplined man of action" who made New Deal ideas come alive. With a hawkish nose and pursed smile, Berle's intelligence seemed emphasized by his high forehead, which extended upward in a wave of gray hair. Cuneo had been to Berle's home and relied on his advice religiously. "I was among his closest friends, almost a member of the family," Cuneo said.

As Assistant Secretary of State, Berle was deeply involved in national security and intelligence. Some didn't understand Roosevelt's reliance on Berle, a man who didn't suffer fools gladly. He could be as somber as the president could be lighthearted. Cuneo understood their successful mix. FDR relied upon Berle "as if he were an instant historical computer," Cuneo said. An avid, voluminous reader, Berle was "fully familiar with the structure and running of nations and empires, from the double crown of the pharaohs to the British Commonwealth."

As Hitler began dominating the world's attention, Cuneo remembered Berle's funereal tone when the Nazis marched into Czechoslovakia in 1938. "The deathwatch for Europe has begun," Berle declared. That same year, Drew Pearson floated an item, in the bottom of his column, that mentioned Cuneo as a possibility for Assistant Secretary of State if Berle moved to another post.

Berle was ambivalent about State taking over intelligence and getting involved with other foreign espionage agencies. In September 1939, when war began in Europe, Sir William Wiseman, a British mentor to Stephenson, approached Berle about forming a UK–USA intelligence partnership, similar to the one Wiseman had headed during World War I. But Berle refused, contending the British had tricked America into joining that earlier conflict. He didn't want it to happen again.

Over time, Berle and Cuneo developed very different views of Winston Churchill's spy operation at Rockefeller Center and its relationship with the United States.

In New York, Cuneo had become close with British spies and shared their concern about the Nazi threat inside prewar America. As Donovan put together the OSS, America's first spy agency, Cuneo encouraged him to rely on the advice of Stephenson.

But Berle worried that the BSC, far from an innocuous passport office, had become a "full size secret police and intelligence service" inside the United States. By mid-1941, he believed hundreds of BSC agents and informants were violating espionage laws. He urged a shutdown of this foreign spy agency in the heart of Midtown Manhattan.

Undoubtedly, Berle felt annoyed about the BSC's very existence. While his wide-ranging State Department portfolio included intelligence matters, he apparently never learned of the BSC presence until after President Roosevelt gave his tacit approval in mid-1940. There is no evidence Cuneo ever took his old friend and mentor into his confidence about this spy arrangement. Perhaps he sensed Berle's skepticism about his own credibility as a spy.

"He [Cuneo] gathers, through Walter Winchell, pretty much all the gossip of the town," Berle recorded privately in his diary, "but a good deal of it is not altogether accurate."

Berle's criticisms of the BSC intensified when he learned about the fake Nazi map of South America that FDR presented to the nation as authentic. He believed Stephenson's staff was forging and falsifying other intelligence they shared with Donovan. After another dubious BSC report—about a German raider off the coast of Dutch Guiana in the Caribbean—Berle advised Hull that they had "to wonder what is really going on."

Berle didn't think much of Donovan either. He expressed concern about Stephenson's abiding influence on America's top spy. BSC agents surrounded Donovan so much that his wife, Ruth, described in her diary the scene at their Georgetown house: "Bill has British Empire for breakfast."

When Berle learned about Stephenson's deputy, Dick Ellis, providing almost daily oversight of OSS, he alerted Under Secretary of State Sumner Welles. Berle's misspelled but otherwise accurate memo got right to the point: "For your confidential information, the really active head of the intelligence section in Donovan's group is Mr. Elliott [sic], who is assistant to Mr. Stevenson [sic]. In other words, Stevenson's assistant in The British intelligence is running Donovan's intelligence service."

Berle concluded that Churchill's spies were steering US policy toward war through faked claims and manipulated news stories. "Without going into a long mess of detail," he explained to Hull and Welles in another memo, "I believe that the British Intelligence probably has been giving attention to creating as many 'incidents' as possible to affect public opinion here."

Hoover also had enough with the BSC. He joined forces with Berle in pushing the White House to halt the BSC's espionage inside America. Hoover was upset that Stephenson had sent seven hundred encrypted messages to London via an American radio transmitter, and yet the BSC would not share his messages with the FBI or other American officials.

Hoover and Berle shared disdain for the wild covert action of BSC spy "Cynthia" and felt they had no control over such outlandish cases. The whole business at Rockefeller Center seemed crazy to Berle, a disaster waiting to happen.

"Why should anyone have a spy system in the United States?" Berle contended. "And what will anyone look like a little later when someone finds out about it?"

In a classic turf battle, both Hoover and Berle, who worked cooperatively on Latin American intelligence cases, felt Stephenson's BSC and now Donovan's OSS posed an intolerable threat to their authority. After the White House ignored their complaints, they secretly lobbied Capitol Hill.

In early 1942, in the wake of Pearl Harbor, Congress voted to amend the Foreign Agents Registration Act so it would, in effect, stop Stephenson's spies from working inside the US. The legislation, which Berle helped write, called for all foreign agents, allies or not, to register with the government.

For Berle, it was the legislative equivalent of hitting the brakes on a runaway car. Under the proposed law, the names of all secret agents were required, along with a detailed description of their activities and how much money would be spent. It said "all records, accounts, and propaganda material would be liable to inspection by US government authorities."

When he learned of it, Stephenson quickly roused Donovan and the British embassy. Donovan sent a memo to the president asking him to veto the bill, which Roosevelt did. In this dispute, Donovan's and Churchill's spies prevailed.

"I am impressed with Donovan's courage," Berle recorded in his diary, "though I don't think much of it in terms of national wisdom."

However, in April 1942, another version—this time exempting the British and other friendly nations during the war—was signed by FDR.

Aside from policy disputes, Berle's personal animus toward Stephenson erupted when he found out a BSC spy named Dennis Paine was digging to "get the dirt" on Berle's private life. Any scandalous material would then be leaked to the press. Unlike with other figures who were compromised this way, Paine's spy mission didn't yield any compromising evidence about Berle—except that he and his wife preferred to use two separate tubs when taking a bath together.

After one of Hoover's top FBI officials alerted him about the BSC's "dirt" investigation, Berle complained bitterly to the British embassy. He called out "the attempt of the British so-called Security Co-ordination to spy upon and thereafter to arrange for a press campaign against a high official" of the US government. He "requested" they never do so again. In the meantime, the FBI ordered Paine out of the country.

Privately, Berle confided this outrage to Cuneo, both as a friend and as the president's liaison with the BSC. "Berle exhibited his iron self-control, but his eyes snapped his anger as he told me that they had tapped his wire, opened his mail and put agents to work to dig up, if they could, any dirt in his past," Cuneo recalled.

Both Berle and Attorney General Biddle showed discomfort with Cuneo's role with this foreign spy operation and Donovan's emerging OSS. They viewed his job as "a respectable front" for surreptitious illegal spying, like "playing the piano at a whorehouse," Cuneo recalled. "Indeed they were old enough friends to ask me, in effect, the age-old question: What's a nice person like you doing in a joint like that?"

Cuneo's fidelity and friendship with the British showed in his reply. He underlined the president's commitment to Donovan and Churchill's intelligence help. Though Berle and Biddle were longtime friends, Cuneo made it clear that "my first mission was to prevent the exclusion of British Security Co-ordination from the country."

Around the same time, a meeting between Cuneo and Hoover was even more confrontational. The FBI boss said the BSC must stop its covert operations, and aimed much of his displeasure at Stephenson's top aide, Dick Ellis, whom he wanted "to get out of the country."

Given his amiable relationship with Hoover, Cuneo was "taken aback by the explosion" between them. For years, Cuneo and Hoover had traded news tips and confidential information with Winchell, both over the phone and in banter at the Stork Club, a New York favorite of Hoover's. In this conversation, Hoover intended to school Cuneo, suggesting he was out of his league in this treacherous world of international espionage.

"He asked me if I had any idea of what they [Stephenson's spies] were doing," Cuneo recalled. "I answered truthfully that I had only a vague idea."

Actually, Cuneo had been an active player for the BSC. He often disseminated information in their propaganda campaign, advised Stephenson about the president's thinking and even aided British ships in their attempts to destroy the Nazis at sea. If he claimed he didn't know of covert action that involved sabotage and other acts of violence, it was only because he looked the other way while it was being discussed.

Cuneo didn't tell Hoover much. He kept his true feelings to himself. "I'd hate like hell to tell him [Hoover] what I would be prepared to do for our country if New York was being bombed" by the Nazis. Instead, Cuneo acted as a defense lawyer with

Hoover, as well as in his talks with Berle and Biddle. "In a sense, in addition to being something of a secret trial of the BSC, Stephenson and Ellis, it was also a poker game," Cuneo said. "I asked that they make known to me the alleged crimes of the BSC."

Their laundry list of wrongdoings by the BSC was considerable, including kidnapping, mail opening and wiretapping. But Cuneo, displaying more knowledge than he originally let on, argued that the kidnappings were of British deserters who were hit on the head and rounded up in handcuffs. "No murders were mentioned," Cuneo insisted. "No Americans had suffered bodily harm."

Then, Cuneo said, he "played my ace." He emphasized that "all of the purported acts" had taken place before Pearl Harbor, before the two nations became allies in the war. He argued that a "moral statute of limitation" applied and that Roosevelt wanted Churchill's spies to remain at Rockefeller Center.

When Cuneo asked Stephenson about these allegations, he "of course denied everything" but "could not hide the smoldering anger in his eyes." Apparently Hoover and these other American ingrates had forgotten Stephenson's tremendous espionage help in catching Nazi spies on their own doorstep.

Although Hoover eventually conceded the BSC could stay—as per the president's directive—he made it clear that Ellis wasn't trustworthy. He was "vehement" on this point. Donovan pushed right back, Cuneo recalled, saying Ellis was "a most experienced professional, utterly vital to the instruction of the OSS."

Cuneo didn't know Ellis much at all, but Donovan's insistence on his presence at such a critical time made him argue for it with Hoover. "In the end, for the only time, I personally had to vouch for him [Ellis]," Cuneo recalled. Cuneo promised he would resign if Ellis acted in anything other than an honorable way as a soldier and gentleman.

During this time, Cuneo met Ellis and discussed the allegations briefly. By reputation, Ellis was known as cordial and friendly, but was not in this circumstance. "Unquestionably one of the ablest men in his field, I was somewhat astonished to find him visibly troubled and vague," Cuneo recalled.

Perhaps the reason for this discomfort was that Ellis didn't want to give any credence to rumors about himself. Cuneo wasn't equipped to determine if Hoover's suspicions were true. In acting as a form of "defense attorney" for the BSC, Cuneo was serving the same purpose for Ellis as well. Cuneo didn't want to hear any admission of guilt about improper spying.

"It would have caused untold trouble if I had had to go back and declare that in truth they [Hoover and Berle] were right: BSC had violated the law," Cuneo said.

In speaking to Ellis, Cuneo avoided doing any fact-finding of his own. "It was necessary for me to preclude him from telling me anything, so I told him that Stephenson had entered a general denial, that any allegations about him were untrue, and he mumbled his agreement with Stephenson," Cuneo recalled of the response from Ellis.

To calm the waters, Lord Halifax and another British embassy official eventually met with Hoover, Berle and Attorney General Francis Biddle. The British argued that Stephenson had lived up to the original mid-1940 agreement—which Cuneo had conveyed from FDR—that allowed the BSC to work undercover at Rockefeller Center and cooperatively with the FBI.

Hoover claimed that while he liked Stephenson personally, the BSC chief kept him in the dark about spy missions and "reported only after the fact what he had been doing, and on occasion not even then." Perhaps Stephenson assumed Hoover already knew his whereabouts—knowing that he'd been under FBI wiretap and physical surveillance for nearly a year.

With war now raging around the world, neither side wanted more trouble. Berle's and Hoover's demands that the BSC be closed were firmly rejected. Halifax, presumably on Churchill's orders from London, sided with Stephenson and found little fault with his efforts. But they did agree "Little Bill" wouldn't pursue any intelligence activity inside the US without Hoover's knowledge.

"The effect of that stricture was to make Stephenson more secretive in the measures he and his service took to elude Hoover's surveillance," wrote intelligence historian Anthony Cave Brown. "As a result, an odd mixture of cordiality, suspicion and irritation developed in Anglo-American intelligence relations within the United States, one that remained for the rest of the war."

Rather than close its doors at Rockefeller Center, Stephenson's spies would rely more on Donovan's OSS, the agency they helped create. After Pearl Harbor, Donovan's OSS would grow dramatically in size almost overnight, with its $10-million budget (more than $200 million in 2025 dollars), six hundred staffers and mandate to spy all over the world in fighting the Axis powers.

Cuneo's friendship with Berle continued on, surviving their differences over the BSC and Cuneo's role as a behind-the-scenes intelligence officer. By the end of 1942, Drew Pearson's column reported on Cuneo's new link to his ambitious mentor. "Assistant Secretary of State Adolf Berle, once an original Roosevelt brain truster, now has a brain trust of his own," it said, "headed by busy as a bird dog Ernest Cuneo."

Even with his name in print, though, Cuneo remained out of sight.

21

THE STORK CLUB

War didn't make a dent in the popularity of the Stork Club, New York's most celebrated nightclub. Despite the anxious nerves and soul-crushing battles of 1942, a steady flow of Hollywood and Broadway stars, glad-handing politicians and out-of-town visitors passed through its doors every night.

Inside this Manhattan club, patrons paid a small fortune for a little enjoyment—a veritable foxhole for fun, away from the death and destruction of the outside world.

Just off Fifth Avenue at East 53rd Street, it reigned as the epicenter of New York's Café Society. According to legend, Ernest Hemingway once paid his bar bill by cashing a huge movie rights check from his novel *For Whom the Bell Tolls* without the club's owner flinching.

On Sunday nights, after his 9:00 p.m. radio broadcast, the Stork Club's most regular customer, Walter Winchell, could be seen at Table 50. He chatted away with his lawyer Ernest Cuneo and whatever luminaries happened to come by. All seemed to pay tribute to America's king of gossip.

Most of the Stork's clientele could be found in its main room. But the elite gathered in the "Cub Room," given its name by Winchell, apropos of nothing but a whim and his fame.

"The Stork Club was the temple of the high priest of this

new cult of fame for fame's sake, the columnist and broadcaster Walter Winchell, who presided over a mélange of stars, athletes, politicians and the merely notable," historian Jon Meacham later described.

Cuneo, a divorced man whose social life revolved around his fascinating work, took in the view and enjoyed himself. The Cub Room's decor, with its rose-pink hue, cast an attractive glow on everyone.

"The Cub Room, the inner sanctum, blazed with wit, champagne, sparkling jewels and even more sparkling and beautiful women," Cuneo recalled. "Against a background of superb decoration, polished crystal and gleaming silver, the female of the species appeared at her alluring best."

Cuneo's rough-hewn banter with Winchell, a carryover from the night's broadcast, had its own appeal. While most feared Winchell's wrath, Cuneo felt he could poke a little fun at his legal client.

"For God sakes, Walter," Cuneo exploded, after listening to a long soliloquy, "don't you ever talk about anything but yourself?"

Winchell deadpanned like a great comedian.

"Name a more interesting subject."

They agreed nothing quite compared to the Stork, their playground for the newly famous—not the Copacabana, not the El Morocco, nor any other club in New York catering to the rich and privileged. "The Stork was the racetrack and showplace of the Meritocracy, the winners, the career people of both sexes," Cuneo recalled.

Their rapport was a game of "can you top this," trading one-liners. Cuneo, the Ivy League grad, traded quips with Winchell, the sixth-grade dropout. Everything was pabulum for the next day's column and broadcast.

"Women are the profession of idle men and the relaxation of warriors," Cuneo once declared to him.

"That's a good line," Winchell said.

"It's not mine—it's George Bernard Shaw's," Ernie corrected.

Winchell scribbled it down in his notebook. "Well, I'll give it some circulation."

Cuneo, now a bear of a man bulkier than his NFL playing days, lived large at the Stork Club. "Champagne for everybody in the house—that was Ernie," remembered Herman Klurfeld, a Winchell rewrite man.

On one occasion, shortly before Pearl Harbor, Cuneo joined Winchell at a table with actor Charlie Chaplin and Assistant Secretary of State Adolf Berle. "I was a mere ego in a whirlwind of superegos," Cuneo said. "I practically had to blow a whistle to insert one word in the conversation."

Yet for all his bluster with Winchell, Cuneo preferred the invisibility of being a sidekick rather than a featured player. He wasn't some actor or budding politico vying to get his name in the paper. His important daytime work with an alphabet soup of government agencies was rarely, if ever, mentioned at night. As Winchell's adviser, he gained first-class access into this glittering emporium. But he kept his government intelligence work a secret.

Not that spying couldn't be done at the Stork Club. Each night, the smoke-filled niterie buzzed with the trading of human intelligence of all sorts. It was like Manhattan's answer to Rick's Café in *Casablanca*. Rumors, news tips, jokes and insights were the coin of the realm for daily chroniclers like Winchell, who repeated it all regularly in the *New York Daily Mirror*, syndicated in newspapers around the country.

The nightspot also reverberated with far more intimate exchanges. Up close in this place packed with patrons, there was the smell of perfume, the sight of warm flesh pressed against another body that young people in wartime couldn't resist. A fatalistic wartime ethos infused the thinking of so many, who wondered what calamity might befall them in the future.

After a few drinks, spending the night with a new acquaintance always seemed possible.

"Naturally, with both great beauty and hard-pressed and high-pressured men in any limited area, there was deep, but not lengthy interest in each other," Cuneo said. "The play of the sexes was a game of its own, with well-known bets. Hearts against heartbreaks, playing the field... For both sexes, the odds were the same: take the fun where you find it and pay off with the agony when it hits you."

Cuneo knew to keep his mouth shut about sensitive matters concerning his top private client. Whatever Winchell, with a common-in-law wife and three children at home, did after hours was his own business.

Decades later, Cuneo would still downplay Winchell's love life when interviewed by biographer Neal Gabler. "He [Winchell] was not promiscuous in sex," Cuneo explained. "He may have had some other encounters...and if he went to bed with them sometimes, it was for the same reason that mountain climbers climb peaks—'It was there.'"

As the war progressed, Cuneo enjoyed the company of his British spy friend Ian Fleming whenever he came to town. Fleming enjoyed the devil-may-care world of Manhattan, with all its seductive trappings. Fleming was an expert on caviar and martinis and, though not a connoisseur, he could tell good wine from bad.

When it came to women, however, Fleming, for all his success as a coldhearted Lothario, still talked as if he were clueless.

"Fleming, though he did not know it and would not accept it, was a knight who could not reconcile himself to the fact that women were not Elaines in ivory towers," Cuneo observed, referring to Arthurian legend, "and that the world was not one of black and white values."

During Fleming's visits to the Rockefeller Center office, the female staffers of the BSC took note of his handsome appearance and debonair style. They swooned a bit, just as they did with Lord Louis Mountbatten, a senior naval officer and cousin to the royals. "Fleming came in from time to time," recalled Stephenson's secretary Grace Garner, "and of course, they [Fleming and Mountbatten] were both so good-looking that just like dominoes, the girls would go down—whoosh, like that."

The British Naval Intelligence brass valued Fleming's unconventional "corkscrew thinking" and his flair for coming up with dramatic coldhearted action plans. Fleming was "charming to be with but would sell his own grandmother," said Ewen Montagu, his fellow British Naval Intelligence officer. "I like him a lot."

In the art of romance, Fleming did have a practical side. During a trip to London, Cuneo brought along some women's nylon stockings for his pal Fleming to give as gifts to his lady friends. When he arrived at Fleming's office, Cuneo tossed a half dozen pairs of the nylon stockings onto his desk, knowing how difficult they were for Englishwomen to obtain during wartime.

"Long, medium and short," Cuneo said, identifying each one. "I assume you're playing the field."

"Actually, I'm not," Fleming replied. He acted rather defensive, not allowing his cool demeanor to be breached. Cuneo recalled "feeling I might have invaded his sensibilities."

But it was all a charade. The two men had shared plenty of personal conversations about women while working together at Rockefeller Center, and especially while entertaining themselves at Manhattan's nightspots. Cuneo knew better. He called Fleming's bluff.

"Good, there are others who are…" Cuneo shot back, reaching for the nylons.

Quickly, Fleming grabbed the silky items off his desk and stuffed them into his Navy jacket. He gave a knowing glance to Cuneo.

"No, *I'm* not…" he explained about playing the field, "but some of my friends *are.*"

After this absurd exchange, Cuneo recalled, the two men "roared with laughter." Given Fleming's satyr-like reputation, his quaint reply seemed particularly amusing.

Sexual relations for spies, even sophisticates like Fleming, could signify more than just one-night stands and tantalizing gifts. Even the simplest of emotions could seem suspect or grounds for compromise. In these exchanges, there was always a question of who was manipulating whom.

Garner said the female staffers at the BSC were well acquainted with Cuneo. "He knew everybody," recalled Garner. "He knew Walter Winchell and the rendezvous for them was The Stork Club… He would be given stories and inside information on what was happening in Britain and so on."

Later in the war, Cuneo convinced Winchell to devote a whole column to singing the praises of British women who had been conscripted into the military. *"British Women—Orchids to Some Gallant Ladies,"* read one story's headline. It described the heroics of several women in the war effort, including Churchill's daughter Mary. Cuneo provided all of the content for this particular column. He claimed Stephenson asked for the tribute as a favor.

But Cuneo wasn't a disinterested party. By that time, Cuneo had met one of these women fighting for Churchill at Rockefeller Center and fallen in love with her.

When she first met Ernest Cuneo, Margaret Emily Watson, the Canadian spy nearly smothered by a Nazi intruder, was about thirty years old, never married, and had been living in Manhattan for nearly three years in a dorm-like apartment. Listed as a secretary clerk, she had been working on secret matters for Stephenson virtually since he opened the BSC offices at Rockefeller Center in summer 1940.

At some point in Room 3603, the quiet, cerebral Watson encountered Cuneo, a fast-talking, self-assured lawyer from New York eight years her senior. They seemed an unlikely pair. But somehow, they were eventually dating.

"She's a knockout," Cuneo boasted to all who would listen, including friends like Fleming and his Italian-American relatives in the New York area. Margaret kept her lengthy brown hair parted down the middle and tied in the back, so that her open face revealed her lively, sensitive eyes, high cheekbones and friendly smile.

The frigid winters of Winnipeg were becoming a distant memory for Watson, especially as the war dragged on. She had left her small Canadian neighborhood shortly after the death of her father, James. She'd been recruited by Stephenson for a top secret assignment in Manhattan that promised something much more exciting than if she'd stayed home. Still, getting involved with a divorced American man probably wasn't what she'd expected.

Despite his strong attraction to her, Cuneo had a lot to lose by entering into a love affair, especially with a foreign spy. Cuneo was in a highly sensitive position dealing with the BSC in New York. He had instructions to use his good judgment, and avoid publicity and any compromising situations. He couldn't afford to let sexual attraction somehow affect his spycraft and possibly bring more attention to himself. Isolationists and critics of FDR would have a field day if they learned of Cuneo's espionage activities with a foreign nation inside America's borders.

By then in his late thirties, Cuneo could feel rightfully proud of his professional accomplishments. He mingled every day with powerful and influential people. Yet Cuneo's introduction to Watson came at a vulnerable time in his personal life.

After his 1939 divorce, Cuneo became involved with another woman for a time but that too didn't work out. Aware that he wasn't particularly handsome, he didn't like to talk about his attempts at romance. Once while discussing their view of women,

Cuneo told his spy friend Fleming that "a true broken love affair is like a spiritual amputation."

Perhaps with his first wife, Zilpha, in mind, Ernie said nothing quite compared with the love between a man and a woman. "These are extremely deep loves and no one can experience it more than two, three or four times in a lifetime," he explained. "This is because the healing takes a very long time and it's so terribly painful."

Whatever the cause of his breakup with Zilpha and the woman after her, Cuneo felt ready to find a new love when introduced to Watson at Stephenson's spy headquarters. "My father would be candid that he was on the rebound," his son Jonathan later recalled. "And for my mother, here he was this very successful, gregarious American Big Guy." Ernie didn't tell Margaret of his failed first marriage until much later.

Watson was impressed with this erudite American lawyer, educated at Columbia University and so familiar with the imposing city of New York. He was nothing like the men she'd known back in Winnipeg, where her father had been in the wholesale tea and coffee business and her mother had stayed at home with the family.

Cuneo seemed to know a lot about everything. He was highly valued by Stephenson, the man she trusted most. She began accompanying Cuneo around Manhattan, meeting his many famous friends at the Stork Club and elsewhere.

"He was very charismatic—absolutely brilliant—he was a man of the world," said Sandra Cuneo, explaining what attracted her mother to her father. "In the old terms, he swept her off her feet. He was probably a lot different than what she was used to in Canada. He was worldly and older than she was."

In a sense, Stephenson was responsible for introducing Cuneo to Watson and implicitly gave his approval for their relationship. Apparently "Intrepid," as Cuneo called him, welcomed this romance without reservation, without some hidden agenda.

The unofficial BSC playbook called for the recruitment and development of any and all personal contacts who could help their cause. Some BSC women were given surveillance assignments when they dated in New York. There was even a spy term for it—a "dangle," the way a fish is lured to a hook.

Older powerful men often had a glazed look in their eyes when they approached younger beautiful women, as Cuneo's unpublished memoir later reflected about other cases, though not his own. These attractions could loosen tongues and allow tightly held state secrets to be obtained.

Margaret Watson never intended to be a "dangle," her family says. There was likely never a conversation with her bosses about deceiving or enticing Cuneo by returning his affections. Perhaps no instructions were necessary other than to let human nature take its course.

But for Stephenson, this wartime connection surely carried an opportunity to further cement his relations with the Americans. It would be a means of keeping Cuneo—the vitally important invisible spy with direct lines to the White House, the FBI, the OSS and America's biggest media megaphone in Winchell— loyal and beholden to the BSC's interests. For him, it would be another kismet example of sexual attraction being used in the name of the Crown.

There remains one certainty about the origins of this love affair—to those who knew her, it was inconceivable that Watson, as a dedicated agent, went ahead with her relationship with Cuneo, the American intelligence liaison, without her boss's knowledge and approval.

"I can't imagine that he [Stephenson] didn't know," said Sandra Cuneo. "Maybe he was happy that this was someone he didn't have to vet. Knowing my mother, if he had disapproved, she would have stopped it immediately."

22

MESSAGES FROM THE DEEP

The Hamptons, best known as a place for the rich to relax along sandy beaches, was the unlikely scene for Hitler's most ambitious strike inside America.

Shortly after midnight on June 13, 1942, four Nazi saboteurs carrying explosives approached Amagansett, New York—a narrow strip of farmland and sand dunes located between East Hampton and Montauk, along the south fork of Long Island. A German submarine dropped them off near the coastline. In inflatable rubber rafts, the men rowed ashore. Then the sub disappeared into the dark waters of the Atlantic.

Quietly, the four saboteurs began their secret mission—just the way Admiral Wilhelm Canaris planned.

As head of the German Abwehr spy agency, Canaris followed Hitler's direct orders to create "Operation Pastorius," a mission designed shortly after Pearl Harbor to cause death and destruction in the United States in one swift blow.

Canaris, who generally preferred espionage to violence, had expressed doubts to Hitler that the plan would work. The arrest of some thirty Nazi agents in the Duquesne spy ring, rounded up by the FBI, had decimated the German espionage network inside America. Previously, Hitler had tried to avoid any provocation of the US while it was still neutral.

However, now that Roosevelt had declared war, Hitler insisted on an immediate response. He didn't want any of Canaris's excuses, even if they were grounded in reality. Hitler reminded Canaris that "there were plenty of loyal German-Americans in the Party who would be only too willing to return to the United States on such a mission, and if need be give their lives for their Fuhrer and their Fatherland."

Without reply, Canaris and his deputy smiled grimly, saluted and left to carry out their leader's orders.

The Abwehr, as the intelligence branch of Germany's armed forces, had traditionally been in charge of spying and counter-intelligence. As a longtime military man, Canaris considered his approach more professional than and different in style from that of the Nazi Party's Security Service (Sicherheitsdienst), answerable to SS leaders like Reinhard Heydrich and Heinrich Himmler, whom he viewed as Hitler's slavish henchmen.

Canaris was appalled at Hitler's treatment of Jews and those the Nazis perceived as enemies of the state. He played a good soldier in front of other top Nazis, but privately, he seethed at the disastrous course destined for his country under Hitler. Canaris's intelligence reports warned of America's industrial strength, but the Führer seemed disinterested in facts. As another German intelligence official later explained, Hitler "really believed he was appointed by fate and did not need the counsel of mere human beings."

Twelve saboteurs were chosen for "Operation Pastorius." (Canaris named it for Francis Daniel Pastorius, the leader of the first organized settlement of Germans in America.) Most of these agents had once lived in the United States or visited extensively. All had been members of the German American Bund and spoke English proficiently.

At a special school outside Berlin, not unlike Camp X, they were trained in skills such as using explosives and timing devices, secret writing in code and blending into a crowd. Their aim was to create sheer chaos—blowing up railroads and bridges, and launching a series of attacks on aluminum plants needed for aircraft and other defense factories. Two other targets were the New York City water supply and Hell Gate Bridge, vital to a New York freight railroad serving as a supply chain between Washington and Boston.

The Nazi spies carried with them a huge amount of US dollars to help bribe potential helpers and pay for expenses, enough money to carry on a two-year campaign of terror. Canaris intended this "Pastorius" attack to be similar to the deadly 1916 Black Tom railroad yard sabotage explosion near the Statue of Liberty, carried out by German agents prior to America's entry into World War I. As Canaris envisioned it, after the first four Nazi spies landed on Long Island, another team would infiltrate Florida. But this grand German plan never got very far.

As they arrived on the Hamptons beach, the first four took off their German uniforms and changed into civilian clothes. They buried some of their supplies in the sand dunes for recovery later. Their suspicious activity caught the attention of James C. Cullen, an unarmed Coast Guard patrolman passing by. Rather than kill him, the Nazi spies offered Cullen a wad of cash to forget what he had seen.

Cullen took the money and ran through the fog, eventually alerting Coast Guard headquarters. His superiors were skeptical about the twenty-one-year-old patrolman's claim until they found a pack of German cigarettes in the wet sand, followed by a canvas bag with uniforms and explosives buried in the dunes. Meanwhile, the Nazi spies fled, taking an early-morning train into New York City.

The next day, two of the Nazi spies decided to quit. One of them, George John Dasch, called the FBI office in New York to give himself up, but the agency thought it was a hoax. A week later, Dasch tried the FBI again in Washington. By then, Hoover's G-men had learned of the Coast Guard report about the Nazi spy landing on the Hamptons beach. The FBI interrogated Dasch, who gave the names of his fellow saboteurs. It led to the arrest of the other three, as well as the other Nazi sabotage team that arrived in Florida.

Hoover turned the saboteurs' capture into a publicity bonanza for his FBI—just like with his manhunt for gangsters during Prohibition—even though it was Dasch's change of heart that prompted the arrests. The *New York Times* heralded the Nazi spies' capture on its front page. *Life* magazine displayed all their arrest photos, and detailed the killing gadgets they'd brought with them, such as electric blasting caps, a detonating device for TNT and small tubes of sulfuric acid for igniting fires.

A cry for retribution arose from a frightened American public. A secret military trial set up by President Roosevelt would result in the quick execution of all the Nazi saboteurs in August 1942, except Dasch and his traveling companion, who were given long prison sentences.

The embarrassed Third Reich refrained from another sabotage attempt in the United States. They wouldn't try again until late in the war, and that would end up failing as well.

Canaris, a proud hero of World War I, had tried to warn Hitler that his plan wouldn't work, but his advice as spymaster had been brushed aside. The mortifying failure of "Operation Pastorius" incensed Hitler. It created a lasting division between him and his top spymaster for the rest of the war.

Just how much Canaris deplored Hitler—and secretly hoped for his removal—was still hidden behind his acquiescent face.

The German sabotage fiasco reminded American officials how much its own international spy agency, the OSS, needed to grow to meet the Axis threat. By mid-1942, undetected Nazi U-boats roaming the Atlantic had sunk dozens of US merchant ships.

On his nationwide broadcast, Walter Winchell told his radio listeners about the brazen sabotage attempt on Long Island. No

doubt reflecting Cuneo's thinking, Winchell lambasted the isolationists who had downplayed Hitler's menace. Pearl Harbor
"woke up a nation of Rip Van Winkles," he chided.

"Now we know that Germany was operating on our street
corners," Winchell said. "That was proven on the witness stand.
And now we know that hate propaganda was paid for by Berlin. That was proven by the FBI. Saboteurs must now come by
submarines instead of luxury liners."

As the OSS liaison with the British and several US agencies,
Cuneo found himself in the mix of many policy discussions and
strategic moves, mostly as a conveyor of intelligence rather than
a decision-maker. Remarkably, he managed to keep good relations with key players, even when they didn't like one another.

For example, Cuneo continued to act as an effective go-
between with the BSC's William Stephenson and the State
Department's Adolf Berle, who despised each other. And he
maintained a friendly demeanor with the FBI's J. Edgar Hoover
despite his bitter rivalry with William Donovan's OSS. "The
Abwehr gets better treatment from the FBI than we do," Donovan complained.

While much of Cuneo's intelligence work involved hand-
holding with various spymasters and government officials, he did
manage some sleuthing of his own. Cuneo's training as a lawyer, instincts as a journalist and love for solving human puzzles
made him a formidable intelligence agent. He displayed these
spy-like skills effectively, for example, when he realized the security risks inherent in the private insurance industry.

It began simply enough. Through a legal client, Cuneo
learned how the private insurance business around the world
relied on pool coverage, shared among different insurers, as a
way of spreading the financial risk. This system required companies applying for fire, casualty, aviation and marine insurance to
provide extensive maps and physical details about their facilities.

While this seemed a dull but natural part of everyday business, Cuneo realized it could provide a huge amount of intelli-

gence about aircraft factories, defense manufacturers, chemical
plants, harbors, railways and other potential targets. In terms
of attacking America, the enemy could cause all sorts of mayhem and disaster using these insurance records, he determined.

Cuneo at first feared the US had given out too much information about its domestic sites to companies with German ties.
Indeed, the private insurance system provided access to even the
floor plans of the White House. In 1941, detailed descriptions
of the new locks installed along the Panama Canal were sent to
a Tokyo insurer. Some of the money from this international insurance system was "used for subversive activities" by Germany
to finance Nazis spies in the United States and throughout the
Western Hemisphere, the OSS later said. "The Insurance people
are the Axis payoff men in the US and Latin America."

Cuneo convinced Allen Dulles, then working at Rockefeller
Center in the OSS's New York office, to create a secret unit
to take advantage of this situation. Offensively, these insurance
records were a gold mine. As Cuneo explained to Dulles, the
details could be a virtual road map for Allied pilots looking to
attack German, Italian and Japanese military-related facilities.
Dulles agreed, and set up a secret OSS insurance unit to tap into
this rich source of information. By late 1942, when the commanders of the Allied forces invading North Africa "wanted to
learn the kind of equipment on the docks at the points chosen
for invasion, the insurance companies proved a reliable source,"
Cuneo said.

Hoover balked when FBI officials learned the OSS wanted
to extend its insurance unit investigations to Latin America. He
considered it poaching on his turf. After an earlier battle between Donovan and Hoover, President Roosevelt instructed the
OSS to concentrate on espionage in Europe, but permitted the
FBI to continue its intelligence work in Latin America. Cuneo
worried about Hoover's recalcitrance but expressed confidence
to OSS colleagues that he could convince the FBI to cooper-

ate. In permitting Cuneo to see the FBI chief on the OSS's behalf, Donovan emphasized in a December 1942 memo, "Please make clear that we do not desire to engage in any 'operations' in South America."

Cuneo's insurance success with Dulles helped establish a good working relationship between the two men, both of them lawyers. Dulles had quickly grasped the importance of Cuneo's insurance warnings. He also believed deeply in the OSS's mission. "Bill Donovan conceived the OSS as a worldwide intelligence organization that could collect the facts necessary to develop our policy and war strategy," Dulles explained.

Cuneo's idea would provide a treasure trove of critical information used in bombing attacks against enemy targets. But he wouldn't get credit for a long time. A half century later, Cuneo was recognized publicly for his initiative. "The idea for the Insurance Intelligence Unit was hatched by Ernest Cuneo, a New York lawyer and OSS operative close to President Franklin D. Roosevelt," reported the *Boston Globe* in November 2001, after the confidential OSS documents about the project were finally released.

Unlike the swashbuckling Donovan, the discreet Dulles seemed better suited to the subtleties of spying. He stressed the importance of "cutouts" as intermediaries in clandestine operations and other go-betweens. His espionage instincts were more sophisticated than those of most US officials—instincts that led him to suspect the Russian spy Walter Krivitsky had been assassinated in his Washington hotel room rather than believe the official version claiming he'd committed suicide. A lifelong fan of spying, Dulles went to bed with a copy of Rudyard Kipling's *Kim* on his night table.

As a young Princeton graduate, Dulles entered the foreign service, spending a year in India and holding posts in Vienna, Berlin, Constantinople and Bern, Switzerland. He returned to

Washington to work in the State Department's Near Eastern Affairs desk and eventually picked up a law degree from George Washington University. Before joining the OSS, Dulles spent sixteen years at the same New York law firm as his brother, John Foster Dulles, who later became US Secretary of State.

After being recruited by Donovan for the OSS at Rockefeller Center, Allen Dulles left New York in fall 1942 to oversee the agency's espionage efforts in Switzerland, where he showed his taste and talent for espionage.

Dulles quickly developed sources that led to remarkable disclosures. On March 10, 1943, his Bern office reported, "The new Nazi policy is to kill Jews on the spot rather than deport them to Poland for extermination there." This shocking information—one of the first clear indications of the ongoing Holocaust behind enemy lines—came "from a Berlin source which our agent considers reliable," said Dulles.

The OSS dispatch mentioned that fifteen thousand Berlin Jews had been arrested, "several hundred children died," "several hundred adults were shot" and that "high officers of the SS reportedly have decided that Berlin shall be liberated of all Jews by mid-March." It warned that the Nazis planned to extend this policy of extermination "to other parts of Germany in the near future."

At first, officials in Washington remained wary of the spy information Dulles squeezed out of neutral Switzerland. After sharing this Holocaust warning with others, including President Roosevelt, Donovan wrote back apologetically to Dulles about the timid response.

"It has been requested of us to inform you that 'All news from Bern these days is being discounted 100% by the War Department,'" Donovan wrote on April 29, 1943. "It is suggested that Switzerland is an ideal location for plants, tendentious intelligence and peace feelers, but no details are given."

Donovan made sure Dulles knew he disagreed with this assessment and that Dulles had his full backing. "You are the one through whom our Swiss reports come," Donovan wrote, "and we believe in your ability to distinguish good intelligence from bad with utmost confidence."

Dulles soon rewarded that faith in his espionage ability and judgment. While in Bern, he learned of Canaris's unhappiness with Hitler and his murderous Third Reich. Along with British spies, Dulles relied on sexual intrigue to help influence the German spymaster.

The OSS provided money to Madame Halina Szymanska, the mistress of Canaris, in an elaborate exchange for information. After her husband, a Polish colonel, was slain, Szymanska and her daughters moved to an apartment in Bern arranged by Canaris. She soon became a valued informant for the OSS. Dulles also developed a double agent—Hans Bernd Gisevius, an Abwehr officer in Switzerland who answered to Canaris and dealt with his mistress—as another key source.

When Canaris slipped away from his duties to visit his mistress Szymanska, they shared information in bedrooms in Switzerland and Italy. "In the course of pillow talk he [Canaris] used to talk to her freely," recalled Nicholas Elliott, later head of the British Secret Intelligence Service in Bern. Their rendezvous provided indications in early 1941 that the long-expected Nazi invasion of England wouldn't happen. Instead, Hitler wanted to invade Russia.

It became clear that Canaris intended this highly classified information to be shared with the Allies because of his increasing anger with Hitler, a disgust he dared not show while in office, even after such fiascos as "Operation Pastorius." Increasingly, Canaris and other top German officers insisted Hitler be removed by any means possible.

Inside the German ranks, the treachery for Canaris only intensified. By early 1942, Reinhard Heydrich, the ruthless chief of the secret police under Heinrich Himmler, requested that

Canaris put the Abwehr under Himmler's control. This plan posed great danger for Canaris.

Heydrich, a young blond officer described as "the apotheosis of the Nazi doctrine of Nordic racial supremacy," projected an evil ambition while overseeing the Gestapo. He possessed "an incredibly acute perception of the moral, human, professional and political weakness of others." Hitler called him "the man with the iron heart," a brutal architect of the Holocaust plans for genocide and deportation of all Jews in German-occupied Europe.

Though Heydrich claimed to be a friend of the older Canaris, his consolidation move with the Abwehr stemmed from Heydrich's suspicion there was unhappiness within the German intelligence corps. He was determined to stamp it out. For the Allies, the removal of Canaris from the Abwehr would severely hurt their efforts to keep track of Hitler's next moves. A decision was made to kill Heydrich before he could expose Canaris.

The assassination plan was ingenious. On May 23, 1942, a repairman came by to fix a broken antique clock in Heydrich's office at Hradčany Castle in Czechoslovakia. The repairman noticed a piece of paper detailing Heydrich's plan to visit a Prague suburb. That information was relayed to Czech resistance leaders working with British intelligence.

Four days later, Heydrich's car blew up, leaving him mortally wounded. At Heydrich's funeral, Canaris cried profusely. "He was a great man," he told another Nazi. "I have lost a friend in him."

Hitler, furious at Heydrich's assassination, ordered the elimination of a whole Czech village in retaliation—all 199 men within it were shot—and ramped up his own security precautions. The British avoided taking any responsibility for the assassination, but documents made public decades later show that Churchill's secret Special Operations Executive was actively involved in Heydrich's killing.

Canaris, leading an incredible double life, remained under

extreme pressure even after Heydrich's assassination. By summer 1943, Canaris was looking to strike a deal with the Allies through secret negotiation.

Several history books claim Canaris reached out through intermediaries for a meeting in Spain with British spymaster Stewart Menzies and the OSS's Donovan. According to these accounts, Canaris asked the two Allied spies about possible peace terms if Hitler wound up dead or captured. Others remain dubious of these accounts—based on information from an Abwehr officer who said he accompanied Canaris to Spain—and stress there are no documents that support this version.

Nonetheless, after the war, Menzies acknowledged that Canaris reached out and "did ask me to meet him on neutral territory with a view to putting an end to the war." The purported plan by Canaris would help bring about a swift end to the war, saving countless lives. Under its terms, however, while fighting would end in Europe, it would continue in the Pacific.

For strategic reasons, Churchill instructed Menzies not pursue such a deal with Canaris. Roosevelt also rejected a similar Canaris-inspired proposal brought to him by Donovan a few months later. The president was appalled at the OSS leader's freelance diplomacy, which made it seem as if he were trying to live up to the nickname "Wild Bill." FDR let Donovan know that he had no intention of negotiating with "these East German Junkers."

In the multidimensional game of chess that leaders must play during wartime, both Churchill and Roosevelt displayed a broader view of the geopolitical picture than their two spymasters. As masterful tacticians, Churchill had dispersed the appeasers in his government while Roosevelt had outmaneuvered the isolationists. They understood the chain reaction a deal with Canaris might cause.

To these two Allied leaders, the Canaris plan didn't account for the Soviet Union's potential response to a coup against Hitler or whether the war would continue along its border. Nor was there any sign the Japanese would stop fighting.

For these reasons and more, Churchill and Roosevelt insisted on "unconditional surrender" as the only terms for ending the war against the Axis powers. "To stop short of total military victory, to allow Germany any doubt of its total defeat, would have been unthinkable on our part," the politically astute Dulles later explained.

With this misstep, Donovan's rising star at the White House began to diminish. For all his unlimited energy in building up the OSS and traveling around the world, his freelance actions with Canaris raised the idea that he needed a shorter leash, something his detractors, like Hoover and Berle in Washington, were only too willing to provide.

In the meantime, Dulles kept his head low in Switzerland, as if running his own spy agency. He pursued his contacts with the German spymaster Canaris—until he finally developed another double agent who would be far more successful.

23

MEETING CHURCHILL

At the Anchorage, where he kept a pied-à-terre apartment, Ernest Cuneo learned personal connections controlled everything in wartime Washington. "Many normal folk, not familiar with the bureaucratic maze, have no idea of how important access is," he explained.

Cuneo stayed at the luxury building, just off Dupont Circle, when he wasn't in New York. The Anchorage became a place of hidden intelligence and influence for Cuneo, who was surrounded by neighbors with enough power to make things happen.

In the adjoining apartment was the powerful Speaker of the House Sam Rayburn. On the floor above was Senator Millard Tydings, chair of the Interior and Insular Affairs Committee. Above Cuneo's place could be found Admiral William Standley, former chief of Naval Operations and the new ambassador to the Soviet Union. And above *him* was former ambassador to France William Bullitt, closely allied with Secretary of State Cordell Hull.

Inside the Anchorage, Cuneo traded favors, big and small, including a personal request he handled from the BSC's William Stephenson. As he described to Cuneo, a British freighter full of explosives had caught fire in Bombay, India, killing about one thousand people and injuring many more, including an

English little girl known to Stephenson. The spymaster said she might have a chance of being saved if transported to America for hospital care.

Cuneo talked to his White House intelligence contact, David Niles, who responded swiftly by getting the president's wife and the US Army's chief of staff involved. "He [Niles] called Mrs. R. and within a few hours Dave called me to say that General Marshall had ordered space cleared in the mail plane for both the child and the mother," Cuneo said.

In a world full of ongoing tragedy, Stephenson relied on his friend Cuneo for this singular favor among spies. Unfortunately, the request came too late. "Word was flashed to Bombay," Cuneo recalled, "but the answer came back that the child had died."

The Anchorage became a clearinghouse for the OSS mainly because George Bowden, its assistant director, also lived there. Trained as a tax lawyer, Bowden was personally recruited by his friend William Donovan. He served as a steady, grounded presence for the agency, especially with Donovan constantly flying around the world.

One morning in early January 1943, Bowden called Cuneo urgently. He told him to rush down to "the Kremlin," their nickname for OSS headquarters in Washington. When Cuneo arrived, he found Donovan looking desperate and worn-out. His face appeared "gray and shaggy," Cuneo remembered. "He looked like a dying man."

Donovan blurted out the death sentence he had received for his infant spy agency.

"He told me OSS was about to be abolished by order of the Joint Chiefs of Staff," Cuneo recalled. "I told him I didn't believe it."

Donovan's prognosis wasn't far off. For months, General George V. Strong, the Army's imperious chief of intelligence (derisively called "George the Fifth" behind his back), had sought

Donovan's ouster. Like the FBI's J. Edgar Hoover, Strong didn't want to contend with the OSS. He resented playing second fiddle to an amateurish rival group of wannabe spies.

Donovan disliked Strong as well, but his own provocative actions had created enough trouble to endanger his OSS job.

Donovan's once shining political star in Washington no longer seemed unassailable. His career as America's top spy had started off with a flourish. The *Washington Star* newspaper even ran a comic strip of Donovan as a heroic character, an international man of mystery. He was praised in the media and publicly supported by the president.

"Mr. President, is Bill Donovan's work still a secret?" asked a reporter at a press conference.

"Oh my, yes," said Roosevelt. "Heavens, he operates all over the world."

At FDR's urging, Donovan offered a steady stream of written ideas for improving US espionage efforts. Some suggestions were well-thought-out—others less so, but delivered with the same urgency.

"Dear Grace, I think the attached memorandum will be of interest to the President," Donovan wrote to Grace Tully, the White House gatekeeper for FDR, on a routine basis. "Will you please see that it gets to his desk."

Many of Donovan's ideas were inspired by Stephenson and what he learned from the BSC spymaster. He embraced Stephenson's love of gadgetry—"the technology of subversion"—made at a supersecret facility in Canada. One spy machine promised to "reproduce faultlessly the imprint of any typewriter on earth," a key to forging documents. Other devices were meant to kill.

At his Washington headquarters, Donovan set up his own technical group for spy devices. They invented innovative apparatuses and electronics, along with sabotage methods for fighting the enemy. They cooked up a new plastic explosive, called "Aunt Jemima," that could be baked safely into pancakes if needed.

The OSS also launched a "Morale Operations Branch" designed to carry out undercover psychological warfare. They called this team of researchers and academics "Donovan's Brain Trust." Each agent ferreted out damaging information and photos that could undermine or embarrass the enemy. Impressed with their skill, Stephenson called the OSS's branch "the most brilliant team of analysts in the history of intelligence."

But Donovan's attempts to emulate Stephenson's propaganda tricks in prewar America didn't work out so well for him in neutral European countries. Some ideas backfired, much to General Strong's muted glee. The OSS dropped leaflets from the sky over German troops, claiming their wives and girlfriends were being unfaithful. A similar effort was tried through the German mails without much result. US Army officials were embarrassed by these stunts.

Donovan's rash plunge into diplomacy particularly rattled the White House. His secret peace deal overtures to Nazis like Canaris, the Abwehr's spymaster, upset Roosevelt and caused too many headaches.

Strong pushed for a presidential order placing the OSS under his command. A stroke of Roosevelt's pen would effectively end Donovan's short tenure. While that order was being drawn up in the White House, Donovan learned about it. His frantic meeting with Cuneo, looking for a way to avert his fate, came about as Donovan considered resigning on the spot. Donovan said the order was on the president's desk awaiting his signature.

Cuneo jumped into action. "I picked up the phone, got the White House, and was told by a person who asked me never to tell that General Donovan was right," he recalled. "The order was the first thing that the President would sign."

That news stunned Cuneo. "Well, put it at the bottom of the pile!" he pleaded.

As a man wearing several hats, Cuneo served not only as the OSS's liaison with the British, but as an unofficial connector to the White House, FBI and Justice Department. He prided himself on being in the know, especially as Winchell's "legman" in Washington—though it was a term he hated. In this case, though, he was as taken aback as Donovan.

Over the phone, Cuneo pleaded for more time. He asked that the order be removed from the top of the paper pile and kept away from Roosevelt's signature as long as possible. "The person answered that I must be mad," Cuneo said, "a war was on, it was out of the question to interfere with the communications of the Joint Chiefs of Staff with the president."

Eventually, after much cajoling, Cuneo's friend at the White House agreed to put the order pushed by General Strong at the bottom of the pile. Grace Tully was most likely the person on the other end of the line with Cuneo (though he kept her confidence and never named her).

Over the next few hours, Donovan, Bowden and others in the OSS called every ally they could find, seeking a reprieve before Roosevelt terminated the nation's first independent spy agency. Cuneo tried to cash in "every political note I had in town" by reaching out to friends in the House and Senate, and "even, in desperation, to the Supreme Court."

Like a movie scene in which an innocent man strapped into the electric chair awaits a last-minute call from the governor, the OSS brass sweated to the end of the day, waiting to find out their fate. Cuneo kept up his frantic pace of reaching out to contacts at the Anchorage and elsewhere.

"I was still yanking them at the 4 p.m. deadline when I got a call to lay-off, the President had rejected the order of the Joint Chiefs," Cuneo recalled.

During this tense Washington drama, Donovan sent a letter to the president in hopes that he would reconsider. He said signing the order prepared by General Strong would "be a valuable gift" to the enemy.

In classic Rooseveltian style, the president had changed his mind—assuming he was initially inclined to agree with Strong—and eventually backed the OSS. He even invited Wild Bill and his wife to join him at a special Sunday service at St. John's Church across from the White House. As if nothing had happened, the president told Donovan that his invitation to church services was offered only "with certain friends."

At least for now, Donovan, the OSS and their quick-thinking liaison Cuneo were still in business as spies.

Since William Stephenson's arrival in mid-1940, most New Yorkers had been completely unaware of his massive intelligence agency perched atop Rockefeller Center. Three years later, that cloak of secrecy still existed, even though the British and the Americans were now partners in war. Intrepid's successful corps of spies and their mission remained a mystery to the American public. Those few US officials aware of his deeds generally weren't happy with him.

The State Department's Adolf Berle had "a strong aversion" to Stephenson's aggressive spycraft, regardless of its effectiveness. Hoover's FBI placed wiretap and physical surveillance on Stephenson personally to see if he'd misstep. At times, it seemed Ernest Cuneo was one of the few friends Stephenson had in the American government.

In December 1943, he accompanied Cuneo on a long flight to London, part of an undercover OSS assignment approved by Donovan. Stephenson surely viewed Cuneo's visit as another way of having a Roosevelt loyalist, like Harry Hopkins and Donovan before him, to see firsthand how Great Britain was handling the war. Cuneo had proven himself to be a friend to Stephenson and had been an early supporter of the BSC's cause. Stephenson wanted to show his appreciation.

The two men sat together during the bumpy ride over the Atlantic. The four engines of the long-range B-24 bomber, known as the "Liberator," hummed loudly, making conversation difficult. The B-24 Liberators were brand-new, state-of-the-art aircraft, armed with radar and an uncanny killing ability. From high above, they could destroy German submarines in the Atlantic. The Liberators also carried high-priority cargo and sometimes top officials, including Prime Minister Winston Churchill.

Midway through their sixteen-hour trip, Stephenson asked Cuneo what he would like most to experience during his visit to England. He didn't have to wait very long for an answer.

"The Great Man, Churchill," Cuneo replied.

Meeting Churchill, he enthused, would be his greatest thrill. For the longest time, he had worked with Churchill's spies in America, and now he wished to shake hands with their leader, a man he admired tremendously from afar.

With his usual air of certainty, Stephenson promised he would arrange an encounter with the prime minister. Given the demands of the war, however, it seemed unlikely to Cuneo.

The long war against the Nazis was building to a climax by December 1943. Only a few weeks before, Churchill had met with President Roosevelt and Soviet leader Joseph Stalin at the Tehran Conference, to map out Allied strategy for the long-awaited European invasion that following June. Dwight Eisenhower was named Supreme Allied Commander, while Hitler chose General Erwin Rommel, the famed "Desert Fox" of the North Africa offensive, to defend "Fortress Europa," the nations seized by Germany. The chances of Churchill being available for a handshake greeting with an American spy with no diplomatic status seemed remote.

When they landed in England, Stephenson arranged for Cuneo to spend time with the American Air Force group at their Goxhill base in Lincolnshire. The Yanks affectionately called it "Goats Hill." During his visit, Cuneo heard emotional stories of pilots lost while fighting in the skies. Each mission came back with fewer planes than they had left with. Later, Cuneo returned to London for a few late-night drinks with Air Force officers near Grosvenor Square.

Meanwhile, Stephenson spent that same day at 10 Downing Street. After leaving Claridge's hotel, he updated Lord Beaverbrook and Lord Leathers, the Minister of War Transport, on the latest strategies and waited to see the prime minister. Stephenson would engage in marathon debriefings until he finally met with Churchill. The conversations continued until 3:30 a.m., when Stephenson headed back to his hotel.

Walking past the corner of Brook Street and Grosvenor Square, Stephenson spotted the dark silhouette of a husky man speaking with two uniformed officers. He immediately recognized Cuneo.

"Come along, Ernie," Stephenson said, remarkably cheery for so late. "We are going to call upon the Prime Minister at No. 10."

Cuneo stared at Stephenson incredulously. "Good God Bill," he explained. "Don't you realize it is four-o'clock in the morning and we cannot possibly break in on the great man at this hour? Why, he may be asleep."

Stephenson knew better. When he left 10 Downing Street a few minutes earlier, Churchill was still in full throttle. The prime minister was a man powered at night by naps taken in the afternoon. Stephenson reminded his American friend of all the Allied forces still awake that night, including those jumping out of planes into enemy territory.

"Why then do you think that their leader should be sleeping at his post?" Stephenson teased.

Cuneo agreed to follow him back to Downing Street. Once they passed through its black oak door, there was little wait. The two men soon met Churchill in an adjoining room, where he was sharing a nightcap with some other colleagues. Churchill smiled warmly when he heard the Italian surname of Stephenson's companion from New York.

"Cuneo..." Churchill repeated, as if the name sprang some spark in his encyclopedic memory. "Are you, by any chance, related to the Cuneo who served as navigator to Christopher Columbus?"

By today's standards, invoking the memory of Michele de Cuneo, the aristocratic traveling companion of his fellow Italian Columbus on his second voyage to the Caribbean, might not have been advisable. Not only did Columbus create a slave trade to Spain, but in de Cuneo's candid 1495 account, he recalled taking "a very beautiful Carib girl" into his private chambers with Columbus's blessings. When the naked woman resisted his advances, Michele de Cuneo whipped and raped her without a second thought. "Eventually we came to such terms, I assure you, that you would have thought she had been brought up in a school for whores," he bragged.

Such outrageous behavior was likely laundered over time, as history turned into legend, enough so that by the time Churchill and Ernest Cuneo met at Downing Street, Michele de Cuneo's memory was described as that of a champion, who found the New World with the fabled Columbus. From this account of their 1943 meeting, it seems neither Churchill nor Ernest Cuneo had any real idea about the sordid side of this Columbus trip— just the mythology.

"Cuneo's chest swelled with pride," according to H. Montgomery Hyde's account of their meeting. "Yes, indeed, he was a direct descendant of that famous Genovese sailor, he assured Churchill."

For the rest of their memorable meeting—the gift that Stephenson promised him—Cuneo shared his time with Churchill "in the warmest possible fashion," said Hyde.

On their way back to Claridge's near dawn, Stephenson savored his Churchill triumph. He asked Cuneo what struck him most in meeting the prime minister.

"I was astonished to find this great [leader]," Cuneo said,

"dressed in such a simple garb as an overall." He meant Churchill's famous "siren suit"—the one-piece garment with a belt he wore while sheltering from the possibility of nightly air raids. Despite his disappointment with Churchill's clothing, Cuneo's admiration for "the great man" never wavered.

While in London, Cuneo accompanied Stephenson to a lunch with Lord Louis Mountbatten at his double-storied penthouse, a palatial residence looking out upon Hyde Park and reachable only by a private express elevator.

Cuneo enjoyed himself immensely. He showed his propensity for fast one-liners that he'd sharpened at the Stork Club in New York. When someone disparaged Italian dictator Benito Mussolini, another guest at the table replied that at least Mussolini made the trains run on time.

"Yes, but perhaps the Italians would prefer that they didn't!" joked Cuneo. It was amusing enough to those at the table that they repeated it afterward.

Foreign Secretary Anthony Eden, also at the luncheon, leaned over to Stephenson and asked in a whisper who the man speaking with the American accent might be. The spymaster told Eden that the husky, gregarious Cuneo was a trusted adviser to President Roosevelt and "a good friend of Britain," serving as a link between the OSS and Churchill's intelligence agency.

Eden seemed content with Stephenson's explanation. But as the group left, Eden posed another similar question, this time to his host, Lord Mountbatten.

In a low voice, Eden asked Mountbatten who was the small quiet man sitting next to him at lunch. Mountbatten, a decorated war hero familiar with British intelligence, seemed stunned by the question.

"Why, don't you know?" Mountbatten exclaimed. "He's your man in New York."

Cuneo's meeting with Churchill is not reflected in any official records, only in the recollections he shared after the war and repeated by British spies like Hyde, who wrote their own account of Stephenson and the BSC's activities.

In his papers at the FDR Library, Cuneo mentioned his trip to London as coming at an important time in the war. "While I was in London, Rome was bombed and Mussolini resigned," he recalled. "It was one of the great turning points of history."

During Cuneo's trip, the British made clear their objections to the strategy agreed upon at the Tehran Conference earlier that month involving the "Big Three"—Churchill, FDR and Stalin, the Russian leader. By then, Hitler's demise appeared on the horizon and the new parameters for a postwar world were already being drawn.

At Tehran, Roosevelt and Stalin decided an Allied "second front" should come through France from the West—effectively squeezing Hitler's troops already fighting on the Russian front to the East. The USSR would join the fight against Japan once Germany was defeated. But Churchill argued unsuccessfully that Anglo-American forces should go through the Balkans to secure more of Eastern Europe now in Hitler's domain. Churchill claimed his approach would cost fewer lives.

However, another reason, largely unspoken in public, was that Churchill's move would keep nations such as Yugoslavia, Bulgaria and Romania—and by extension, even Poland, Hungary, Czechoslovakia and the future East Germany—from becoming Communist bloc nations dominated by the Soviets after the war.

While in London, Cuneo's curiosity about the Tehran agreement couldn't be contained. Late one evening, while descending the stairs along the Duke of York Column, he asked Desmond Morton, Churchill's longtime intelligence adviser, about it.

"Why is the Prime Minister so anxious to go up through the Balkans?" inquired Cuneo, acting as Donovan's surrogate on this trip.

Excitedly, Morton stopped on the stairs. He faced Cuneo, grabbing his shoulders.

"Because The Prime Minister says that if we send ten divisions up the Vardan Valley, we can crush the retreating right flank of German armies and save middle Europe from the Russians!"

Morton asked if Cuneo, a liaison for the president's new spy agency, could have any influence on changing policy. "Deeply as I sympathized with the British, I could do nothing," Cuneo recalled.

It's not clear if Cuneo knew about the discussion concerning Donovan's possible OSS role in the Balkans, bandied about a few months earlier on cables exchanged between Roosevelt and Churchill.

The exchange reflects the differing views on Donovan's effectiveness. On October 22, 1943, Roosevelt wrote that "the chaotic condition developing in the Balkans causes me concern." He said resistance forces in Greece and Yugoslavia were more prone to fighting each other than they were the Nazis. The president suggested that "an aggressive and qualified officer" was needed to go there and straighten out the mess.

"The only man I can think of now who might have a chance of success is Donovan," wrote FDR in a top secret cable. "I do not believe he can do any harm and being a fearless and aggressive character he might do much good." Roosevelt said he was willing to place "all agencies of ours now working in the Balkans" under Donovan's command if Churchill agreed.

In his response using an impromptu code name as "Former Naval Person," Churchill begged to differ with the president, and declined the offer of Donovan's help. He said his own forces were managing the Balkan conflict as well as possible.

"I have great admiration for Donovan, but I do not see any centre in the Balkans from which he could grip the situation," Churchill explained bluntly but diplomatically. "It would take a long time to move from one of the many centres of guerilla activity to another."

Whether FDR was trying to get rid of Donovan by sending him on this assignment is debatable, but clearly Churchill didn't think much of America's spymaster, certainly not enough to change his strategy for the region.

Although Cuneo likely espoused the president's position during his London trip, he eventually came around to the British view that the "second front" should have been launched through the Balkans and not Normandy—a fateful turn of events in Eastern Europe that, in Cuneo's view, would define the world for decades to come.

"The error of the Second Front was the first tragic domino in a series by which Communism was to sweep from the Baltic and the Adriatic to the China Seas—virtually without the loss of a man," Cuneo bemoaned.

After the war, Churchill would air that same view publicly, the way he'd once warned about Hitler. As the consequences of the Tehran agreement became clear, Churchill bemoaned the loss of Eastern European nations seized by the Soviets and put behind what he called an "Iron Curtain."

24

ON THE OUTSIDE LOOKING IN

"I am invisible, understand, simply because people refuse to see me."

—Ralph Ellison, *Invisible Man*

The Nazis offended Fiorello LaGuardi, deeply and personally, as one of the first major American officials to speak out against them. At a 1934 Madison Square Garden rally called the "Mock Trial of Adolf Hitler," sponsored by the American Jewish Congress, the city's newly elected mayor warned about Nazi beliefs concerning racial superiority.

"Hitlerism cannot destroy the contribution to civilization of the Jew," LaGuardia told the crowd, wary of the Führer's anti-Semitic influence in America. Indeed, this event was held in the same place where, five years later, a hateful German American Bund rally would praise the Nazis.

LaGuardia understood prejudice as the son of Italian-American and Jewish immigrants—his father raised Roman Catholic in southern Italy, his mother born a Jew from Trieste in the north. Throughout the war, LaGuardia would do everything possible to fight the Axis powers, just like his former aide, Ernest Cuneo.

Of all his influences in public life, Cuneo felt closest to La-Guardia. The mayor had opened the door to the exciting world Cuneo now inhabited as a White House insider and OSS intelligence official, when it could have so easily remained closed to him due to bigotry.

In politics, as in life, both Cuneo and LaGuardia had the constant vantage of the outsider looking in.

"Cuneo shared with LaGuardia his ethnicity—not, however, in the sense of prideful hyperbole but rather an enduring sensitivity," observed historian Salvatore J. LaGumina. "Both men were aware of the prevailing anti-immigrant atmosphere reflected in quota laws limiting Italian immigration at a time when surveys indicated that Italian Americans ranked among the lowest in social acceptance. In the public mind, they were associated with utter poverty, educational deficiencies, religious superstition, and criminality."

For his own reasons, Cuneo kept his distance from the Roman Catholic faith of his immigrant forebears. He spoke angrily about its strictures. He later preferred the Episcopal Church on holidays like Christmas. He could feel proud of his Italian ancestry but also inherited the newcomer's desire to fit in with the prevailing culture. "He encouraged me constantly to change my name and be a WASP," recalled his son Jonathan.

Given his position at the OSS spy agency, Cuneo maintained the lowest profile possible for a man jockeying through the high-profile thoroughfares of national politics, international relations and the media. On occasions, though, he did exert whatever influence he had on matters close to his heart, such as fighting bigotry.

When Cuneo learned about the suppressed story of Doris "Dorie" Miller, a heroic sailor at Pearl Harbor denied a medal because he was Black, he reacted swiftly. "Over at Navy, there was an appearance of nasty prejudice," he recalled. "The liberals believed the Navy was the most racially biased of the services."

On December 7, 1941, Miller's actions aboard the battleship *West Virginia*, where 130 were killed, were extraordinarily bold and valiant. During the Japanese attack, Miller commandeered the anti-aircraft machine gun of a dead gunner. Without any prior training, he shot down as many as four enemy planes from the sky. He also carried several wounded sailors to safety.

"I had watched the others with these guns," explained Miller, a strapping twenty-two-year-old from Waco, Texas, who played fullback in high school. "I guess I fired her for about fifteen minutes." He kept shooting until ordered off the sinking ship.

A month later, the Navy announced the names of several sailors awarded commendations for their courageous actions at Pearl Harbor. But it didn't reveal the name of the sole Black seaman receiving the honor. The Navy's refusal to recognize Miller's heroism publicly was a reflection of its deeply biased system. At the time, the Navy generally relegated Black people to jobs like mess attendant, the job assigned to Miller, and didn't train them to be in higher positions on board, such as those operating guns.

Cuneo worked on the seaman's case with Attorney General Francis Biddle, who was similarly outraged at the Navy's muted response. "Seldom have I so eagerly joined forces," Cuneo recalled. "I opened up a sustained attack of heavy journalistic artillery on the Admirals." Exactly who Cuneo alerted in the media is not clear in documents, but stories about Miller soon started to appear in the press.

Miller's name was recognized publicly four months after those of the white sailors were announced. At a May 27, 1942 ceremony, he received the Navy Cross from Admiral Chester W. Nimitz, becoming the first Black man to gain such an honor in the history of the Navy. Nimitz noted that Miller's medal was a first "to a member of his race and I'm sure that the future will see others similarly honored for brave acts."

Before the formal announcement, Cuneo heard from the Attorney General, who indicated that they'd been successful in getting the admirals to change their decision. "Biddle, with calm satisfaction, called me and told me that Miller was going to get the Navy Cross," he recalled.

For a time, Miller went home to Texas and was praised as a hero. The repentant Navy even created a recruiting poster featuring Miller's portrait with the tagline "Above and beyond the call of duty."

Eventually, Miller returned to the war, assigned to a new ship, still in a lowly position as a cook. He soon met with tragedy. In November 1943, Miller was lost at sea when Japanese torpedoes hit and sank his escort carrier. The blast killed 646 seamen, including Miller. His case remained a *cause celebre* among Black newspapers and writers like Langston Hughes, who eulogized him in verse: "When Dorie Miller took gun in hand/Jim Crow started his last stand."

A year after Miller's death, Winchell again invoked his name when Congressman John E. Rankin, a Southern segregationist, insulted American citizens whose names had sounded foreign. "The name of Dorie Miller, our Negro messman hero who manned a machine gun at Pearl Harbor, will be more valuable to American history than the name of John E. Rankin of Mississippi," Winchell declared.

The *Pittsburgh Courier*, a weekly African-American newspaper that championed recognition of Miller's bravery, applauded the columnist with the headline, "We Agree With You, Walter Winchell."

As much as he loathed the Navy's prejudice, Cuneo soon learned that "when it came to mass race bigotry, the War Department far outdid the Navy." A precursor to today's Defense Department, the War Department was then run by Henry Stimson and his top assistant, John J. McCloy.

Shortly after Pearl Harbor, they decided to order the removal of more than one hundred thousand Japanese-American citizens from their West Coast homes and relocate them to internment camps away from Pacific ports. In addition, more than a half million foreign-born Italian Americans also had some type of restrictions placed on them because of their "enemy alien" status. Eventually, about four hundred Italian nationals wound up in internment camps, along with some eleven thousand German nationals.

The fear of sabotage—a threat emphasized by Hoover's FBI's arrests of double agent spies—fueled this government decision, with its legality later upheld by the US Supreme Court. In Cuneo's view, however, the creation of these "concentration camps" was "one of the most heartless acts" in American history. It hit particularly close to home for Cuneo. The relocation strategy planned by Stimson and McCloy for Italian-born citizens could include Cuneo's parents, John and Louisa, and many of their friends and family. For decades, the extended Cuneo family had been living in northern New Jersey, New York City and Long Island, thinking of themselves as patriotic full-fledged citizens. Italian Americans made up about 18 percent of New York City's population.

When Cuneo first heard this plan, he went directly to his friend, Attorney General Biddle. He met with Biddle inside his Justice Department office suite. Already aware of the plan, Biddle's narrow face appeared stricken as Cuneo sputtered out what he'd learned.

"The Attorney General was in a cold rage," Cuneo recalled. "Stimson had actually told the Cabinet he intended" to soon remove many German and Italian immigrants from their East Coast homes.

Cuneo immediately contacted Winchell, who broke the news. "In most careful language, Winchell breathlessly informed the nation that Stimson was considering moving more than a half million," Cuneo recalled. "As expected, the reaction was instantaneous." Up and down the Eastern Seaboard, he said, "the news convulsed—and panicked" whole neighborhoods.

Stimson, a Republican put into his post as a bipartisan nod by Roosevelt, immediately denied there was any such plan. He declared that Winchell's report, based largely on Cuneo's information, was erroneous. Winchell fought back, pointing out that he only said Stimson was "considering" the internment order. "He [Winchell] called upon Stimson to deny that—if he dared," Cuneo said. "He [Stimson] was, morally, lying, which Winchell called to his attention... Stimson slinked away behind a barrier of silence."

Cuneo fought this proposed order with all his might. "I didn't know at the time that John McCloy was the prime mover, but journalistically and politically speaking, I blew Stimson out of the water." However, in reaction, he said, Stimson and McCloy "redoubled their attack on the helpless Japanese Americans."

Nonetheless, Biddle was pleased with his collaboration with Cuneo. One day, he called Cuneo over to his Justice Department office to ask his opinion about a plan to declare all Italian Americans "non-enemy" aliens, ensuring that they'd not be moved from their homes.

"It's a ten-strike," Cuneo declared. The president also embraced Biddle's plan and "actually told him he wished he had thought of it first."

LaGuardia, though he supported Japanese-American internment in New York, stepped forward to protect Italian Americans against this bigotry. The rallying point occurred on October 12, 1942—Columbus Day—when the mayor appeared before a packed audience at Carnegie Hall. LaGuardia talked onstage with Biddle and Adolf Berle—all three close friends of Cuneo.

The program was beamed on shortwave radio to Italy as part of the OSS's psychological warfare program. Cuneo later learned through OSS spy sources that the Italian underground felt "the effect was profound" in building support for the United States.

But the bureaucratic war wasn't over. In Cuneo's view, Stimson got his revenge by successfully pressuring the White House to prevent LaGuardia from being appointed as the new military governor of Italy, after Mussolini's government fell. Stimson "personally and meanly intervened" with the president over the Little Flower's appointment, he said.

"There is much to this dirty Stimson-McCloy business which has yet to meet the eye," Cuneo later summarized, "but in the liberal circles in which I moved, Stimson became a verb; to Stimson a man was to wreck a man's business, throw a man out of his home and shanghai [sic] him and his family to a concentration camp."

The internment of ethnic Americans proved to be the shame of Roosevelt's administration, a stain on his otherwise stellar wartime record. The fear of sabotage by "aliens" and outside forces could turn the most fair-minded American, even the president, into a suspicious bigot. As FDR wrote to the FBI's Hoover in an April 1942 memo: "Have you pretty well cleaned out the alien waiters in the principal Washington hotels? Altogether too much conversation in the dining rooms!"

Nevertheless, in this White House struggle, Cuneo and his supporters like Biddle felt victorious. "The Germans and Italians descended were saved from the Stimson treatment," Cuneo summarized, "thereby adding, it was estimated, 600,000 to the wartime work force."

During the war, Hitler's propaganda machine tried to divide America along racial and ethnic lines, tearing at its social fabric. "Nazi espionage chiefs concentrate on propaganda," warned Winchell in a December 1943 broadcast, informed by Cuneo's experience. "The Nazis know it's the cheapest and best form of espionage."

Despite their internment, Japanese Americans never proved to be a threat. The State Department's Adolf Berle and others in FDR's administration worried that harsh measures like these internment camps would boomerang and actually undermine security rather than protect it. Berle favored radio programs and

leaflets designed to show how American minorities were helping the war effort.

Still, Hoover's FBI kept a wary eye on possible foreign spies
hiding within the US ethnic minority communities. He publicized their capture at every opportunity. Following Pearl Harbor,
Japanese embassy and consul officials in the United States were
promptly deported. Whatever spy activities they'd had going
were presumed discontinued. But at least one Japanese spy operation remained intact, based within a doll shop in Manhattan.

Stephenson's British spies provided the FBI with its initial
evidence of the so-called "Doll Woman" spy. It began with a
series of suspicious letters with coded messages detailing US
ship movements. They were discovered by Stephenson's mail
inspectors in Bermuda. The chatty letters from a female writer,
ostensibly about doll repair, didn't seem to make sense on their
own. However, the coded messages—spelled out in plain letters
rather than numeric symbols—were easier than most to decipher.

In one example, the sentence "I have just secured information about a lovely Siamese Temple Dancer, it had been damaged, that is torn on the middle" was decoded to mean that
the USS *Saratoga*, with a tear in its middle, was being repaired.
"Fish nets" in another letter referred to submarine nets. "Balloons" referred to military installations. Her description of the
"old fisherman with a net over his back" pointed in code to an
aircraft carrier protected by an anti-submarine net.

Copies of the letters were analyzed by Hoover's FBI, which
ran down a number of clues until they finally traced them to a
doll shop on Madison Avenue run by Velvalee Dickinson. This
Stanford-educated doll collector with expensive tastes had first
made contact with Japanese spies while living in San Francisco.
She stepped up her espionage when she moved to New York.

Dickinson's fancy shop, with foreign and antique dolls in the
display window, advertised in magazines like *Town & Country*
and was featured in the *New Yorker*. The large awning over its

entrance touted her name in bold lettering. Despite her successes, she had difficulty paying for her expensive lifestyle.

After her arrest, Dickinson pled guilty and admitted to taking cash from the Japanese naval intelligence in return for her spying on shipyards. While the *New York Times* called her the "Doll Woman" in its headlines, the prosecutor labeled her a traitor in court. "One finds it difficult to believe that a native-born American, no matter how degraded and low, could be guilty of such acts," said US attorney James McNally at Dickinson's sentencing. Reflecting the bitter racial undertone of the era, McNally called her "a woman who sold her country to the Japs for money." A federal judge agreed and ordered Dickinson to prison for ten years.

The fear of German sabotage in America remained high throughout the war. The "Fifth Column" groups—such as the German American Bund, which showed up in large numbers at the Madison Square Garden rally in 1939—had gone mostly underground. But Winchell and Cuneo remained on the lookout for Nazi influence inside the United States.

The alarming tenor of the times was reflected in the case of Gerald B. Winrod, a political and religious extremist, swept up in the "Great Sedition Trial." Winrod was arrested in July 1942, along with George Sylvester Viereck and more than two dozen others, charged with publishing propaganda designed to undermine America's war against Germany.

Critics of Winrod, an evangelical Christian preacher from Wichita, Kansas, nicknamed him "the Jayhawk Nazi." His anti-Semitic sermons and hateful views could be found in the flagship magazine of his group, the Defenders of the Faith. A political isolationist, Winrod unsuccessfully sought the 1938 Republican US Senate nomination in Kansas. The party's regulars blocked him as an unacceptable candidate who, they said, "might possibly lean toward a Fascist program."

In December 1943, more than a year after Winrod's arrest, Winchell offered a scoop about the Jayhawk Nazi. The broadcaster claimed one of those charged with seditious activities "is, to use the underworld slang for snitching, singing madly to the Department of Justice right now to save himself."

Winchell didn't name the snitch, but shared that this person had recently filed a libel lawsuit against him, and also admitted to the Justice Department that "he was in the pay of Berlin, Germany." He clearly meant Winrod, whose lawsuit objected to Winchell calling him a Nazi collaborator.

The FBI, like the rest of America, listened to Winchell's broadcast and took notes. In a flurry of internal memos, the agency tried to find out the sources of the leak to Winchell. That search invariably led to Cuneo, the man of many hats. According to a very defensive FBI memo, O. John Rogge, of the Department of Justice's Criminal Division, "advised that apparently a telephone call which he received yesterday afternoon from Mr. Ernest Cuneo, Winchell's attorney, was the basis for Winchell's remark."

The memo provided an insight into Cuneo's approach as a private media attorney for Winchell who also happened to have access to government secrets.

"He [Rogge] stated that Cuneo called concerning other matters and advised that he understood one of the defendants in this case wanted to turn Government witness and was 'singing' to the Department," the FBI memo said. "Mr. Rogge informed Mr. Cuneo this was not true; that he didn't know what Cuneo was talking about; and that the matter was thereupon dropped."

This "cover-your-rear" FBI memo, addressed to higher-ups, didn't identify Cuneo as a liaison for the OSS. Nor did it mention his personal contacts within the Justice Department, including Hoover and Attorney General Biddle. Instead, the memo said "Mr. Rogge advised that he was amazed that Winchell should use this information in his broadcast after this conversation with Mr. Cuneo."

Eventually, the weak legal case against Winrod and many others in the so-called "Great Sedition Trial" fell apart. But Winchell and his lawyer Cuneo were far from finished trying to root out Nazi sympathizers and other isolationists in America who might impede FDR's war effort.

To insulate himself from criticism, Cuneo decided to give up his government salary and work for the OSS without compensation, just as Donovan did. Since August 1942, Cuneo had been paid $6,000 annually (roughly $100,000 in today's dollars), but gave it up in April 1943, OSS records show. Cuneo's decision came about after a Navy admiral, a favorite of the isolationists, became angry at something in Winchell's column. He complained to Donovan, asking why he couldn't "control" Cuneo.

By not appearing on the government payroll, Cuneo realized he could act more independently and express his private views more freely. As an operative for the president, he'd still be an insider. He retained a handsome income as a private attorney for Winchell and others. But foregoing a government salary made him that much more invisible, less of a target for foes.

"Thereafter I functioned as an unpaid volunteer at OSS," said Cuneo. Echoing an old newspaper adage, he said, "I didn't owe anyone a damn cent and there wasn't a man I couldn't tell to go to hell, though, in reverse, I'd have gone to hell and back for FDR."

25

THE SLAP HEARD AROUND THE WORLD

With help from Cuneo, columnist Drew Pearson broke the wartime news story of how General George Patton was compelled to apologize for slapping soldiers hospitalized for trauma and calling them "cowards." One of these scenes was later re-created in the 1970 Oscar-winning movie Patton.

"I won't have cowards in my Army."

—from *Patton*, a 1970 film written by Francis Ford Coppola
and Edmund H. North

During his tough campaign through Sicily, General George S. Patton Jr. stopped to inspect a field hospital in August 1943. He wanted to personally express his gratitude to injured troops for their bravery.

"There were some three hundred and fifty badly wounded men in the hospital, all of whom were very heroic under their sufferings, and all of whom were interested in the success of the operation," Patton recalled.

Since the war began, Patton—nicknamed "Old Blood and Guts"—had generated constant headlines as his armored forces tore through Hitler's military, first in North Africa and then across the Mediterranean into Sicily. It seemed only a matter of time until Patton reached Berlin.

Brash and often profane, the nearly sixty-year-old West Point graduate was considered a brilliant field tactician and a kick-ass motivator of soldiers in combat. Patton could be difficult, as the Army brass understood all too well, but he always got impressive results.

"His manner was extrovert, his appearance flamboyant and his dealings with people emphatic to the point of theatricality," described military historian John Keegan.

Inside the hospital ward, Patton shook hands and spoke with soldiers who'd been shot in combat. Many were lying in make-shift beds, with their injured bodies, heads and limbs covered in white bandages. A group of medical officers accompanied the general.

At one point, he spotted Private Charles H. Kuhl, seemingly unhurt, squatting on a box next to the wounded. When Patton asked about his injury, Kuhl shrugged and said he felt "nervous." It was his third time complaining of exhaustion after being on the front.

"I guess I can't take it," Kuhl admitted. He couldn't stand being shot at.

Patton became enraged. He'd been warned about "shirkers" who complained about "battle fatigue," a more psychological twist on the old World War I term "shell shock." Now Patton found himself facing what he considered a combat evader.

"You mean that you are malingering here?" Patton demanded. The private burst out in tears.

The general slapped Kuhl's cheek with his glove. Then he yanked him up and dragged him to the entrance of the hospital tent. With a swift kick in the pants, he pushed him outside.

"Don't admit this son of a bitch," Patton screamed at the flustered medics and nurses. He ended his tirade by vowing to send Kuhl back into combat.

"You hear me, you gutless bastard?" he ranted. "You're going back to the front!"

Undeterred, Patton erupted again the following week in a similar scenario while visiting a different evacuation hospital. When asked, Private Paul G. Bennett complained of combat fatigue and nervousness to the general. Once more, Patton slapped the offending soldier and promised to return him to the front.

"You may get shot and killed, but you're going to fight," Patton swore at him. "If you don't, I'll stand you up against a wall and have a firing squad kill you on purpose. In fact, I ought to shoot you myself, you goddamned whimpering coward."

Patton grabbed his own pearl-handled pistol and started waving it about, as if he might carry out his threat. A hospital commander stepped in and ended the confrontation.

The controversy didn't end there. One of the hospital surgeons filed a formal complaint about Patton's wild action, which eventually made its way to the top commander, General Dwight Eisenhower. Under orders, Patton was directed to apologize for his boorish behavior to his troops, especially the two soldiers whose faces he'd slapped.

Word of the two incidents spread slowly, reaching the ears of some reporters. In a private meeting, Eisenhower asked them to suppress the story for the good of the war effort, arguing that the Allied cause could not afford to lose a fighting general as talented as Patton. The reporters agreed to keep quiet.

Several weeks went by, with no public mention of the Patton slappings, until columnist Drew Pearson broke the story, based on an inside tip from his longtime friend and lawyer—Ernest Cuneo.

Drew Pearson was a man of many contradictions. Born a pacifist Quaker, he nonetheless liked to fight. While seeking the truth, he often lied. He cowrote his first book anonymously, only to be fired when his newspaper employer found out about his outside gig.

Eventually, Pearson became a famous newspaper and radio columnist—second only to Walter Winchell in popularity. And like Winchell, Pearson relied on Cuneo for legal counsel and as an occasional intelligence source. By that point, they'd been friends for twenty years.

"Pearson was the great American gadfly," Cuneo explained. "It has been said, and often, that if you had him for a friend, you didn't need any enemies."

At Columbia, Cuneo and Pearson, then student and teacher, debated various heady, esoteric subjects, such as comparing different world cultures, "starting a lifelong conversation without interruption." They wondered why, for instance, the ancient Greeks of Athens and the "California Indians" turned out so differently, even though they had similar climates. "The Columbia campus was not only an arsenal of ideas, old and new, but it was a reevaluation of the accepted, entrenched ideas," Cuneo recalled.

By 1940, Pearson's transformation seemed remarkable to Cuneo. No longer a college professor at Columbia, Pearson became a top-rated newspaper and radio commentator in Washington, his liberal viewpoint syndicated around the country. If Pearson didn't like a piece of legislation or White House action, his broadcast and column "Washington Merry-Go-Round" could kill it with a single bulleted item.

Unafraid to express opinions, Pearson didn't play the game of "on one hand, then the other hand" approach favored by most Washington journalists, who considered themselves "neutral" and "objective." Pearson sometimes mixed rumor with fact, and used information about a subject's private life or sexual proclivities to gain an advantage.

Early on, both Pearson and Cuneo were convinced that the evil powers of Nazism and fascism had to be stopped.

"We were the closest of friends," Cuneo later wrote. "From 1933 on, we were intent on bringing down Hitler/Mussolini and...had been waging all out journalistic and legal war on them."

Pearson freely traded information with British intelligence officers, so long as he gained a tidbit for his column. He often showed the British spies all the information he had gathered relating to them before printing it. Once he even let the BSC write the words for his column (extolling the role of British women in the war, similar to Winchell's column on the same subject).

According to the BSC's secret history, the White House instructed the FBI "to penetrate Pearson's intelligence system." But Hoover, also a good source for Pearson, deflected the order.

"Of course, Hoover came along and told me about it," Pearson told a BSC officer, as if brushing off a fly from his lapel. "So I was able to take the necessary precautions."

The British were upset when Pearson published "hot" news from Assistant Secretary of State John McCloy claiming that Churchill wanted to delay opening up a second front. Pearson couldn't be talked out of running it. He soon learned the British could parry right back.

"Pearson, who had no scruples himself in publishing unauthorized information, was nevertheless enraged when BSC succeeded in penetrating his own intelligence organization, although he never discovered how or by whom this was done," according to the agency's history.

Churchill's spies, who were constrained from any public comment by the British Official Secrets Acts, were amazed at Pearson's wartime freedom of the press. But that didn't change their feelings about the tall, thin-lipped American gossip columnist with his bloodlust for scoops.

"He had a goatish indifference to the feelings of others," observed the authors of the BSC history, "and was quite unperturbed if one of his disclosures cost a friend or acquaintance his job."

Cuneo acted every bit the tough New York lawyer for Pearson. Anyone saying something bad about his client could expect to get sued.

During the 1940 presidential campaign, Cuneo threatened a University of Chicago official with a lawsuit for "viciously attacking the professional integrity of my client" by claiming that something Pearson had said on nationwide radio wasn't true. "Unless proper apologies are made to Mr. Pearson, immediate legal proceedings will be instituted," Cuneo warned.

Most of the legal attacks, however, were aimed *at* Pearson. A *Time* magazine cover story profiling the controversial columnist said his "feuding and crusading has erupted into some whopping libel suits"—yet Pearson always seemed to walk away unscathed with Cuneo by his side.

"Cagey Drew Pearson, a match for most libel lawyers, brags that he has not yet paid a judgment (though his attorneys' fees are huge)," *Time* said. "He will work hours to make an item libel-proof, or to tone down the libel until it is not worth suing over."

If compelled to show up at a libel trial, Pearson made sure to shake the hands of each accusing witness to confuse the jury. Pearson's confidential files of personal secrets were notorious and feared, supposedly more scandalous than Hoover's FBI dossiers. In one notable example, General Douglas MacArthur dropped his libel suit when Pearson threatened to make public the military man's love letters to his mistress.

"When Drew went after an 'enemy,' he was as consecrated to bringing him down as a St. George slaying the dragon," Cuneo described. "No matter how badly battle went against him, he hung in like an English bull-dog to the locked-jaw death. This perhaps is why he nearly always won."

Cuneo's greatest public display of friendship with Pearson came during a libel lawsuit. In 1941, Congressman Martin L. Sweeney of Cleveland accused Pearson's column of making up the claim that he opposed a foreign-born Jew, Emerich Freed, for a federal judgeship because of his religion. Sweeney also denied Pearson's assertion that he was the spokesman for Father Charles Coughlin, the notoriously anti-Semitic Roman Catholic radio priest.

Pearson took the stand in his own defense. But according to published news reports, the "most sensational testimony" at the Sweeney libel trial came from Cuneo. He swore that while at Harvey's Restaurant in Washington in May 1939, he heard Congressman Sweeney say that "Roosevelt had sold out to the Jews" and attacked the character of "all Jewish girls." Pearson won the lawsuit.

Cuneo came to Pearson's rescue again in late 1943, after Roosevelt accused the columnist of being a serial liar.

The dispute stemmed from the Quebec Conference, held in August 1943 and attended by FDR and Churchill—but, for military reasons, not Stalin. The two leaders discussed the long-awaited Allied invasion of France and Italy, but without a resolution. Pearson was frustrated by the lack of results.

On his radio show with 3.5 million listeners, Pearson accused Secretary of State Cordell Hull of deliberately stalling the invasion plans because he was "anti-Soviet" and "would like to see Russia bled white—and the Russians know it." At the time,

Stalin's troops were suffering large losses in fighting the Nazis along the Eastern Front.

A furious Hull condemned Pearson's item as a "monstrous and diabolical falsehood." Hull convinced Roosevelt to issue an unusual rebuke of the columnist as "a chronic liar," a particularly odd charge given Pearson's longtime support for FDR's policies. Roosevelt suggested Pearson's column was full of falsities and very detrimental to keeping the Allied nations together and winning the war.

The president's tongue-lashing of Pearson didn't rally the press to the columnist's side, but rather put the spotlight on Pearson's frequent mixing of unverified rumors into his reporting. "He is frequently guilty of colossal errors of fact, often reports cocktail gossip as gospel truth," *Time* magazine said of the Pearson affair.

Pearson quickly defended himself, offering no apologies. But the White House condemnation seemed to hurt Pearson's reputation, a costly problem for a syndicated columnist heard so widely on popular radio.

Privately, Cuneo didn't agree with Pearson's column and felt going ahead with it was a mistake. "It was a most unfortunate charge because paranoiac Stalin was shrieking the same thing," Cuneo wrote in his unpublished memoir. But Cuneo added that calling Pearson a chronic liar "also was untrue and certainly was monumental ingratitude" by the president. After all, many scoops favoring the New Deal over the years first appeared in Pearson's column and had been fed by Cuneo himself.

Like a master spy, Cuneo came up with an alternative plan designed to deflect attention away from this controversy and protect Pearson, a most valued asset for Cuneo's own propaganda needs at the OSS. This diversion plan would involve Patton.

The prickly general, who had his own military spies, was known for causing difficulties for OSS intelligence agents trying to gather intelligence in Sicily. Cuneo felt the general was a glory hunter, unnecessarily costing American lives with his reckless actions. So Cuneo didn't feel bad about putting the heat on Patton.

"To take Drew off the spot, the report of an OSS man was given to him, namely that General Patton had slapped the face of a shell-shocked soldier. It was true," Cuneo wrote in his memoir, without admitting that he was the one who arranged to share the OSS report with Pearson.

In checking out the tip, Pearson learned the Patton slapping incidents were well-known among the troops in Europe and some of their relatives back home. He also learned the war correspondents had suppressed the slapping story. Pearson submitted his own version to the US Office of Censorship for approval. The War Department again argued it would hurt morale.

But the censorship panel disagreed, saying there was nothing in the broadcast or press code that prohibited information "about the conduct or shortcoming of military officers or any official of the Government." The panel director said "it seems to me that suppressing would do more harm than good."

Pearson's blockbuster scoop on the Sunday evening of November 21, 1943, caused a sensation. In relaying the slapping incidents, Pearson called for Patton's removal because he was "a bit too bloody for the morale of the Army."

At first, Eisenhower's chief of staff, Walter Bedell Smith, denied its veracity. But the embarrassed war correspondents, who'd previously agreed to keep quiet, now jumped all over it. "The General's crime was no greater than the Army's in hushing it up for so long," concluded *Time* magazine.

Cuneo's high-stakes diversion plan worked like a charm. "Drew's luck was with him," he recalled. "Patton and Eisenhower denied it—then had to admit it. Drew made the point that others, not he, were liars. That made the headlines too. Patton and not Pearson was the headline."

In the wake of the controversy, some in the press, like *Newsweek*, called for Patton to be fired. "It seemed as if all those who had enjoyed Georgie as a hero-warrior enjoyed even more pulling him off the pedestal they had built for him and sneering at his feet of clay," described Patton's daughter Ruth.

Although he apologized publicly, Patton, the old horse soldier, remained defiantly unrepentant in private. To his diary, Patton complained: "If the fate of the only successful general in the war depends on the statements of a discredited writer like Drew Pearson, we are in a bad fix."

Ultimately, Patton survived his crisis, going on to lead the Third Army through France on its intended march to Berlin. The slapping incident became part of Patton folklore, dramatized vividly in the Academy Award–winning 1970 film about his life starring George C. Scott.

For the moment, Pearson survived the controversy as well, thanks to his friend Cuneo. Once again, Cuneo remained anonymous, without a trace of the fact that he had handed the damning OSS spy agency report about Patton to the columnist and caused a nationwide sensation. With it, Pearson restored his reputation as a hard-charging journalist.

The following year, however, the syndicate carrying Pearson's column refused to renew. FBI documents later showed that complaints by Hull and Patton to Pearson's syndicate company may have had an effect. Because of his popularity with the American public, though, Pearson soon found another home for his column.

26
VICE

"Spies? Yes. All the other chocolate makers, you see, had begun to grow jealous of the wonderful candies that Mr. Wonka was making, and they started sending in spies to steal his secret recipes."

—Roald Dahl, *Charlie and the Chocolate Factory*

In Washington, at dinner parties and in salons, Vice President Henry Wallace enjoyed himself like a man who knew he'd soon be king.

Wallace was a frequent guest at the five-story mansion of millionaire Charles Marsh, an elegant place along Embassy Row with a white sandstone facade and Parisian-style wrought grillwork. Inside, its airy, expansive rooms—with several fireplaces, Palladian windows and hardwood floors—were perfect for hosting weekly soirees. They buzzed with gossip and the clatter of mixed drinks among journalists, academics and politicians devoted to President Roosevelt.

"You could sit at Charles's house and hear more of what was going on than you'd hear practically any other place in town," said Creekmore Fath, then a young FDR aide.

With a wave of full hair, piercing blue eyes and a corn-fed Midwest idealism about himself, Wallace was touted as the next in line for the presidency. When Wallace took office in 1941, the *New York Times* columnist James Reston called him the "assistant President." By late 1943, when Wallace attended the Marsh parties, many in the press assumed he would be renominated again in 1944 on the same Democratic ticket with FDR.

The British were keenly aware that President Roosevelt's heart condition could render him disabled or dead at any moment. With Wallace the potential heir to America's political throne, the BSC assigned a young charismatic spy, Roald Dahl, to keep an eye on him.

Later the famous writer of well-known children's books (such as Charlie and the Chocolate Factory), Roald Dahl served in WWII as a suave undercover agent for the British in Washington, becoming intimate with women like congresswoman Clare Boothe Luce and warning about the pro-Russian tendencies of Vice President Henry Wallace.

Years later, Dahl would become the beloved author of children's books. But at this point, Dahl was known only as a brave injured combat pilot working in Washington as an "assistant air attaché" at the British embassy. That job title provided enough cover for the fact that he'd also joined the BSC as a spy, collecting intelligence at various social gatherings, including those at Marsh's place.

Tall, charming and good-looking in his RAF uniform, Dahl

had a unique talent for integrating himself with powerful people in the most intimate ways and learning their secrets.

Marsh, a strong Roosevelt supporter, treated Dahl, at age twenty-seven, like a son or younger brother. They were close enough that Marsh confided his jealous worries about the outside romances of his beautiful wife, Alice Glass, whose affairs included a young congressman named Lyndon Johnson, a Marsh protégé.

One night before a dinner at his house, Marsh revealed another secret to Dahl.

"You're a flying chap," said Marsh, clutching papers clasped together in his hand, "what do you think of that?"

Marsh dropped the documents in front of Dahl. He suggested the young man could read them in his downstairs study if he liked while dinner was being prepared.

The paper pamphlet was entitled "Our Job in the Pacific" and written by Henry Wallace. The vice president was not only a frequent visitor to Marsh's parties but would, from time to time, solicit opinions from Marsh, the owner of several newspapers and oil wells in Texas.

Privately, Wallace had shared this draft with Marsh, probably never dreaming his host would offer it to Dahl, a friendly chap who also happened to be a British spy.

"Marsh in his political naïveté handed it to me that evening for comments," Dahl recalled. "I saw immediately its importance from the British point of view and excused myself saying that I was going downstairs to read it."

In a quick perusal that made his "hair stand on end," Dahl realized that the vice president proposed to cut Great Britain out of the world of commercial aviation after the war.

Wallace's plan would internationalize airports in the name of world peace and give the United States a tremendous advantage. Critics also disliked Wallace's call for "the emancipation of colonial subjects" in places like India, and how he portrayed the Soviet Union in a sympathetic light.

Despite the Anglo-American alliance necessary to defeat the Axis powers, Dahl knew that progressives like Wallace were less tolerant of the British Empire that Churchill was trying to maintain. Wallace, a former Secretary of Agriculture, belonged to the left-leaning portion of the Roosevelt coalition, a big political tent that included conservative Southern Democrats and big-city mayors with large ethnic constituencies.

Previously, at a White House meeting in 1943, Wallace confronted Churchill about his future view of the world. "I said bluntly that I thought the notion of Anglo-Saxon superiority, inherent in Churchill's approach, would be offensive to many of the nations of the world as well as to a number of people in the United States," Wallace wrote in his diary.

Churchill frowned on his suggestion to bring Latin America into this plan. "He said if we took all the colors on the painter's palette and mix them up together, we get just a smudgy grayish brown," Wallace recounted.

"And so you believe in the pure Anglo-Saxon race or Anglo-Saxon *über Alles*," the vice president replied.

Churchill rebuffed him, he said, "which caused the British to reach the conclusion that I am not playing their game of arranging matters so that the Anglo-Saxons will rule the world." In his diary, Wallace said "British policy clearly is to provoke the maximum distrust between the United States and Russia and thus prepare the groundwork for World War III."

Cuneo was dubious about Wallace. From his start in politics, Cuneo had been part of the liberal "Brain Trust" who came of age during the New Deal of the 1930s. But from his 1940s experiences with Stephenson's BSC, Cuneo found himself siding with Churchill's camp, adamantly opposed to Hitler but also wary of Stalin's totalitarian grip.

"The most intimate group around the President, Mrs. Roosevelt, [presidential advisor Harry] Hopkins and Wallace, took a strong stance against 'imperialism,'" recalled Cuneo, whose circle of British acquaintances would soon include Dahl as well as friends Ian Fleming and Ivar Bryce. "The difficulty was that a host of very good people, leading American citizens in fact, did not conceive of Russia or Communism as evil. Many, in fact, thought of the Russian Communists as the great liberators."

While Wallace's plan reflected his idealist views, Dahl realized it would be seen in London as a deep betrayal by a wartime ally.

"I thought, my goodness, I've got to do something about this," Dahl later said. "This would make them rock back at home."

From Marsh's study, Dahl discreetly made a telephone call for help so that a copy of the vice president's papers could be made.

"I quickly phoned the only contact I knew in BSC and told him to meet me on the road outside Marsh's house fast," he recalled. "I handed the pamphlet through the car window and told him he must be back with it in fifteen minutes. The man buzzed off to the BSC Washington offices and duly returned the pamphlet to me on the dot."

With Wallace's document back in hand, Dahl went upstairs again to see Marsh. His host was none the wiser. Like a good spy, Dahl didn't say much, and gave no indication that he'd been "very much excited" by its contents.

A copy of Wallace's purloined document swiftly made its way to Stephenson at Rockefeller Center, and then to London, where Churchill read it and reacted with "cataclysms of wrath." It seemed to confirm all of the British's concerns about the American who might be next in the Oval Office.

When Wallace published his plan in early 1944, the British objections surfaced publicly. During Dahl's conversations with Marsh, still unaware of the clandestine spy maneuver in his own house, the young agent contended that the pamphlet would cost Wallace his job. He said Churchill would surely urge FDR to select a new vice president.

Marsh, the veteran of many political soirees, acted as though Dahl were the naive one.

"Don't be a child—grow up," Marsh scolded. "Don't you know that the most certain way to be sure Wallace will continue to be vice-president is for the word to get around that Churchill is against him?"

The BSC's satellite office in Washington, where Dahl was assigned, had opened up two years earlier, shortly before Pearl Harbor, when Donovan created America's first intelligence agency. While Stephenson's BSC headquarters remained at Rockefeller Center, Donovan worked primarily in the nation's capital, with a smaller OSS outpost in New York. Stephenson made sure his BSC Washington staffers worked cooperatively with the Americans.

"Donovan's organization rapidly taking shape," Stephenson telegraphed on August 9, 1941, to his boss, Stewart Menzies, head of MI6, the British Secret Intelligence Services in London. "Central offices in Washington now working with staff and liaison is established and functioning."

Cuneo, as OSS liaison, continued to travel back and forth between New York and Washington. He gained a unique understanding of how the two spy agencies analyzed Hitler and his armed forces. From his own education, Cuneo knew the "modus operandi" of an adversary—whether in college sports, police detective work or international espionage—should be studied carefully to determine what might happen next.

When Cuneo mentioned "modus operandi" theories to Stephenson, the Canadian spymaster "astonished me by his encyclopedic knowledge of it," Cuneo recalled. He cited Sir Llewellyn William Atcherley—the main "MO" proponent among police in Scotland—and how it'd been adapted by British intelligence. Little details, he learned, often provided large clues about future behavior.

"As a result, they had a modus operandi dossier on every major military staff officer in the world, including Hitler's generals," Cuneo recalled. While the Nazi MO was relatively easy to decipher, figuring out the cagey intent of the enigmatic Stalin would prove to be the biggest challenge in espionage. The Russian leader was a masterful player of realpolitik during the war.

"What this meant, early in 1943, was that even as Stalin was hoping for a break in the British-American alliance, he would accept the peace terms the British-American alliance would insist upon, rather than go to war against them," Cuneo contended.

In Washington, Stephenson relied on Dahl as his eyes and ears to report on the "MO" of Vice President Wallace and other Americans deemed not to be acting in British best interests.

Dahl became a spy by accident rather than design. As a pilot, Dahl's plane crash-landed in the Egyptian desert in 1940 and he fractured his skull. He pushed himself out of the wreckage before the plane's fuel tanks exploded. Unable to return to flying, he transferred to Washington.

After his impressive bit of quick thinking at Marsh's mansion, Dahl was summoned to New York by the BSC chief for a visit. Inside the giant skyscraper at Rockefeller Center, with its impressive bank of elevators, Dahl journeyed up to the thirty-sixth floor at what seemed lightning speed.

"They go up and down faster than I have ever dived in an airplane," Dahl wrote to his mother. "Your ears pop and your stomach either comes out of your mouth or drops out of your arse according to whether you're going up or down."

With his vivid imagination, Dahl fancied the BSC's stylish headquarters and viewed Stephenson as some "small unknown creature, hiding in a dark room somewhere in New York." Stephenson's modest, soft demeanor struck young Dahl as rather dull and awkward in conversation. Nevertheless, Dahl's spy assignment certainly proved stimulating.

"What the hell are you doing here?" demanded one of the

top British officers after stumbling upon Dahl at one particularly grand social event.

"I'm afraid, sir, you'll have to ask Bill Stephenson," he replied adroitly.

After the war, Dahl would gain worldwide fame for his fantasy books, selling millions of copies of such stories as *James and the Giant Peach*, *Matilda*, *The Witches*, *Charlie and the Chocolate Factory*, and *The BFG*. Biographers of Dahl later suggested the Rockefeller Center elevator rides up to the BSC headquarters on the thirty-sixth floor inspired the Great Glass Elevators in the Willie Wonka world of *Charlie and the Chocolate Factory*.

Although later beloved by children, Dahl was known during the war as "a killer with women" because of his suave good looks. The BSC encouraged him to cultivate influential women, usually older and wealthier ones, who might share official secrets during intimate moments. "The war had created a shortage of eligible young men in both cities," explained David Sturrock, a Dahl biographer, who said the young British spy "found himself constantly in demand as a guest."

One of his affairs was with Republican congresswoman Clare Boothe Luce, a critic of FDR and Britain's handling of the war. Her husband, Henry Luce, then owned the influential *Time* and *Life* magazine companies. "I hope to be able to make her change her views a little and say something better next time she speaks," Dahl explained.

After three nights in bed with Luce, Dahl complained about exhaustion from a task above and beyond the call of duty.

"I am all fucked out," he told an American friend. "That goddam woman has absolutely screwed me from one end of the room to another."

His complaints fell on deaf ears at the British embassy.

"You know it's a great assignment, but I just can't go on," Dahl wearily informed his superiors.

"Roald, did you see the Charles Laughton movie of Henry

VIII?" asked Lord Halifax, the British ambassador in Washington. Indeed, Dahl said, he had watched the famous 1933 Alexander Korda film *The Private Life of Henry VIII*.

"Well," Halifax continued, "do you remember the scene with Henry going into the bedroom with Anne of Cleves, and he turns and says, 'The things I've done for England'? Well, that's what you've got to do."

Not all of Dahl's rendezvous as a spy involved sex. Purely on charm, Dahl wrangled himself an invitation from First Lady Eleanor Roosevelt to visit the family's home in Hyde Park, where the young spy managed to converse with the president. "I was able to ask pointed questions and get equally pointed replies because, theoretically, I was a nobody," he recalled.

One relaxed Sunday morning in 1943, Dahl walked into a little side room where FDR was preparing a martini. "Good morning, Mr. President," Dahl said cheerily. Roosevelt engaged in idle chatter with the young Welshman he perceived as his wife's social friend.

"I had an interesting conversation today from Winston..." the president began, with some comments that provided insights into the current MO of the president. Dahl quickly reported these comments to Stephenson in a ten-page report.

"Bleeding this information on the highest level from the Americans was not for nefarious purposes, but for the war effort," Dahl later explained. "That's why Bill [Stephenson] planted fellows like us."

Vice President Wallace also befriended Dahl, going for walks and playing tennis with him on occasion. Among his many interests, Wallace was an agrarian expert on plant seeds who sent Dahl a bag of fertilizer for Christmas. "He is a nice boy and I am very fond of him," Wallace wrote in his diary, though he disagreed with Dahl over British policy.

In their conversations, Wallace said Dahl pointed out that "of the 20 German saboteurs discovered by the FBI, 17 of them had been apprehended because of advance information given by the British Secret Service to the FBI." Dahl praised the OSS's work and said future Anglo-American cooperation was necessary "to prevent destructive possibilities of the atomic bomb."

Dahl considered Wallace naive, a smart country bumpkin. Menzies, Churchill's spymaster, deemed Wallace dangerous, and insisted on monitoring him the way the BSC might with a Nazi spy in America.

The British complained bitterly about Wallace's controversial pamphlet, which appeared publicly as the two countries were preparing in 1944 for the D-Day invasion. It prompted Secretary of State Cordell Hull to apologize for his vice president's ill-timed and off-base comments.

Through private channels, Cuneo carried the message of concern from Churchill's government about Wallace's future in American politics. "I came to regard Wallace as a menace," said Stephenson, in comments relayed by the OSS liaison, "and I took action to ensure that the White House was aware that the British government would view Wallace's appearance on the ticket at the 1944 presidential elections" as troubling.

Both the BSC and J. Edgar Hoover's FBI felt there was good reason to doubt Wallace's judgment. During his tenure, Wallace "frequently made speeches before organizations allegedly subject to Communist or Soviet control," summarized a 1945 FBI memo. Although much of the FBI's so-called "evidence" was guilt by association, Wallace's rhetoric was indeed favorable to friendly ties with the Soviet Union and critical of British imperialism. The FBI said the American Communist Party considered "the highly idealistic Wallace as a quite easily manipulated pawn." Hoover made sure the White House knew that assessment. The BSC came to the same conclusion. As Cuneo bluntly observed, "the Russians had subtly wormed their way" into FDR's left-leaning group of advisers, including Wallace, "now completely surrounding the President intent on their own program—the destruction of European imperialism, especially the British Empire."

The security concerns about Wallace came to a head when a German double agent, working at the Berlin foreign desk, discovered Wallace had been talking indiscriminately about top secret matters to his brother-in-law, a Swiss diplomat. The confidential information wound up in the hands of the Nazis.

The astute German double agent told his OSS contact in Bern, Allen Dulles, about Wallace's willy-nilly disclosures. Dulles then alerted his boss, OSS chief William Donovan. Eventually, the president's military chief of staff, Admiral William Leahy, stunned by this breach of security, brought the Wallace matter to Roosevelt. The president looked at the OSS report and, without any emotion, replied calmly that it was "quite interesting."

By that point, without yet showing his hand, Roosevelt had likely made up his mind to reshuffle and get rid of Wallace on the 1944 ticket. The Democratic bosses and party regulars, including Mayor of Chicago Ed Kelly, were telling him that the vice president must go. Such awkward departures required a certain political dexterity, of which FDR was a master.

Cuneo kept Stephenson informed of the inside politics, especially about whether the British worries about Wallace might come true. But by February 14, 1944, the BSC let London know that "Roosevelt has undertaken to Party that he will jettison Wallace as Vice-Presidential candidate."

Dahl was of two minds about the fate of his social friend Wallace. Initially to his mother, Dahl wrote that "Wallace has temporarily lost his prestige, but I think he is on the way up the ladder—not down it, as so many people seem to think."

But the BSC's secret history, apparently relying on Dahl's input, noted his awareness of Wallace's imminent downfall. "A British officer in Washington, who was in frequent consultation with Wallace, reported that Wallace was unaware of this almost to the day of his rejection by the Democratic Convention five months later," it said.

Roosevelt's method of getting rid of a troublesome figure like Wallace was to send him abroad, just as he'd shipped off Joe Kennedy to London years earlier. In late May 1944, FDR dispatched Wallace on a long tour of China and Soviet Asia, while he made arrangements to replace him at home.

By the time Wallace returned to Washington in early July, even the Russians knew he was a goner. "Wallace has set the business circles against himself," Soviet Andrei Gromyko informed Moscow. "He has also set the Southern Democrats representing the influential right wing of the Democratic Party against himself. Their influence in the Congress and in the party apparatus is very high."

Late in July at the Democratic National Convention, delegates selected little-known Senator Harry S. Truman of Missouri, a compromise candidate, to replace Wallace as Roosevelt's running mate. Roosevelt never told Wallace personally of his intentions and even wrote to him, "I hope it will be the same old team."

As the convention started in Chicago, however, Roosevelt said publicly he'd vote for Wallace if he were a delegate but didn't want to unduly influence others. Privately, the politically astute Cuneo was amused by this exchange.

As Cuneo recounted, the president "declared that he himself would not accept the nomination of anything but an open convention, one of his laughable little pleasantries and he certainly would not accept a Vice President who wasn't the choice of an open convention. He knew very well that he was throwing Wallace to the wolves by mere acquiescence. Aware that Wallace could never be renominated, FDR at first endorsed him, thereby retaining the loyalty of Wallace's followers. This process of endorsing a hopeless candidate to gain the support of his followers was then known as goldbricking."

Wallace, once the crowd favorite, lost to Truman on the second ballot.

Roosevelt's chances of reelection in the fall remained a matter of concern in London. Churchill "was naturally most interested in the result of this election, which came at the final critical stage in the war," recalled H. Montgomery Hyde, in his book about the BSC agency.

To Stephenson's surprise, a poll by the Gallup organization showed Republican challenger Thomas Dewey to be leading. For a long time, the Gallup pollsters had been helpful to the British in their propaganda campaign against American isolationists, even after Pearl Harbor when public opinion for the war cooled because of mounting casualties.

Stephenson decided that George Gallup, a staunch Dewey supporter, had fixed things against FDR. "As WS learned, there was little doubt that Gallup deliberately adjusted his figures in Dewey's favour in the hope of stampeding the electorate," said the BSC history.

Filled with suspicions, Stephenson asked Donovan to analyze the Gallup polling data. With FDR's approval, the OSS's statistical expert, David Seiferheld, reviewed the raw data. He concluded that Gallup had miscalculated and the president was ahead. Cuneo let Stephenson know the president's own analysis showed a comfortable lead and predicted Dewey's campaign would be embarrassed with the final results.

"It's unbelievable, there are going to be some whitefaced boys in this country," crowed Cuneo in a conversation that was secretly recorded and later transcribed by the BSC. "Dewey is calling up Gallup so often they have to have a clerk to answer him. Imagine a guy shaking so much."

"And Gallup is trying to give Dewey service, I suppose?" Stephenson replied.

"Sure," said Cuneo, the secret sharer of information, "he's one of Gallup's principal clients."

Stephenson later prepared a memo to London that quite accurately detailed how Roosevelt would win state by state based on the OSS analysis. At that moment, a week before Election Day, Churchill's spymaster shared his trepidation with Cuneo.

Laughing as he sent off the telegram, Stephenson told his American friend that history would decide whether he "would be branded either an idiot or a genius."

27

SLAUGHTERING THE INNOCENTS

"I may no longer shield or shelter thee,
But must forsake thee in the fateful hour.
O shame on him who wrought me this sword,
And shaped it for my ruin and disgrace!"

—*The Valkyrie* by Richard Wagner, translated from his Ring cycle

Spying's impact on the war, for all its subtle and seemingly imperceptible ways, was becoming increasingly clear by 1944. The OSS of "Wild Bill" Donovan and the BSC of "Intrepid" Stephenson—the spymasters whom Ernest Cuneo helped discreetly in the background—had achieved remarkable success, making victory for the Allies more certain.

Stephenson had inspired America to create its first spy agency and kept the Nazi threat from taking root in the Western Hemisphere. By September that year, Donovan had built up a staff of nearly twenty thousand—outpacing Churchill's spy network—with some two hundred and fifty secret agents in Germany and Austria alone.

"I must express my most sincere admiration," Stephenson told Donovan in a heartfelt note, "for the way your whole S.I. [secret intelligence] organization has been developed in what is, compared to the development of the various established secret intelligence organizations elsewhere, a phenomenally short space of time."

Stephenson's note anticipated a future with Donovan still running his spy agency after the war. "I look beyond the satisfaction which has been given to me to play some role of minor assistance in its beginning, to a profound hope and faith that the organization which you have so effectively created and developed will continue into the days of peace," he wrote.

The most noteworthy part of Stephenson's hand-delivered letter—marked "personal" and "top secret"—was its mention of the remarkable espionage by Allen Dulles in Switzerland and his cultivation of a double agent spy known by the code name "George Wood."

"This is certainly one of the greatest secret intelligence achievements of this war," lauded Stephenson, who first met Dulles during his early days at Rockefeller Center.

Indeed, it was high praise coming from a man whose British bosses ran Bletchley Park fifty miles outside of London, the code-breaking home of cipher machinery and early computers that intercepted German messages without the Nazis discovering their weakness. This "Ultra" intelligence, as it was known, was a triumph of high technology in spying, credited with shortening the war by at least two years.

But the "George Wood" success harkened back to the most fundamental form of spying: the trading of secrets between human beings.

The code name "George Wood" pertained to Fritz Kolbe, a bald, finicky bureaucrat placed in a sensitive position by the Germans even though he had refused to join the Nazi Party. One of his coups as a double agent for Dulles involved the warning about Henry Wallace. But Kolbe delivered so many more secrets, and his influence became legendary.

"Our best intelligence source on Germany materialized in the summer of 1943, in the person of a diplomat, one who had the kind of access which is the intelligence officer's dream," Dulles wrote decades later. "George Wood (our code name for him) was not only our best source on Germany but undoubtedly one of the best secret agents any intelligence service has ever had."

Early in the war, Kolbe became repulsed by Hitler's savage actions, which he believed would be ruinous for Germany. Carefully, Kolbe sought out ways to provide confidential information he handled to the Allied forces without getting caught.

Kolbe worked as an assistant to Karl Ritter, an influential Nazi official who answered directly to Foreign Minister Joachim von Ribbentrop. With brusque, unmatched efficiency, Kolbe screened important diplomatic cables, as well as top secret messages from generals in the field, and prepared them for review.

Despite having the personality of a porcupine, Kolbe somehow evaded the paranoid suspicion that pervaded German intelligence. "It was like a comedy," Kolbe recalled. "I who, without any compromises, rejected and fought the Nazis, even hated them, had...ended up in their inner circle."

Kolbe managed to visit neutral Switzerland in August 1943, with confidential documents strapped to his legs. The British were suspicious of Kolbe's offerings. But Dulles—who still rued how he had dismissed a chance to meet with Lenin during World War I—didn't make the same mistake this time as head of the OSS's Bern office. Dulles decided to listen to Kolbe, though he remained wary of being trapped in a double cross.

"This could be an attempt to break our code," Dulles worried, as he later recalled. "The Germans figure we'll bite, cipher this stuff and radio it to Washington. They monitor everything, including Swiss commercial wireless channels... Or perhaps our friend is an *agent provocateur*. He plants the information with us and then tips off the Swiss police that we are spying. His rendezvous with us is proof and we are kicked out of the country. Still, there is just the glimmer of a chance that this man is on the square."

In a private meeting, the professorial, pipe-smoking Dulles

debriefed Kolbe, who freely shared his story. Kolbe provided an encyclopedic amount of information about the German war machine, including a key factory near Berlin that made high-tech plane equipment. He also revealed the location of Hitler's secret headquarters, called the Wolfsschanze ("Wolf's Lair"), in East Prussia. He identified German spies, gave details on weapons systems and talked about German strategy discussed in his Foreign Office.

Dulles was impressed by Kolbe's answers but still fretted that he might be a double agent. He asked Kolbe about his motives for turning on his country.

"I hate the Nazis—to me they are the enemy," Kolbe insisted. "I have a similar feeling about the Bolsheviks. They both menace the world. But we are in the middle of a war and this is no time to bargain. Try to believe me that I am a patriotic German with a human conscience and that there are others. All we ask as payment for our services is help and encouragement and support after the war."

Dulles couldn't make any promises. "We can hardly divine now what will happen after the war," he replied. "It must be won first."

After their lengthy debrief, Kolbe returned to Germany, but Dulles managed to meet him again several times. Kolbe proved to be an extraordinary spy for the OSS, providing sixteen hundred pages of copied documents over the next two years. They detailed the German war plans and various leaks in American and British espionage systems.

By January 1944, Donovan alerted Roosevelt that the OSS had cultivated a spy who was the "first important penetration" into the heart of the Nazi hierarchy. He kept his name secret from the president.

The "George Wood" operation was a welcome coup for American intelligence, which began the war so flat-footed with the Pearl Harbor attack. Kolbe's information was a gold mine, as Stephenson said in his effusive note to Donovan after meeting with Dulles.

"The visit here of your very able representative in Switzerland reminds me of the fact that when I was in London recently I had the opportunity of going into the history and product of the 'Wood' traffic," wrote Stephenson, who marveled at its contents.

The lion's share of the credit went to "Agent 110," the code name for Dulles, who cultivated other Nazi spies. He learned valuable information about the German resistance movement and the development of the V-1 and V-2 weapons aimed at London.

Most importantly, Dulles secretly negotiated with a German lieutenant general for the surrender of more than six hundred thousand German troops in northern Italy, five days before Germany's total surrender. The OSS effort with "Operation Sunrise" by Dulles likely saved thousands of lives among those on the front lines, prevented prisoners of war from being used as bargaining chips, and kept Italy's priceless art and antiques from being destroyed.

Not everything for Dulles turned out a success, however.

Like Kolbe, Admiral Wilhelm Canaris of the Abwehr privately loathed Hitler and eventually became a double agent for Dulles and British intelligence—initially a spying triumph for the Allies. "An intelligence service is the ideal vehicle for a conspiracy," Dulles later explained. "Its members can travel about at home and abroad under secret orders, and no questions are asked."

The German spymaster's transformation was truly remarkable. Early in the war, Canaris seemed a loyal career officer, a supporter of Hitler. But his professional instincts were undermined by amateurish Nazi orders and his own ambition that demanded he go along with questionable decisions. A typical example was the disastrous "Operation Pastorius" submarine sabotage attempt in the United States that he'd warned wouldn't work.

Taking advantage of Canaris's doubts about Hitler, the Allied spies made several impressive strides. Dulles and the British had recruited Halina Szymanska, Canaris's Polish mistress, to their side. Churchill's spies had also assisted the Czech assassins who'd blown up the car of Canaris's main rival, Reinhard Heydrich.

But late in the war, an attempt by Canaris and other coconspirators to get rid of Hitler became a tragic failure.

On July 20, 1944, Hitler presided over a strategy meeting at the Wolf's Lair, desperate to fend off defeat on the Russian front. Into the room came Colonel Claus Schenk von Stauffenberg— carrying a briefcase with a time bomb inside.

Stauffenberg, a handsome German count and war hero, was undoubtedly brave. During the North African campaign, he'd lost an eye and parts of both hands. Like Canaris, Stauffenberg became repulsed by Hitler and horrified by the Nazis treatment of its perceived enemies, especially the wholesale killing of Jews.

A fellow officer once asked Stauffenberg why he had a photo of Hitler hanging above his office desk.

"I put it up so that whoever comes here shall see the man's expression of madness and the lack of any sense of proportion," he replied. When asked what could be done about Hitler, he replied, "Kill him."

Stauffenberg became convinced something must be done to stop Hitler, even if it involved risking his own life. The thirty-nine-year-old colonel, part of an organized coup attempt, had agreed to place the briefcase under the table where Hitler was sitting. His foot activated the trip wire.

Then Stauffenberg departed the room, called away momentarily by a prearranged phone call from another conspirator. In a few seconds, according to his plan, the bomb would go off and the Führer would be dead.

This certainly wasn't the first scheme to assassinate Hitler. It had been contemplated many times, including by William Stephenson himself in the late 1930s, before he took over the BSC.

Earlier in 1944, the British Special Operations Executive started "Operation Foxley," proposing a smorgasbord of ways to poison Hitler, kill him by a sniper's attack or annihilate him with explosives. Its top secret plan, not made public until 1998, bluntly stated its objective: "the elimination of HITLER and any high-ranking Nazis or members of the Fuhrer's entourage who may be present at the attempt."

While the British debated how and when they should assassinate Hitler, other top Germans were planning his demise. In March 1943, Canaris's Abwehr obtained an English-made bomb, which was planted in Hitler's plane during a trip to the Wolf's Lair. But the bomb never went off. Another group of officers conspired to shoot Hitler without regard for their own safety the next time he visited the front. But Hitler never came.

Dulles became aware of the German underground's efforts to assassinate Hitler through private meetings in Switzerland with Hans Bernd Gisevius, an Abwehr associate of Canaris assigned to the German consulate in Zurich. Gisevius provided information gleaned from Abwehr couriers and passed it along to Dulles. He offered clues to help spot the Peenemünde test site near the Baltic Coast where the Nazis developed guided missiles and rockets.

Most significantly, Gisevius was one of the coconspirators in "Operation Valkyrie," the code name for the Hitler assassination plot carried out by Stauffenberg. "To him, a victory for Hitler meant the end of Christian civilization, and of Western culture in Europe and possibly in the world," recalled Dulles, who met with Gisevius in advance about the coup attempt against the German dictator.

But killing Hitler at the Wolf's Lair wouldn't be easy. Loyal Nazi troops lined the whole compound. Concrete safe houses, hidden under pine trees bunched together like a shield, made it hard to detect from the air for Allied fighter planes. What was needed was an assassin with security clearance like Colonel

Stauffenberg. Three times before July 20, he'd tried unsuccessfully to find the chance to kill Hitler.

The fate of his beloved Germany seemed in his hands. Like his other coconspirators, Stauffenberg wondered what Roosevelt and Churchill would do if Hitler was suddenly eliminated. Would the Allies insist on unconditional surrender, or would they agree to negotiate a peace settlement with a new German government? "I must know how England and the United States would act if Germany were forced to negotiate at short notice," he insisted. Blowing up Hitler at the Wolf's Lair seemed like a last chance.

After Stauffenberg left the meeting room, someone kicked the briefcase by mistake, far enough away to shield Hitler. When the bomb exploded, four people were killed. But the Nazi leader escaped with only minor injuries.

From a distance, Stauffenberg saw some bodies blown up and assumed Hitler was dead. He took off by airplane to Berlin to help launch the coup as it'd been planned. But by the time he arrived, news from the Wolf Lair declared the Führer had miraculously survived.

"Today an attempt was made on the Führer's life with explosives," announced a short radio broadcast that night, prepared by Joseph Goebbels, the Third Reich's chief propagandist. "The Fuhrer himself suffered no injuries beyond light burns and bruises. He resumed his work immediately…"

The coup never got off the ground. The next day, Stauffenberg and other coconspirators were lined up in front of a firing squad and executed. "Long live sacred Germany," Stauffenberg cried before dying.

The Gestapo received the names of many other military and political officers who were part of the Valkyrie conspiracy plan and they went on a killing spree. Gisevius managed to escape to Switzerland with the help of Dulles and the OSS. But nearly five thousand were executed directly because of the plot. One who came under suspicion was Canaris.

By 1944, the Abwehr overseen by Canaris—once with a staff of twenty-two thousand—had been replaced in Nazi circles by SS chief Heinrich Himmler's own intelligence agency. In denouncing Canaris, Himmler claimed that because of his "positive attitude to Jewry," the head of the Abwehr used the services of countless Jewish contact men and intermediaries both in Germany itself and abroad. Unaware of his former spymaster's intent to get rid of him, Hitler was content to push Canaris aside with no further action.

After the Wolf's Lair explosion, the rabid investigation into plots against Hitler revealed Canaris's own involvement. Canaris's diaries also detailed his complicity in earlier coup attempts against Hitler. Many of the July 20 conspirators were his friends. Stauffenberg had telephoned Canaris five days before the blast.

After being found guilty by the Nazis' so-called "People's Court," Canaris was imprisoned at Flossenburg Concentration Camp, tortured and eventually executed.

"This is the end," Canaris tapped out in a coded message before his death to a prisoner in the next cell. "Badly mishandled. My nose broken. I have done nothing against Germany. If you survive, please tell my wife… I only did my duty to my country when I tried to oppose the criminal folly of Hitler."

With an extra touch of cruelty, Hitler's thugs strangled the unrepentant spymaster, stripping Canaris naked before the gallows and lynching him with a piano wire. It was a slow and particularly gruesome way to die.

Despite the failure of Valkyrie, Dulles's intelligence work in Switzerland showcased his talents, which were most impressive to the Allies, as Stephenson said in his laudatory note to Donovan. Dulles demonstrated political savvy as well as great skills as a spy, to an even greater degree than the more flamboyant

Donovan. Not only did Dulles develop contacts with the German underground, he also fielded unofficial peace settlement inquiries from the Japanese.

Dulles met with German-born businessman and arms dealer Friedrich "Fritz" Hack, who acted as a go-between with the Japanese navy, particularly Commander Yoshiro Fujimura, a naval attaché in Switzerland. The secret peace talks went on for months, but had not reached a resolution by the time the US dropped atomic bombs at Hiroshima and Nagasaki.

As the war in Europe entered its final stages, the British were insistent that the terms of "unconditional surrender" against Germany not be undermined by softening American public opinion, as people became anxious for an ending through a negotiated settlement.

In December 1944, Stephenson handed to Ernest Cuneo a provocative column intended for publication by Walter Winchell, entitled "Humanity vs. the German People." While both Donovan and Dulles at the OSS had seemed open at times to the idea of a negotiated peace, their official liaison Cuneo was willing to act as the conduit for the BSC with a very different stance.

"It was a cogent argument against leniency, based on facts," the BSC's secret history recalled. "Winchell published it as it stood." In this account, Cuneo was identified only as "WS's intermediary."

With Cuneo's help, Winchell once again proved an effective megaphone for the British viewpoint in America. He gave voice to Churchill's spies—their involvement undisclosed in the column—who couldn't understand why some US officials might consider peace terms at this point.

"Soft peace peddlers who want leniency for the Germans would clasp blood-stained hands that in five years have slaughtered more innocents than were killed in all the world's wars up to 1939," Winchell began. His column didn't argue in diplomatic policy language. Rather it spoke up for individual people victimized by Hitler.

Vividly, Winchell illustrated one atrocity after another.

"Should we negotiate with the stormtroopers in Danzig who tore out the tongue of Mr. Lendzien, a deputy to the Polish parliament?... Or with the German soldiers who murdered six Polish farmers and 20 women and children in the village of Wisniewo by binding their hands and feet and then running tanks over them?... Or the Nazis of Breukelen in Holland, who tied five young boys to their car and dragged them through the streets until they were dead?"

The stunning examples Winchell provided were only a prelude to the ugly truth about the Holocaust that the world witnessed as the Nazi concentration camps were opened. Winchell reported on the huge number of Polish victims already found "systematically exterminated in murder cells" at Treblinka— more than the combined population of Arizona, Nevada, Montana, Idaho, Delaware and New Hampshire.

"The 'master race' has undertaken the worst religious persecutions since early Christians were fed to lions at Roman circuses," Winchell's column said. "Staggering figures of Jews burned, gassed, tortured, maimed, have shocked all civilized people—almost immunizing them to further shock."

The following month, in January 1945, Auschwitz would be liberated, with shocking photos of starving, skeletal prisoners in the place where more than a million had been murdered by the Nazis.

Some details in Winchell's column reflected the insider spy knowledge of Cuneo's OSS, including a prominent case handled by Donovan and Dulles. "How many towns have the Nazis wiped off the map?" Winchell asked. "1,600 innocent Czechs executed for 'having approved of Heydrich's assassination' because the Nazis had to cover up the fact that Heydrich was killed with the assistance of his own associates in the Gestapo."

Winchell, who once warned of isolationist complacency in combating the Nazi influence in America, now warned about not being vigilant enough in the name of peace abroad.

"Despising democracy and hating the word 'republic,' Germans devised 'reich' to replace it," Winchell argued. "When self-styled 'good Germans' weep crocodile tears and demand 'democratic justice' they must be reminded of German crimes. Let's remember that nine-tenths of all Germans supported Hitler vigorously ever since they elected—yes, ELECTED—him head of the German state... Maybe the soft peace boys can prove the Germans would die for democracy tomorrow if we let them run their own affairs. But past performance talks—and says No."

This particular Winchell column was so successful with the American public that BSC officers helped prepare three more installments on the same subject. Winchell called them "Humanity vs. the German People" Parts 2, 3 and 4.

In talking about the consequences of war, Winchell gave his vast American audience a glimpse at the bloody reality of espionage—the world Cuneo inhabited, so often invisible to the public. And while the British later claimed secret authorship of these Winchell columns, their all-American phrasing and journalistic lingo suggested that Cuneo had more than a hand in their creation.

28

DAYS OF DECISION

They jumped out of a plane into the black, velvety unknown of the nighttime sky. The group of Allied spy commandos descended into Nazi-occupied France, several hours before thousands of troops would storm Normandy's beaches at dawn on D-Day.

Falling through the cold dark air, these intelligence agents hoped their parachutes would work and that they wouldn't be spotted by the enemy on the ground. Most of them—but not all—would land safely and survive this incredibly risky maneuver.

They would be the first.

Their covert mission, called "Project Jedburgh," involved the American OSS, the British Special Operation Executive and paramilitary forces of the French Resistance. From behind enemy lines in France, they intended to blow up rails, block roads and destroy bridges.

The valiant effort of "the Jeds" to keep Nazi fighters at bay was all part of the deception surrounding D-Day.

Prior to the massive June 6, 1944 attack, the Allies fooled Hitler into thinking their invasion would come at Pas-de-Calais, about one hundred and eighty miles north, rather than Normandy. In Dover, across the English Channel from Pas-de-Calais, they created fake tanks, dummy landing craft and an entire phony Army headed by General George Patton to deceive the Nazis.

Leading up to D-Day, double agents—especially the German spy code-named "Garbo" by the British—further misled the Nazi high command by promoting lies that pointed to Pas-de-Calais. Code breakers at Bletchley Park confirmed the success of this deception by reading the encrypted "Enigma" messages of the Germans without them knowing it.

Of all the Allied espionage operations on D-Day, the "Jeds" had the boldest and arguably most dangerous assignment. As the huge black-painted B-24 Liberator aircraft neared their landing spot, the first group waited for the word to leave. A sergeant on board yelled, "Action stations!" in preparation as the plane lowered, and then "Go!" as they were above their destination.

"We'd be looking for a meadow, then flashes from a couple of flashlights would appear," recalled Lieutenant Eugene Polinsky, a navigator from Maywood, New Jersey. "We would drop down to 200 to 400 feet, open the bomb bay doors and send out supplies, munitions, etc. in parachute containers—or insert an agent."

Once on the ground, the Jeds became guerilla warriors. Each team had three fully armed commandos in uniform, including a radio operator. If they were caught, they expected to be shot by the Nazis as spies. They looked to join up with local French Resistance fighters. The Jeds' hit-and-run approach was epitomized by their motto: "Surprise, kill and vanish."

One of the Jed paratroopers in France that summer was thirty-year-old Stewart Alsop, a future national news columnist. A graduate of Groton and Yale, and then an editor at Doubleday book publishing, Alsop suddenly found himself in the deadly chaos of guerilla warfare as a secret agent for Donovan. He'd just gotten married to an Englishwoman the month before he landed.

"There is something to be said for facing the possibility of death when you're young and finding out what your own reaction is and what kind of a guy you are," Alsop described.

Nearly all the key leaders who plotted D-Day wanted to be there firsthand to witness this historic event. Winston Churchill planned to watch the landings, the culmination of all his efforts against Hitler, from aboard a battleship, HMS *Belfast*. But the British monarch insisted in a letter that Churchill remain . in London.

"Dear Winston, I want to ask you one more time not to go to sea on D-Day," wrote King George VI, outlining his reasons. "If you went, you'd cause me and your fellow ministers a lot of anxiety."

After much worry by his king and cabinet, the seventy-year-old prime minister conceded.

William Stephenson of the BSC was determined to be part of the "second front" created on D-Day. For one day, he served as a pilot instead of a spy. Stephenson flew as a rear gunner over the coastline during the invasion, on the hunt for the Luftwaffe in the skies.

"Harking back to his days as a fighter pilot in the First World War, he was annoyed because he encountered no German aircraft to shoot at," recalled his colleague H. Montgomery Hyde.

Stephenson could take heart that much of the espionage and political work he'd provided during the past four years in America had contributed mightily to this historic moment.

The OSS's "Wild Bill" Donovan also wanted to be at the forefront of the D-Day first-day force. He had traveled with Stephenson to London and insisted on joining the action at Normandy as well. He intended to wear the Congressional Medal of Honor that he'd earned for heroism in the last war.

But Supreme Commander Dwight D. Eisenhower and the other generals didn't want Donovan mucking around the battle site. Some were tired of Donovan's antics, while others were concerned for his safety.

When one admiral tried to stop him, Donovan couldn't control himself. "We ought to die together on the beach with enemy bullets through our bellies!" Donovan told him.

US Secretary of the Navy James Forrestal sent a strict written directive ordering him not to get on any boat for the assault. But Donovan blew it off. "I'll read it later," he told his top aide, Colonel David K. E. Bruce, head of the OSS European office in London.

Donovan managed to find a ride aboard a cruiser for Bruce and himself. They didn't make it to the Normandy shoreline until the following day, June 7. With little regard for his own safety, Donovan roamed around the bloody beachfront without a clear agenda.

At one point, Donovan and Bruce encountered machine gun fire from nearby Germans, pinning them down on the ground.

"You understand, David, that neither of us must be captured," Donovan insisted. "We know too much."

In an almost comedic exchange, they realized neither one of them had brought along their suicide pills for such desperate situations. Donovan had left his L-tablet, a poison pill with potassium cyanide, back in his Claridge's hotel room in London. Donovan ordered Bruce to, should they get out of this jam, contact the hotel and warn that its servants shouldn't touch his lethal pills in the medicine cabinet.

"If we are about to be captured, I'll shoot you first," Donovan whispered to the usually unflappable Bruce. "After all, I am your commanding officer. Then I'll shoot myself, so there's nothing to worry about."

Luckily, when Allied forces came by with a new line of attack, Donovan and Bruce managed to evade the Nazi gunfire. Wandering around, they eventually found General Omar Bradley and his staff inside a deserted barn, planning their next move.

Interrupting Bradley without regard, Donovan began talking obsessively about trying to contact OSS agents involved in the D-Day assault. Bradley listened politely to the gray-haired, decorated World War I hero and said he'd tend to his request later.

"But suppose you now go back to wherever you came from," Bradley added. By day's end, Donovan was back on a warship, enjoying a hot meal.

While Donovan's own judgment was suspect, his well-funded

OSS did offer considerable assistance to the D-Day invasion. With "the Jeds," for example, the British provided much of the training and espionage expertise, but the OSS provided the necessary manpower. "This was an arrangement of which advantage could be taken only sparingly and very discreetly, for the OSS had difficulty in securing a sufficient number of agents to fulfill their own needs," the BSC secret history explained.

What Donovan's band of amateur spies lacked in experience, they often tried to make up for with daring and creative enthusiasm. As *Life* magazine described, "In the field, the OSS men jumped at midnight from planes, landed on the hostile coasts from rubber boats, swam underwater to attach explosive 'limpets' to enemy ships, infiltrated past sentries to carry radio sets to Maquis and guerillas, set up high-powered telescopes on the mountainous Mediterranean islands and slipped into German Paris with a pistol in hand and cyanide pills in the other."

Overall, their bravery came with a high cost in blood. The OSS deployed 523 special operations agents in France surrounding D-Day, including 83 Jedburgh officers. They suffered 18 killed, another 17 missing or captured, and 51 wounded. Some were tortured by the Gestapo. Others died while landing at night, their bodies caught in the trees.

The rousing victory of D-Day was described by Donovan in a typically enthusiastic memo he sent to the president on June 14. "Having just returned from the beachhead in France," Donovan detailed the flaws in the German strategy, their military equipment, the Luftwaffe's once feared aircraft and even their defeatist spirit.

"All these various elements of disintegration, spiritual as well as physical, might result in a speedy break-up of the whole German defense," Donovan predicted, based on his own observations as well as intelligence reports. "Everything that I saw made clear that the Germans no longer have an Air Force that belongs in the Big League."

However, Donovan's freelance wanderings through the Normandy battlefield and his off-the-cuff comments wore thin with British officials, just as they did with the US military. His impulsive decisions were far more than a liaison like Cuneo could control or mitigate. Three years earlier, Churchill's intelligence advisers applauded Donovan's selection as Stephenson's favored choice to run America's intelligence system. But during the war, the British endured constant conflicts with the strong-willed OSS chief.

A week before D-Day, Churchill's intelligence adviser Desmond Morton warned Churchill that Donovan had arrived in London, hoping to meet with the prime minister. "As usual, General Donovan holds strong views about everything in the strategic and political field," Morton advised. "When he gets back to Washington, he will certainly talk to the President."

After the D-Day invasion, Donovan sent Churchill some statistical maps and charts as a memento of the great day. "These maps have been found most useful," Churchill wrote back, adding the odd rejoinder "Believe me" before his signature.

When Donovan returned to the States, Eisenhower's chief of staff, Walter Bedell Smith, dropped a note to the prime minister, informing him that the OSS spymaster had finally left London, much to their mutual relief.

"I have always been worried by his predilection for political intrigue, and I have kept a firm hand on him when I could," Smith admitted to Churchill about Donovan, "so he keeps away from me as much as possible."

Increasingly, as Donovan's liaison, Cuneo realized he was in a similar position.

29

LAST GOODBYE

In October 1944, Cuneo met privately with President Roosevelt in the Oval Office to discuss polling research for the upcoming election. "As I glimpsed at the president, I was almost visibly startled," Cuneo recalled. "I hadn't seen him in nearly a year. The change was ghastly, literally ghastly." FDR's deteriorating health concerned Churchill. Shortly after the two leaders attended the 1945 Yalta Conference with the Soviet Union's Joseph Stalin, FDR died at age sixty-three.

A few months after D-Day, Ernest Cuneo, the anonymous go-between, arrived at the White House to meet with Franklin Roosevelt in a rare face-to-face encounter. It would be their last.

The sixty-two-year-old president was in the final stages of a fourth presidential reelection campaign, promising to bring the biggest war in America's history to a victorious completion. But after witnessing the president's frail condition, Cuneo worried his hero wouldn't make it to the finish line.

On October 19, 1944, Cuneo arrived promptly for a 12:45 p.m. briefing about the latest poll results taken shortly before the upcoming election. "I entered the Oval Room," he recalled. "The door silently closed behind me, and I was alone with President Roosevelt."

FDR sat behind the magnificent mahogany desk, inherited from his immediate predecessor, Herbert Hoover. Framed photos of the president's four sons, all serving in the military, sat on his desk, reminders of his own vulnerability to the war's consequences.

Within arm's length, the president kept handy a telephone, a letter opener and various knickknacks to amuse himself. An American flag stood behind him, ahead of the dramatic drapes that gave his office the theatrical appearance of a stage.

A White House calendar record of this meeting, with Cuneo's name scribbled down in the president's appointment book, still exists today. There is no other documentation of their Oval Office discussion than the vivid details Cuneo wrote down later from memory.

President Roosevelt was a towering figure in Cuneo's life. While LaGuardia provided Cuneo's initial entrée into New York politics, Roosevelt opened the door to a much wider field of domestic policy and international intrigue. Cuneo befriended "Brain Trust" figures like Tom Corcoran and Adolf Berle who were central to FDR's early presidency. And because of his connection to FDR, he became Walter Winchell's lawyer and a conduit with Churchill's spies at Rockefeller Center.

"I admired the President very much indeed; but it was short of worship," Cuneo recalled. He stopped short of complete adoration only because he was exposed so often to the political sausage-making of the Roosevelt administration.

Throughout the war, as Donovan's official OSS liaison with

the FBI and British intelligence, Cuneo served as a middleman with various agencies. He acted as an able fixer whenever Secretary of State Cordell Hull, Assistant Secretary of State Adolf Berle or Attorney General Francis Biddle objected to Donovan's latest game plan. They "were sticklers for form," he recalled, and "very much more often than not expressed personal as well as official outrage at proposed 'projects' of the Strategic Services."

Although Berle and Biddle were longtime personal friends of his, Cuneo tried to remain professionally loyal to Donovan, at times a very hard task. Often it seemed Berle and Biddle preferred to remain in the dark about Donovan's spy endeavors.

"OSS gave them as little information as possible, and they were glad to receive none at all," Cuneo said. "If a 'project' was successful, they needn't know. If it failed, particularly in security, it was officially embarrassing, and, of course, we were disavowed on the spot."

In a way, this very meeting with Roosevelt was a rather questionable venture, involving foreign influence in American politics. Cuneo was on a mission initiated by the British.

"Oddly enough, that which brought me to the President's desk originated in London," Cuneo later acknowledged. Several weeks earlier, the head of the BSC, William Stephenson, requested private details on polling information for the ongoing 1944 presidential campaign. Whitehall wanted to know whether they'd still have a partner in FDR or have to deal with a new president in Republican Thomas Dewey. "Mr. Churchill had asked for it," Cuneo said. "General Donovan cleared it with the President who expressed interest in the result."

Bearing good news about the polling data, Cuneo looked forward to his meeting with Roosevelt, whom he considered the most gifted political player of his time. The president juggled competing interests with assurance, the same way stars from the old NFL handled the pigskin.

"He reminded me of Bronko Nagurski, Ernie Nevers or Ken

Strong, the class of the field when I played football," Cuneo recalled. "He could kick, run or pass superbly, was incredibly canny in his use of interference, and once past the line of scrimmage, a tackler couldn't put a hand on him. FDR was the greatest broken-field runner in American history."

As he sat down in the Oval Office to debrief the president, Cuneo noticed FDR gazed at him with some degree of familiarity. He was not completely invisible, despite the Brain Truster's desire for anonymity. "I was not unknown to Mr. Roosevelt," he said. "He recognized me as an outrider of his Palace Guard, a member in good standing of the Right Honorable Company of Expendables."

Cuneo tried not to show his shock at the appearance of Roosevelt. Once the picture of vibrancy, FDR now looked like a mere shadow of his campaign photo.

"As I glimpsed at the President, I was almost visibly startled," he wrote. "I hadn't seen him in nearly a year. The change was ghastly, literally ghastly."

The president's congestive heart failure and the strains of his office had taken their toll. His eyes were dark and sullen, his body wan. Cuneo kept staring as the president spoke, realizing that he was talking to a doomed man.

"Worse than the wasting of his body, it was apparent that his tremendous spirit was calling on his once-great physique for more than it had, and wasn't getting it," Cuneo recalled. "I was startled because I thought the death mask was on his face."

Roosevelt motioned for Cuneo to sit at the chair to the left of his desk. He began talking "in a lively fashion" though his body seemed to fail him. Twice his arm fell limply to his desk. After three futile tries, he finally reached his lit cigarette to his lips. Watching his hero stumble, Cuneo felt it was "one of the most awful moments in my life."

Still, with more verve than most Americans, Roosevelt carried on as if nothing was amiss.

"So, you think we'll win," he began. It sounded more like a declarative statement than a question.

"I do, Mr. President," Cuneo replied.

When asked why, Cuneo explained the public was pleased that the war in Europe was going well. He said General MacArthur's pending attack in the Philippines would also be of comfort to worried voters on the West Coast, and would "pull out the rug from the core of the Midwest opposition" from the GOP. In Cuneo's mind, MacArthur had been a potential political rival to FDR, just as General George McClellan had been for Lincoln during the Civil War.

The upbeat poll results were of little comfort to FDR. "Well, I wish I felt as confident as you do," the president concluded.

Cuneo didn't believe he had made any guarantees of victory. Rather, he was just giving Roosevelt the odds of reelection, "like reporting the morning line at the Belmont or Santa Anita racetracks."

Then, looking at Cuneo, the president turned to another topic. He wanted to know Cuneo's estimate of "possible defections of the Italian-American vote," especially in New York, Massachusetts and California.

Clearly, the president identified Cuneo as an Italian American, perhaps because of his surname or appearance, or remembering his previous ties to LaGuardia in New York. Cuneo didn't take offense, as he might have under different circumstances, and instead answered simply as a tactician.

Cuneo pointed out why Italian Americans still favored the president. During the war, Attorney General Biddle declared some six hundred thousand Italian Americans exempt from "enemy alien" status—unlike many of Japanese descent who remained in internment camps. Before Biddle's October 12, 1942 edict, some Italian Americans had been subject to detention and surveillance, targeted as traitors. The president also favored continued sovereignty for Italy, thanks largely to Berle's efforts.

Cuneo expressed confidence that "the President's fears here were groundless," as much as he could speak for all Italian Americans.

"No," the president countered. "Certain Catholic churchmen have told me that everything I am trying to do in Italy is opposed by the British."

Cuneo shrugged his shoulders, though he understood what Roosevelt meant. During the Allied battle swing through Italy, FDR had instructed bombing flights to avoid church sites in Italy, especially near the Vatican in Rome. Churchill resisted putting too many restrictions on his fighting forces.

"Of course, I knew that neither Churchill nor [British Foreign Minister Anthony] Eden were vitally concerned about Italy as we were," Cuneo wrote in his unpublished memoir. "Few descendants of Rome vote from Epping Forest," the ancient woodland outside London.

Roosevelt let a random personal thought fly from his mouth. "My father fought with Garibaldi!" he declared suddenly and proudly.

"Really?" Cuneo replied, a bit incredulous.

The president told a phlegmatic story of how his father, James Roosevelt, while a student in Naples during the mid-nineteenth century, helped the fabled Redshirts of Italian patriot Giuseppe Garibaldi in the effort for Italian unification.

"As a lark, he helped the Redshirts drag up the cannon," FDR recalled with a laugh. The ailing president seemed enlivened by this fond family memory, Cuneo noticed, "as if his father's boyish action were a good Groton prank."

Cuneo joined right in. "Several of the Cuneos are supposed to have been there—the number grows with the years—and more particularly my great-grandfather," he told him about Garibaldi. He spared Roosevelt the story about a Cuneo decendant and Christopher Columbus that he'd shared with Churchill.

They returned for a moment to the politics of the day. Roosevelt asked Cuneo what he thought would happen after the election, a standard inquiry from the president. He seemed pleased when Cuneo replied with an old adage by President Theodore Roosevelt, a distant cousin of FDR.

"The most valuable patronage at his disposal was an invitation to the White House," Cuneo told the president, repeating TR verbatim. "It swelled men's egos to believe they were giving the President advice."

Having watched Franklin Roosevelt's political climb, from the New York governor's mansion to the White House, Cuneo came to one central conclusion about his motivation. "FDR ran against only one opponent in his life—Teddy Roosevelt, his relative," Cuneo concluded. "He admired Teddy's maverick tactics and his bold attacks on his own party."

Given the rosy election outlook for the Democrats in 1944, Cuneo felt compelled to ask FDR the most pressing question of the campaign—"What about the South?" During his presidency, some of the most pointed criticism came from Southern Democrats on Capitol Hill opposed to desegregation and other New Deal reforms.

"Let it go," Roosevelt said, without a tinge of regret. "It's going anyhow, and so are we!"

After nearly an hour, the meeting wrapped up, with the next presidential visitor queued up in the wings. Cuneo walked to the exit and turned toward the president once more before leaving.

"I want to see you again, and soon," the president said in his mellifluous voice. Cuneo wished him adieu as well. He noticed Roosevelt waved goodbye with the same arm that earlier had difficulty lifting the cigarette.

"We never met face to face again," Cuneo later recalled. "I knew as I left, that we wouldn't; it was both awful and sad, as I crossed Executive Avenue over to State, to think that the President, before long, would be with the Ages."

Six months later, after winning his fourth presidential election, Roosevelt died at his retreat in Warm Springs, Georgia, a shock to his nation still at war. Harry Truman, the man who'd replaced Vice President Henry Wallace on the 1944 ticket, became the new president. He'd be faced with a world full of problems. There were many secrets to learn, including about the newly developed atomic bomb, which had been kept from him.

For Cuneo, the image of President Roosevelt that October 1944 afternoon at the White House remained with him forever, "an image which never varied from my original one." To him, FDR was a man of "extreme gallantry and conviction." He saved democracy in World War II and won four terms to the presidency, more than anyone in US history. Perhaps most remarkably, Roosevelt wasn't afraid to secretly support Churchill and his spies in their clandestine effort to get America into the war.

Whether from the bleacher seats or in the scrum of history, Cuneo knew greatness when he saw it. Whether as a spy or a political "liaison," he was grateful to have been on Roosevelt's team. As Cuneo reflected years later, "Not even his enemies would deny that the tremendous force of his personality never left any doubt as to whom was Commander-in-Chief."

PART IV

Cold Warriors

As "liaison" for America's fledgling spy agency, the Office of Strategic Services, Cuneo dealt with the British, the FBI, the attorney general, the military, and the White House. As a lawyer for the media's two top influential voices—Walter Winchell and Drew Pearson—he could help affect both government policy and public opinion.

JONATHAN CUNEO

"I am afraid that if you want to go down in history you'll have to do something for it."

—Joseph Conrad, *The Secret Agent*

"Among the increasingly intricate arsenals across the world, intelligence is an essential weapon, perhaps the most important."

—Sir William Stephenson

30

BETRAYALS

A wartime American spy seduced by the Russians, Elizabeth Bentley handled several moles inside the US government and the OSS, where Cuneo was a top official. Afraid of being murdered by her Soviet bosses, Bentley eventually exposed her spy ring to the FBI, which caused a Cold War sensation.

Elizabeth Bentley was in a terrible bind.

After spending much of the war as an undercover spy for the Russians, the American-born Bentley decided to confess to the FBI in 1945, detailing the full extent of her disloyalty. At the same time, her Russian handlers debated whether to kill Bentley to stop her from revealing their secrets.

"I found myself in the grip of terror," Bentley, then thirty-seven, recalled. "My time is running out, I said to myself desperately. It won't be long before I, too, am six feet under."

Bentley decided she must flee to someplace safe. In Manhattan, worried that she was being tailed by a Soviet assassin, Bentley followed a circuitous route through the city streets—ducking in and out of stores—before taking a train ride to an FBI satellite office in New Haven, Connecticut.

Bentley's desperate flight to the distant FBI office took place shortly after the United States dropped two devastating atomic bombs on Japan, bringing the long war to an end. After Germany's surrender in 1945, Russian spies continued to vie for information that could provide a nuclear advantage. A new struggle between the US and its former ally the Soviet Union quickly escalated, with both sides more reliant than ever on espionage. Bentley's damaging revelations to the FBI would help define this developing era called "the Cold War."

"I realized that I had a job to do before I died—I must get this information to the FBI," recalled Bentley, a Vassar graduate whose family roots reached back to Connecticut's earliest settlers. "Instead of serving the cause of humanity I was a tool for the enslavement of the people... I decided this was my country and that it was a good country. I felt I had been on borrowed time."

For several years, one of World War II's biggest secrets was America's development of nuclear weaponry at a remote site in New Mexico. The race to create the first atomic bomb began when scientist Albert Einstein warned FDR in 1939 that the Nazis might be first to figure out how to turn uranium into a devastating explosive device unless the US acted swiftly.

In the immediate wake of the Hiroshima and Nagasaki bombings, the United States refused to share its nuclear technology with other Allied partners—not Great Britain and especially not the Soviet Union. American officials, aware of Joseph Stalin's expansionist goals in Europe and elsewhere, worried Soviet spies would steal the secrets to the A-bomb. Espionage could no longer be ignored to the degree it once was.

"With the advent of a weapon of unprecedented destructive force, it became paramount to acquire information about an enemy's scientists, research laboratories, universities, and over-all scientific infrastructure to correctly assess the immenseness of dire strategic threat," observed Vince Houghton, a historian at the International Spy Museum in Washington, DC, in 2019. "Such information was indeed crucial to national survival."

To the FBI agents who questioned her, Bentley's firsthand knowledge of Soviet espionage activity inside America—including double agents hidden within both the OSS and the BSC—was stunning. Her revelations also proved a political coup for J. Edgar Hoover in the turf battle over the future of America's national security.

Bentley revealed how the Soviets ran an elaborate US spy network, housed in a modest-looking travel agency in Manhattan called World Tourists. Through her clandestine work, she learned of numerous American plans: a secret plastic explosive more powerful than TNT, development of a new B-29 "Superfortress" bomber plane and how the US was cracking into the Soviet cipher codes. She even provided confidential details of the D-Day invasion plans to the Soviets.

Bentley, a former schoolteacher with a master's degree from Columbia, seemed an unlikely spy. A shy, lonely woman who sympathized with the US Communist Party, Bentley entered into a sexual affair in 1941 with Jacob Golos, the Soviet agent running the Manhattan travel agency. Golos recruited her as a courier, assigned to several clandestine missions between New York and Washington.

By Bentley's account, Golos, an older, heavyset Russian spy with "startling blue eyes," was quite a lover, flattering her into submission. During her seduction by Golos, Bentley said, she felt herself "float away into an ecstasy that seemed to have no beginning and no end."

Their undercover romance didn't last long. After Golos died of a heart attack in late 1943, Bentley was assigned another Soviet handler, Anatoly Gorsky, whom she detested and likened to a gangster. Code-named "VADIM," Gorsky was short, fat and ruthless, without any of Golos's personal appeal. Her disgust at Gorsky's cruelty prompted Bentley to reveal all to the FBI. In doing so, Bentley suspected, quite accurately, that she might soon wind up dead.

When Gorsky told his Moscow bosses that Bentley had declined an offer to defect to the Soviet Union, he also offered a lethal solution. "She may damage us here very seriously," Gorsky said. "Only one remedy is left—the most drastic one—to get rid of her."

Shooting and poisoning were considered—even faking a suicide like the suspected 1941 Washington hotel murder of Soviet spy defector Walter Krivitsky. The tiny FBI office in New Haven became Bentley's refuge.

Hoover's G-men compiled Bentley's spy disclosures—including a lengthy list of suspected double agents inside the US—and put them into a lengthy deposition. Hoover soon shared it with William Stephenson of the BSC. Immediately, the New York–based spymaster informed London.

One of the double agents identified by Bentley was BSC intelligence officer Cedric Belfrage, who came to Rockefeller Center around the time of Pearl Harbor. A talented writer and film critic, Belfrage worked in the propaganda arm of the BSC. Records later showed that sensitive Allied information handled by Belfrage wound up in the hands of the Russians—a fact unknown to the BSC's Stephenson and American OSS figures like Donovan and Cuneo.

"For some time, Cedric had been turning over to us extremely valuable information from the files of the British Intelligence Service, most of which I saw before it was relayed on to the Russians," Bentley described.

Years later, in the Soviet archives, researchers found a 1948 memo by Gorsky about the damage done by Bentley disclosures, which identified Belfrage as a double agent for the Soviets. Between 1942 and 1943, Belfrage and other New York agents greatly increased the rolls of microfilm with secret information sent to Moscow's spy center, providing the Russian with a distinct advantage.

"Given the unprecedented number of wartime secrets exchanged by the British and the American intelligence communities, Belfrage had access to an unusually wide range of intelligence," wrote Christopher Andrew in his 1999 history of the Russian spy archive.

Throughout the 1940s, Belfrage remained elusive. When asked about Bentley's allegations, Belfrage said he passed along only "certain things of a really trifling nature," in the hopes of gaining access to Russian intelligence. Belfrage managed to avoid being charged as a spy. Along the way, he had help.

Belfrage's effort to cover his tracks was aided by another Soviet spy implanted in the heart of British intelligence. Kim Philby, a high-ranking member of MI6 during World War II and the early days of the Cold War, vouched for his fellow double agent. "Belfrage's career…is well known to our New York office, by whom, in fact, he has been employed," wrote Philby to his British bosses, who were eager to avoid public embarrassment.

With legendary guile, Philby also avoided detection. During World War II and the early days of the Cold War, he betrayed his country as a top double agent for the Russians. A product of the finest schools in England, Philby would serve as a highly regarded liaison between the British and US intelligence services, making him privy to many secrets.

Not only did he vouch for Belfrage, Philby also provided cover for another alleged Soviet double agent who'd worked in a top position at Rockefeller Center with Stephenson. That arrangement, however, would take another two decades to reveal.

In the meantime, Philby's treachery included secretly alerting the Soviet intelligence agency about Bentley's defection in late 1945. The security leak sounded like a game of telephone gone awry.

Philby, then overseeing British counterespionage against the USSR, first learned of Bentley's flight from a memo prepared by Stephenson. Earlier, the BSC chief had heard about her defection from the FBI's Hoover, who bragged about his latest espionage coup. Hoover assigned Bentley the male code name of "Gregory" to help secure her safety. But Hoover's excitement about what she revealed apparently couldn't be contained.

After Philby's warning, the Soviets turned sharply against Bentley, attacking her credibility. To avoid further detection, the Russians ordered their spy network in the United States to remain silent for several months. Bentley's sex life and her penchant for drinking were raised by those looking to discredit her.

Nevertheless, Bentley's disclosures raised troubling questions. In the massive effort by Stephenson and Donovan to combat the Nazis, were the security precautions inside both the BSC and the OSS good enough to prevent infiltration by Soviet spies? In their rush to combat the Nazis, had these spy agencies welcomed the help of Communist agents without thoroughly checking their backgrounds?

In London, the long knives had been out for quite a while against Stephenson. During the war, Stewart Menzies, the head of MI6, was never a fan. Although Menzies consulted Churchill almost daily, he didn't share the prime minister's enthusiasm for Stephenson's unconventional approach. Menzies was tired of complaints from the US State Department and FBI about Stephenson's maverick actions.

Eventually, Menzies expressed enough doubts about Stephenson that the prime minister decided to seek Roosevelt's opinion.

At a May 1943 conference in Washington, Churchill posed the question about his own spymaster in New York. FDR promised to get back to him with a report.

Attorney General Francis Biddle received the assignment. He quizzed Cuneo about the BSC chief in strictest confidence. Cuneo was the natural person to ask, as the OSS liaison with Donovan, but even more so, as the American who had worked with Stephenson the longest, dating back many months before Pearl Harbor.

Cuneo was surprised by this presidential request out of the blue. As Winchell might say, he smelled a rat.

"I sensed an end run and I was correct," Cuneo said, invoking football terms once again. "Enquiry [sic] revealed that the person who wanted to know was not the President but the Prime Minister."

Cuneo pushed back when his friend Biddle insisted that Roosevelt was the key motivator for this request.

"I asked him why the hell the President should be interested in how Stephenson was getting on," Cuneo recalled. The Attorney General fessed up. "Biddle said the President didn't care, but Churchill had asked him to find out."

Further snooping by Cuneo revealed that the same turf-minded critics of Donovan's OSS had extended their doubts to Stephenson as well, looking to eliminate both agencies as rivals. "It seemed to me we were back at square one," Cuneo decided, realizing the inside politics at play. "Failing to bring down the OSS, its bureaucratic enemies would get the British to bring down Stephenson."

Responding to Biddle's request, Cuneo replied with a glowing report. "I wrote the appraisal of Stephenson that he was in all respects first class," he recalled. "Stephenson's tact and integrity rated highly with Americans." If Intrepid had any faults, Cuneo claimed, it was that "his uncritical admiration for the Prime Minister lacked his usual objectivity."

Though the inquiry was confidential, Cuneo informed his Canadian friend about the White House request. "I gave Stephenson an A+ and told him in general terms that there had been inquiries from on high about him," Cuneo recalled.

Most fascinating to Cuneo was Churchill's "secret line of communication" for this evaluation of Stephenson. Rather than the usual channels—through the White House or diplomatic pouches—Churchill wanted it sent to him by an American official of Lloyds, the famous private insurer, to ensure that no one else would learn about it.

But other spies did find out. Secretly, the Russians also knew about Stephenson's situation, according to Soviet Archives documents released years later. That same month in May 1943, an encrypted message sent to Moscow contained secret information from Belfrage, the BSC double agent inside Rockefeller Center.

Betraying his own boss, Belfrage reported that Stephenson had traveled from England with Churchill (on his way to attend a White House war planning conference). Belfrage said the FBI complained about Stephenson's "subversive activity" within the United States, including propaganda efforts and covert operations aimed at isolationists. But for now, he added, Stephenson's job seemed secure.

Elizabeth Bentley's accusations showed how Russian infiltration plagued the American OSS—enough to raise troubling questions about Director Donovan's judgment and oversight. During the war, more than forty OSS officials shared confidential information with the Soviets—sometimes beyond the restrictions set by the White House.

Most prominent on Bentley's list of OSS double agents was Duncan Lee, a Rhodes Scholar and Yale-educated lawyer, personally recruited by Donovan to serve as his top assistant inside his spy agency. During the war, Bentley said, Lee provided her with confidential information that she shared with Moscow.

Donovan had no idea of his betrayal. "You have put your brains, your imagination and your doggedness into everything you have done," Donovan commended Lee. "You have reason to be proud of what you have done, and we are proud of you." Lee later testified he "never divulged classified information to any unauthorized person."

But fifty years later, Bentley's accusations were confirmed by the CIA's release of once secret Soviet encrypted correspondence. They showed that Lee, code-named "Koch," passed along information about American strategy, OSS operations in Europe and a confidential "Red list" that the OSS kept of suspected Soviet spies in its own ranks.

At the time, Bentley and Golos were delighted to have a top Donovan aide as their secret source. "All of the agent information from Europe and the rest of the world comes through his hands," gloated Golos in a message to Moscow.

As friendly spies, Bentley socialized with Lee and his wife in Washington. During one walk through their neighborhood in November 1944, she said, Lee alluded to "something very secret going on" at Oak Ridge, Tennessee. "He said it must be something super secret because it was shrouded in such mystery and so heavily guarded." Indeed, Oak Ridge was the protected Manhattan Project site used for enriched uranium in developing the atom bombs soon dropped on Japan.

The Bentley revelations confirmed the security doubts that led to Donovan's fall from political grace by the war's end. The OSS's future seemed in doubt as well.

The FBI's Hoover and other critics had strongly opposed Donovan's proposal to turn the OSS into a permanent intelligence agency, likening it to "an American Gestapo." Donovan had raised the idea several times during the war. He argued that a unified intelligence agency might have prevented Pearl Harbor. But Roosevelt, usually a Donovan supporter, never made a commitment to this proposal.

Instead, FDR instructed an aide, Colonel Richard Park Jr., to informally investigate the OSS. Park's report sharply rebuked Donovan's agency for its bumbling oversight and lax security, recommending it be dismantled. As Cuneo recalled, the army colonel's report listed the "illegalities and improprieties attributable to OSS, and a Congressional investigation was threatened."

Cuneo had been on the receiving end of one such security bumble. When Donovan asked for a special entry visa for a new hire, the FBI blocked it. He asked Cuneo to intervene with Attorney General Francis Biddle. Dismissive of the FBI's reasons, Donovan told Cuneo that his new hire was guilty of only "a few youthful mistakes."

Cuneo repeated that explanation to Biddle, who promised to check it out. Shortly after, Cuneo received an angry telephone call from Biddle, demanding he return to his Justice Department office.

"A few youthful mistakes?" Biddle shouted at his friend Cuneo as he walked in. "Tell him, Edgar!"

Waiting in Biddle's office was FBI Director Hoover, Donovan's biggest critic, ready to pounce.

The FBI chief recited aloud the criminal history of Donovan's proposed new hire. Two homicide convictions, two manslaughters and other allegations were on the rap sheet. Donovan's description of "a few youthful mistakes" soon became a joke shared within the intelligence community.

Despite his hope the two nations might get along after the war, Donovan eventually adopted a more cautious view about Russia and its long-term threat to America. An OSS report, dated April 2, 1945, warned: "Russia will emerge from the present conflict as by far the strongest nation in Europe and Asia—strong enough, if the United States should stand aside, to dominate Europe and at the same time to establish her hegemony over Asia."

But Roosevelt never read it, dying a few days later. FDR collapsed from a cerebral hemorrhage while sitting for a portrait at his retreat in Warm Springs, Georgia. His death at age sixty-three shocked a world still at war, enough so that Churchill described hearing the news as having "been struck a physical blow."

Donovan understood what the passing of the president, his old law school classmate from Columbia, meant for his agency.

"I am afraid it's the end," he surmised.

He was right. The following month, the new president, Harry S. Truman, shut down the OSS and thanked Donovan for his service.

Unlike before, Cuneo couldn't prevent its closure. He no longer had anyone to call in the Oval Office. Thus ended the spying career of Major General William J. Donovan, America's most decorated hero.

31

A KNOCK AT THE DOOR

Both Stephenson and Cuneo were disturbed by the 1945 defection of Russian spy Igor Gouzenko in Canada, which revealed the extent to which the Soviet Union was spying on its Allied partners and set the tone for the Cold War. Gouzenko, fearing for his life, wore a hood to protect his identity when in public.

LIBRARY AND ARCHIVES CANADA

Igor Gouzenko knew the NKVD, the Russian secret police, were coming for him. Hiding during the night, the twenty-six-year-old Soviet spy and his pregnant wife stayed with a neighbor across the hall so they could keep an eye on their apartment.

Gouzenko, a cipher expert, had just defected from the Russian embassy in Ottawa, Canada, with secret codes in his pocket. He watched anxiously to see if Soviet agents would show up.

When they did, the secret police ravaged through Gouzenko's apartment in Ottawa, looking for the top secret documents he had taken. Most of all, they were searching in vain for him.

"Through the keyhole, I could see our door clearly," he later recalled. "Knocking on it was [Vitali] Pavlov, the NKVD chief!"

As these agents called out his name, Gouzenko watched helplessly, his life at risk. He knew if the NKVD investigators found him, he'd be returned to Russia and executed.

Like Elizabeth Bentley, Gouzenko renounced being a Russian spy at the end of World War II. Given his oppressive experiences at their embassy—and the taste of freedom he'd had in Canada—Gouzenko decided he must seek political asylum for the sake of his family and his own sanity.

"Any criticism, no matter how minor, was interpreted as 'anti-Soviet sentiment' and generally resulted in the offender being dispatched forthwith to Moscow," he described about the embassy's paranoid atmosphere. "Our greatest fear was the constant danger of some action or word placing us on the 'black list.'"

On September 5, 1945, three days after Japan's formal surrender, Gouzenko walked out of the embassy with more than a hundred documents under his clothing. In remarkable detail, they revealed the Soviet effort to steal nuclear secrets and a list of double agents in "sleeper cells" in Canada, Britain and the United States.

That day, Gouzenko first sought refuge with Canadian authorities, but they turned him down as a crackpot. Even the local newspaper refused him. It wasn't until Ottawa police stopped the Soviet agents rummaging through Gouzenko's apartment at night that he finally found safety.

When questioned, the Russians gave a phony excuse to local cops about why they had busted into Gouzenko's home.

"He left some documents here and we have his permission to look for them," claimed Pavlov, the top agent. The lie was apparently not convincing to the police, who shooed them away.

Gouzenko and his wife were taken into protective custody. Eventually Gouzenko was moved to Camp X—the training compound in Canada run by BSC spymaster William Stephenson—where intelligence experts debriefed him.

Over the next several months, the Gouzenko revelations, like those of Bentley, underlined the treachery of the Soviet Union, with Stalin's intention to dominate the postwar world shocking their Allied partners. Stephenson later called Gouzenko's defection a "heaven sent opportunity to put the whole world on warning."

Cuneo felt Gouzenko's flight to freedom resembled a movie thriller. "Alfred Hitchcock at his zenith could not have imagined more terrifying escapades," he said.

Before Gouzenko, America seemed ready to go back to sleep in an isolationist trance, dropping its guard toward Stalin. "Even as we dismantled our armed forces and dismissed our allies," Cuneo wrote, "we were fairly supplicating the Kremlin, an enemy which was already waging war against us, to give us its worthless word that it would help in keeping the peace."

For Stephenson, the Gouzenko case revived his mission at a time when the Rockefeller Center offices were expected to close with the war's end. Much of his staff had already gone home. For example, BSC deputy Dick Ellis returned to London in 1944, to serve in a highly secretive MI6 role overseeing businessmen and journalists who were "assets," and later on a top committee meant to reorganize British intelligence.

On his own, Stephenson got involved in the Gouzenko matter, even though his main supporter, Winston Churchill, was no longer prime minister. Two months earlier, in a stunning reversal, Churchill's Conservative Party was rejected at the polls when Great Britain—tired of war and looking for a change—voted in the Labour Party of Clement Atlee. The change in prime ministers left some wondering if the Churchillian reliance on espionage as a vital weapon would also wane.

However, the Gouzenko case showed that battle lines were not erased with the Axis powers' defeat, just merely redrawn in a new world order.

"The Gouzenko revelations served to ramp up the good-versus-evil dichotomy that was emerging; historians have categorized the affair as the spark that began the Cold War," observed Canadian intelligence writer Dennis Molinaro in 2017. "In fact, Winston Churchill's famous 'Iron Curtain' speech came right in the middle of the scandal, in March 1946."

The Gouzenko case proved to be Stephenson's last mission.

According to his BSC colleague H. Montgomery Hyde, Stephenson happened to be in Ottawa on September 6, 1945, for a routine official visit, when he heard scuttlebutt about Gouzenko's desperate effort earlier that day seeking asylum as a defector. Stephenson's instincts compelled him to check it out right away. (Other accounts suggest Stephenson heard about it in New York and then flew up to Ottawa immediately.)

"Stephenson immediately realized that this man [Gouzenko] might well provide a unique opportunity for obtaining important details of the operation of the Soviet intelligence system in the Western Hemisphere," wrote Hyde. "He also realized that the Russian's life might be in serious danger, if he had indeed defected, since the Soviet secret police in the Embassy would undoubtedly attempt to 'liquidate' him and would almost certainly succeed unless some prompt action were taken to protect him."

Stephenson made sure Gouzenko and his family were treated well while in Canadian custody. Nervous and exhausted, Gouzenko's initial account was difficult to believe until his stash of stolen documents were reviewed and verified.

Meanwhile, under Canadian police guard, pregnant Anna Gouzenko gave birth to the couple's second child. At the hospital, they posed as Polish farmers to avoid detection. Like an unofficial godfather, Stephenson ordered a layette for the baby girl as a gift, which was sent by his staff at Rockefeller Center.

During Gouzenko's stay at Camp X and a nearby country house, a sharp debate ensued over what to do with him. Some suggested Canada should not offend Stalin, their wartime ally, and ought to deny him asylum. Truman and Atlee were brought into the debate amid fears of provoking another world war. Nothing leaked out publicly about the Soviet defection for four months.

While in London to see Atlee, Canadian Prime Minister William Lyon Mackenzie King visited Churchill at his Chartwell home, privately asking for his counsel about what to do with Gouzenko. Churchill firmly said Soviet espionage against the West must be revealed rather than covered up. He strongly advised Anglo-American unity in sending a strong message to Stalin. "It must not be written," Churchill said about dealing with the Russian dictator, "it must be understood."

During the debate, Stephenson wrote to "C," the code name for his London boss, Stewart Menzies, urging that "the story of what has been discovered in Canada can be published to the world. This should enlighten the public of the Western Democracies as to the situation vis-a-vis the Russians that we are all facing."

Over time, Gouzenko and the evidence he'd carried from the Russian embassy would fuel several investigations and thirty-nine arrests. The most sensational involved the US treason trial of Julius and Ethel Rosenberg, leading to their 1953 executions. Security was so tight around Gouzenko that he later appeared on television with a white hood over his head to conceal his face. He lived the rest of his life in Canada under the alias "George Brown."

Admirers of Stephenson, like Cuneo, remembered how he stepped forward to support Gouzenko when other top Allied officials were reluctant to get involved in the Soviet defector case.

"It marks a turning point in history," said Cuneo. "He quickly took charge, rescued Gouzenko and then delivered the evidence which resulted in the conviction of the A-bomb spies."

★ ★ ★

The Gouzenko affair rippled through America's postwar security system, causing great unease. With Donovan's OSS already dissolved by Truman, the FBI's J. Edgar Hoover recognized his opportunity to extend his realm of domestic investigations into international intelligence.

During the war, Hoover had complained bitterly about Stephenson's BSC activities in the United States, but now the two put aside their differences because of Gouzenko's revelations. The FBI chief met privately with Stephenson, both convinced that this serious spying breach should not be buried.

With the help of Cuneo, a friend of both men, a plan was devised to let the world know about Gouzenko. As Stephenson later said, "After consultation with Hoover and President Roosevelt's so-called brain trust co-ordinator, Ernest Cuneo, we agreed that the story should be released by way of Drew Pearson."

This pathway to public release would be roundabout, full of deception like a spy drama. As a masterful media manipulator and knowing Pearson's sympathetic view of the Soviets, Cuneo didn't leak the confidential Gouzenko information directly to the columnist. Instead, he planted it.

"I did not give it to Drew, as Stephenson believes, because Drew and I did not agree: he favored the pro-world peace through cooperation with the Kremlin and probably would not have used it because it came from me, BUT I put it where I knew Drew would find it and he blew it sky high," Cuneo later described, without identifying his go-between.

On February 3, 1946, Pearson's nationwide radio show began with a blockbuster. "The biggest story of espionage and intrigue is about to break," Pearson announced to his fifteen million listeners. He explained "the Canadians have taken over a Russian agent"—without naming Gouzenko—who "has put the finger on certain officials inside the American and Canadian governments cooperating with the Soviets."

Drew Pearson's scoop reverberated around the world, like some gong sending shock waves throughout the intelligence community. The Canadian government soon rounded up more than two dozen suspects. In the United States and Great Britain, the investigative trail led to such spies as Klaus Fuchs, a German physicist who had fled the Nazis. Fuchs eventually confessed he had provided vital nuclear bomb information to the Soviets during and after the war.

"The Soviet penetration in the USA was so widespread," Stephenson later explained, "and their agents were preparing to escape."

British spy Ian Fleming admired the tenacity of Stephenson in ferreting out these moles. "Bill Stephenson worked himself almost to death during the war, carrying out undercover operations and often dangerous assignments (they culminated with the Gouzenko case that put Fuchs in the bag)," wrote Fleming.

The revelations from Gouzenko and Bentley raised a nagging question: Just how high up did the Russian infiltration of the US government reach? Counterintelligence security measures—meant to detect double agents—were generally weak during the war. The Roosevelt administration was hesitant to upset the Soviets, who bore the brunt of the Nazi attacks in Eastern Europe and were so crucial to winning.

Roosevelt ignored some early warnings himself. From the British, he heard suspicions about Harry Dexter White, Assistant Secretary of the Treasury and a longtime adviser. In 1941, Lord Halifax, the British ambassador in Washington, discussed the White matter during a private meeting with Roosevelt.

"Mr. President, there is a highly placed Russian agent in your organization," the British diplomat warned.

Roosevelt asked for the spy's name.

"Harry Dexter White," replied Lord Halifax.

FDR rejected it out of hand. He felt such a betrayal by his friend couldn't be true.

"Why, I've known Harry White for a long time—[that's] impossible," Roosevelt responded. "Now, what did you want to see me about?"

Five years later, rumors escalated once again when White was nominated by Truman and approved by the Senate in February 1946 to become the next US director of the International Monetary Fund, a key institution in rebuilding the world after the war. White remained in that post for more than a year, while suspicions about him came to a boil.

White's name arose at congressional hearings focused on alleged Communist infiltration within the US government, part of the so-called "McCarthy era." Without strong proof, Bentley accused White of being part of an undercover spy ring within the American government that had provided information and documents to the Soviets during the war. White suffered a heart attack immediately after testifying at a House Un-American Activities Committee hearing, where he adamantly denied Bentley's charges. He died days afterward at age fifty-five.

White's disloyalty became even clearer years later. Decrypted Soviet archive messages, made public as part of the Venona Project by the US Justice Department, identified White as "LAWYER" and other code names in his dealings with the Russians. Documents show White met with high-level Russian spies at people's homes and in his car. He discussed matters of US policy and information he gleaned as Treasury's liaison with the OSS spy agency.

Family and supporters claimed White didn't provide any valuable information and was trying to be helpful to the Soviets as an ally. But more recent scholars offer a darker conclusion.

"There is no explaining away that White knew very well that his continued contact with the Soviet underground was potentially dangerous for him," historian R. Bruce Craig, a White biographer, wrote in 2004. "The Venona decrypts provide convincing corroborating evidence about the general nature and extent of the Soviet espionage activities in North America, and document Harry Dexter White's specific role in the Communist conspiracy."

After the Gouzenko case, Stephenson returned to New York to say his goodbyes. He'd already begun plans to dismantle the British Security Coordination offices—the secret agency he put together under Churchill's command—so that its doors at Rockefeller Center would close by mid-1946.

At that time, Stephenson declined to talk about his triumphs. He felt bound by his own personal code of honor, as well as the United Kingdom's Official Secrets Acts. He even refused to comment about the highly publicized Gouzenko defection case, where his actions were so important.

"It is not so generally known that but for the intervention at a critical moment of another Canadian, who never sought the limelight, Igor Gouzenko might not have been alive to tell his dramatic story," Hyde contended.

Stephenson slowly made some concessions to history. He didn't publish his official papers in bestselling volumes, as Churchill did after the war, earning himself a fortune in the process. Proud of the extraordinary work of the BSC, however, Stephenson commissioned a book-length narrative of all they achieved. Given the controversial nature of his spy agency, including potential illegal actions within the United States, Stephenson decided in 1944 to ship all the BSC records at night in an armed security convoy to Camp X in his native Canada. They would serve as the basis for this BSC account.

The secret history would be written by a small group of staffers, including Roald Dahl, building on an earlier study prepared by Hyde. In the last months of the war, Dahl found himself sent to Camp X to work on the manuscript. Stephenson felt the early drafts by his former deputy Dick Ellis were dry and too academic. He asked Dahl to add more human detail to this narrative, which made some parts read like a spy thriller.

However, Dahl was soon bored at lonely, remote Camp X—by then not much more than a storage site for records. It was too far from the high life he'd enjoyed in Washington and Manhattan.

"I wrote a little bit of crap," Dahl recalled, "and then thought, 'I'm not going to do this, it's an historian's job.'" He called and complained to Stephenson, who agreed to let him come back to Rockefeller Center. By February 1946, Dahl was headed home to England.

The BSC history was meant to be released in the distant future, long after Stephenson was dead. By then, the official tale of these spies and their covert actions would no longer have any immediate legal consequence or cause security risks, but would make clear the record.

Only a few copies of the final version of the BSC history were printed. They were kept secured and locked away from public review. Fatefully, Stephenson said he ordered the top secret files, loaded with code names and secret operations, destroyed. Virtually all of the existing records were soon gone, impossible to recover.

"We had to improvise," Stephenson later explained about his actions, "and anyhow we burned everything."

The secret BSC history itself wouldn't be revealed publicly for another fifty years.

In those last days at Rockefeller Center, Stephenson received well wishes from numerous figures, including some with whom he'd had bitter disputes.

"When the full story can be told I am quite certain that your contribution will be among the foremost in having brought victory finally to the united nations cause," wrote the FBI's Hoover, constrained by the same secrecy as Stephenson.

In November 1946, the US Presidential Medal of Merit, then the nation's highest civilian honor, was awarded at a small ceremony held inside Stephenson's apartment suite at the Dorset Hotel. It was the same place where he'd once shared drinks and bon mots with Cuneo and Ian Fleming. Representing the president was William Donovan, now a major general, who felt tremendous gratitude toward his Canadian friend.

Donovan pinned the medal on Stephenson and gave him a photograph of himself, with an inscription thanking the BSC spymaster for helping to create America's first intelligence agency. A small newspaper article about the award appeared in the *New York Times*—mentioning Stephenson for the first time after so many years of war and espionage—but no interview was granted. True to his word, Stephenson remained invisible as much as he could.

But the insiders knew of his impact. Buckingham Palace had already recognized Stephenson's extraordinary contributions by knighting him in the New Year Honours list in 1945. When Churchill reviewed the list of honorees, he made note of Stephenson's name and wrote, "This one is dear to my heart."

From today's available records, it's not clear if Cuneo attended any of these Stephenson ceremonies, though it's likely he was among those at the private Dorset Hotel event. Stephenson had tried to return Cuneo's loyalty with a significant gesture.

When Churchill came to New York in March 1946, after making his famous "Iron Curtain" speech in Missouri, Stephenson tried to set up a meeting between Cuneo and the former prime minister. The correspondence about Cuneo is now in the Churchill archival records in Cambridge, England.

"Before leaving New York, I suggest you might find it of interest to see 'A,'" Stephenson said in a telegram to Churchill sent from Jamaica, where the spymaster would make his future home. In this missive, Cuneo's name remained a secret, identified only by the letter *A*.

Stephenson further explained to the former prime minister about "A," that "he is a New York Attorney, one of Britain's staunchest and most helpful friends throughout the war." It also described Cuneo's influence in the United States, including his ties to "certain of the most widely read newspaper columnists and radio commentators in the country," and with certain minority groups.

"The associations, combined with boundless energy and shrewd ability in the handling of delicate situations, gave him ready entrée into the White House during the Administration of the late President Roosevelt," Stephenson recalled. He assured Churchill that "A" still had sway with President Truman and remained a big proponent of Anglo-American unity.

A follow-up letter to Churchill was sent from Rockefeller Center by one of Stephenson's assistants, Elinore Little, a close BSC friend of Margaret Watson, who was dating Cuneo by that time. That follow-up letter, also in Churchill's archives, is much more direct. It refers to Cuneo by name.

"If Mr. Churchill should wish a meeting arranged with Mr. Cuneo," Stephenson said in this note, "I should be very pleased to help if he will telephone me."

There are no other records indicating if Cuneo ever met Churchill during his stay at the Waldorf Astoria in Manhattan. While in town, Churchill gave a luncheon speech defending his views, attended a Broadway play and posed for a painting with his wife, Clementine.

But unlike Cuneo's wartime visit to London, circumstances in New York apparently never allowed for a meeting with Cuneo, the spy identified as "A," and the former prime minister, credited by history with saving Western civilization. Nevertheless, for many years after, Cuneo remained an admirer of Churchill's legacy and a lasting friend of Bill Stephenson.

32

THE CENTER OF EVERYTHING

Tim was not sure how best to play Ernest Cuneo. After three months of asking questions, he had come to think of Cuneo as somehow the center of everything; certainly he kept cropping up in the oddest places... He was also involved, somehow, with British intelligence and the American interventionists. He was said to be close to J. Edgar Hoover of the FBI, also to the country's other powerful journalist, Walter Winchell.

"I'm Drew's legal adviser." Cuneo ordered chipped beef on toast; inspired by Mrs. Nesbitt's cuisine, Tim did the same.

"'Adviser' is a safer word than 'lawyer,'" Cuneo chuckled. "Drew is sued for libel about once a week, and now that he's on the radio he's sued for slander too. The lawsuits never stop. Luckily, he loves a fight, good Quaker that he is. I give him advice on how to win the suits. I also tend to pick up odds and ends of information that are useful to people."

—Gore Vidal, *The Golden Age*, a 2000 novel

War changed Ernest Cuneo and his worldview. He was no longer the progressive New Deal lawyer who in the 1930s filed ACLU legal briefs supporting the Loyalists in the Spanish Civil War. He became more critical of the Soviet Union, certainly more than other American liberals who envisioned living in peace with Stalin. He now viewed America's Communist wartime ally with greater suspicion.

Cuneo's eyes were opened by all that he'd witnessed working with Stephenson's BSC and Donovan's OSS. He found himself more aligned with the Churchillian internationalist view rather than the old US isolationists or the naive pro-Russian rhetoric of someone like Vice President Henry Wallace.

In Cuneo's view, Stalin waged a constant diplomatic war against British and American allies to serve his long-term agenda. The Soviet leader, he said, "insisted on a second front in France, resisted Churchill's plan for an allied attack across the Balkans, thus seizing Middle Europe and East Germany for Russia."

With the start of this new Cold War in 1946, Cuneo worried the British Lion was being replaced by the Russian Bear.

"Stalin was looking for power vacuums to fill and he found them beyond his wildest expectations," Cuneo later wrote. "Capitalizing on the deep desire of the American people for world peace, Stalin launched a vast propaganda and diplomatic offense to get the United States to disarm unilaterally. It succeeded. The United States 'brought the boys home,' demobilized its armies, dismantled its air force and mothballed its fleets."

On a personal level, this change in Cuneo's perspective toward the Soviet Union was most reflected in his postwar relationship with Drew Pearson, the nationally known radio commentator and newspaper columnist.

For years, Pearson, his old teacher from Columbia, had been a valued guide through the byzantine world of Washington politics and the media. Throughout the war, Cuneo served as Pearson's lawyer and provided many insights, including the blockbuster news tip about Patton slapping a soldier.

Although the two men had vastly different backgrounds, they remained loyal friends. When the Chief of Naval Operations gave Cuneo difficulty about press coverage, Pearson lashed out at the offending admiral in his column and "gave him very rough sledding for the rest of the war," Cuneo recalled.

Toward the war's end, however, Pearson and Cuneo began to differ. While Cuneo remained supportive of the British government, Pearson veered toward anti-colonialism. He expressed strong support for India's independence from the British Empire. In December 1944, his "Washington Merry-Go-Round" column also published a US State Department message that quoted Churchill instructing his British general in Athens to shoot leftist demonstrators if they got out of hand.

Churchill complained bitterly about Pearson's exposé. Under Great Britain's Official Secrets Acts, Pearson's publication of leaked secret documents might well have landed him in jail if he were British—but in America, he received plaudits and a bigger audience.

"Drew Pearson's article is a specimen of the kind of stuff that fits in with the campaign of the OSS against the British," Churchill complained to William Donovan, essentially accusing the then OSS chief of involvement. As a result, the home office in London instructed Stephenson to place a spy on Pearson to discover his source.

Roald Dahl, the dapper BSC agent then stationed in Washington, received the assignment. As he did with Charles Marsh and others, Dahl ingratiated himself with Pearson. He was invited to the columnist's home repeatedly. "We became very good friends and we exchanged information openly," Dahl recalled. "He wanted it for his column, and he knew I wanted it for other reasons."

Undoubtedly, this smoothing of Anglo-American feathers benefitted Cuneo, a friend of both Pearson and Dahl. But Ernie realized a bigger schism was emerging. His two major media clients—Winchell and Pearson—once unified in supporting America's entry into the war, were now drifting apart on the question of Russia. "On this critical point of foreign policy, Winchell and Pearson took different directions," he said.

Winchell, a weathervane for public opinion, became increasingly critical of "the Commies," his Runyonesque phrase for the Soviet Union. "This is the truth—during the war we did not receive the cooperation of the Kremlin," Winchell falsely told his huge radio audience. "On the contrary, they distrusted us completely."

Even though he provided political information to him, Cuneo felt Winchell was fundamentally an entertainer holding court from the Stork Club. He wasn't a serious political commentator, not compared to Pearson.

"He was a Broadway-Showbiz headliner, brilliant and honest, but essentially a primitive, streetwise street-fighter," Cuneo said of Winchell. "Drew, by contrast, was a first-class scholar, a Phi Beta."

Cuneo believed the preachy, didactic tone to Pearson's reporting reflected his background as a Quaker (he used "Thou" and "Thee" around his home) and the summers young Drew spent with his distinguished father on the Chautauqua circuit, a popular Christian cultural fair that stressed elevating the spirit and intellect of the masses.

"At the slightest call of 'Onward and Upward,' Drew took off like a homesick angel," Cuneo described, "eager to breathe the rarified atmosphere of pure culture."

While Pearson wasn't a Communist, Cuneo said, the utopian dream of world peace, throwing off the yoke of colonial imperialism, appealed to him as a journalistic crusader. Pearson always perceived the Russians as "underdogs" rather than oppressors. He had supported Vice President Wallace and aligned himself with the more left-leaning members of Roosevelt's inner circle, such as Harry Hopkins, who felt Russia could be trusted.

However, after five years of world war, trust in Russia wasn't the takeaway for Cuneo. Through his experience as a spy, he

knew of the Soviets' malevolent behavior, including their espionage in the United States. In the postwar world, he felt the
US couldn't afford to be naive or weak. Stalin's aggressive actions would only get worse.

Pearson and his backers "did not conceive of Communist
Russia as a totalitarian Empire, expanding its domain in the
same manner as the Nazis, as intent on a Communist world empire as much as the Nazis," Cuneo wrote. "A host of very good
people, leading American citizens in fact, did not conceive of
Russians or Communism as evil. Many, in fact, thought of the
Russian Communists as the great liberators."

Cuneo's differences with Pearson could only be wallpapered
over in legal documents and hefty fees for so long. "This impending war between Drew and me distressed me terribly," he
recalled. "Drew was like my older brother. But the issue had to
be met: Drew was damned if he was going to see imperialism-
colonialism perpetuated and I was damned if I was going to see
the British American alliance broken."

Their biggest dispute involved David Karr, a member of Pearson's team of investigators.

Based on his own contacts, Cuneo informed his old friend
that Karr was a known liar and suspected to be a Soviet spy. He
told Pearson that Karr was listed by both British intelligence
and the FBI as an "outright" Russian double agent "of highest
effectiveness."

Pearson immediately came to Karr's defense. "Drew just
couldn't believe it," Cuneo recalled.

Then in his early twenties, Karr certainly didn't seem like a
double agent. He appeared "an utterly winsome fellow in per-
petual good humor and a mind as fast as a jackrabbit," Cuneo
recalled. "He was super-intelligent, thoroughly knowledgeable,
flexible as an eel, and he had the nerve of a bank robber."

Pearson admired Karr's skill at ferreting out information from
various sources on Capitol Hill, even if he bent a few ethical

rules. One story had Karr sitting in the stalls of a men's room, eavesdropping on State Department officials chatting as they relieved themselves and washed their hands.

Karr viewed Pearson in heroic terms, earning the older man's loyalty—however misplaced it may be. Pearson didn't want to heed Cuneo's warning. After so many years of successfully avoiding libel suits and fending off presidential criticism for reporting the truth, Cuneo argued, why invite disaster with a young man who could give his enemies a sword?

One sign of trouble could be found in Hoover's files. In 1944, Karr's false claim that he worked for Vice President Wallace prompted an FBI "impersonation investigation," reports show. When agents interviewed Wallace, he denied Karr was ever an employee. Before the FBI left, however, Wallace mentioned that "he liked David Karr personally and frankly admired him because of his continuous action on behalf of liberalism." Karr escaped any charges.

The previous year, Karr told a House Un-American Activities committee that he was an FBI informant, which also wasn't true. Soon after, Karr resigned from his government job with the Office of War Information and joined Pearson's team of investigators as a "legman."

At a time of increasing paranoia, the FBI investigation found that Karr had been a reporter for the Communist Party USA's *Daily Worker* publication and still had contacts with other suspected Soviet spies in the United States. Years later, the Venona Project's analysis of decrypted Soviet messages revealed that Karr provided information in 1944 to the NKVD, the Soviet spy agency. Long before that confirmation was possible, though, Cuneo decided he must force the issue with Pearson.

"In a last desperate effort," Cuneo said, he contacted Pearson's wife, Luvie. He convinced her that a "showdown" about Karr was needed for her husband's sake. Cuneo told her that he

considered Karr "without exception, the most amoral, unprin-
cipled and faithless man I have ever known."

Eventually, Cuneo met with Pearson along with the young
man in question. The political schism between them broke into
full view.

"Drew said he was sick of having people called Commies,"
Cuneo recalled, "and if we didn't like it, we could both go."

Karr stayed.

"I never hated to fight anyone more than I did Drew, but we
sure went at it," Cuneo recalled. Slowly, Cuneo disengaged from
Pearson as a client, but still considered him a friend.

Cuneo's relationship with Winchell also changed as the
Truman administration took root in Washington. Like others
identified as FDR insiders, Cuneo and America's most famous
columnist no longer received the favored treatment they once
had at the White House—no presidential exclusives and no political ammunition to fire at enemies.

Truman's appeasement of the segregationist Southern Dix-
iecrats in the name of party unity appalled Cuneo. "He's like
a man whom you tell, 'I've just shot your two brothers in the
back,' and he says, 'That's fine, let's all be friends,'" Cuneo said.

Stung by Truman's rebuke, Winchell eventually erupted before the 1952 Democratic Party's national convention. Given
the corruption allegations swirling around some Democrats,
Winchell joked the conclave should be held at Alcatraz, the notorious prison in San Francisco Bay.

Pearson was curious about Winchell's furious split with Truman's Democrats and his support for such right-wingers as Senator Joseph McCarthy and General Douglas MacArthur. So
Pearson called his old friend Cuneo and asked why.

"Cuneo is frank to say that it's because: 'we're not consulted,'"
Pearson recorded in his diary. "In other words, Roosevelt used
to get Winchell down [to the White House] and hold his hand

once a month so that Walter became his great companion. Now Cuneo can't get near the White House or in to see the Secretary of State."

Pearson, ever the investigator, sensed there was more at play than just presidential access.

"I think the real reason for Winchell's ire goes deeper, and back to the fact that Truman once called him a k★★★ [an anti-Semitic slur]," Pearson surmised. "Also Walter sees which way the wind is blowing and wants to get on the bandwagon."

The days of Winchell and Pearson—the double-barreled propaganda machine—were slowly coming to an end for Cuneo. He had been a brilliant intelligence agent during the war, able to weaponize and influence public opinion through the mass media. He had helped Stephenson establish his spy headquarters at Rockefeller Center and served as the official liaison for Donovan in creating America's first spy agency. Though lacking any major standing, Cuneo had learned to act as a go-between and fixer in a maze of government egos and competitions over turf. He even managed to meet two of his heroes, Roosevelt and Churchill, before the war was through.

Unknown to virtually everyone, Cuneo handled a remarkable number of clandestine missions without detection. The history books, like the one prepared by the BSC, would allude to his actions but never mention him by name. He was sworn to secrecy and anonymity. Even if he were inclined to talk about his spy experience, Cuneo felt he still couldn't tell anyone about it.

33

A SHOT IN THE DARK

After the war, Ian Fleming proved a lasting friend to Ernest Cuneo. They'd met as spies at Rockefeller Center before Pearl Harbor and stayed in touch throughout the conflict—an unlikely alliance of two men from distant countries and backgrounds.

When the fighting finished, they felt at a loss, even though their side had won. Both still craved the intrigue of their spy work, its sheer intensity on a worldwide stage. They were surprised to find within themselves a sense of emptiness.

"We almost suffered emotional 'bends' the day the war ended—tension went out like a power line turned off," Cuneo recalled. "Like it or leave it, aside from its horrors, you missed the frightful challenge of war. I think Fleming missed it as much as most; he seemed both grumpy and disconsolate."

Now middle-aged, both men set out to find a place for themselves in this new peacetime existence. Nothing would ever match the thrill of their experiences in wartime espionage, which had drawn upon so many of their inventive skills. But in the years to come, both Fleming and Cuneo would try, in their own shared way, to replicate this sense of being spies in a new Cold War atmosphere.

When he came to New York, Fleming still shared drinks and

laughs with Cuneo at their favorite Manhattan bars and restaurants, just as they had done before. By 1946, however, things had changed. Bill Stephenson had moved out of his spacious suite at the Dorset Hotel. He now spent much of winter in the Caribbean warmth of Jamaica. Most of the tensions and rivalries between intelligence agencies, kept at bay during the war, resurfaced as the battles ended.

"Bill Stephenson was gone and much of the British-American rapport evaporated with his departure," Cuneo recalled. "This deeply affected my British-American friends. Fleming and I were no exception… I discovered this when he was more or less savagely attacking the White House. I took on Buckingham Palace, deriding the monarchy as a fantastic anachronism."

Saddled with enormous debts, the British Empire had been seriously depleted by the years-long conflict, leaving its economy and cities in ruin. It seemed as if the magnificent United Kingdom would never be the same again.

In his flippant New Yorkese, Cuneo suggested that the trooping of colors at Buckingham Palace, once a symbol of imperial power, was now just a tourist attraction.

"No, Ernie," Fleming insisted, his eyes reflecting all the sadness of those who had risked and lost their lives for the Crown, including members of his own family. "It's a ballet, maybe, but a beautiful one."

While most of his teasing with Fleming was in a good-natured fashion, Cuneo realized he'd gone too far with a comment about the Royal Navy's wartime reliance on dirty old lend-lease ships from the United States. "The Royal Navy was too close to [Ian's] heart for thrusting, even by banter," Cuneo wrote.

Fleming had suffered terrible personal losses during the war. His younger brother, Michael Fleming, died from his wounds following the retreat from Dunkirk in 1940. It was an awful reminder of the way their father, Major Valentine Fleming, had been killed on the Western Front in World War I.

Fleming had also endured tragedy in his romantic life. In March 1944, a beautiful young woman Ian had dated, Muriel Wright, was killed during an air raid in London. Authorities asked him to identify her body. Fleming told friends that Muriel had been the love of his life. He predicted he'd never marry.

Instead, Fleming engaged in a number of affairs with women whom he treated in a cool and sometimes masochistic way. "He took elaborate steps to make sure that no sexual relationship ever developed to the point where he had to give anything of himself away," said biographer John Pearson. Fleming pursued and seduced women with no promise of permanence. As he told one paramour, "You must treat our love as a glass of champagne."

Unlike his American friend Cuneo, Fleming wasn't inclined toward domestic life. "I couldn't bear my wife's eyes gradually going dull after the honeymoon and only lighting up again when she talked to her friends," Fleming wrote.

By contrast, Cuneo created a new life for himself with his wartime lover, Margaret Watson, who'd worked for the British Security Coordination as an aide to Stephenson. Both were intent on starting a family together.

Margaret wasn't like the other young Canadian women who went home dutifully to Winnipeg after serving on Churchill's spy staff at Rockefeller Center. As the war wound down, Margaret's younger sister Jean in Winnipeg married a returning officer from the Royal Canadian Air Force. Watson's widowed mother and other family members still lived in her remote hometown, so different from the vast metropolis she discovered with Cuneo. But Margaret decided to stay in New York.

On October 22, 1946, a week before her thirty-second birthday, Margaret married forty-one-year-old Ernie. They took up residence at 2 Sutton Place South in Manhattan, an elegant apartment building with views of the East River.

This second marriage for Cuneo seemed far different from his previous one with Zilpha Bentley, whom he'd met as a Columbia football star bursting with energy. Now Cuneo appeared much older and out of shape. The life-or-death burdens of the past five years felt like, in his words, "a heavy overcoat" that he'd only recently taken off, after the end of the war's stresses.

"War has been a terrible education for me; my hair has turned snow white," he observed. "The tension was so high that even the forearms felt like cables of strong piano wire."

In victorious postwar America, Ernie was now an accomplished, well-connected lawyer capable of earning a small fortune. In private papers, he described himself as "very happily married" to a "splendid" woman.

The following summer of 1947, Margaret journeyed with her new husband to Bermuda, for a kind of honeymoon where they were joined by some of their wartime compatriots. On their way home, manifest records show, they flew in a small plane with former OSS boss William Donovan, Sir William Stephenson and his wife, Mary, arriving together at LaGuardia Airport.

In Jamaica, Cuneo enjoyed visiting with Stephenson at his "Hillerton" mountaintop estate overlooking Montego Bay. Stephenson invited Cuneo to ride the mountain trails on his prize horse, a chestnut-colored beast named Winston.

When Cuneo jumped on, the horse bolted. Winston ran around, up and down the mountain, until exhausted and brought under control.

"You say this is the best horse on the island?" Cuneo said accusingly when dismounting.

Stephenson burst out laughing. "Yes sir!" he replied. "Winston is the best *polo pony* in Jamaica."

In the succeeding years, the Cuneos' two children, Sandra and

Jonathan, came along for repeat trips. They were familiar enough with the knighted spymaster to call him "Uncle Bill" and his wife "Lady Mary." In messages to his pals, Cuneo shared his delight in becoming a father.

"Dear Walter, Many thanks for your kind wire," Cuneo sent to Winchell via Western Union in November 1948, after Sandra's birth. "Baby has Margaret's long body and my head. There is simply astonishing resemblance to me. I will anticipate you by saying it must be a hell of a handicap for a girl. Matter of fact she is very cute. Regards, Ernie."

As a private attorney, Cuneo earned enough money that the couple eventually purchased an airy two-story summer home in upstate New York, near the Vermont border and the Green Mountains. A short ride from their place was Black Hole Hollow Farm, a nine-hundred-acre property resembling an English country estate. It was owned by Ivar Bryce, Fleming's childhood friend and a member of Stephenson's spy staff, and his third wife, Marie-Josephine "Jo" Hartford, heiress of the A&P supermarket chain. For Fleming, summer visits to Vermont with his two friends soon became an annual ritual.

"I thought you might like to walk to the top of Goose Egg," Fleming said cheerily, early one morning with a knock at Cuneo's front door. As if he were Sir Baden-Powell, Fleming trekked up the large hill like a good scout, with his groggy, heavyset friend following along.

At certain points, Fleming stopped and pointed out the peaks and vistas of the Adirondacks. They reminded him of Scotland's beauty, with scenes of mountains, lakes and endless pine forests in upstate New York that he would later recall in his writing.

When they reached the top, Cuneo ridiculed Fleming's cockamamie theory that it took more energy to descend a hill than climb up. As if silly schoolboys, they raced down Goose Egg to prove their point. "Like two whirling dervishes," Cuneo recalled, "sweated and happy...laughing like mad."

When they reached the bottom, Fleming turned serious.

"Let me tell you, Ernie, I was worried..." Ian said, pausing for Cuneo to wonder why. "About how the hell I'd ever get a mule like you down the mountain if you had broken a leg."

In the 1950s, Cuneo went into business with his wartime spy pals, Ivar Bryce and Ian Fleming, running a newspaper syndicate. Bryce, a childhood friend of Fleming's, was wealthy and had a summer place near Cuneo's home in upstate New York, which Fleming visited occasionally. Cuneo and Fleming went on a cross-country tour of the US that informed the James Bond novels.

JONATHAN CUNEO

Summers of laughter and good times helped solidify the friendship between Cuneo, Fleming and Bryce, who banded together in a business venture. In 1951, Cuneo convinced Bryce, a man of considerable wealth, to take over the North American Newspaper Alliance (NANA), a long-established news syndicate that had fallen on hard times with the advent of television. "I thought it would be rather fun to get involved with," Bryce explained.

NANA had an impressive legacy. Ernest Hemingway wrote for it during the Spanish Civil War. Ira Wolfert won a Pulitzer Prize for his international reporting during World War II fighting in the Solomon Islands. With his newspaper experience and wide array of contacts in New York, Cuneo believed he could turn around NANA's fortunes, bolstered by Bryce's financial backing.

As an added bonus, they offered Fleming the job of heading NANA's European office based in London, where he already worked with the Kemsley newspaper group. Cuneo assured his friends that owning a media company was a convincing way to meet any influential person they wanted, especially in the intelligence community.

Nothing compared to the satisfaction Fleming derived from being a wartime spy, but the NANA job gave more focus to his career filled with wanderlust, after trying his hand variously as a naval officer, stockbroker, banker and travel writer. During the anti-Communist McCarthy era, Fleming suggested that celebrated British writer Rebecca West write for NANA, getting interviews with former Soviet spies Elizabeth Bentley and Whittaker Chambers, who testified in the perjury trial of Alger Hiss.

"She [West] sees a Communist under every single bed and to have her interviewing Bentley and Chambers would surely be a great feather in your cap," Fleming wrote to Cuneo with his usual cheek.

Among the three friends, the NANA business became like a boys' club fraternity, reflecting their interests in sex and spying. In a note to Cuneo, Fleming salaciously described "a pretty secretary," who sat on the knees of NANA executives at one meeting, as a "Turkish sandwich." From his cushy NANA office in the New York Times Building, Cuneo joked back with another sexual reference. "As [Alfred] Kinsey could have told you, it is a hell of a lot more fun to take a girl to a hotel than to go off to a cave by yourself."

However, improving NANA's fortunes proved difficult, leaving Fleming frustrated when his suggestions weren't adopted. "I have put forward a lot of excellent ideas in a constant stream of

offerings, none of which have been favored on the grounds that
they cost a few dollars," Fleming complained to Bryce. "Even
the accreditation of all my correspondence to NANA has been
fraught for me with nothing but brickbats."

Business difficulties, though, didn't impact their friendship,
especially in the wintertime, when both Fleming and Bryce
traveled to Jamaica. During the war, the BSC's Stephenson had
assigned Bryce to monitor Nazi influence in Latin America,
with Bryce running missions from Jamaica, where he had a
beach house. In 1941, Fleming became enamored by this tropical paradise while accompanying Admiral Godfrey, the Royal
Navy's top spy, to a wartime conference.

"When we have won this blasted war, I am going to live in
Jamaica," Fleming promised his pal Bryce. "Just live in Jamaica
and lap it up, and swim in the sea and write books."

True to his word, Fleming, with money from his family in-
heritance, bought a sandy twelve-acre parcel along the beachfront in 1945 with Bryce's help. Fleming built a new home which
he called Goldeneye, named for the spy and sabotage mission
Operation Goldeneye, one of several highlights of Fleming's intelligence career during the war. It was near Stephenson's house
in Montego Bay.

During a tropical sojourn in January 1952, Fleming turned
his attention to writing a spy novel, an ambition he had talked
about for years. In effect, he created an alter ego, transforming
his knowledge of international espionage and his own wartime
missions into memorable Cold War fiction.

The hero of his novel would be a British secret agent, inspired by various real-life figures—notably Stephenson for his
bold moves, inventive killing gadgets, and coolheaded fearless-
ness. This fictional secret agent would have a boss called "M"
not unlike his own Royal Navy boss Admiral Godfrey. Fleming called his protagonist James Bond—"the simplest, dullest,
plainest sounding name I could find," he later explained—with

a fascinating world of evil characters, beautiful women and daring, violent plots swirling around him.

Bond's suave, devil-may-care attitude would recall Duško Popov, the elegant wartime double agent who fooled the German Abwehr by playing for big stakes at a Portuguese casino. In the novel, entitled *Casino Royale*, Fleming evoked similar, fictionalized scenes of Bond playing high-stakes baccarat in an attempt to bankrupt and vanquish a Cold War evildoer.

"The clues to the Second World War are everywhere, yet Bond is fighting an emphatically new war, against a looming communist threat," writer Ben Macintyre observed of Fleming's work. "Once again, Fleming drew on reality and reshaped it to lend credibility to this imagined combat. The people, the weapons, the scenes, all carried deliberate echoes of real wartime events."

One tellingly dramatic scene in the novel took place at Rockefeller Center, where Bond shot and killed "a Japanese cipher expert cracking our codes." It was Bond's first deadly assignment, earning him the code name of "007" and a license to kill.

This scene was an embellished version of Stephenson's real-life late-night break-in to steal cipher codes at the Japanese consulate in 1941, in which no one was killed but Navy intelligence agent Fleming was thrilled to watch as a tag-along. (James Bond is "a highly romanticized version of the true spy," Fleming later explained. "The real thing is... William Stephenson.")

In the novel, Bond placed himself in an adjacent skyscraper and aimed his Remington rifle, with a telescopic sight and silencer, at the unsuspecting cipher expert. With an initial shot, another British agent first shattered a thirty-sixth-floor window of the Japanese consulate (another fictional tip of the hat to Stephenson, whose own Rockefeller Center office was on the thirty-sixth floor). Then, as the cipher expert turned to gape out the broken window, Bond fired away from four stories above.

"They have tough windows at Rockefeller Center to keep the

noise out," Bond explained matter-of-factly to the reader about his maiden assassination. "It worked very well."

Fleming didn't feel that way about his book. *Casino Royale* almost never appeared. After writing it in a rush in Jamaica, Fleming tucked the manuscript away when he returned to London and considered abandoning it. He called his novel a "dreadful oafish opus." Eventually, an editor friend and Fleming's older brother, a successful travel writer, convinced a publisher to take it on.

Near publication, Fleming urged Cuneo to promote *Casino Royale* in Walter Winchell's column. He also enlisted another British spy friend, Roald Dahl, in his publicity effort. "If you get a chance of putting in a word with the TV tycoons for *Casino*, I shall be very grateful," he wrote. "Money is despicable stuff but it buys Renoirs."

Like winning some bet out of the blue, Fleming's novel-writing career was launched. Sooner than they ever imagined, the real-life spy stories that Ian shared with his pals Ernie and Ivar—mentioned only discreetly over drinks and laughs in New York, Vermont and Jamaica—would now be known to millions, albeit through the veneer of fiction.

Fleming had turned his wartime secrets into art—and cash.

34

TRIP TO THE ANGELS

Cuneo encouraged his friend Ian Fleming to turn their real-life war-time experiences into the fictional James Bond tales. For one movie treatment, Fleming suggested Cuneo play a mobster—an idea that offended Cuneo's Italian American sensibilities. Actor Sean Connery played the first James Bond in film, and the series became one of the greatest movie franchises in history.

Aboard the sleek Super Chief train—hurtling through the Midwest on its way from Chicago to Los Angeles—Ian Fleming wanted to get a sense of the heartland, with his friend Ernest Cuneo as a guide.

Cuneo wasn't a world chronicler like Alexis de Tocqueville

or a traveling hipster like Jack Kerouac. But he'd promised to take his British novelist pal on this roadshow across America at his request, as if they were on some grand expedition.

"Fleming was at this time all but unknown," Cuneo recalled. "He was, in his own words, 'waffling about' not even conceiving remotely of the fame to come."

On this November 1954 ride, with a notebook in hand, Fleming wrote down as many insights as possible, background notes for future James Bond escapades. As always, he was a stickler for details.

"We were halfway to Iowa before the Super Chief's stewards had fully absorbed their instructions on how to make his Martinis," Cuneo said, recalling Fleming's routines. "He was off at every stop through New Mexico and Arizona, talking to the men serving the train, walking briskly around the desert architecture stations, taking mental photographs by the score."

The year before, Fleming's first novel, *Casino Royale*, enjoyed some initial success in Britain. His new novel, *Live and Let Die*, had just been published, and his third in the Bond series, *Moonraker*, would come out in 1955. But sales in America were so far disappointing.

Like a good intelligence officer, Fleming resolved to improve in this foreign land through more reconnaissance.

"I would love to see Las Vegas and then perhaps the Hollywood world very briefly," Fleming wrote to Cuneo, two months before they departed. "I would also very much like to make the trans-continental trip by train in the luxury to which you and I are accustomed and then perhaps fly back. What do you think of all of this? "

Fleming was aware of Cuneo's pressing business matters at home with NANA, but argued the trip would pay personal dividends. "It would take you away from your desk for about ten days and I wondered if you can spare the time to chaperone me. I do hope so, as my education is now only incomplete with respect to the West Coast of America."

It wasn't a hard bargain. Though now married with two small children, Cuneo was only too delighted to reunite with his wartime spy buddies, Fleming and Ivar Bryce, for an extended holiday. They rallied at Bryce's Vermont home near the Saratoga Springs racetrack, where Ivar's wife owned and raced thoroughbred horses. From there, Fleming and Cuneo journeyed to Chicago, as the first step in their sightseeing tour.

For many Brits, the Windy City was known as the land of Al Capone. Churchill famously posed for a much-publicized photo holding a tommy gun, just like the notorious mobster. When Fleming arrived with Cuneo, he expressed eagerness to visit one particular site on Chicago's North Side.

"Off we go to America's great shrine—the scene of the St. Valentine's Day Massacre!" Fleming yelped, joyously like a kid.

Cuneo didn't share his enthusiasm. He and other respectable Italian Americans he'd known, like Fiorello LaGuardia, resented this gangland slur, implying that anyone with their shared heritage was somehow a Mafia criminal. Cuneo recalled that Fleming "at once discerned that he had something in mind that would infuriate me."

Cuneo refused the offer to visit. "Not me," he growled. He insisted Fleming go by himself if he must pay homage to this mob shootout scene. "But before you do, let's drop in at a little place they have here."

They visited the Chicago Art Institute, home to a large collection of Impressionist and other paintings comparable to the Louvre's. Cuneo wanted to make sure Fleming knew the Midwest wasn't entirely made up of cowboys and hicks.

"Fleming was entranced, completely enveloped by the masterpieces," Cuneo recalled. More so than Ernie, Ian gazed at the Rembrandts and Picassos with genuine appreciation. He commented on the artistry in hushed, reverent tones as though in a cathedral.

"He forgot St. Valentine's," Cuneo recalled. "I almost had to drag him out."

Out on the street, though, Fleming's "enchantment evaporated... He went to the St. Valentine's scene—alone."

The long ride out West aboard the Super Chief—touted as "the Train of the Stars" because of the celebrities it carried out to Hollywood—provided a place for the two friends to converse. Although they were business partners in the NANA syndicate, most of their talk centered on personal affairs. As both men acknowledged, Ian's life was certainly more complicated than Ernie's.

Marriage was now part of the equation. Fleming had wed socialite Ann Charteris in 1952, shortly after he finished *Casino Royale.* "After being a bachelor for 44 years, I was on the edge of marrying and the prospect was so horrifying that I was in urgent need of some activity to take my mind off of it—so I wrote a book," Fleming later explained, seemingly in jest.

Since the late 1930s, the couple had carried on a longtime on-and-off affair while Ann was married to one man, then another. In 1944, Ann's first husband, Lord Shane O'Neill, died while fighting in Italy during the war. She then married Lord Rothermere, Esmond Harmsworth, the owner of London's *Daily Mail,* who'd also been her surreptitious lover. But that second union ended in divorce in 1951, when Rothermere realized she was seeing Fleming in Jamaica rather than Noël Coward.

Though admittedly incompatible, Ann married Ian while she was pregnant by Fleming and they moved in together in London. Their only child, Caspar, was born in August 1952, a month before Cuneo's son, Jonathan, arrived. The two pals had vowed jokingly during the war that whoever sired a son first would call him Caspar. The uncommon name was an obscure reference to a poem, "The Battle of Blenheim," about a famous victory won by Churchill's ancestor, the Duke of Marlborough.

Ian made good on the bet. His marriage, though, didn't fare as well.

"By almost any count, the Flemings' marriage was ill-fated from the first," Cuneo said years later. "There is evidence that Anne [sic] and Ian did not drift apart; they tore each other apart instead."

Yet during their train ride, Fleming spoke of his new family with hopefulness.

"I think it is possible that Ian carried the image of the ideal damsel throughout his life, and found his adult ideal in Anne," Cuneo wrote, "that Anne was the ideal superwoman, the super-sophisticate, the toast of Mayfair."

Cuneo wondered how much of James Bond's extravagant sexual conquests were a reflection of Fleming's real life. Growing up in puritanical New Jersey, Cuneo had been taught "that evil 'thoughts' were as bad as evil 'deeds.'" His own marriage to Margaret reflected more the postwar desire for domestic tranquility of the 1950s than the sexual callousness James Bond exhibited toward bikini-clad single women in the 1960s films.

"What came to Bond's mind, I assure him, would be the last to enter mine, or in fact, anyone I knew or had ever known," Cuneo told his friend. But Fleming simply laughed. To him, Bond was a creative concoction, not to be taken too seriously. He spoke with detachment about his fictional spy, the way a scientist might talk about constructing a human robot.

Both men shared a *carpe diem* perspective about the world. As young men during the war, they had witnessed tragedy and impending doom. Like passengers on a sinking ship, they assumed their existence would be short. "You might just as well have a hell of a time while the voyage lasted," Cuneo said, summarizing their view, "grinding out the juice of each day as if it were the last grape on the vine."

Fatherhood, however, noticeably changed Fleming, as it did Cuneo. "Men do not like to use the word 'love,'" Cuneo explained. "Fleming and I spoke often of our children, and neither used the term; but it was clear to me that Ian 'loved' his son Caspar deeply, more deeply, possibly, than most fathers."

Arriving in Los Angeles, the moveable feast of conversation between Cuneo and Fleming continued at a UCLA college football game. Up in the grandstands, amid the cheers and groans of the crowd, they talked philosophically about other all-American pursuits: violence, sex, and the most addicting narcotic of all in Cuneo's mind—fame.

The violence of football, with its helmeted combat in dirty gridiron trenches, could mimic the battles of war, though Cuneo knew it was nothing like the real thing. Both he and Fleming had friends and relatives impacted by war. They were well aware that their own actions were responsible, directly and indirectly, for enemy deaths.

"Fleming never killed a man with his own hand, though of course, during the war, like everyone else, we were engaged in helping to kill thousands," Cuneo said.

Death was no stranger to them. In the Great War, which claimed Fleming's much-admired father, Cuneo's older brother, Lawrence, had been "knocked unconscious by a land mine and mustard-gassed and blinded" from its effect, he recalled. "His lungs and stomach were never the same and he died young."

As the UCLA game marched on, Cuneo told his British friend about his own days playing at Columbia and for start-up franchises in the National Football League. By the 1950s, the NFL was quickly surpassing baseball as America's favorite pastime. Cuneo said the sheer action and brute force of football—"a vast spectacle" rousing a crowd—was intoxicating to any young man seeking glory.

"The popularity, the publicity, the roar and smell of the Stadium, whip him up like a shot of cocaine," he explained. "When a man can't play anymore, withdrawal of applause induces an effect akin to persecution and neglect."

Cuneo told Ian about the bad gash on his head that had forced his early retirement from the Brooklyn Dodgers, and how badly he missed the applause and the fame after his football career was over. Only after he felt "cured" of being a glory hunter—"broken the love of applause," as he explained to Fleming—could Cuneo adopt the cloak of anonymity needed to be a successful intelligence operative.

Ian gave him a quizzical look. "Fleming saw no particular reason for considering this a deep emotional experience, or if he did, he concealed it well," Cuneo recalled.

"Too bad you don't like applause," Fleming responded dryly.

Cuneo tried again. "You missed the point," he explained. "I shun applause because I like it too much. It might be like going back on dope."

"That's good," Fleming replied with a dismissive nod. "Nothing like being aware of your defects of character. A sound approach. You don't usually admit them, you know."

Cuneo grunted a simple cuss at him.

When they arrived in Southern California, the two friends visited Santa Anita racetrack, where Ernie placed a few bets on the ponies. Ian scribbled down many details in his notebook, observations stretching from the paddock to the receiving barns.

Hollywood, this playland of fantasy, also meant a discussion of sex between the two middle-aged married men, who spoke like locker-room mates. With his usual flourish, Cuneo declared to Fleming that "sex was a sport in New York, a profession in Hollywood, an art in Paris and a heavy industry in London." Ernie enjoyed coming up with aphorisms, the pithy kind that could be quoted in *Bartlett's* or a newspaper column.

Fleming jumped in, perhaps remembering his time as a spy. "And a damned nuisance in Washington," he added.

While passing through Beverly Hills, they dined at Chasen's restaurant, a favorite among celebrities. They bumped into Mert Wertheimer, a big Detroit and Miami gambling operator with a new casino in Reno, Nevada. Cuneo knew Wertheimer as an "affable and urbane" character from his days campaigning with Michigan governor Frank Murphy. In its secret files, the FBI also recognized Wertheimer as a "front man" business associate for gangster Meyer Lansky and other organized crime figures.

Intrigued by this likable rogue, Fleming immediately showered Wertheimer with questions about the inner workings of casinos.

"Do big-time gamblers have 'systems' to beat the house?" Fleming asked him.

"All the time," said Wertheimer, amused by his curiosity.

"How do you handle them?" Ian asked.

"We send a car to the airport to meet them," Wertheimer guffawed.

Fleming persisted. "How do you make your real money?"

It was the type of question that could get some wiseguy knee-capped or worse for asking. But Wertheimer, charmed by the novelist, gave him an honest answer.

"On the loser who's just going to stay until he gets even," he explained. "He's our boy."

Fleming's desire to learn more shady insider details for his spy novels took the two friends to the Los Angeles Police Department. Cuneo arranged a conversation with Captain James Hamilton, a tall, trim investigator with the LAPD's intelligence unit. Invariably, the subject turned to the hidden hand of organized crime. Cuneo cast doubt on any such notion.

"Captain, Mr. Fleming here has the usual distorted view of an Englishman," said Cuneo, a bit patronizingly, of his pal. "They believe, you know, our country is laced by organized gangs of racketeers, of tremendous wealth and enormous influence."

Hamilton frowned at Cuneo. "Don't *you*?" he asked incredulously, as if Ernie were a country bumpkin rather than a man-about-town.

"Well, no," Cuneo replied. "I just don't think you can carry on a large business on a basis of corruption." His reply contained more than a dash of naivete.

"Have you ever been to Las Vegas?" Hamilton demanded.

"No, but we're going," Cuneo said, referring to the last leg of their journey.

Delighted by this introduction, Fleming dived into a long conversation with the LA cop about all aspects of the criminal underworld. Hamilton pulled out investigative charts outlining the Mafia's hierarchical structure with its capos and soldiers, the names of each majordomo, and their different territories. "It was clear he watched Las Vegas like a hawk," Cuneo recalled.

Hamilton regaled them with gruesome details of murders his intelligence detectives had solved but "couldn't legally prove" in court. He explained how an anonymous man stationed at the airport, wearing a tourist shirt and carrying a shaving kit with a camera inside, was actually an undercover agent, who tracked and photographed the movements of each mobster arriving and departing by plane.

Their discussion about narcotics trafficking was "revolting," Cuneo remembered, but Fleming "was fascinated by the various kinds of drugs and the ingenious methods of concealing them." Ian kept scribbling these details into his notebook.

Flying into Las Vegas, America's gambling mecca carved out of the desert, the two unpacked at the Sands, the hotel casino favored by Frank Sinatra. It was run by Jack Entratter, a friendly face Cuneo knew from the Copacabana, another favorite New York nightlife spot during the war—that was, when Cuneo wasn't hanging out with Walter Winchell at the Stork Club.

Walking up to Cuneo, Entratter offered some unsolicited advice after watching him lose a hand at the blackjack table.

"You should have stood," Entratter said from behind him.

Staring down intently at his chips, Cuneo didn't look up at the stranger.

"Listen guy, if you want to play, take a couple of my chips, but for [blank] sake leave me alone," cried an annoyed Cuneo. He then turned to the stranger behind him and suddenly laughed aloud with recognition, realizing it was "Big Jack."

The casino's gregarious front man treated Cuneo and Fleming like VIPs. "He moved us into a fine suite and made available to us the private barber shop," Cuneo recalled.

Most importantly, Entratter explained to Fleming the inner workings of a big-time Las Vegas casino, with its famous entertainers, "schmaltzy" floor shows and other over-the-top offerings designed to please an American mass audience looking for a good time.

Fleming learned about the hidden security cameras in the ceiling of the Sands's massive gambling room, which kept an eye on the blackjack tables and other games of chance. If a player appeared to somehow be cheating, Fleming learned that security guards soon appeared. They had a convincing way of "leaning" on the player to ensure the games weren't rigged and the house wasn't being swindled.

Before the night was through, Cuneo and Fleming decided to play at every major casino on the Strip, the gaudy, fluorescent-lit Las Vegas thoroughfare. They won a single dollar playing blackjack at the Sands, each downed a glass of champagne and then left. They repeated the same small bets at the Sahara, the Old Frontier and every other casino, laughing that they were winners.

"One buck ahead and we quit—grandly, announcing that we had beaten the house to everyone's amazement," Cuneo recalled. "Took a drink and whisked out, as if there were another notch on our guns."

The two finished their gambling parade at Steamboat Springs, leaving at 4:00 a.m. The next day, they flew to Denver on their way back to New York.

The tour around America had been a success for both men. "Ian used a lot of the material he gathered in his next book," Cuneo said. Fleming explained to him his formula for novel writing, which relied on eight hundred words of notes and observations each day for his next work.

"Figure it out for yourself," he told Cuneo. "At the end of a year, I have about 250 or 300 of these daily memos, and when I go down to Jamaica, I weave them into a book."

Days after his arrival home in New York, Cuneo received a gift from Fleming: a small plain gold bill-clip, a memento of their quest together. Engraved into the metal, Fleming's inscription read as though written by James Bond himself:

"To Ernie—
my guide on a trip to the Angels and back.
007."

35

FACT INTO FICTION

Cuneo encouraged his friend Ian Fleming to turn their real-life wartime experiences into the fictional James Bond tales. For one movie treatment, Fleming suggested Cuneo play a mobster— an idea that offended Cuneo's Italian American sensibilities. Actor Sean Connery played the first James Bond in film, and the series became one of the greatest movie franchises in history.

> *"You must know thrilling things before you can write about them."*
>
> —Ian Fleming

Opening his mail one day in March 1956, Ernest Cuneo found a complimentary copy of Ian Fleming's new spy book, *Diamonds Are Forever*. He gobbled up each page, assured that part of this fourth novel in the James Bond series would reflect their journey across the United States.

Cuneo hit a roadblock when he arrived at the name of a minor character in Fleming's text.

"He sent me a first copy, as always, nicely inscribed," Cuneo recalled. "I was slightly chagrined to find it contained a character called Ernie Cureo, a taxicab driver."

The "Cureo" character, a Las Vegas cabbie and underground CIA informant, appeared briefly before driving offstage. Inside the cab, a verbal exchange between "Cureo" and James Bond very much reflected Fleming's own trip to Las Vegas with his pal.

In the novel, "Cureo" told Bond about the real-life gangster Bugsy Siegel, who "saw the possibilities" of Las Vegas and built the first big casino, the Flamingo, in 1946 before getting murdered by other mobsters. Driving along with Bond, "Cureo" also pointed out another casino where Fleming did his homework.

"Here's the Sands," said "Cureo" to the British secret agent. "Plenty of hot money behind that one. Don't rightly know whose. Front guy is a nice feller name of Jack Intratter. Used to be at the Copa in New York. Mebbe you heard of him?"

The fictitious mention of a "Jack Intratter" alluded to the real-life Jack Entratter from the Sands who'd treated Fleming and Cuneo as VIPs during their 1954 trip.

Earlier in the novel, another major character in the Bond series, CIA operative Felix Leiter, described "Cureo" as an Agency asset planted in Vegas.

"We've got a good man there," explained Leiter to Bond. "Undercover. Cab-driver by the name of Cureo, Ernie Cureo. Good guy, and I'll pass the word you're coming and he'll look after you. He knows all the dirt, where the big fixes are, who's in town from the outside mob. He even knows where you can find the one armed bandits that pay the best percentages."

The slight switch in names was Fleming's knowing wink to his American friend who'd transported him all around Vegas and other parts of the country. (Leiter's first name of "Felix" derived from the middle name of another friend, Ivar Bryce.)

Before the novel's end, poor "Cureo" is shot while helping to save Bond from villains. Of course, Fleming's titular hero survives to live another day in his next spy installment.

While Fleming likely chuckled to himself while writing this in Jamaica, turning their Las Vegas romp into fictional gold, Cuneo wasn't so pleased reading this passage in New York. As an Italian American, he didn't like to be associated with any hint of the Mafia, any suggestion that he knew their whereabouts. Even if it had been meant in good fun, Cuneo expressed his objections to Fleming, who ignored them. Annoyed at the reference to himself, Cuneo "made a routine protest" to Fleming, he recalled, "well knowing that I could do nothing about it, that he knew I could do nothing about it and so what the hell."

Bryce wasn't so offended when he found a Fleming tip-of-the-hat reference to himself in other James Bond novels. "He enjoyed using the names of his friends, or even those whom he knew only slightly," Bryce recalled. "It certainly amused me to discover that Mr. and Mrs. Bryce signed the visitors' book in *Dr. No*, as well as traveling incognito by train together in *Live and Let Die*."

Fleming's own meticulous preparation of cocktails—seen often at Stephenson's duplex penthouse during the war—was reflected in Bond's repeated instruction that his martini drink be "shaken, not stirred."

Whether in Jamaica, London, New York or elsewhere, Fleming seemed intent on converting his spy feats and general observations into his fictional work. "Like all writers, I suppose, he viewed every incident of life with an appraising eye, judging what would be of use in the next book, or the next but one," said Bryce. "He took immense trouble with names and plots, although the names sometimes came before the plots."

Diamonds Are Forever reflected other memories, from Fleming's summer stays in the Adirondacks with his pals Bryce and Cuneo. Using their initials, the book is dedicated to Bryce ("J.F.C.B.," referring to John Felix Charles "Ivar" Bryce), Cuneo ("E.L.C.") and "the memory of W.W. Jr.," referring to a horse-racing friend, William Woodward Jr., who'd met with an untimely demise.

Woodward advised Fleming about thoroughbred racing scenes in his novel and provided an inspiration for Bond's revved-up cars. He owned the champion colt Nashua at a nearby upstate stable. Fleming was particularly impressed by Woodward's "Studillac," a hybrid car with a powerful Cadillac engine. Unfortunately, in a much-publicized case months later, Woodward was shot by his wife inside their Long Island mansion. She claimed to have mistaken him for a prowler.

Diamonds also drew upon other Fleming memories from his 1954 trip, including when he and Cuneo accidentally visited a low-rent version of the famous mud baths in Saratoga Springs.

The Bond novels were a fanciful way for Fleming and his pals, like Bryce and Cuneo, to relive their memories of World War II without getting into trouble. For example, Fleming incorporated what he'd learned of Camp X's unarmed combat and underwater demolition exercises, replicating them in his *Live and Let Die* tale.

Most provocatively, Fleming provided insights taken from Station M, the British spy lab in Canada, with its many gadgets, forgeries, operational details and killing strategies used by the British secret services. Ordinarily, such secrets would have been prohibited from being disclosed publicly. Fiction made these secrets safe to disclose, without the threat of going to jail. As Fleming once joked, "If the quality of these books, or their degree of veracity, had been any higher, the author would certainly have been prosecuted under the Official Secrets Act."

Indeed, most serving the Crown as spies were asked to sign an Official Secrets Acts document, keeping them mum for decades afterward. Fleming's description of James Bond and his spy world were an imaginative way around any Cold War restrictions.

Cuneo was happy to spitball creative ideas with Fleming. From his own spook sources in the government, Ernie rattled off various real-life anecdotes. He told Fleming how the Russians "were able to take a man's fingerprints from a glass and put them on a rubber glove—excellent for framing a false clue." He mentioned "rumors about cyanide cigarettes—one whiff and the victim would die without a clue." And he described "a compressed air revolver which would shoot a needle into a man's heart without leaving a visible wound."

Fleming later expressed regret to Cuneo that he didn't give him enough credit beyond the rather anonymous dedication with his initials.

"I think it is very friendly of you not to sue me over *Diamonds Are Forever,*" joked Fleming in a May 14, 1956 letter. "Your role in the book, while respectable enough, was not as distinguished as it should have been and that wife you keep out in Las Vegas might need a bit of explaining if Margaret cut up rough."

Fleming rectified this omission with his 1961 novel *Thunderball,* which he dedicated solely to "Ernest Cuneo—Muse."

The genesis of that novel emerged from a friendly gabfest between Fleming, Bryce and Cuneo about making a James Bond movie. There'd already been a CBS live television version of *Casino Royale* featuring "Jimmy Bond" in 1954, but it hadn't been very satisfying. On an April 1959 business trip, Cuneo gathered with Fleming at Bryce's house and they tried to do better.

The three friends were now more than a decade removed from their service as intelligence agents. By coming up with a fictional spy story based on their wartime experiences, they "visited this haunted forest of memory," as Fleming described it. Their gung-ho sensibility can be heard in the voice of James Bond in *Thunderball,* when he exclaims, "The war just doesn't seem to have ended for us."

To reflect the new geopolitical climate, however, *Thunderball's* plot revolved around a blackmail attempt involving stolen atomic bombs by a terrorist criminal group called SPECTRE. The three friends, along with a young Irish writer and director, Kevin McClory, decided to form a company called Xanadu Productions to make this Bond film.

At the outset, Cuneo "scribbled off" an initial outline of the movie, providing a plotline "capable of great flexibility" with the Russians as villains, Fleming later recalled. Cuneo suggested "just the right degree of fantasy" with a lot of suspense, and urged that it feature many well-known guest stars. As a goodwill gesture, Cuneo sold his copyright claim on the initial movie treatment to Fleming's production company for only a dollar. He never had any later regrets.

Working off Cuneo's first draft, Fleming prepared a sixty-seven-page "rough suggested treatment" for a motion picture, to be called *James Bond of the Secret Service*. In this version, the Mafia would be the bad guys rather than the Russians or the fantastical SPECTRE name eventually adopted. In an introductory note to this treatment, Fleming recommended that actor Burl Ives play the top Mafia figure. And then Fleming made a surprise acting pitch for his American friend who'd come up with this original idea.

"Ernest Cuneo is mentioned as the Capo Mafiosi in Sicily," Fleming explained in his treatment. "He is a New York lawyer, legal advisor to Xanadu Films, and has a more fabulous gangster face than has ever been seen on the films."

Cuneo, with his hooded eyes and stocky appearance, did resemble actors like Ernest Borgnine and James Gandolfini. Years afterward, Cuneo's adult children remembered that Fleming floated the idea of putting their father into a Bond film. But it's unlikely Cuneo was agreeable to becoming a Mafia capo on screen, and he never did so.

Eventually, Fleming decided to turn the movie treatment into a full-fledged novel called *Thunderball*, published in 1963. The development of a film was slowed by a legal challenge by a writer and producer claiming partial credit for the *Thunderball* script. In the meantime, Hollywood decided to turn another Bond novel, *Dr. No*, into a movie, which premiered in October 1962.

Fleming doubted that he'd ever profit from any James Bond film. As he wrote to his old spymaster friend, William Stephenson, "As you know producers profits have a curious way of melting like snow in summer sunshine when anyone else has a share of them, and I think the days of my becoming a millionaire are still in some way distant."

But James Bond's transition from the printed page to the drive-in movies proved unstoppable. Various actors—including Richard Burton, James Stewart and James Mason—were contemplated to play 007. The final selection met with Fleming's approval. "The man they have chosen for Bond, Sean Connery, is a real charmer," he wrote to another friend, "fairly unknown but a good actor with the right looks and physique."

The Bond films—*Dr. No* in 1962, *Goldfinger* in 1964, and eventually *Thunderball* in 1965—would launch one of the most popular Hollywood franchises in history. They would expand Fleming's literary success around the world. His fictional creation James Bond—inspired in part by the shadowy real-life spies he'd met at Rockefeller Center and elsewhere during World War II— achieved the kind of celebrity that would last for generations.

Beneath the glossy surface, the 007 adventures seemed like a modern interpretation of old romantic English fables. In Fleming's fictitious world, Great Britain still reigned as a mighty empire, the equal of the United States and Russia, despite its new reality as a depleted country encumbered by war debts. And Bond was its superhero, overcoming those who might challenge him.

"This is all true Secret Service history that is yet in the higher realm of fantasy, and James Bond's ventures into this realm are perfectly legitimate," Fleming explained, citing as fodder for his novels the real-life Gouzenko spy case in Canada and the corpse with the false invasion plans found by the Nazis on the Spanish coast. "So you see the line between fact and fantasy is a very narrow one and, if I had time, I think I could trace most of the central incidents in my books to some such real happenings as I have described."

Yet even though *Thunderball* was dedicated to Cuneo, he remained largely unknown to the James Bond–reading public and is mentioned only fleetingly in various biographies about Fleming.

Fame—the kind that Fleming had dreamed of when he talked with Cuneo on their train ride across America—had finally arrived for him, almost miraculously, at age fifty. And though some of this success resulted from Cuneo's help, his American friend didn't fight for credit as others did. Instead, Cuneo preferred to remain, once again, out of the limelight.

36

PRESENTATIONS

Inside his Central Intelligence Agency headquarters, director Allen Dulles received a telephone call in June 1954 from a familiar source, Ernest Cuneo, warning him about a possible security problem. Both had learned not to discount any threat of Communist infiltration.

A decade earlier, Dulles and Cuneo had been wartime colleagues at Rockefeller Center, part of the early spy staff put together by the OSS's chief, William Donovan. In 1942, Dulles had moved to Switzerland, where he'd handled top secret cases involving Nazi double agents and the negotiated surrender of Axis troops in Italy.

By the time he received this call from Cuneo, Dulles had become America's top spy, appointed to lead the CIA by President Dwight D. Eisenhower. Dulles thought enough of Cuneo's security tip that he filed a memo about it with the agency's Inspector General. It referred to a probe conducted by a rabid anti-Communist, William E. Jenner, chair of the US Senate's Internal Security Subcommittee.

"I wish to note for the record that Mr. Ernest Cuneo advised me by telephone that he understood that the Jenner Committee was making an investigation of an organization named Presentations, Inc., which was allegedly organized by former CIA

(OSS) and State Department personnel, and was allegedly making movies on behalf of certain Communist or fellow-traveler organizations and Communist labor unions," Dulles wrote.

In his memo, Dulles said he told Cuneo that he'd never heard of the Presentations firm but promised the CIA would check out his warning.

At first, the government investigation into the Presentations company by Senator Jenner didn't seem to get very far. One former official of the OSS's Presentation Branch—which made movies and charts for the military—said the "Presentations" company was merely a desire by his buddies to go into business together privately, without any hint of politics involved.

But Cuneo's tip about potential trouble eventually paid off. During congressional testimony, another former top OSS official, Carl Aldo Marzani, invoked his Fifth Amendment privilege when asked about the Presentations firm. Marzani was later sentenced to prison for concealing his previous membership in the Communist Party USA and eventually revealed as a paid Soviet KGB collaborator.

Cuneo's warning call to Dulles underlined his political savvy as well as his concern about Soviet infiltration of Allied intelligence, stemming back to the Gouzenko spy case at the end of the war. Like many others, he felt betrayed by Russia's clandestine behavior as an ally.

However, as America's anti-Communist fervor metastasized into the McCarthy era of the early 1950s, Cuneo was appalled by its excesses. "[Senator Joseph] McCarthy, a psychopathic alcoholic, falsely accused innocent people by the dozen," Cuneo recalled. "He launched one of the most vicious Red Hunts, little short of a civic lynching mob."

McCarthy's loutish behavior sidetracked attention from the genuine problem, at least in Cuneo's mind, of Russian "moles" and "double agents" planted in the ranks of American intelligence. The public pushback against "McCarthyism," he said,

"gave the American Communist cadres both projective color-
ing and a magnificent battle slogan."

Dulles shared Cuneo's concerns about Russian espionage. He
was well aware of criticisms that "Wild Bill" Donovan had been
too slow or blind to Moscow's infiltration of the OSS, something he resolved not to repeat at the postwar CIA. There still
existed a wartime tension between Dulles and Donovan that was
never resolved. When Eisenhower nominated him for the post,
Dulles sought out advice from his old OSS boss before taking
on the CIA job—something Donovan had once thought would
one day be his own. Wild Bill wasn't encouraging.

"You did a wonderful intelligence job in Switzerland during
the war, but, Al, this CIA job needs an expert organizer, and
you're no good whatever at that," Donovan told him.

Another bureaucratic enemy, the FBI's J. Edgar Hoover, kept
a confidential file on Dulles. It detailed his extramarital affair
with Mary Bancroft, a glamorous relative of the *Wall Street Journal* founder and an OSS spy assigned to him during the war.
Hoover knew how to play dirty—he spread the unfounded
rumor when Donovan died in 1959 that the cause was syphilis.

During this time, Cuneo managed to straddle all of these egos
and avoid many pitfalls. He felt a sense of loyalty to Donovan for
creating his role in 1940 as OSS "liaison" with Churchill's spies
at Rockefeller Center, codifying his place as the first American
spy of World War II. On a personal level, by being assigned to
work with Stephenson in Manhattan, he had met his wife Margaret and eventually started a family. He felt a lasting bond to
Stephenson, built on genuine admiration.

But Cuneo was never blind to Donovan's flaws at the OSS.
The old warhorse preferred to constantly run off to hot zones
in the field instead of remaining at his office. Cuneo believed
Donovan wanted to die in a glorious fight rather than doze off
at his desk.

"I consider him to be a great military leader—his love of
a battle, however, militated against him as an administrator,"

Cuneo concluded about Donovan. "I count it one of the lucki-
est things of my life that I was enabled to serve under what I
regard as a great soldier, most lovable leader, poor administrator
and the worst politician I have ever encountered."

*William "Wild Bill" Donovan led the OSS, America's first intelligence agency, through WWII
with Cuneo as a key adviser. Donovan never got his wish to lead the permanent Central Intelligence Agency, though a statue stands there today in his honor.*

Dulles proved himself a much better politician and diplomat. Cuneo continued to cultivate his connections with him,
such as with the "Presentations" phone call. Despite his NANA
news syndicate's dwindling finances, Cuneo realized that good
contacts within the US intelligence community were an important source of news "scoops" and a way to maintain his personal influence.

After all these years, Ernie still thought like a spook.

By 1960, when John F. Kennedy won the presidency, Dulles
wanted to keep his CIA job as a Republican holdover in the

new Democratic administration. Dulles knew JFK's father, former ambassador Joseph Kennedy, from their shared winter social circles in Palm Beach, Florida. The elder Kennedy convinced his son to keep the CIA director in place.

In a sense, Cuneo's pal Ian Fleming, with his James Bond spy novels, helped cement Dulles's relationship with the Kennedys. JFK first met Fleming as a last-minute guest to a small Washington dinner party the Kennedys hosted in spring 1960. JFK was already a fan of the 007 novels, having read *Casino Royale*. Dulles had been invited to this party but couldn't attend.

After dinner, Kennedy asked Fleming how he might handle the brewing controversy of Fidel Castro's Communist takeover of Cuba.

"Ridicule, chiefly," Fleming replied wryly.

The former British spy then outlined several Bond-like spy techniques to "deflate" Castro's reputation that sounded right out of Bill Stephenson's BSC playbook. One idea called for American scientists to shoot off some kind of rocket to form a cross in the sky, aimed at convincing Cubans that it was a heavenly sign that Castro should be replaced.

Fleming also suggested US planes drop leaflets, purportedly from the Soviet Union, claiming that American atomic testing had contaminated Cuba's island. This alarming propaganda would say that A-bomb radioactivity would collect in men's beards and make them impotent unless they shaved off all their facial hair.

Kennedy seemed amused by Fleming's farfetched suggestions. But a deadly serious reaction came soon after from Dulles, inside the agency's headquarters.

Apprised of JFK's dinner conversation, the CIA director realized the Bond books were a favorite with the Kennedy clan. Around this time, Dulles received a copy of Fleming's *From Russia with Love* from Kennedy's wife, Jacqueline, with the inscription, *"Here is a book you should have, Mr. Director."* (Later, once in the White House, the Kennedys hosted a private screening of the Bond movie *Dr. No.*)

Without much prompting, Dulles directed scientists in the agency to see if Bond's gadgets and high-tech killing devices could be adopted in real-life spying.

Cuneo, always attuned to Washington rumors, was well aware of Fleming's influence on the new president's style and outlook. During the Kennedy administration, Cuneo later learned, the CIA tried several Bond-like ways to shoot, poison and blow up the Cuban dictator, all without luck.

"Jack Kennedy, professing his preference for James Bond, certainly imitated him to a degree no president had even remotely approached before," Cuneo observed. "President Kennedy's death duel with Cuba's [leader Fidel] Castro has James Bond overtones."

Although Fleming's spy novels already enjoyed success, the James Bond saga soared in popularity when boosted with a public endorsement by the new president. In March 1961, *Life* magazine listed *From Russia with Love* as one of JFK's favorite books.

Even the usually low-profile CIA basked in Bond's glow. "Kennedy gave the CIA a dash and elan it had not known with the public," recalled Jack Valenti, an aide to Lyndon Johnson who later headed the Motion Picture Association of America. "Dulles, [CIA official Richard] Bissell and the others in the intelligence community were Ivy League and urbane. They were perceived as pretty stuffy. Suddenly they became mavericks, loose cannons—real exciting guys. They were our James Bonds."

Those close to Fleming realized his James Bond novels had sprung from his own spy experiences, but certainly weren't factual enough to base public policy on. His biographer John Pearson called the Bond adventures "an experiment in the autobiography of dreams." For all his contributions to them, Cuneo knew the tales of 007 were "ludicrous depictions of intelligence services" and enjoyed a good laugh at their expense.

In the wake of the CIA's disastrous 1961 Bay of Pigs fiasco in Cuba, Dulles lost his top post, but he continued to enjoy the Bond associations. At a 1963 American booksellers convention, he praised Fleming's 007. And the 1965 movie version of *The Man with the Golden Gun* combined fantasy and fact in a scene where James Bond, relaxing in a chair, is seen reading Dulles's real-life book, *The Craft of Intelligence.*

The Kennedy era held great promise for Cuneo, as a fellow Democrat with ties to the old OSS and the Roosevelt administration. His wife, Margaret, was a member of the JFK inaugural committee, assigned to the "Hostesses for Governor's Receptions" around town. Reflecting the mores of the times, Margaret was listed as "Mrs. Ernest Cuneo" in that group, which included the wives of other Washington luminaries such as William O. Douglas, Tom Clark, David Bruce and Dean Acheson.

Now in his midfifties, Cuneo seemed a font of tantalizing Kennedy stories from the old days, when the president's father was the US ambassador in London and a source of news and confidential tips passed along to Walter Winchell. At one private dinner in the 1960s, Drew Pearson called Cuneo "the expert on Joe Kennedy." He urged him to describe the old man's affair with Hollywood star Gloria Swanson for his dinner guests. "I was closer to Joe Kennedy than Rose Kennedy ever was," Swanson told Cuneo, as Pearson recorded in his diary.

Details about the president's own extramarital affairs, none of which appeared in the media, were freely discussed at these dinner parties. Early in 1961, Margaret and Ernie were invited over to the home of Drew Pearson and his wife, Luvie, where plenty of steamy gossip was served. As Pearson recalled, "We spent most of the evening discussing the favorite topic of conversation: the sex life of the president of the United States."

With a jaundiced eye, Cuneo also followed the inner workings of the spy world during the Kennedy administration, sharing a healthy skepticism with his friend Fleming. Both knew things weren't always as they seemed in the newspapers.

Shortly after the May 1961 assassination of Dominican dictator Rafael Trujillo, reportedly by local killers, Fleming wrote to Cuneo in a cryptic way, as if he suspected the CIA's involvement.

"Sorry about old Trujillo," Fleming wrote. "He really managed to survive quite splendidly as top monster and I shall be interested to read details of how they finally blew him to pieces."

The Cold War, with its deadly covert operations, carried a mixed sense of morality, influenced by what had happened before with Hitler. This ambivalence was reflected in the dark novels of John le Carré and Graham Greene, rather than the heroic but cartoonish shootings in Fleming's books. Cuneo, like JFK and other Democrats who'd come of age during World War II, believed the spread of Soviet Communism must be thwarted in Latin America as well as the rest of the world. Rather than remaining in the shadows, Cuneo became increasingly willing to put his name out in public to stop it.

By May 1963, Cuneo would be listed as a member of the Citizens Committee for a Free Cuba, along with several other hawkish anti-Communist Americans like Clare Boothe Luce. Although the *New York Times* described the committee as "non-partisan," warning of "the growing Castro-Communist influence in Latin America," critics called it a front group pushing for decisive action against Castro.

Cuneo didn't believe in state-sanctioned assassination—despite the fictional violence found in the James Bond tales, or the real-life whispers of a "disposal squad" used by the British agents of Rockefeller Center against suspected Nazi spies. While talk of Mata Hari and 007 made spying sound sexy, he said "key intelligence is much more prosaic," like figuring out the amount of Nazi steel production for military use.

"There was never a Bond nor could there be one," Cuneo insisted years later. "There was killing and presumably it continues by all major powers. But generally speaking this is very low echelon stuff and even at that infrequent. Obviously, if major Chiefs of State were targets, their life spans would be much shorter, since at the expense of one life another life can be taken in open countries, quite easily."

That lesson in vulnerability would be underlined in front of a Texas schoolbook depository building and define a new era for America. JFK's assassination on November 22, 1963, shocked Cuneo as it did the rest of the world. The killing in Dallas made it seem as if the dark underworld of fictional spies had become an awful reality, full of bitter ironies. As author Ben Macintyre noted, the night before Kennedy was killed, he'd been reading a James Bond novel; so had his assassin, Lee Harvey Oswald.

To investigate the president's killing, former CIA director Allen Dulles became part of a seven-member commission, headed by the US Supreme Court chief justice Earl Warren. In accepting the assignment from JFK's successor, Lyndon Johnson, Dulles promised complete confidentiality on his part, according to a tape-recording of their conversation released decades later.

"I'll keep this entirely quiet," Dulles assured the new president.

Former CIA director Allen Dulles (third from right) was a member of the Warren Commission investigating President Kennedy's assassination. According to 1964 FBI records, Cuneo claimed Dulles was sharing information with him about the Warren panel's internal deliberations for a proposed magazine story.

GERALD R. FORD PRESIDENTIAL LIBRARY

"Please do," said Johnson. "Please do."

But by June 1964, three months before the lengthy Warren Commission Report was presented to Johnson and the public, FBI records suggest Dulles was sharing details about the commission's investigation with a friend—Ernest Cuneo.

When Cuneo came by the FBI office on June 19, 1964, he told top Hoover aide Cartha "Deke" DeLoach that he was preparing "a lengthy article about the Kennedy assassination with emphasis on the Warren report." Cuneo asked for the Bureau's cooperation in preparing his story. He wanted to confirm what he'd heard from a member of the Warren Commission.

"He stated that Allen Dulles was to be a principal source of information for him prior to the time the report was issued," DeLoach summarized in a June 23 FBI memo. "Cuneo specified again that he thought he could get sufficient information from Allen Dulles to write his article; however, it would be helpful if he could call us from time to time."

Remarkably, Cuneo's effort to gain an inside scoop about the Kennedy killing—the biggest story since World War II—began shortly after the assassination, records show. On December 27, 1963, Cuneo came by FBI headquarters to meet with DeLoach, the top FBI official assigned to the Warren probe, according to DeLoach's memo. It was marked "Assassination of the President" and filed the same day.

At that time, DeLoach was upset with a Drew Pearson column that had criticized security measures surrounding Kennedy's fatal Dallas visit. Cuneo expressed sympathy to DeLoach—who claimed that Cuneo agreed with him about errors in Pearson's column—and promised to stay in touch.

By June 22, 1964, Hoover wrote his own memo about Cuneo. It said Cuneo had signed a contract with Curtis Publishing Company—owner of the *Saturday Evening Post* and other magazines—to write a thirty-five-thousand-word "book of the week type of thing" about the Warren Report examining the JFK assassination.

The source of Hoover's memo was federal court judge Edward A. Tamm, who called the FBI immediately after speaking with Cuneo. Tamm admitted he didn't understand everything Cuneo had mentioned about the Warren panel. But the judge was alarmed.

"Judge Tamm stated that Mr. Cuneo apparently has talked to Allen Dulles, who says the report is going to be a complete exoneration of the FBI for any responsibility because of the Secret Service's claims that the FBI should have notified them about Lee Harvey Oswald being there and of his background, etcetera," said Hoover's memo.

Concerned about the upcoming Warren report, Hoover feared his bureau might be blamed. Maybe critics would find his G-men didn't respond adequately enough to Oswald's alleged Communist ties, including his time in Russia in 1959. In this Hoover memo, addressed to his top staff, the FBI director said he had defended the Bureau's actions during his own testimony to the Warren Commission.

"I stated that Oswald had been playing around with communism, had defected to Russia, but there was no evidence of violence in his makeup, but [sic] we are now sending all names of this type of person to Secret Service," Hoover wrote.

In trying to find out about the closed-door Warren Commission deliberations, Cuneo's friends and loyal sources in the intelligence community gave him a distinct advantage. According to the same Hoover memo, Tamm told him that "Cuneo has interviewed a number of people, including as he had mentioned, Dulles, and he has substantial knowledge of what is going to be in the report."

The following day, DeLoach filed another memo. It said Cuneo had asked DeLoach if he could show him "in strictest confidence" what the FBI had sent to the Warren Commission. Cuneo reminded DeLoach that "he had gone to bat for us with Drew Pearson when Pearson was criticizing the FBI," the memo recalled.

But DeLoach wasn't willing to share anything with the former OSS liaison, acting in this case more as a journalist than a spy.

"I told Cuneo that we respected his friendship highly and appreciate his need for information," DeLoach described in his note. "However, he should know that the Warren Commission has specifically requested that we refrain from making any statements whatsoever until the release of their report. I told him that obviously it would be out of the question for me to show him our report."

Cuneo left FBI headquarters empty-handed. As Hoover's deputy DeLoach recalled, Cuneo "stated he was leaving my office to go over and see Allen Dulles at that particular time."

The Warren Commission Report finally appeared in late September of 1964. The massive document concluded Oswald was the lone assassin of the fallen president, a contention that would set off controversy for decades to come for those who questioned it.

But there was no preemptive article by Cuneo featuring Dulles, nothing with his byline examining the commission's deliberations before its conclusions had been announced. What would have been a bombshell news story never appeared.

The reasons why are not clear from the available records. Perhaps the former CIA director didn't cooperate as Cuneo had hoped he might. Or perhaps the claim of his willingness to cooperate had been a bluff by Cuneo to get Hoover's people to talk to him. No one could question Cuneo's bona fides as a former spy still friendly from the outside to intelligence agencies.

Though unknown to the public, Cuneo was certainly identifiable to Hoover as a man trusted by the spymasters of both Roosevelt and Churchill to keep secrets during the war. With this most closely guarded of investigations—of the death of a president—he still seemed able to enter the corridors of power virtually undetected, as if hidden from view.

The desire to get a headline-grabbing scoop—in this case, about the JFK murder investigation—seemed something Cuneo learned from gossip columnist Walter Winchell, or even earlier as a city desk reporter for the *New York Daily News*, chasing down much less famous murders. However, the reasons why Cuneo believed he could learn the secrets of the inner workings of the Warren Commission remain a mystery.

The 1964 FBI memos made it clear that Cuneo worked for the North American Newspaper Alliance, a seemingly legitimate news outlet. But by then, the syndicate's shrunken finances had forced it to merge with another company and shed employees, including their man in London, Ian Fleming.

The collapse of NANA barely made a dent in the friendship between Cuneo and Fleming, largely because of James Bond's phenomenal success around the world. Everyone seemed to want a piece of Bond, including the producer and scriptwriter who sued Fleming for screen credit with *Thunderball*.

During the legal fight, Fleming suffered a heart attack. Cuneo flew over to London to help his friend during the proceedings. Eventually, they settled the lawsuit to avoid further endangering Ian's health.

Fleming was no longer the physical specimen who could outclass and outrun Cuneo, the former NFL pro player, when they raced up Goose Egg hill near Ivar Bryce's place in Vermont. Booze and nonstop smoking had corroded Fleming's insides. Ironically, the creator of the ever-resilient James Bond character complained of his "ludicrous health troubles" in candid letters to his American friend.

"These are now resolving themselves and I am more or less erect (in a respectable way)," Fleming quipped about his maladies. "But I am afraid with an endless vista of twenty cigarettes and three ounces of liquor a day and, worst of all, no women, scrambled eggs or golf… In the meantime, I look out the window at the rain and eat food cooked in kosher margarine. What a life!"

Now internationally famous but lacking the ability to enjoy it, Fleming seemed trapped and inescapably diminished to Cuneo. Fleming "suffered a great deal in his last few years," he said, especially from excruciatingly painful bouts of sciatica, which rendered him immobile. The emotional strains of Fleming's marriage also seemed to hasten his decline, draining whatever flickering hope he held for finding lasting love.

"Most of all, he suffered from the curtailment of action necessitated by his cigarette-weakened heart," Cuneo observed. "He declined to take the advice of his doctors. He resented growing old. He preferred the Roman death, sudden—preferably killed in action and to a certain extent he was."

Noël Coward, Fleming's wartime spy friend and neighbor in Jamaica, was pained to see him wither away, no longer able to pursue his Bond-like reputation with women.

"Of course, he loved fucking women—it was as simple as that and he was quite unscrupulous about it," Coward recalled. "That was the great shock after his first heart attack when he began to discover that he couldn't any more. The great stallion couldn't do the stallion's work and I think—I'm sure—that this was one of the reasons why he went on smoking his cigarettes and drinking and began not caring."

On August 12, 1964, Fleming died at age fifty-six following a second attack. His passing came a few months after the movie *To Russia with Love*—based on the late President Kennedy's favorite spy novel by Fleming—opened in Times Square. It soon played to rapturous audiences around the world. By only a few weeks, Fleming's death preceded the Warren Commission's presentation.

In Cuneo's memory, Fleming remained that force of nature he'd first met at Rockefeller Center, sharing a drink and a laugh alongside Stephenson and dreaming up ways to defeat the Nazis. Fleming was a great spy who set the world afire with his literary imagination.

His lion-hearted friend seemed "a knight out of phase," Cuneo wrote, "a knight errant searching for the Round Table and possibly the Holy Grail, and unable to reconcile himself that Camelot was gone and still less that it had probably never existed."

37

SEEKING RECOGNITION

Cuneo's book about his old boss, Fiorello LaGuardia, became the impetus for the 1960 Pulitzer Prize–winning musical Fiorello!, but typically Cuneo didn't seek any credit.

LIBRARY OF CONGRESS

"It would be absolutely intolerable if...ex-agents of the secret service were to be allowed, after they retired, without fear of consequence to publish secrets. It is far easier for them to invent... fairy tales in many cases than to give authentic facts."

—Winston Churchill

Up in lights, the name "Fiorello!" appeared outside the Broadhurst Theatre, right off Times Square and Broadway, where fame is touted in big bold letters. The musical version of Mayor Fiorello LaGuardia's early life attracted large crowds and critical acclaim, including a Tony Award and the 1960 Pulitzer Prize for Drama.

"It is obvious that LaGuardia is a natural subject for musical comedy," wrote the *New York Times* critic Brooks Atkinson, in a rave review that credited the play's four listed creators, including the legendary George Abbott. "Why did no one think of him before?"

But someone *had* told LaGuardia's story beforehand—Ernest Cuneo.

In 1955, Cuneo published a small book called *Life with Fiorello*, more of a memoir than a full-fledged biography. With a warm, often humorous style, Cuneo recalled working for congressman LaGuardia, before he became the city's well-known mayor. His book captured the heart and rough-and-tumble spirit of "the Little Flower." It inspired Abbott and his other producers to bring *Fiorello* to Broadway.

"I did give him [Abbott] a thin little book on LaGuardia by Ernest Cuneo," Jerome Weidman, the play's coauthor, explained to the *Times*. "He took it away for the weekend, then came back with a proprietary interest in the Mayor. He even bawled me out for getting a fact wrong."

The producers secured the life rights from the mayor's widow, and so Cuneo's book was not mentioned in the show's credits. Nevertheless, Cuneo's influence was felt throughout the show.

According to a biography of the show's composer and lyricist, Jerry Bock and Sheldon Harnick respectively, the musical reprised various scenes from Cuneo's book, including the tripped fire alarm to disrupt a LaGuardia campaign appearance. The title of one song, "On the Side of the Angels," was inspired by a Cuneo description of his boss. The show also modeled a character named "Neil" on young Cuneo himself.

At one point, the LaGuardia character exclaimed, "When people think of Italians, I want them to think of Michelangelo, Caruso, Garibaldi; not of Ponzi and the Mafia." That quote echoed Cuneo's book, which described LaGuardia's loathing of gangsters and that he prayed the kidnapper of Lindbergh's baby "doesn't turn out to be Italian."

Cuneo last saw LaGuardia in 1946, when both were in Paris. The former mayor, who'd championed New York's downtrodden ethnic minorities, was then in charge of a United Nations program designed to feed Europe's starving refugees. The following year, LaGuardia died. Cuneo felt determined to recount LaGuardia's story, giving his hero the recognition he deserved.

"My only aim has been to talk in my own way about Fiorello as I remember him, and to suggest as well as I can the magnificent human outlines of the man before they are lost in the well meaning monuments to his great work," Cuneo explained.

Cuneo's book writing went slowly during the early 1950s, weighed down by his own business obligations as well as family duties with Margaret and their two children. His friend Ian Fleming—who himself dawdled before launching his James Bond novels—urged Cuneo to quicken his glacial pace. By September 1953, Fleming offered to ask his agent to take a look at "the manuscript as it stands, otherwise you will go on tinkering with it until LaGuardia is just a page in history books."

The LaGuardia book's success, though, proved worth the wait. Through his writings, Cuneo showed a desire to understand the extraordinary times in which LaGuardia had lived, and to recognize those who'd affected him. "Fiorello really was the kind of man he reputed to be; the myth and the reality were one and the same in almost every particular," he attested.

Cuneo followed with other writings. In 1963, he published the high-minded book called *Science and History*, a theoretical attempt to apply scientific method to the study of history. Citing a range of political philosophers and various past empires, Cuneo seemed as if he were trying to make sense of all he'd witnessed during World War II. "I actually think I have cracked the code of history," he confided to Walter Winchell, who mentioned the new book in his gossip column.

If Cuneo's memoir about LaGuardia was a paean to politics, the book he helped assemble about Winchell, published after Winchell's death in 1972, seemed a cautionary tale about the dangers of fame, propaganda and the power of mass media. It was called *Winchell Exclusive: "Things That Happened to Me—And Me to Them."* In an introductory essay, Cuneo described Winchell at his peak as "the only man who could simultaneously elevate FDR back into the White House and meet Goebbels, Hitler's propaganda chief, down in the gutter and stomp him and his lies into the mud."

Winchell died a broken man, his finances drained and his fame proved fleeting. Despite their bitter parting as friends, Cuneo later made sure this memoir by his media client got published.

JONATHAN CUNEO

Cuneo's own relationship with Winchell didn't end well. During the Cold War, Cuneo warned Winchell about his support of Senator Joseph McCarthy, the anti-Communist demagogue, but his advice was ignored. During the height of his popularity, Winchell paid Cuneo handsomely for his legal counsel, though increasingly he didn't pay at all.

Their true breaking point occurred with a 1951 incident at the Stork Club, when singer Josephine Baker said she was denied service because of her race. Baker blamed Winchell for supporting the club's manager. Cuneo tried to broker a truce.

Instead, Winchell accused Baker, who'd been a wartime spy for the French Resistance, of being a Communist. This unfounded charge against the stylish singer, who dressed in Dior haute couture at her concerts, caused Baker to lose her US work visa. But it also meant "the beginning of the end," as Winchell rapidly lost his popularity, Cuneo recalled. "The silence of the phones in his suite was awful."

Cuneo kept his distance from the columnist but never cut ties completely. After Winchell's death in 1972, Cuneo helped get his former friend's autobiography published posthumously and even wrote an introduction for it. Winchell's showbizzy book regaled readers with short, punchy anecdotes about all the famous and infamous people he'd known. Only in aggregate, like some pointillist painting, did these gossipy nuggets provide a greater portrait of Winchell and his era.

"Historians will be unable to explain the 20th century without understanding Winchell," Cuneo eulogized at his 1972 memorial.

More than anyone, Winchell showed the power of gossip as a self-created creature of the American mass media. But what the public didn't realize was how much Winchell relied on propaganda from the British with Cuneo's help, and the dominant voice Winchell provided in readying the United States for World War II.

"Winchell became the firepoint," Cuneo said, quoted in Neal Gabler's biography of Winchell. "His rolling barrages could and did clear the way for the President and the preparation of war."

Spying remained the most enigmatic part of Cuneo's life, the most difficult to track, document and understand. Slowly, historians pieced together the extraordinary espionage operation at Rockefeller Center, the biggest foreign spy operation ever inside the United States. Many classified documents were kept locked up for years or were destroyed. Most agents stayed quiet, sworn to secrecy by law or bound by honor not to speak of their exploits.

Over time, Cuneo played a supportive role with respect to the desire for recognition among Churchill's spies, especially William Stephenson. After the war, the spymaster known as "Intrepid" retired to Jamaica, his Shangri-la in the Caribbean, where friends such as Lord Beaverbrook, Noël Coward and Ian Fleming also had homes.

"For a year or so, he [Stephenson] showed little interest in the outside world and was content to enjoy life on this island in the sun," recalled H. Montgomery Hyde about his former BSC boss. Gradually, Stephenson became involved in private business ventures and more determined to burnish his legacy.

In 1962, Hyde published *The Quiet Canadian* in England, an eye-opening account of Stephenson's handling of the British Security Coordination Office in New York, with chapters such as "Spies, Saboteurs and Propagandists." (The American version of the book was entitled *Room 3603*, named for the main office at Rockefeller Center.)

Unlike the fictional James Bond novels, Hyde's book provided many factual details about the real-life British and Canadian spies who had worked for Stephenson during the war. His book described the inner workings of the Rockefeller Center operation and Churchill's clandestine effort to bring America into the war. It revealed the various efforts to combat Nazis spies in America, including the one killed in Times Square.

The book's escapades highlighted the romantic romps of "Cynthia," the BSC's Mata Hari; the creation of Camp X and the fake map given to FDR; and the campaign to undermine isolationist US politicians opposed to joining Britain in the fight against Hitler. With surprising candor, the book explained the feeding of propaganda to Winchell, Drew Pearson and other American journalists.

In his acknowledgments, Hyde thanked Stephenson, who "put his files and private papers unreservedly at my disposal." These documents clearly included the voluminous BSC history that Stephenson ordered prepared at the end of the war before ordering all the rest destroyed.

Hyde also credited Stephenson's second-in-command, Colonel C. H. "Dick" Ellis, who'd carefully read his manuscript and made many suggestions for improvements. "His experience and knowledge of the intelligence background of the story have been invaluable," Hyde said of Ellis, who was highly regarded among the BSC staff.

In a rare moment of public recognition, Cuneo was thanked by Hyde for recalling how he'd been the middleman between the BSC and such US officials as Bill Donovan and J. Edgar Hoover. "If it had not been for Stephenson and his organization in the US, there would've been many more gold star mothers in America at the end of the war," declared Cuneo, the "dynamic link" given the last word in Hyde's book.

For the American version, Ian Fleming provided a special foreword, vouching for its "fascinating" contents. Fleming marveled at Stephenson's accomplishments as a spymaster.

"Only the removal of the cloak of anonymity he has worn since 1940 allows us to realise to our astonishment that men of super-qualities *can* exist, and that such men can be super-spies and, by any standard, heroes," Fleming said, more than two decades after first working with Stephenson. Fleming compared him to his fictitious character James Bond, which undoubtedly heightened the book's appeal among spy readers.

The Hyde book wasn't much of a financial success, said intelligence expert Nigel West, who criticized some of its descriptions, "but it did accomplish Stephenson's objective, to gain recognition as having played a pivotal role in the clandestine war."

To the chagrin of some and the amazement of others, the wall of silence surrounding British spy operations during the war was now eroding. Although the supersensitive Bletchley Park code rooms still remained unknown to the public, the naming of actual spies and events in Hyde's book upset top British officials. Initially, they considered banning it and perhaps filing criminal charges against Hyde, like others who had broken the British Official Secrets Acts and were punished.

But when confronted, Hyde slyly pointed out the book was essentially about Stephenson, who was Canadian and therefore not subject to the same rules as Brits. He claimed his sources were not from MI6 nor any other British agency. As White-hall officials feared, the Hyde book led to several more by others that further pushed the espionage door open, including a 1974 book that revealed the "Ultra" code-breaking program at Bletchley Park.

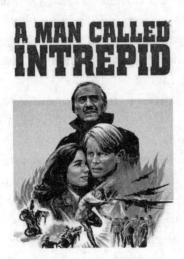

Spymaster William Stephenson insisted on secrecy at Rockefeller Center but in later years seemed concerned about his public legacy. A controversial 1976 book about Stephenson became a popular TV miniseries starring actor David Niven but was criticized for exaggerations made by the aging war hero.

AUTHOR COLLECTION

The most controversial, *A Man Called Intrepid*, appeared in 1976 and once again focused on Bill Stephenson. The book (written by a Canadian journalist with virtually the same name, William Stevenson) became a bestseller—and was later the basis for an NBC television miniseries starring actor David Niven as "Intrepid."

"For some men, intelligence work is an extension of life's illusion," novelist John le Carré said in his *New York Times* review of this book. "Intrepid took to it as the very element of war."

This time, Stephenson's more extravagant claims—like taking credit for spying that led to the stealing of German codes used in the Ultra program—were called into question. Supporters defended Stephenson as unquestionably a war hero who had since suffered two serious strokes that had fuzzied his memory.

But critics, like historian Timothy J. Naftali, detailed how Stephenson, out of a seeming need for recognition, exaggerated his closeness to Churchill and Roosevelt and other important details in both the Hyde and *Intrepid* books. Naftali even pointed out that "Intrepid" was not Stephenson's secret code name but rather the telegraphic address for his BSC office.

"Sir William Stephenson's restless attitude toward his place in history tainted that legacy, despite the fact that his indulgent biographer bears some of the responsibility for the myths," said Naftali. Nevertheless, adding to the spymaster's enigma, Naftali conceded that "there can be no doubt" that Stephenson's "exploits were great" during the war.

Ironically, the *Intrepid* book erased Cuneo from a significant moment in the history of the British-American spy alliance. It portrayed the newly arrived Stephenson as being at a White House meeting in 1940, talking directly with FDR, who would promise "the closest possible marriage" between the FBI and the BSC. But, as Naftali noted, it was Cuneo, as the sole White House intermediary, who actually shared this presidential message with Stephenson.

Cuneo became aware of the controversial book about his friend and decided to shun it. "I did not read [*A Man Called Intrepid*] because I have no recollection of the events in which I am described as having taken part," he said.

Despite these doubts, Stephenson received plenty of laudatory official recognition for his wartime achievements before he died in 1989 at the age of ninety-two. Canadians embraced him as one of their greatest wartime heroes. They eventually erected a statue in his honor in his hometown of Winnipeg. And in Ontario, an "Intrepid Park" was carved out of the Camp X site once supervised by Stephenson's spies.

Most notably, in September 1983, Stephenson came to New York to receive the coveted William J. Donovan Award before seven hundred guests at a dinner held by the Veterans of OSS, a group of former intelligence agents that included Cuneo. Its previous award winners included Allen Dulles and Dwight D. Eisenhower.

Now an old man in his seventies, Cuneo didn't want his own actions to go unnoticed. He appealed to Stephenson as the only one still alive who could speak on his behalf.

"My war record is obscure…and I should like a written document to indicate that, when my days are over," his wartime contributions be acknowledged, Cuneo wrote to Stephenson in 1975, around the same time period when the bestselling book and TV movie about "Intrepid" appeared. "You are the only high authority who is in a position to describe my services," Cuneo added.

Although he had insisted on anonymity for most of his career, Cuneo knew that such a nebulous status as "liaison" to a foreign intelligence agency left him bereft of any recognition. He had taken the spying equivalent of a vow of silence by a priest or omertà by a mobster, only to find that others had sold their stories for fame and fortune.

After the war, Cuneo had provided memorable accounts of Fiorello LaGuardia, Walter Winchell and other famous people on the public stage with whom he'd worked. But this process underlined the lack of public recognition regarding his own secret career and what he had accomplished on behalf of his country as a spy.

Eventually, Cuneo started to write his own memoir, a scattershot effort that was never published. He made provisions so his private papers would be donated to the FDR Library in upstate New York. However, there remained one urgent question for Cuneo in seeking recognition: Was it all too late?

38

KEEPING SECRETS

"We all think our own secrets are the only ones that matter...
Other people's secrets are never quite as important as one's own."

—James Bond in Ian Fleming's *Goldfinger*

Margaret Watson Cuneo faced death with the same stoic strength that she'd brought to her wartime work with Churchill's spies at Rockefeller Center, the place that changed her life.

Margaret and Ernie had been married for nearly thirty years when she learned in the 1970s of her terminal illness.

By then, the Cuneos had raised a family and moved from New York to Washington. They still maintained the summer home in the Adirondacks, where Margaret stayed for long stretches, and Ernie still kept a pied-à-terre in Manhattan, primarily for business reasons.

But instead of enjoying retirement with fond memories of the past, Margaret developed ovarian cancer and began a long ordeal of suffering until its insurmountable end. In 1976, she died at the age of sixty-two inside Georgetown University's hospital.

"Stoicism does not begin to describe her—she was one of the most stoic people I know, in terms of pain," recalled her daughter, Sandra, who took care of her while she was dying. "She was also a tremendously kind and empathetic person."

Both Sandra and her brother, Jonathan, were distinguished

lawyers who had handled delicate matters in business, politics and even Hollywood, just like their father. But their respect for confidentiality couldn't compare to their mother's tight-lipped secrecy about her career at Rockefeller Center, where she worked for five years with hundreds of spies. Her only mention of what went on there was a fond memory of ice-skating at its outdoor rink.

"My mother did not keep a diary," said Jonathan, recalling the intelligence work of his mother up on the thirty-sixth floor. "She would no more write down something that was secret than she would stab you in the eye."

Margaret's obituary in the *New York Times* said she "first met her husband" while working for "the British security office" in New York, but it never mentioned spying or what she did there.

"I had no idea of Room 3603," said Sandra. "She never talked about it, never ever talked about it, nor did my father."

As adults, the two Cuneo siblings maintained an abiding curiosity about their parents' lives in "the Great Game" of spying. Jonathan said he still has a keepsake letter sent to Margaret after the war by Bill Stephenson, the man known in their family as "Intrepid," another reminder of his mother's very secret service to the Crown.

Kept in a frame, Stephenson's May 1945 letter to "Miss Margaret E. Watson" suggests her unspecified spy duties were more than secretarial and that, as far as BSC employees went, she was "a valuable one, particularly so because of the confidential and very difficult nature of your work."

Margaret had been part of a remarkable group of young Canadian women enlisted by Stephenson for the British Security Coordination. They uprooted their lives to work undercover in New York. For years afterward, Margaret kept in contact with her close BSC sisters, like fellow Canadian Merle Cameron, who'd had a boyfriend killed in the war, and Stephenson's top secretary Grace Garner, who later moved to London.

After his wife's death, Ernest wrote a note to one of Margaret's closest BSC friends, Elinore Little, who had married and moved to New Jersey. "Margaret always loved you so much and talked so often of the years you were together," he said.

In Margaret's memory, Cuneo donated a grove of trees to be planted at a local school near his family's former summer home in upstate New York, where they'd spent many pleasurable times with Ian Fleming, Ivar Bryce and other friends. During that time, Margaret had been on the summer concert committee for the Saratoga Spa, a historic state park, that included the wives of Governor Nelson Rockefeller and Cornelius Vanderbilt Whitney.

Despite Margaret's intense and successful work with British intelligence, she didn't pursue a professional career after the war. Like many women in the 1950s, she stayed home and focused on the needs of her family. "That was the unspoken contract with my father," recalled Sandra. Margaret later took a travel agent job, but only after her youngest child Jonathan left home for school.

Ernie's restlessness and wide-ranging interests seemed to leave little room in the Cuneo household for more than one career. He was constantly busy, part of his hard-driving personality. At home, he could at times be mercurial, even harsh in his judgments. Despite these difficulties, Cuneo's two children grew up with admiration for their father's idealism and deep sense of patriotism. "He didn't do things for the praise and glory," explained Sandra. "He wasn't interested in glorifying himself."

Along with his numerous legal and business clients, Cuneo stayed in contact with the intelligence community, and kept up his love of politics and writing about public affairs. Occasionally he found time for a feature in such magazines as *American Legion*, read by many World War II veterans, or wrote articles about the good old days of the early NFL and playing for the Orange Tornadoes and Brooklyn Dodgers. Most notably, he penned an opinion column syndicated to various local newspapers about politics. He rarely revealed anything about his former life as a spy.

Perhaps the closest he came to doing so was with his reaction to the so-called "Pentagon Papers" case. Cuneo frowned on the landmark 1971 US Supreme Court decision, supporting the First Amendment right of newspapers like the *New York Times* and the *Washington Post* to publish the government's classified history of the Vietnam War. He reminded his column readers that other nations had official secrets acts that would have sent such journalists to jail for publishing confidential documents. "It is considered a great disgrace for a government official to leak or plant a story in the press," wrote Cuneo, with little sense of irony or disclosure that he was one of the biggest leakers to the press during World War II.

As he grew older, Cuneo had no difficulty talking publicly about Winchell, LaGuardia and the Roosevelt years. But he remained reticent about discussing too much of his work for the OSS or with Churchill's spies. Gradually, however, he revisited his past as a spy, discovering more secrets about those memorable times and the friends he'd known.

In the early 1980s, he befriended Raymond Benson, a young writer preparing a large compendium book about James Bond and its creator, Ian Fleming. "He was just fantastic and so talkative—we really hit it off," recalled Benson about Cuneo. "He would call me every week just to chat. I think he was lonely. I guess, in me, he saw a kindred interest. He loved talking about Ian Fleming."

Benson asked Cuneo to write his book's introduction. In doing so, Cuneo called Fleming "the warmest kind of friend, a man of ready laughter, and a great companion (everything James Bond is not!)."

But Cuneo admitted to being "annoyed" when learning a few of Fleming's secrets, revealed in a biography after his death.

He realized that Fleming had never graduated from either Eton or the military academy Sandhurst, as he led Cuneo to believe. (Other biographers claimed Fleming left Sandhurst after contracting gonorrhea from a London prostitute.) Fleming had also lied about once fighting as a boxer. His crooked nose had fooled him, Cuneo said.

"I thought I knew Ian Fleming thoroughly, in and out," wrote Cuneo, with lasting amusement about his old friend. "Thus, I was surprised, and a trifle miffed with Ian."

In this world of spy secrets, however, Cuneo's biggest surprise involved C. H. "Dick" Ellis, Stephenson's trusted second-in-command at the BSC.

During the war, Ellis, a short man with a friendly demeanor, acted as an omnipresent figure. He was always ready to help, always seemingly in the know. Neither an Englishman, a Canadian nor an American, Ellis might seem an outsider as an Australian at BSC. But over time, Ellis became the ultimate insider.

As a true intelligence professional with years of experience, Ellis earned the trust of Stephenson in setting up the BSC and later that of Donovan in establishing the OSS, the American precursor to the modern CIA.

Traveling to Washington, Ellis provided influential advice to Donovan in the nuts-and-bolts creation of the new US spy agency. Donovan's sense of gratitude to Stephenson extended as well to his deputy director, Ellis, "without whose assistance American intelligence could not have gotten off the ground in World War II," concluded CIA historian Thomas Troy in a secret report finally released in 2000.

Not everyone was so admiring of Ellis. During the 1942 Duško Popov spy investigation, J. Edgar Hoover had complained that Ellis was untrustworthy. Ellis had chastised Popov for talking to the FBI about British funding of his spy activities.

"Hell, you shouldn't have told them [the FBI] that," Ellis told Popov, "that's none of their business."

Cagily, Ellis turned Hoover's priggish reputation against him. As a smoke screen, Ellis suggested the FBI leader disapproved of Popov's playboy sex life and was jealous of the BSC's involvement in espionage cases that Hoover considered his own.

Like most at Rockefeller Center, Cuneo then thought of Ellis as an amiable fellow based on their experiences together. Cuneo had followed Donovan's instructions to keep Ellis from being booted out of the US by vouching for his integrity. As Cuneo later recalled, "My first assignment in the OSS was to block the expulsion of Colonel C.H. "Dickie" Ellis, second-in-command to Stevenson and then prime instructor of the OSS."

Throughout the war, Dickie's fingers seemed to be in every pie. Ellis oversaw the BSC's Manhattan headquarters when Stephenson was away, and involved himself in Camp X training in Canada. He later opened up the BSC's satellite office in Washington. As the war wound down, Ellis provided input for the secret BSC history, kept under wraps for nearly fifty years.

In his 1962 book about Stephenson, Hyde praised Ellis and his ability to speak Russian without difficulty. For years afterward, Ellis remained friendly with Stephenson, visiting him and his neighbor Ian Fleming in Jamaica. None of them seemed to harbor any deep suspicions about Dickie.

Slowly, the truth revealed itself, an accretion of suspicion and solid evidence. The first sign appeared right after the war. Walter Schellenberg, a top ex-Nazi official for foreign intelligence, said during interrogation that British intelligence had been compromised by "a man named Ellis." Despite this damning clue, not much resulted.

Over the next decade, some claimed Ellis admitted selling "vast quantities of information" to the Germans up to 1940, while others pointed to Ellis as a Soviet mole. Colleagues of

Ellis, his fair hair now turned white, simply couldn't conceive of him being a traitor.

Most tellingly, Ellis was friends with Kim Philby, finally revealed in 1963 as the most notorious Soviet double agent in British intelligence history. Philby emerged as the key figure in the "Cambridge Five" spy ring that provided countless secrets to the Soviets during World War II and the Cold War, causing the deaths of dozens of British agents and assets. When made public, the scandal rocked both the British and American governments.

"Philby's name is synonymous with treachery on a colossal scale," *The Economist* magazine later observed. "Philby played his high-stakes game of double-cross so ruthlessly, so successfully and for so long that he acquired a different level of infamy after he was unmasked."

For years, Philby's upper-class, cosmopolitan manner and subtle maneuvering had helped him evade suspicion, just like Ellis.

The spy link between them first emerged in the early 1950s. British counterintelligence investigators suspected the two men tipped off the Soviets to the impending defection of KGB officer Vladimir Petrov and his wife to Australia. When Ellis learned that an internal British security probe focused on Philby, he apparently warned his double agent friend at a hastily arranged lunch.

Despite suspicion surrounding them for years, the two double agents managed to evade any official action until Philby defected to Moscow in 1963. By then, British officials had interrogated Philby with evidence of his disloyalty, prompting him to flee.

Ellis proved more elusive. Eventually, in the mid-1960s, British intelligence officials confronted Ellis with their proof against him. "Ellis denied everything for several days," British counterintelligence agent Peter Wright later recalled in a book. "He blustered and blamed the whole thing on jealous colleagues. But as we produced the evidence…he began to wilt."

Ellis admitted to taking money from the Nazis—selling infor-

mation used by the Gestapo for a planned invasion of Britain—
though he denied being a Soviet mole. He claimed that at
Rockefeller Center he never betrayed Stephenson or the other
Allied intelligence officials, like Donovan and Cuneo, who came
into contact with him.

After three decades, though, the evidence caught up with
Dick Ellis. The small friendly BSC deputy who once appeared
so helpful and knowledgeable was now viewed as a dissembling
traitor by his interrogators.

"Ellis was a venal, sly man," Wright said with disgust. "Never
once did I hear an apology. I could understand how a man might
choose the Soviets through ideological conviction. But to sell
colleagues out to the Germans for a few pounds in time of war?
I told him that had he been caught in 1939–40 he would have
been hanged."

Most historians who examined the Ellis evidence in later years
saw through his duplicity. "Ellis had spied for Russia after the
war, not for ideological motives but because he would be under
heavy blackmail pressure from the KGB," said author Chapman
Pincher, summarizing the British conclusions. "It would never
be possible to make a detailed assessment of the damage he had
done, but if, as seemed likely, his treachery had covered something like thirty years, it would have put Philby's in the shade."

Never charged with any offense, Ellis died in 1975 at the age
of eighty inside the Australian home where he'd retired. A few
years later, when Pincher's allegations about Ellis appeared, British Prime Minister Margaret Thatcher refused to confirm or
deny them, rejecting a request by Ellis's family to clear his name.

The debate about Ellis continued even after his death. Some
defenders, including Ellis biographer Jesse Fink as late as 2023,
would point out there was never an Ellis confession to being a
Soviet mole, and that the accusations against him were never de-
finitively proven. However, for others well-versed in Cold War
espionage, the signs of Ellis's guilt were unmistakable.

"As a spy for the Germans, Ellis had obviously done immense harm," concluded intelligence expert Nigel West in 2016. "As a spy for the Soviets, the ramifications were incalculable."

During the 1980s, when the allegations were still in doubt, old friends from their halcyon days at Room 3603 refused to believe Ellis had hoodwinked them. Stephenson offered to sue anyone who besmirched Ellis's record. Hyde wrote a letter in his defense to the *Times of London*. It seemed unbelievable to Cuneo as well.

"If the charge against Ellis is true...it would mean that the OSS, and to some extent its successor, the CIA, in effect was a branch of the Soviet KGB," Cuneo declared, remembering how Ellis oversaw the origins of America's secret message system. "Since clandestine communications is the very lifeline of any intelligence system, it follows that the charges against Colonel Ellis, if true, could mean that the communications of the OSS were vulnerable and possibly compromised since birth."

Initially, Cuneo would "scorn the idea of 'Dickie' Ellis being a mole" based on weak circumstantial evidence. But eventually he acknowledged that "in this vale of tears, anything is possible. Indeed, there may be some merit to H.L. Mencken's dismal observation that while it is a sin to think evil of people, it is seldom a mistake."

Revelations about Ellis sent a seismic shiver down Cuneo's spine, as if he'd been bamboozled beyond comprehension, his confidence both shaken and stirred. After all, he'd vouched for Ellis over the FBI's objections.

As a discreet middleman of secrets, Cuneo had prided himself on being careful inside the intelligence worlds of Stephenson and Donovan. He considered himself a good judge of character and a true patriot in the fight against tyranny. So how could he have not detected such a double cross, not even with the slightest suspicion?

For if these allegations were true, Dick Ellis was the most invisible spy of all.

In the last few years of his life, Ernest Cuneo's sense of anonymity gave way to a willingness to have his remarkable career noticed publicly, a cause picked up and carried by friends and admirers.

Never forgetting his own roots, Cuneo was praised for his wartime efforts on behalf of people of Italian descent who immigrated to America like his own family. In 1963, the *New York Times* had recognized Cuneo as the main "animator" putting together an international convention in New York of the Italian American Academy of Forensic Medicine, featuring Attorney General Robert F. Kennedy.

Years later, Cuneo championed a public service award named for Fiorello LaGuardia, given out by the National Italian American Foundation. He was thanked by its first recipient, Representative Peter Rodino, chair of the House Judiciary Committee. By the 1980s, Italian Americans like Mario Cuomo, Geraldine Ferraro and Antonin Scalia had found prominent places on the national political scene, in a way that once seemed closed to Cuneo and other Italian Americans a generation earlier.

Cuneo's intelligence friends and legal colleagues in Washington, who called themselves "Ernie's Gang," petitioned for him to receive the Presidential Medal of Freedom, the nation's highest civilian honor. They wanted to make sure America recognized his extraordinarily intelligence work for the US in dealing with Churchill's spies at Rockefeller Center and in the early days of the OSS.

These friends "vowed to correct the oversight while Cuneo still lived, not at Cuneo's request, or even with his specific approval, but solely to satisfy an ideal," recalled Army Colonel M. Cordell Hart, one of the sixteen petitioners. Their petition underlined Cuneo's unique role as the OSS's liaison and included support from Sir William Stephenson.

Fairly or not, history has a way of favoring those in the limelight rather than those who keep secrets in anonymity. An ironic reminder was the large bust of famous aviator Charles Lindbergh installed in 1975 inside the lobby of Rockefeller Center's International Building—once home to the BSC during the war, the same place where Stephenson and Cuneo fought surreptitiously against Lindbergh's America First isolationists' pro-Nazi views. As one last favor to their friend, "Ernie's Gang" tried to pull Cuneo's name out of the dustbin of history.

Cuneo and Churchill's spies, who worked on the thirty-sixth floor of the International Building at Rockefeller Center, are now forgotten without a trace, but a memorial to their key American nemesis—aviator Charles A. Lindbergh, an isolationist—ironically stands at the building's entrance.

AUTHOR COLLECTION

But the lobbying effort for this presidential honor was indeed too little, too late. The petition papers were still being reviewed at the White House when Cuneo died in March 1988 after suffering a heart attack at his home in Arlington, Virginia. His remains were interred at Arlington National Cemetery with full military honors. Though he'd not served in the armed forces, a presidential exception allowed Cuneo's ashes to rest there in recognition of his contributions to the OSS's war effort.

The nonstop force of energy that was Ernest Cuneo—the former NFL player who became an invaluable spy for his country—was now at rest. His wide-ranging interests and fields of endeavor during one lifetime were awe-inspiring to his friends, such as Senator Claiborne Pell, who called him "truly a modern day Renaissance man."

In expressing sympathy, Ernie's friends alluded to his code of anonymity and how it helped him achieve so much as a team player. As one admirer wrote to Cuneo's family about his favorite adage, "His line was always on the matter of how much we might accomplish in life if there was not the need to take credit."

Seasoned Washington observers, like novelist Gore Vidal, knew Cuneo to be an influential behind-the-scenes figure at a key moment in history. Cuneo's secret alliance with Churchill's spies to get America into World War II was part of "the largest, most intricate, and finally most successful" conspiracy of the 20th century, Vidal said.

Yet publicly, Cuneo remained an enigma, with no clear appreciation of what he had done. There were no awards or statues giving him credit or recognition. Newspaper obituaries didn't seem to know what to make of his life. The *New York Times* headline read—"Ernest L. Cuneo, 82; Owned News Service"—with only a fleeting mention of his intelligence work and what had happened at Rockefeller Center. The perfunctory obit contained no sense of his real accomplishments or his impact during the war. It all remained invisible to the paper of record.

Following his death, Cuneo was mentioned fleetingly in histories and biographies about far more famous people. His name appeared almost as an afterthought. His unique role as a spy—traceable through his collected papers at the FDR Library and other declassified documents—remained largely ignored, much to his family's puzzlement. Cuneo's adult children, Jonathan and

Sandra, became custodians of their father's legacy. (Both were interviewed extensively for this book, with Jonathan providing a copy of his father's unpublished memoir.)

"It's one of the most amazing stories," said Jonathan, a prominent Washington attorney, who tried to piece together the intricate details of his father's life before he died in July 2023. "The interactions between Winchell and British intelligence—and the effort for hearts and minds—was a big intersection between what Stephenson was trying to accomplish and what my father was trying to accomplish. I think there's a lot there."

Sandra Cuneo, who once served in Governor Mario Cuomo's Washington office in the 1990s, said she didn't really know what her father did with Winchell—including the "leaks" from the British intelligence that appeared in the American press—until she read Neal Gabler's 1994 biography of the famous columnist. Her mother's spy career was even more of a mystery.

On the most personal level, the Cuneo siblings remained in the dark, with so many unresolved questions about their parents' time at Rockefeller Center. They learned that other adult children of those who'd once worked for "Intrepid" had a similar unfulfilled curiosity.

Around 2007, Eliza Nascarella, the grown daughter of Margaret's BSC friend Elinore Little, contacted Sandra, then living in Los Angeles, and asked about getting together. It was a request made for old time's sake.

In the early 1940s, Elinore Little considered Margaret Watson to be her best friend. They were young women from Canada who'd moved to New York to serve undercover in the British Security Coordination office. The two women stayed friends after the war but were now long gone.

Over the phone, Elinore's daughter expressed a strong desire to know more. "She looked me up out of the blue," recalled Sandra. "She said, 'I'm coming to LA with my two daughters.' And she stayed with us."

When they finally sat down to compare notes, the two daughters of these female BSC staffers hoped to find some answers. The threat of punishment for violating wartime secrets no longer applied. What happened at Rockefeller Center was now a part of history, even if certain details were still in dispute.

Despite their daughters' curiosity, however, Elinore and Margaret took their wartime secrets with them to the grave, having rarely spoken about their special wartime service after they came home. As former spies, they too remained invisible, even to their own children.

"We asked, 'What did our mothers do during the war?'" Sandra recalled.

After a short discussion, the two daughters came to the same conclusion.

"Beats the hell out of me," Sandra said, laughing.

It was a Runyonesque phrase that sounded very much like Ernest Cuneo.

★ ★ ★ ★ ★

ENDNOTES

In assembling this book, I relied on Ernest Cuneo's unpublished memoir, many of his files stored at the FDR Presidential Library and interviews with his two adult children, Sandra and Jonathan Cuneo. This effort was supplemented by dozens of published books, newspaper, magazine and scholarly articles—including some written by Cuneo himself—as well as various documents from the Library of Congress, the Truman, Kennedy and LBJ presidential libraries, the National Archives, the FBI, OSS and CIA archives, the Columbia University library, Indiana University library, Princeton University library and the Churchill Archives in Cambridge, England. Where there was a difference of opinion (and sometimes even fact) between sources, I relied on the most contemporaneous account and used my best judgment.

I owe heartfelt thanks to my longtime entertainment attorney Scott E. Schwimer, literary agent Joe Veltre of the Gersh Agency, editor Peter Joseph and his Hanover Square staff at HarperCollins, and my family, friends and colleagues, particularly Taylor Maier, Mark Harrington, Tom Mitchell, Reade Maier, Emily

Schmitt, Andrew Maier and his wife, Leah Jackson. Most of all, I'm forever grateful to my wife, Joyce McGurrin, for all her wise advice and abiding love. With Joyce as my inspiration and companion, it's been quite a journey.

—*Thomas Maier, Long Island, New York*

ABBREVIATIONS

ECM—Ernest Cuneo Unpublished Memoir

FDR—Ernest Cuneo Papers at FDR Presidential Library

BSC—*British Security Coordination: The Secret History of British Intelligence in the Americas, 1940–1945*. Edited by William Stephenson, introduction by Nigel West. Fromm International, 1999. First published in Great Britain, 1998.

HYDE—Hyde, H. Montgomery. *Room 3603: The Incredible True Story of Secret Intelligence Operations During World War II*. Farrar, Straus and Giroux, 1962.

PART I

"Today, Winston Churchill is the center": *American Monthly Review of Reviews*, May 1905.

"Never say 'no' to adventures": Fleming, Fergus, ed. *The Man with the Golden Typewriter: Ian Fleming's James Bond Letters*. Bloomsbury Publishing USA, 2015, p. 263.

CHAPTER 1

"Nazi forces": Presidential Speeches, Franklin D. Roosevelt Presidency, On Lend Lease file, Mar. 15, 1941, *https://millercenter.org*.

"Senor Don Julio Lopez Lido": Ludwig Spy Ring file, *https://www.fbi.gov*.

"The British are many things": ECM.

"I have said this before": Goodwin, Doris Kearns. *No Ordinary Time: Franklin & Eleanor Roosevelt: The Home Front in World War II*. Simon & Schuster, 2008, p. 187.

"He [Stephenson] is a man of few words": HYDE, p. x.

"Few of the thousands": le Carré, John. "England's Spy in America." *New York Times*, Feb. 29, 1976.

"Know what I'd like": Fleming, Fergus, ed. *The Man with the Golden Typewriter: Ian Fleming's James Bond Letters*. Bloomsbury Publishing USA, 2015, p. 85.

"Cuneo not only belonged": HYDE, p. 191.

"Tangle within tangle": Churchill, Winston S. "My Own True Spy Story by the Man Who Has the Best Right to Tell One." *The Cosmopolitan*, Vol. 77. Schlicht & Field, 1924, p. 76.

"For the British": Troy, Thomas F. "The Coordination of Information and British Intelligence." Secret document approved for release Apr. 21, 2005, p. 55, *https://www.cia.gov/library/readingroom*.

"British Passport Control": Lovell, Mary S. *Cast No Shadow: The Life of the American Spy Who Changed the Course of World War II*. Pantheon Books, 1992, p. 338.

"My father": Int. with Jonathan Cuneo.

"Disposal squad": Gentry, Curt. *J. Edgar Hoover: The Man and the Secrets*. W. W. Norton & Company, 2001, p. 271.

"For security reasons": Marrin, Albert. *FDR and the American Crisis*. Knopf, 2015, p. 156.

CHAPTER 2

"Men have a solicitude about fame": Boswell, James. *The Life of Samuel Johnson, Vol. 2*. London: J. Davis, 1817, p. 208.

"Both teams": "Football Giants in Tie at Orange." *New York Times*, Sept. 30, 1929.

"It was a bruising game", **"We weren't playing for the money"**, **"For the addicted football player"**, **"Like the other teams"**, **"Piggy was"**: Cuneo, Ernest. "Present at the Creation: Professional Football in the Twenties." *American Scholar*, Autumn 1987, Vol. 56, No. 4, pp. 487–501.

"Socially I think": Int. with Sandra Cuneo.

"I saw myself always as an alien": Talese, Gay. *Unto the Sons*. Random House, 2014, p. 4.

"A remarkable lack": "Columbia Matmen Top Harvard." *New York Times*, Jan. 15, 1928, p. 149.

"Recuperation and setting": ECM, Part 1–3, pp. 68–73.

"Crusader": LaGumina, Salvatore J. "Ernest Cuneo, the Forgotten Brain Truster." *Italian American Review*, Jul. 1, 2021, Vol. 11, Issue 2, pp. 141–148.

"Commercial geography": Applegate, Edd. *Muckrakers: A Biographical Dictionary of Writers and Editors*. Scarecrow Press, 2008, p. 136.

"Sort of a run of the mill player": Cuneo, Ernest. "Present at the Creation: Professional Football in the Twenties." *American Scholar*, Autumn 1987, Vol. 56, No. 4, pp. 492–493.

"A deep forehead cut", **"I decided to quit"**: ECM, Part 1–3, p. 339.

CHAPTER 3

"We seldom discussed", **"It was embarrassing"**: LaGumina, Salvatore J. "Ernest Cuneo, the Forgotten Brain Truster." *Italian American Review*, Jul. 1, 2021, Vol. 11, Issue 2, pp. 141–148.

"Fiorello's office": Cuneo, Ernest. *Life with Fiorello*. Avon Book, 1960, p. 9.

"We can protect", **"The people turned out"**: LaGumina, Salvatore J. "Ernest Cuneo, the Forgotten Brain Truster." *Italian American Review*, Jul. 1, 2021, Vol. 11, Issue 2, pp. 141–148.

"Ernie is wonderful to talk to": Thomas G. Corcoran, interview 3 (III), 9/9/1969, by Joe B. Frantz, LBJ Library Oral Histories, LBJ Presidential Library, p. 14.

"Lord Lothian", **"Britain will marry Hitler"**: Gabler, Neal. *Winchell: Gossip, Power and the Culture of Celebrity*. Alfred A. Knopf, 1994, p. 287.

"Tom bitched a bit": Winchell, Walter, with introduction by Ernest Cuneo. *Winchell Exclusive*. Prentice-Hall, 1975, p. ix.

"Legal services", **"Cuneo raised"**: Gabler, Neal. *Winchell: Gossip, Power and the Culture of Celebrity*. Alfred A. Knopf, 1994, p. 288.

"An infallible combination": FDR, Against OSS and BSC file, p. 77.

"John [J. Edgar Hoover] wouldn't tap": ECM.

"Short speech", **"I had Walter"**: FDR, Crusader to Intrepid file, p. 48.

"The President feels", **"Look Walter"**: Gabler, Neal. *Winchell: Gossip, Power and the Culture of Celebrity*. Alfred A. Knopf, 1994, pp. 287–288.

"Walter Winchell was uniquely influential": Weiner, Richard. *Syndicated Columnists*. Public Relations Publishing Company, 1979, p. 57.

"There was a lawyer named Ernest Cuneo": LBJ Library, Oral history transcript, James H. Rowe Jr., interview 5 (V), 5/10/1983, by Michael L. Gillette, p. 3.

CHAPTER 4

"Far away": "Text of Address by Winston Churchill Replying to Chancellor Hitler." *New York Times*, Oct. 17, 1938.

"Displayed cautious interest": Brown, Anthony Cave. *C: The Secret Life of Sir Stewart Graham Menzies, Spymaster to Winston Churchill*. Macmillan, 1987, p. 195.

"Volunteered to assassinate Hitler": Int. with H. Montgomery Hyde, "After Dark: British Intelligence," Open Media Production, Channel 4, 1988.

"Easy rifle shot": *Gibraltar Magazine*, March 2009, pp. 32–33.

"We have not reached": Grehan, John. *The Hitler Assassination Attempts: The Plots, Places and People That Almost Changed History*. Frontline Books, 2022, p. 71.

"Could have sent": "Personal History," The Intrepid Society, *http://intrepid-society.org/W4/personal-history*.

"Horrible bloodbath": Churchill, Winston. Churchill Archives, CHAR 8/518A/33 Oct–Dec 1935, "The Truth About Hitler" pamphlet. The article is reprinted from WSC's article for the November 1935 *Strand Magazine* and includes the text of his article.

"I think I see my way through": Hastings, Max. "Privately Churchill called them 'bloody Yankees'—but with a lover's ardour he fawned, flattered and flirted to woo the U.S." *Daily Mail*, Aug. 20, 2009.

"I shall drag the United States": Gilbert, Martin. *Churchill and America*. Simon & Schuster, 2005, p. 186.

"I was sent": Stephenson in 1973 CBC Interview, *Secret Secretaries: The Women of British Security Co-ordination*.

"Churchill's vision": Gage, Beverly. *G-Man: J. Edgar Hoover and the Making of the American Century*. Penguin, 2022, p. 245.

"Quietly and with no fanfare": Troy, Thomas F. "The Coordination of Information and British Intelligence." Secret report approved for release Apr. 21, 2005, pp. 22–23.

"I cannot contravene": Gentry, Curt. *J. Edgar Hoover: The Man and the Secrets.* W. W. Norton & Company, 2001, p. 265.

"Stephenson agreed", "Welcomed the idea enthusiastically": HYDE, p. 26.

"There should be the closest possible marriage": Troy, Thomas F. *Wild Bill and Intrepid: Donovan, Stephenson, and the Origin of CIA.* Yale University Press, 1996, p. 39.

"Counter-espionage, political warfare", "Your duty lies there", "If we do go down": HYDE, pp. 26–32.

CHAPTER 5

"Since the only time": FDR, Crusader to Intrepid file, p. 86.

"Had instant communication": Troy, Thomas F. *Wild Bill and Intrepid: Donovan, Stephenson, and the Origin of CIA.* Yale University Press, 1996, p. 185.

"A curious no-man's land": ECM.

"We had reached": Persico, Joseph E. *Roosevelt's Secret War: FDR and World War II Espionage.* Random House, 2002, p. 30.

"Lindbergh dropped in at the embassy", "It was the decisive factor": Klurfeld, Herman. *Winchell, His Life and Times.* Praeger, 1976, p. 81.

"The Crown": MacDonnell, Francis. *Insidious Foes: The Axis Fifth Column and the American Home Front.* Oxford University Press, 1995, pp. 53–58.

"It was hardly a roaring success": FBI History, "Rumrich Nazi Spy Case," *https://www.fbi.gov/history/famous-cases/rumrich-nazi-spy-case.*

"The Ratzis": "The time Walter Winchell condemned an American Nazi rally," *American Masters, https://www.pbs.org.*

"One of those lethal chariot races": ECM, Part 1–3, p. 1207.

"Today's threat": Daniels, Roger. *Franklin D. Roosevelt: The War Years, 1939–1945.* University of Illinois Press, 2016, p. 67.

"Those with whom": MacDonnell, Francis. *Insidious Foes: The Axis Fifth Column and the American Home Front.* Oxford University Press, 1995, p. 101.

"When it came to protecting": FDR, OSS Stephenson Boys file, p. 6.

CHAPTER 6

Details of Donovan's arrival and "He laughed": "British Plane Here on Regular Flight." *New York Times*, Aug. 5, 1940, p. 1.

"Wild Bill": Waller, Douglas. *Wild Bill Donovan: The Spymaster Who Created the OSS and Modern American Espionage.* Free Press, 2011, p. 23.

"My secret legs": Dunlop, Richard. "The Wartime OSS." *American Legion Magazine*, June 1984, p. 15.

"I arranged that": HYDE, p. 37.

"Mr. President, with great respect": Kimball, Warren F. *Churchill and Roosevelt, Volume 1: The Complete Correspondence—Three Volumes.* Princeton University Press, 2015, p. 57.

"Frankly and honestly": Wapshott, Nicholas. *The Sphinx: Franklin Roosevelt, the Isolationists, and the Road to World War II.* W. W. Norton & Company, 2014.

"Doing much to combat": HYDE, p. 38.

"In the United States", "Nazi Germany is a conspiracy": Congressional Record, 76th Congress, Vol. 86, Part 10, p. 10781.

"He [Donovan] has carried": United States. Department of State, "Foreign Relations of the United States: Diplomatic Papers, Volume 2," p. 952.

"A novel attempt": Troy, Thomas, quoted in "The Office of Strategic Services: America's First Intelligence Agency," CIA Publication, May 2000, pp. 5–10.

"If they ever": Benson, Robert Louis, and Michael Warner. "Venona: Soviet Espionage and the American Response 1939–1957," National Security Agency, 1996, p. 91.

"I shall never accept": Allen Dulles FBI file, File 1, Section 4, p. 29, contains Giniger, K.S. "Chief Spy: The Story of Allen Dulles." *Washington Post*, Jul. 3, 1960.

"Liaison": "Ernest L. Cuneo, 82; Owned News Service" obituary. *New York Times*, Mar. 5, 1988.

"If things went", "Murphy was visibly nervous", "FDR had reached the limit": FDR, Box 108, OSS and Stephenson file, p. 53; FRD, Crusader to Intrepid file, p. 90.

CHAPTER 7

"Stephenson knew": Pearson, John. *The Life of Ian Fleming*. Bantam, 1967, p. 104.

"To Stephenson": Pearson, John. "James Bond Alias Ian Fleming." *Life*, Oct. 7, 1966, p. 102.

"It was a pretty sound job": Fleming, Ian. *Casino Royale*. Signet, 1953, p. 109.

"There was a huge fireplace": FDR, Box 5, Fleming, Ian, (Folder 2 of 2), p. 5.

"Do you question", "All but tirelessly": Fleming, Fergus, ed. *The Man with the Golden Typewriter: Ian Fleming's James Bond Letters*. Bloomsbury Publishing USA, 2015, pp. 75–76.

"All but blind": Conant, Jennet. *The Irregulars: Roald Dahl and the British Spy Ring in Wartime Washington*. Simon & Schuster, 2008, p. 98.

"Recalling the Battle": ECM, p. 30.

"This is Mortimer": HYDE, p. 182.

"Stephenson insisted I meet Colonel Ellis": FDR, Crusader to Intrepid file, p. 91.

"I had been 20": "Patriot or spy?" *Toronto Sun*, Jul. 14, 1981, contained in CIA file released 2010, *https://www.cia.gov/readingroom/docs/CIA-RDP90-00552R000201770001-5.pdf*.

"With the outbreak of war": Troy, Thomas F. *Wild Bill and Intrepid: Donovan, Stephenson, and the Origin of CIA*. Yale University Press, 1996, p. 240.

"Donovan told me": FDR, Crusader to Intrepid file, p. 91.

"Dickie": FDR, Box 108, OSS and Stephenson file, p. 51; Matthews, Owen. *An Impeccable Spy: Richard Sorge, Stalin's Master Agent*. Bloomsbury, 2019, p. 362.

"No fool": Jeffery, Keith. *MI6: The History of the Secret Intelligence Service 1909–1949*. Penguin, 2011, p. 195.

"Colonel Ellis": FDR, Box 108, OSS and Stephenson file, p. 51.

"Ellis was at the center": Brown, Anthony Cave. *C: The Secret Life of Sir Stewart Graham Menzies, Spymaster to Winston Churchill*. Macmillan, 1987, p. 366.

"One of the very few": *Newsweek*, 1981, Vol. 97, Issue 2, p. 60.

"In addition": FDR, OSS Stephenson Boys file, p. 36.

"With such a large organization", **"Gogarty never showed"**, **"He in turn"**: HYDE, pp. 182–193.

CHAPTER 8

"It is essential": Tzu, Sun. *The Art of War*. Oxford University Press, 1963, p. 148.

"Is it really the Norden Bombsight?", **"The Americans are so secretive"**, **"My message"**: Farago, Ladislas. *The Game of the Foxes*. Hodder & Stoughton, 1974, pp. 41–45.

"It was comparatively easy": HYDE, p. 27.

"The greatest spy roundup": Moynihan, Daniel Patrick. *Secrecy: The American Experience*. Yale University Press, 1998, p. 126.

"The secret": Farago, Ladislas. *The Game of the Foxes*. Hodder & Stoughton, 1974, p. 459.

"Whose tiptoe trail zigzagged": "National Affairs: Spies!" *Time*, Jul. 7, 1941.

"Gentlemen, the time": Simon, Joe, and Jack Kirby. *Captain America, No. 2*. Marvel Comics.

"Sabotage, assassination, and 'Fifth Column'": Daniels, Roger, Sandra C. Taylor, and Harry H. L. Kitano. *Japanese Americans: From Relocation to Redress*. University of Washington Press, 2013, p. 83.

"One of those priceless possessions": Kessner, Thomas. *The Flight of the Century: Charles Lindbergh and the Rise of American Aviation*. Oxford University Press, 2010, p. 230.

"New and effective": BSC, p. 73.

"You are a double agent", **"You have the makings,"** **"I don't know what devil"**: Popov, Dusko. *Spy/Counterspy: The Autobiography of Dusko Popov*. Grosset & Dunlap, 1974, pp. 74–75, 151.

"You're like all double agents": Loftis, Larry. *Into the Lion's Mouth: The True Story of Dusko Popov: World War II Spy, Patriot, and the Real-Life Inspiration for James Bond*. Penguin, 2022, p. 107.

"I don't think a choir boy": Levine, Joshua. *Operation Fortitude: The Story of the Spies and the Spy Operation That Saved D-Day.* Rowman & Littlefield, 2011, p. 126.

"America is still uncommitted": Popov, Dusko. *Spy/Counterspy: The Autobiography of Dusko Popov.* Grosset & Dunlap, 1974, p. 172.

"How, I asked myself, how?": Haufler, Hervie. *The Spies Who Never Were: The True Story of the Nazi Spies Who Were Actually Allied Double Agents.* Open Road Media, 2014, p. 105.

"I had no doubt": Brown, Anthony Cave. *C: The Secret Life of Sir Stewart Graham Menzies, Spymaster to Winston Churchill.* Macmillan, 1987, p. 373.

CHAPTER 9

"An invisible man": Nowlan, Robert A., and Gwendolyn W. Nowlan. *Film Quotations: 11,000 Lines Spoken on Screen, Arranged by Subject, and Indexed.* McFarland & Co., 2016, p. 529.

"Sh-h-h—don't tell anyone", "The brilliant New York attorney": *San Bernardino Sun,* Vol. 45, Oct. 2, 1938, p. 19.

"My experience in combat journalism": ECM, Part 1–3, p. 8.

"One of the first Italian Americans", "Gratefully acknowledged": LaGumina, Salvatore J. "Ernest Cuneo, the Forgotten Brain Truster." *Italian American Review,* Jul. 1, 2021, Vol. 11, Issue 2, pp. 141–148.

"Having served": ECM, Part 1–3, p. 617.

"I am a juggler": Goodwin, Doris Kearns. *No Ordinary Time: Franklin and Eleanor Roosevelt: The Home Front in World War II.* Simon & Schuster, 1994, p. 137.

"I saw many champions": FDR, Against OSS and BSC file, p. 16.

"He was FDR's Field Marshal", "The security of": ECM, Part 1–3, p. 655.

"I'm too Irish": FDR, Against OSS and BSC file, pp. 25–27.

"My own lines": FDR, Crusader to Intrepid file, pp. 49–50.

"Almost no one": Pearson, Drew, and Robert S. Allen. "Washington Merry-Go-Round," syndicated column, Feb. 3, 1939.

"Bob, you can send": ECM, Part 1–3, p. 1272.

"I told him": FDR, Crusader to Intrepid file, p. 89.

"I needed little": FDR, OSS, the Structure of Ernie's Role file, p. 5.

"I have a very great fondness": Oral history transcript, Ernest Cuneo, interview 2 (II), 4/23/1970, by Joe B. Frantz, LBJ Library Oral Histories, LBJ Presidential Library.

"When they started", "I was annoyed somewhat": FDR, OSS, the Structure of Ernie's Role file, p. 2.

CHAPTER 10

"All propaganda": Orwell, George, quoted in Ricks, Thomas E. *Churchill and Orwell: The Fight for Freedom.* Penguin, 2017, p. 162.

"That phenomena peculiar": ECM, Part 1–3, pp. 1135–1137.

"The predicament of Britain": Shirer, William L. *The Rise and Fall of the Third Reich: A History of Nazi Germany.* 50th anniversary ed. Simon & Schuster, 2011, p. 827.

"The propaganda war", "Since the might": ECM, Part 1–3, pp. 1135–1137.

"An excellent intermediary", "He was an American lawyer", "As the alliance": BSC, p. 125.

"The principal difficulty": ECM, Part 1–3, p. 1074.

"Should be cultivated", "Political changes", "This is terrific", "Got any more stuff": BSC, pp. 126–130.

"Great care": Ibid., p. 83.

"Dear Ernie", "I have been asked": Mahl, Thomas E. *Desperate Deception: British Covert Operations in the United States, 1939–44.* Potomac Books, 2000, p. 94.

"The most effective": Ibid., p. 27.

"Propaganda is a truly terrible": Davidson, Eugene. *The Trial of the Germans.* Macmillan, 1966, p. 526.

"The British were desperate": Mahl, Thomas E. *Desperate Deception: British Covert Operations in the United States, 1939–44.* Potomac Books, 2000, pp. 124–125.

PART II

"War ought to be": "Congressional Record: Proceedings and Debates of the Congress," Vol. 85, Part 1, 1939, p. 812.

"We knew almost nothing": Kent, Sherman. "Sherman Kent and the Board of National Estimates: Collected Essays," History Staff, Center for the Study of Intelligence, Central Intelligence Agency, 1994.

CHAPTER 11

"Why, by interweaving": Packard, Frederick Clifton. *They Spoke for Democracy: Classic Statements of the American Way.* Scribner, 1958, p. 48.

"It sounded like": INS. "25 Die in Airplane Crash." *Zanesville Signal Ohio*, Sept. 1, 1940.

"As a member": Memorial Services Held in the House of Representatives and Senate of the United States, Together with Remarks Presented in Eulogy of Ernest Lundeen, Late a Senator from Minnesota, U.S. Government Printing Office, 1942, p. 36.

"If federal authorities", **"A rabid pro-German isolationist"**, **"Lundeen was one"**: Pearson, Drew, and Robert S. Allen. "Washington Merry-Go-Round," syndicated column, Sept. 12, 1940.

"This man, if he lives": Viereck, George Sylvester, Biography at the University of Iowa Libraries, Special Collections.

"Meticulous neatness", **"In any other age"**: "George Sylvester Viereck, 77, Pro-German Propagandist, Dies." *New York Times*, Mar. 20, 1962, p. 37.

"Viereck started": *Editor & Publisher*, 1918, Vol. 51, Issue 1, p. 8.

"Small but dangerous": Johnson, Niel M. *George Sylvester Viereck, German-American Propagandist.* University of Illinois, 1972, p. 87.

"It is clear that you accept": "Viereck Rushes to Harding's Aid." *New York Times*, Sept. 25, 1920.

"A man with two loves": Solomon, Harvey. *Such Splendid Prisons: Diplomatic Detainment in America During World War II.* University of Nebraska Press, 2020, p. 71.

"The agents who are known", **"Viereck succeeded in spinning"**: Farago, Ladislas. *The Game of the Foxes.* Hodder & Stoughton, 1974, p. 431, 378.

"I have never heard": Maddow, Rachel. Transcript: Rachel Maddow Presents: Ultra, Episode 4: A Bad Angle, Oct. 24, 2022, *https://www.msnbc.com/msnbc-podcast/rachel-maddow-presents-ultra/transcript-bad-angle-n1300107*.

"My real crime": Keller, Phyllis. *States of Belonging: German-American Intellectuals and the First World War*. Harvard University Press, 1979, p. 182.

"He had his lawyer": Winchell, Walter, syndicated column, appearing in *Sausalito News*, Vol. 56, No. 1, Jan. 2, 1941.

"Stripped": "Says Mrs. Lundeen Took Viereck Data; Former Secretary to Senator Testifies That Widow 'Stripped' Files of Records." *New York Times*, Feb. 25, 1942, p. 10.

"Stephenson's liaison officer": HYDE, p. 92.

"Smear was the word": Walter Winchell file, Part 18 of 58, FBI Vault.

"Watched him [Viereck] from the very beginning": HYDE, p. 185.

"It made a considerable impression": BSC, p. 224.

"Just as the journalist Drew Pearson predicted:" Maddow, Rachel. Transcript: Rachel Maddow Presents: Ultra, Episode 1: Trip 19, *https://www.msnbc.com/msnbc-podcast/rachel-maddow-presents-ultra/transcript-trip-19-n1299418*.

CHAPTER 12

"Oh, how the ghost": Gottlieb, Robert, and Robert Kimball. *Reading Lyrics: More Than 1,000 of the Twentieth Century's Finest Song Lyrics*. Knopf Doubleday Publishing Group, 2000, p. 345.

"The tremendous bond": FDR, Box 5, Fleming, Ian, (Folder 2 of 2), p. 68.

"Three measures of Gordon's": Fleming, Ian. *Casino Royale*. J. Cape, 1953, p. 60.

"Operation Mincemeat": Macintyre, Ben. *Operation Mincemeat: How a Dead Man and a Bizarre Plan Fooled the Nazis and Assured an Allied Victory*, Crown, 2010, pp. 11–12.

"Of the possible changes": Bryce, Ivar. *You Only Live Once: Memories of Ian Fleming*. Weidenfeld & Nicolson, 1984, pp. 3–4.

"And now, go": Holland, James. *The Battle of Britain: Five Months That Changed History; May–October 1940*. Macmillan, 2011, p. 408.

"Churchill felt this": Roberts, Andrew. *Churchill: Walking with Destiny.* Penguin, 2018, pp. 580–581.

"When Donovan informed": Bratzel, John F., and Leslie B. Rout Jr. "FDR and the 'Secret Map.'" *Wilson Quarterly*, 1985, Vol. 9, No. 1, pp. 167–173.

"Manufacturing documents": Persico, Joseph E. *Roosevelt's Secret War: FDR and World War II Espionage.* Random House, 2002, p. 128.

"Hitler has often": "Text of President Roosevelt's Navy Day Address." *San Bernardino Daily Sun*, Oct. 28, 1941, p. 2.

"What would you say": Bratzel, John F., and Leslie B. Rout Jr. "FDR and the 'Secret Map.'" *Wilson Quarterly*, 1985, Vol. 9, No. 1, pp. 167–173.

"Nazi Ire": Kluckhohn, Frank L. "Nazi Ire Over 'Secret Map' Is a 'Scream' to Roosevelt; He Enjoys 'Faker' and Other Denunciations—Cannot Make Documents Public Lest He Reveal Data Source." *New York Times*, Oct. 29, 1941.

"If Donovan had been told", **"It was Roosevelt's policy"**: Bratzel, John F., and Leslie B. Rout Jr. "FDR and the 'Secret Map.'" *Wilson Quarterly*, 1985, Vol. 9, No. 1, pp. 167–173.

"Given the time": Mahl, Thomas E. *Desperate Deception: British Covert Operations in the United States, 1939–44.* Potomac Books, 2000, p. 16.

CHAPTER 13

"All my possessions": Gilbert, Martin, Winston Churchill, and Emery Reves. *Winston Churchill and Emery Reves: Correspondence, 1937–1964.* University of Texas Press, 1997, p. 12.

"I strongly hope": Churchill Archives, Char 2/410 image 12.

"There is a large field": Churchill Archives, Char 2/410 image 6-7.

"The principal sources": FDR, Against OSS and BSC file, p. 7.

"This was a private", **"That a certain person"**, **"Who is the mysterious"**: Gilbert, Martin, Winston Churchill, and Emery Reves. *Winston Churchill and Emery Reves: Correspondence, 1937–1964.* University of Texas Press, 1997, p. 238.

"My celebrity": Clemons, Walter. "Superspies." *Newsweek*, Mar. 22, 1976.

"Bill [Stephenson] would ask": Macdonald, Bill. *The True Intrepid: Sir William Stephenson and the Unknown Agents*. Timberholme Books, 1998, p. 262.

"I had a gnawing suspicion": Koch, Stephen. "The Playboy Was a Spy." *New York Times*, Apr. 13, 2008.

"Sliding remark": HYDE, p. 187.

"Contacted friends": Winchell, Walter, with introduction by Ernest Cuneo. *Winchell Exclusive*. Prentice-Hall, 1975, p. 182.

"We were in 1941": MacDonnell, Francis. *Insidious Foes: The Axis Fifth Column and the American Home Front*. Oxford University Press, 1995, pp. 103–104.

"It tells the truth": *Life*, Jan. 31, 1938, p. 24.

"An imperial film": Stafford, David. *Oblivion or Glory: 1921 and the Making of Winston Churchill*. Yale University Press, 2019.

"The pictures": Churchill, Winston. "The Future of Publicity," Collier's Weekly, CHAR 8/521, Churchill Archives.

"I strongly suspect": Eyman, Scott. *Cary Grant: A Brilliant Disguise*. Simon & Schuster, 2021, pp. 179–180.

"On the one hand": Gabler, Neal. *Winchell: Gossip, Power and the Culture of Celebrity*. Alfred A. Knopf, 1994, p. 291.

"Newspapers, always": ECM, Part 3, p. 45.

"Beyond hope": BSC, p. 21.

"One of the principal methods": BSC, p. 58.

CHAPTER 14

"She had top secret": Int. with Sandra Cuneo.

"Her role": Int. with Jonathan Cuneo.

"The first time": *Secret Secretaries: The Women of British Security Coordination*, (video 28:10).

"I didn't think": Macdonald, Bill. *The True Intrepid: Sir William Stephenson and the Unknown Agents*. Timberholme Books, 1998, p. 190.

"Thousands of our agents": A Historical Note Introduction by Charles

Howard Ellis to William Stevenson's *A Man Called Intrepid*. Simon & Schuster, 2013, p. 10.

"No one thought": Macdonald, Bill. *The True Intrepid: Sir William Stephenson and the Unknown Agents*. Timberholme Books, 1998, p. 170.

"Canada left": ECM, Part 1–3, p. 1203.

"Another most secret": Brown, Anthony Cave. *C: The Secret Life of Sir Stewart Graham Menzies, Spymaster to Winston Churchill*. Macmillan, 1987, p. 359.

"We were aware": *Secret Secretaries: The Women of British Security Coordination*, (video 1:13).

"He had that quality": "Personal History", The Intrepid Society, *http://intrepid-society.org/W4/personal-history/*.

"If I am killed": Macintyre, Ben. *Ben Macintyre's World War II Espionage Files: Agent Zigzag, Operation Mincemeat*. Crown, 2012, p. 38.

CHAPTER 15

"She was learning": de Maupassant, Guy. *The Complete Works of Guy de Maupassant—Volume 12, 1917*. Brunswick Subscription Company, 1917, p. 247.

"In the higher ranges": Churchill, Winston. *The Cosmopolitan*, 1924, Vol. 77, p. 76.

"Very earthy": ECM, Part 1–3, p. 1275.

"Indicated that not only Mata Hari": Ibid., Part 1–3, p. 1176.

"It would be difficult": BSC, p. 194.

"I commuted back": *Secret Secretaries: The Women of British Security Coordination*, (video 32:00).

"Ashamed?", "Unusually beautiful": Hyde, H. Montgomery. *Cynthia: The Spy Who Changed the Course of the War*. H. Hamilton, 1966, p. 2.

"Several well-known agents": Lovell, Mary S. *Cast No Shadow: The Life of the American Spy Who Changed the Course of World War II*. Pantheon Books, 1992, p. 157.

"Springbok", "A man of powerful attraction": HYDE, pp. 222–223.

"Particularly irritated": HYDE, p. xiii.

"As a bedtime story": BSC, p. 198.

"In a lot of ways": Macdonald, Bill. *The True Intrepid: Sir William Stephenson and the Unknown Agents.* Timberholme Books, 1998, p. 263.

"I was dating": *Secret Secretaries: The Women of British Security Co-ordination,* (video 25:50).

CHAPTER 16

"If Bill Donovan": Troy, Thomas F. "Donovan and the CIA: A History of the Establishment of the Central Intelligence Agency," Part 71, CIA Center for the Study of Intelligence, 1981, p. 26.

"Although the Federal": HYDE, p. 85.

"We likewise decided": Berle, Adolf A. *Navigating the Rapids, 1918–1971: From the Papers of Adolf A. Berle.* Harcourt Brace Jovanovich, 1973, p. 321.

"Gentlemen do not": Stimson, Henry Lewis. *On Active Service in Peace and War, Vol. 2.* Harper & Row, 1948, p. 188.

"You can imagine": Dunlop, Richard. *Donovan: America's Master Spy.* Rand McNally, 1982, p. 287.

"Women spies": Breuer, William B. *War and American Women: Heroism, Deeds, and Controversy.* Greenwood Publishing Group, 1997, p. 46.

"In Donovan's rush": Waller, Douglas. *Wild Bill Donovan: The Spymaster Who Created the OSS and Modern American Espionage.* Free Press, 2011, p. 94.

"England was not": Conant, Jennet. *The Irregulars: Roald Dahl and the British Spy Ring in Wartime Washington.* Simon & Schuster, 2008, p. 306.

"Ghosting is": Winchell, Walter, with introduction by Ernest Cuneo. *Winchell Exclusive.* Prentice-Hall, 1975, p. viii.

"The sort of guy": Wills, Garry. *John Wayne's America.* Simon & Schuster, 2013, p. 162.

"And you can ask": CIA Report on Interviews with Sir William S. Stephenson in Paget, Bermuda, Feb. 11–15, 1969, declassified and released by CIA in 2002, p. 4.

"Running a radio": BSC, p. 60.

"A society": Ignatius, David. "How Churchill's Agents Secretly Manipulated the U.S. Before Pearl Harbor." *Washington Post*, Sept. 17, 1989.

"The Astrological Tendencies": Campbell, Christy. "How Hitler's defeat really was down to the stars." *Daily Mail*, Mar. 7, 2008.

"An ever-growing audience": Jacobsen, Annie. *Phenomena: The Secret History of the U.S. Government's Investigations into Extrasensory Perception and Psychokinesis*. Little, Brown, 2017, p. 15.

"A period of embitterment": BSC, p. 49.

"Silent killing": Winks, Robin W. *Cloak & Gown: Scholars in the Secret War, 1939–1961*. Yale University Press, 1996, p. 168.

"Practically delirious": Waller, Douglas. *Wild Bill Donovan: The Spymaster Who Created the OSS and Modern American Espionage*. Free Press, 2011, p. 126.

"It was typical": Ranelagh, John. *The Agency: The Rise and Decline of the CIA*. Simon & Schuster, 1987, p. 83.

"He [FDR] himself had": FDR, Against OSS and BSC file, pp. 12–13.

CHAPTER 17

"There is required": Churchill, Winston. *The World Crisis*. Simon & Schuster, 2005, p. 293.

"The clenched fist": Thomas, Gordon, and Greg Lewis. *Shadow Warriors of World War II: The Daring Women of the OSS and SOE*. Chicago Review Press, 2017, p. 66.

"Was taught how": Horn, Bernd. *A Most Ungentlemanly Way of War: The SOE and the Canadian Connection*. Dundurn, 2016, p. 91.

"We have to admit": Casey, William J. "Remarks of William J. Casey Director of Central Intelligence Before Veterans of Office of Strategic Services Aboard the Intrepid in New York City," Sept. 22, 1983, *https://www.cia.gov/readingroom/*.

"Paul [Dehn] actually": Kipen, David. "Tinker Tailor Soldier Schreiber: The Unsung Achievement of Screenwriter Paul Dehn." *VQR—A National Journal of Literature & Discussion*, Winter 2013, *https://www.vqronline.org/articles/*.

"Churchill's support for SOE": Stafford, David. *Churchill and Secret Service*. Lume Books, 2021, p. 188.

"God damn", "One of the most", "When I told Halifax": FDR, OSS Stephenson Boys file, pp. 7–8.

"Fiction of the law": FDR, OSS, the Structure of Ernie's Role file, pp. 5–6.

"Both they [Stephenson's BSC] and the Germans": ECM, Part 1–3, p. 1232.

"Own disposal squads": Gentry, Curt. *J. Edgar Hoover: The Man and the Secrets.* W. W. Norton & Company, 2001, p. 271.

"I remember things": Macdonald, Bill. *The True Intrepid: Sir William Stephenson and the Unknown Agents.* Timberholme Books, 1998, p. 298.

"Knocked off": Int. with H. Montgomery Hyde, "After Dark: British Intelligence," Open Media Production, Channel 4, 1988.

"They reached their long arm": U.S. Senate, Congressional Record: Proceedings and Debates of the… Congress, Vol. 87, Part 8, 1941, pp. 8497–8498.

CHAPTER 18

Joe Kennedy in Hollywood and "It would probably be advisable": Maier, Thomas. *When Lions Roar.* Crown, 2014, pp. 301–302.

"One of ex-ambassador": Logevall, Fredrik. *JFK: Coming of Age in the American Century, 1917–1956.* Random House, 2021, p. 307.

"Put the fear", "I suggest you", "I enclose" and Cuneo's dealings with Sandy Griffith and his deputy Francis Henson: Mahl, Thomas E. *Desperate Deception: British Covert Operations in the United States, 1939–44.* Potomac Books, 2000, pp. 82–101.

Campaign against Hamilton Fish: HYDE, p. 73.

"George Hill is 100%": "Not Fish, But Foul." *Time*, Jan. 26, 1942, p, 14.

"Where selfish": Yogerst, Chris. "When the US Government Went After Anti-Nazi Hollywood." *Los Angeles Review of Books*, Jul. 27, 2020.

"Nazi lover": Lovell, Mary S. *Cast No Shadow: The Life of the American Spy Who Changed the Course of World War II.* Pantheon Books, 1992, pp. 342–343.

"Do all that": BSC, p. 74.

"Senator X" and Winchell's "swastika swishery": RealClear Politics. "Politicians and Prostitutes," Mar. 4, 2013.

"One of the most despicable": Kirchick, James. "How World War II Led to Washington's First Outing," *Washington Post Magazine*, Jun. 15, 2022.

"All this and much more": BSC, p. 74.

"Actually, the British, wise in these matters", "Dunderheads": ECM, Part 1–3, p. 1232.

"Imagine it", "If Wheeler gets killed": Winchell, Walter, with introduction by Ernest Cuneo. *Winchell Exclusive*. Prentice-Hall, 1975, p. xiv.

"Extremely careful": ECM, Part 1–3, p. 1232.

PART III

"They say": Shakespeare, William. *Measure for Measure*. Cambridge University Press, 1991, p. 188.

"I'd put Stalin": Schlesinger, Arthur M., Jr. *A Life in the Twentieth Century: Innocent Beginnings, 1917–1950*. Houghton Mifflin Harcourt, 2000, p. 305.

CHAPTER 19

"An ominous buzzing": Effrat, Louis. "Tuffy Leemans Receives the Gifts, But Two Dodgers Steal Spotlight." *New York Times*, Dec. 8, 1941.

"To think that": HYDE, p. 192.

"It's a good thing": Waller, Douglas. *Wild Bill Donovan: The Spymaster Who Created the OSS and Modern American Espionage*. Free Press, 2012, p. 85.

"We are all in": Gilbert, Martin. *Winston S. Churchill: Finest Hour, 1939–1941*. Rosetta Books, 2015, p. 65.

"It is just": BSC, p. 75.

"Very few": Waller, Douglas. *Wild Bill Donovan: The Spymaster Who Created the OSS and Modern American Espionage*. Free Press, 2012, p. 90.

"Drew Pearson was absolute", "I knew what they could do": FDR, Against OSS and BSC file, pp. 11–12.

"Good evening, Mr. and Mrs. America": Gabler, Neal. *Winchell: Gossip, Power and the Culture of Celebrity*. Alfred A. Knopf, 1994, p. 303.

CHAPTER 20

"Assistant Secretary": Winchell, Walter, with introduction by Ernest Cuneo. *Winchell Exclusive*. Prentice-Hall, 1975, p. xii.

"An original Brainstruster": FDR, OSS and Stephenson Boys file, pp. 11–13.

"Instant historical computer", **"Fully familiar"**: ECM, Part 1–3, p. 353.

"The deathwatch": FDR, Against OSS and BSC file, p. 11.

"Full size secret": Troy, Thomas F. "Donovan and the CIA: A History of the Establishment of the Central Intelligence Agency." Approved for release April 2000 by the CIA, p. 83.

"He [Cuneo] gathers": Berle, Adolf A. *Navigating the Rapids, 1918–1971: From the Papers of Adolf A. Berle*. Harcourt Brace Jovanovich, 1973, p. 288.

"Bill has British Empire for breakfast": Brown, Anthony Cave. *The Last Hero: Wild Bill Donovan: The biography and political experience of Major General William J. Donovan, founder of the OSS and "father" of the CIA, from his personal and secret papers and the diaries of Ruth Donovan*. Vintage Books, 1984, p. 159.

"For your confidential": Mahl, Thomas E. *Desperate Deception: British Covert Operations in the United States, 1939–44*. Potomac Books, 2000, p.19.

"Without going": Brown, Anthony Cave. *C: The Secret Life of Sir Stewart Graham Menzies, Spymaster to Winston Churchill*. Macmillan, 1987, p. 368.

"Why should": Ibid., p. 391.

"All records": Persico, Joseph E. *Roosevelt's Secret War: FDR and World War II Espionage*. Random House, 2002, p. 173.

"I am impressed": Brown, Anthony Cave. *C: The Secret Life of Sir Stewart Graham Menzies, Spymaster to Winston Churchill*. Macmillan, 1987, p. 391.

"Get the dirt": Gentry, Curt. *J. Edgar Hoover: The Man and the Secrets*. W. W. Norton & Company, 2001, p. 268.

"Berle exhibited": FDR, OSS, the Structure of Ernie's Role file, pp. 7–8.

"A respectable front", **"Playing the piano"**, **"To get out"**, **"He asked me"**, **"I'd hate"**, **"No murders"**, **"In the end"**, **"Unquestionably"**: FDR, OSS, the Structure of Ernie's Role file, pp. 5–11.

"The effect": Brown, Anthony Cave. *C: The Secret Life of Sir Stewart Graham Menzies, Spymaster to Winston Churchill.* Macmillan, 1987, p. 393.

"Assistant Secretary": Pearson, Drew. "Washington Merry Go Round." *Los Angeles Daily News*, Dec. 1, 1942.

CHAPTER 21

"The Stork Club": Meacham, Jon. "The Man to Blame for Our Culture of Fame." *New York Times Book Review*, Apr. 26, 2017, p. 17.

"The Cub Room": ECM, Part 1–3, pp. 1120–1126.

"For God sakes", **"Women are"**: Winchell, Walter, with introduction by Ernest Cuneo. *Winchell Exclusive.* Prentice-Hall, 1975, pp. ix–x.

"It was Roosevelt's policy": Gabler, Neal. *Winchell: Gossip, Power and the Culture of Celebrity.* Alfred A. Knopf, 1994, p. 285.

"I was a mere ego": Pearson, Drew. "Washington Merry-Go-Round," syndicated column in *Fulton Patriot*, Dec. 5, 1940, p. 13.

"He [Winchell] was not promiscuous": Gabler, Neal. *Winchell: Gossip, Power and the Culture of Celebrity.* Alfred A. Knopf, 1994, p. 391.

"Fleming, though he": Fleming, Fergus, ed. *The Man with the Golden Typewriter: Ian Fleming's James Bond Letters.* Bloomsbury Publishing USA, 2015, pp. 74–91.

"Fleming came in": "British Security Coordination—1941 FDR Speech," *https://www.mygen.com.*

"Corkscrew thinking", **"Charming to be"**: Macintyre, Ben. *Operation Mincemeat: How a Dead Man and a Bizarre Plan Fooled the Nazis and Assured an Allied Victory.* Crown, 2010, p. 12.

"Long, medium and short": Fleming, Fergus, ed. *The Man with the Golden Typewriter: Ian Fleming's James Bond Letters.* Bloomsbury Publishing USA, 2015, p. 76.

"He knew everybody": Macdonald, Bill. *The True Intrepid: Sir William Stephenson and the Unknown Agents.* Timberholme Books, 1998, p. 278.

"British women": HYDE, p, 203; Goldstein, Richard. *Helluva Town: The Story of New York City During World War II.* Simon & Schuster, 2010, p. 48.

"A true broken love affair, "These are extremely deep loves": FDR, Ian Fleming-Correspondence and Miscellaneous file, p. 102.

"My father": Int. with Jonathan Cuneo.

"He was very charismatic": Int. with Sandra Cuneo.

"Dangle": Trahair, Richard. *Encyclopedia of Cold War Espionage, Spies, and Secret Operations.* Enigma Books, 2012, p. 461.

"I can't imagine": Int. with Sandra Cuneo.

CHAPTER 22

"Operation Pastorius": Trefousse, Hans L. "Failure of German Intelligence in the United States, 1935–1945." *Mississippi Valley Historical Review,* June 1955, Vol. 42, No. 1, pp. 84–100.

"There were plenty": Wighton, Charles, and Günter Peis. *They Spied on England: Based on the German Secret Service War Diary of General Von Lahousen.* Odhams Press, 1958, p. 196.

"Really believed": Trefousse, Hans L. "Failure of German Intelligence in the United States, 1935–1945." *Mississippi Valley Historical Review,* June 1955, Vol. 42, No. 1, pp. 84–100.

"The Abwehr gets better": Persico, Joseph E. *Roosevelt's Secret War: FDR and World War II Espionage.* Random House, 2002, p. 198.

"The idea for": Fritz, Mark. "Cloaked Business Newly Declassified Files Show How Allied Firms Dealt with Axis Through Cover of Other Companies." *Boston Globe,* Nov. 19, 2001, p. 1.

"Please make clear": Memo from William J. Donovan, declassified and released Oct. 18, 2013, *https://www.cia.gov/library/readingroom/.*

"Bill Donovan": Dunlop, Richard. "The Wartime OSS." *American Legion Magazine,* June 1984, p. 15.

"The new Nazi policy", "High officers of the SS": Memo from Brig. Gen. John Magruder, Deputy Director of OSS, Mar. 17, 1943.

"It has been requested": Grose, Peter. *Gentleman Spy: The Life of Allen Dulles.* University of Massachusetts Press, 1996, pp. 184–189.

"You are the one", "In the course of pillow talk": Srodes, James. *Allen Dulles: Master of Spies.* Regnery, 1999, pp. 268, 234.

"The apotheosis", **"An incredibly acute"**: Brown, Anthony Cave. *C: The Secret Life of Sir Stewart Graham Menzies, Spymaster to Winston Churchill.* Macmillan, 1987, p. 409.

"He was a great man": Whiting, Charles. *The Spymasters: The True Story of Anglo-American Intelligence Operations Within Nazi Germany, 1939–1945.* Saturday Review Press, 1976, p. 74.

"Did ask me": The Intelligence War in 1941: A 50th Anniversary Perspective: An Intelligence Monograph, Center for the Study of Intelligence (U.S.). Office of Training and Education, Central Intelligence Agency, 1992, p. 19.

"To stop short": Thomas, Gordon, and Greg Lewis. *Defying Hitler: The Germans Who Resisted Nazi Rule.* Penguin, 2019, p. 358.

CHAPTER 23

"Many normal folk": Oral history transcript, Ernest Cuneo, interview 2 (II), 4/23/1970, by Joe B. Frantz, LBJ Library Oral Histories, LBJ Presidential Library.

"Mr. President, is Bill": *Public Papers of the Presidents of the United States: F.D. Roosevelt, 1942, Volume 11.* Best Books, 1950, p. 466.

"Dear Grace": Persico, Joseph E. *Roosevelt's Secret War: FDR and World War II Espionage.* Random House, 2002, p. 249.

"The technology of subversion", **"Reproduce faultlessly"**: Pearson, John. *The Life of Ian Fleming.* Bantam, 1967, p. 115.

"Aunt Jemima": Dunlop, Richard. "The Wartime OSS." *American Legion Magazine*, June 1984, p. 15.

"The most brilliant": Dunlop, Richard. *Donovan: America's Master Spy.* Simon & Schuster, 2014, p. 309.

"I picked up", **"Well, put it"**: LaGumina, Salvatore J. "Ernest Cuneo, the Forgotten Brain Truster." *Italian American Review*, Jul. 1, 2021, Vol. 11, Issue 2, pp. 141–148.

"With certain friends": Brown, Anthony Cave. *The Last Hero: Wild Bill Donovan: The biography and political experience of Major General William J. Donovan, founder of the OSS and "father" of the CIA, from his personal and secret papers and the diaries of Ruth Donovan.* Vintage Books, 1984, pp. 159, 344.

"A strong aversion": Troy, Thomas F. "Donovan and the CIA: A History of the Establishment of the Central Intelligence Agency." Approved for release April 2000 by the CIA, p. 94.

"The Great Man, Churchill", "Come along, Ernie", "Are you, by any chance": HYDE, pp. 184–185.

"A very beautiful Carib girl": Morison, Samuel Eliot, and Mauricio Obregón. *The Caribbean as Columbus Saw It.* Little, Brown, 1964, p. 138.

"Cuneo's chest", "I was astonished", "A good friend of Britain": HYDE, pp. 185–186.

"Why, don't you": Lovell, Mary S. *Cast No Shadow: The Life of the American Spy Who Changed the Course of World War II.* Pantheon Books, 1992, p. 339.

"While I was in London": FDR, Against OSS and BSC file, p. 35.

"Why is the Prime Minister": Persico, Joseph E. *Roosevelt's Secret War: FDR and World War II Espionage.* Random House, 2002, p. 279.

"Deeply as I": FDR, Against OSS and BSC file, p. 36.

"The chaotic condition", "The only man": Churchill Archives, Char 20/121/125, image 1.

"I have great admiration": Churchill Archives, Char 20/122/6, image 1.

"The error of the Second Front": FDR, OSS and Stephenson file, p. 54.

"Iron Curtain": Applebaum, Anne. *Iron Curtain: The Crushing of Eastern Europe, 1944–1956.* Knopf Doubleday, 2012, p. 111.

CHAPTER 24

"I am invisible": Ellison, Ralph. *Invisible Man.* Vintage Books, 1972, p. 3.

"Mock Trial", "Hitlerism cannot destroy": Anthes, Louis. "Publicly Deliberative Drama: The 1934 Mock Trial of Adolf Hitler for 'Crimes against Civilization.'" *American Journal of Legal History,* October 1998, Vol. 42, No. 4, pp. 391–410.

"Cuneo shared": LaGumina, Salvatore J. "Ernest Cuneo, the Forgotten Brain Truster." *Italian American Review,* Jul. 1, 2021, Vol. 11, Issue 2, pp. 141–148.

"He encouraged me": Int. with Jonathan Cuneo.

"Over at Navy": FDR, OSS Stephenson Boys file, p. 16.

"I had watched": Cutrer, Thomas W., and T. Michael Parrish. *Doris Miller, Pearl Harbor, and the Birth of the Civil Rights Movement*. Texas A&M University Press, 2018, p. 22.

"Seldom have I": FDR, OSS Stephenson Boys file, p. 16.

"To a member": Miller biography, Naval History and Heritage Command, *https://www.history.navy.mil/*.

"Biddle, with calm": FDR, OSS Stephenson Boys file, pp. 16–18.

"When Dorie Miller": Cutrer, Thomas W., and T. Michael Parrish. *Doris Miller, Pearl Harbor, and the Birth of the Civil Rights Movement*. Texas A&M University Press, 2018, p. 89.

"The name of Dorie Miller": "We Agree with You, Walter Winchell." *Pittsburgh Courier*, Feb. 5, 1944, p. 1.

"When it came", "One of the most heartless", "The Attorney General", "The news convulsed": FDR, OSS Stephenson Boys file, pp. 16–18.

"He [Winchell] called upon", "It's a ten-strike", "There is much": FDR, OSS and Stephenson file, pp. 43–44.

"Nazi espionage chiefs": Walter Winchell FBI File, Part 19, p. 30.

"Doll Woman": FBI Biography, "Velvalee Dickinson, the 'Doll Woman,'" *https://www.fbi.gov/history/famous-cases/velvalee-dickinson-the-doll-woman*.

"One finds it": Soldiers, Vol. 42, Department of the Army, 1987.

"Is, to use", "He was in the pay": Walter Winchell FBI File, Part 19, p. 4.

"Advised that apparently", "He [Rogge] stated that": Memorandum for Mr. Ladd, Dec. 20, 1943, Walter Winchell FBI File, Part 19 of 58.

"Thereafter I functioned": FDR, Against OSS and BSC file, p. 32.

CHAPTER 25

"I won't have cowards": Donald, Ralph, and Karen MacDonald. *Reel Men at War: Masculinity and the American War Film*. Scarecrow Press, 2011, p. 164.

"There were some": Patton, George Smith, Paul Donal Harkins, and Beatrice Ayer Patton. *War as I Knew It*. Houghton Mifflin Harcourt, 1995, p. 381.

"Old Blood and Guts": Royle, Trevor. *Patton: Old Blood and Guts.* Weidenfeld & Nicolson, 2005, p. 1.

"His manner was extrovert": Keegan, John, ed. *Who's Who in World War II.* Routledge, 2002, p. 119.

"Nervous", "I guess I can't take it": Atkinson, Rick. *The Day of Battle: The War in Sicily and Italy, 1943–1944.* Macmillan, 2008, p. 147.

"You mean that you are malingering here?": Patton, George Smith, Paul Donal Harkins, and Beatrice Ayer Patton. *War as I Knew It.* Houghton Mifflin Harcourt, 1995, p. 381.

"You may get shot": Whiting, Charles. *Patton.* Random House, 1976, p. 44.

"Pearson was the great American gadfly": ECM, Part 1–3, p. 50.

"Starting a lifelong": Treglown, Jeremy. *Roald Dahl: A Biography.* Harvest, 1995, p. 136.

"We were the closest": Mahl, Thomas E. *Desperate Deception: British Covert Operations in the United States, 1939–44.* Brassey's, 1998, p. 49.

"To penetrate": BSC, p. 129.

"Of course, Hoover": HYDE, p. 140.

"Pearson, who had no scruples", "He had a goatish": BSC, pp. 131, 128.

"Viciously attacking", "Feuding and crusading": *Time,* 1939, Vol. 34, p. 45.

"Most sensational testimony": *Editor & Publisher,* 1941, Vol. 74, p. 30.

"Would like to see Russia bled white", "He is frequently guilty": *Time,* 1943, Vol. 42, pp. 19, 20.

"About the conduct": Lovelace, Alexander G. "The Image of a General: The Wartime Relationship between General George S. Patton Jr. and the American Media." *Journalism History,* Summer 2014, Vol. 40, Issue 2, pp. 108–120.

"A bit too bloody": Ritchie, Donald A. *The Columnist.* Oxford University Press, 2021, p. 56.

"The General's crime": *Time,* 1943, Vol. 42, Part 2, p. 65.

"It seemed as": Totten, Ruth Ellen Patton. *The Button Box: A Daughter's Loving Memoir of Mrs. George S. Patton.* University of Missouri Press, 2005, p. 333.

"If the fate": Ritchie, Donald A. *The Columnist.* Oxford University Press, 2021, p. 56.

CHAPTER 26

"Spies? Yes": Dahl, Roald. *Charlie and the Chocolate Factory: The Golden Edition.* Penguin, 2021, p. 15.

"You could sit": Sturrock, Donald. *Storyteller: The Authorized Biography of Roald Dahl.* Simon & Schuster, 2011, p. 216.

"Assistant President", "You're a flying chap": Conant, Jennet. *The Irregulars: Roald Dahl and the British Spy Ring in Wartime Washington.* Simon & Schuster, 2008, pp. 63, 356; Wallace, Henry. "Our Job in the Pacific," Issue 12, American Council, Institute of Pacific Relations, 1944.

"Marsh in his political naïveté": Sturrock, Donald. *Storyteller: The Authorized Biography of Roald Dahl.* Simon & Schuster, 2011, p. 216.

"The emancipation of colonial subjects": Walton, Richard J. *Henry Wallace, Harry Truman and the Cold War.* Viking, 1976, p. 23.

"I said bluntly", "He said if", "British policy clearly": Wallace, Henry Agard, and John Morton Blum. *The Price of Vision: The Diary of Henry A. Wallace, 1942–46.* Houghton Mifflin, 1973, pp. 208–210.

"The most intimate": FDR, Against OSS and BSC file, p. 59.

"I thought, my goodness": Conant, Jennet. *The Irregulars: Roald Dahl and the British Spy Ring in Wartime Washington.* Simon & Schuster, 2009, p. 121.

"I quickly phoned", "Cataclysms of wrath", "Don't be a child": Sturrock, Donald. *Storyteller: The Authorized Biography of Roald Dahl.* Simon & Schuster, 2011, pp. 216–217.

"Donovan's organization": BSC, p. 26.

"What this meant": Cuneo, Ernest. "The Russian Anaconda." *American Legion Magazine,* April 1980, p. 12.

"They go up", "What the hell": Sturrock, Donald. *Storyteller: The Authorized Biography of Roald Dahl.* Simon & Schuster, 2011, p. 227.

"A killer with women": Conant, Jennet. *The Irregulars: Roald Dahl and the British Spy Ring in Wartime Washington.* Simon & Schuster, 2009, p. 98.

"I hope to be": Sturrock, Donald. *Storyteller: The Authorized Biography of Roald Dahl.* Simon & Schuster, 2011, p. 233.

"I am all fucked out", "Roald, did you see", "Well," Halifax continued, "do you remember": Conant, Jennet. *The Irregulars: Roald Dahl and the British Spy Ring in Wartime Washington.* Simon & Schuster, 2009, pp. 120–121.

"I was able", "Good morning", "Bleeding this information": Sturrock, Donald. *Storyteller: The Authorized Biography of Roald Dahl.* Simon & Schuster, 2011, pp. 228–229.

"He is a nice boy", "Of the 20 German saboteurs": Wallace, Henry Agard, and John Morton Blum. *The Price of Vision: The Diary of Henry A. Wallace, 1942–46.* Houghton Mifflin, 1973, p. 492.

"I came to regard": Brown, Anthony Cave. *C: The Secret Life of Sir Stewart Graham Menzies, Spymaster to Winston Churchill.* Macmillan, 1987, p. 484.

"Frequently made speeches", "The highly idealistic Wallace": 1945 FBI memo, Henry Wallace File, p. 138, Section 1, *https://vault.fbi.gov.*

"The Russians had subtly wormed": FDR, Against OSS and BSC file, p. 68.

"Quite interesting": Persico, Joseph E. *Roosevelt's Secret War: FDR and World War II Espionage.* Random House, 2002, pp. 344–345.

"Roosevelt has undertaken to Party": BSC, p. 220.

"Wallace has temporarily": Sturrock, Donald. *Storyteller: The Authorized Biography of Roald Dahl.* Simon & Schuster, 2011, p. 218.

"A British officer": BSC, p. 220.

"Wallace has set": A letter of A. A. Gromyko to the USSR Foreign Affairs Commissar V. M. Molotov, dated Jul. 14, 1944. Document no. 244 in "Sovetsko-amerikanskie Otnosheniya, 1939–1945" [Soviet-American Relationships: 1939–1945] (Moscow: Materik, 2004), pp. 539–555 (in Russian); a letter of A. A. Gromyko to V. M. Molotov, dated Jul. 24, 1944. Document no. 246 in ibid., pp. 559–561.

"I hope it will be": Lelyveld, Joseph. *His Final Battle: The Last Months of Franklin Roosevelt.* Knopf Doubleday, 2017, p. 162.

"Declared that he", "Goldbricking": FDR, Against OSS and BSC file, p. 38.

"Was naturally": HYDE, p. 193.

"As WS learned", "It's unbelievable": BSC, p. 222.

"Would be branded": HYDE, p. 193.

CHAPTER 27

"I may no longer shield": Wagner, Richard, and Oliver Huckel. *The Valkyrie: A Dramatic Poem.* Thomas Y. Crowell & Co., 1909, p. 60.

"I must express", "I look beyond": HYDE, p. 177.

"This is certainly": William Stephenson's Nov. 15, 1944, letter to William Donovan, approved for release by CIA in 2001, Special Collection, *https://www.cia.gov/readingroom/.*

"Our best intelligence source": Dulles, Allen. *The Secret Surrender.* Harper & Row, 1966, p. 22.

"It was like a comedy", "This could be", "I hate the Nazis", "We can hardly divine": Ibid., pp. 11–20.

"First important penetration": Brown, Anthony Cave. *The Last Hero: Wild Bill Donovan: The biography and political experience of Major General William J. Donovan, founder of the OSS and "father" of the CIA, from his personal and secret papers and the diaries of Ruth Donovan.* Vintage Books, 1984, p. 280.

"An intelligence service": Dulles, Allen. *Germany's Underground.* Macmillan, 1947, p. 70.

"I put it up": Baigent, Michael, and Richard Leigh. *Secret Germany: Stauffenberg and the True Story of Operation Valkyrie.* Skyhorse Publishing, 2008, p. 195.

"The elimination of HITLER": Lee, Eric. *Britain's Plot to Kill Hitler: The True Story of Operation Foxley and SOE.* Greenhill Books, 2022, p. 70.

"To him, a victory": Gisevius, Hans Bernd. *To the Bitter End.* Houghton Mifflin,1947, p. xiv.

"Today an attempt": Jones, Nigel. *Countdown to Valkyrie: The July Plot to Assassinate Hitler.* Frontline Books, 2008, p. 216.

"Long live sacred": Fest, Joachim. *Plotting Hitler's Death: The Story of German Resistance.* Macmillan, 1997, p. 278.

"Positive attitude": Mueller, Michael. *Canaris: The Life and Death of Hitler's Spymaster.* Casemate Publishers, 2017, p. v.

"This is the end": Bartz, Karl. *The Downfall of the German Secret Service.* William Kimber & Co., 1956, p. 189.

"It was a cogent": BSC, p. 126.

"Soft peace peddlers": Winchell, Walter, syndicated column, Dec. 8, 1944. "Humanity vs. the German people," BSC, p. 126.

CHAPTER 28

"We'd be looking": Polinsky int. in "OSS in Action The Mediterranean and European Theaters," *https://www.nps.gov/articles/oss-in-action-the-mediterranean-and-european-theaters.htm.*

"Surprise, kill and vanish": Hagerman, Bart. *U.S.A. Airborne: 50th Anniversary, 1940–1990.* Turner Publishing, 1990, p. 353.

"There is something": Alsop, Stewart. *Stay of Execution: A Sort of Memoir.* Lippincott, 1973, p. 129.

"Dear Winston": *Life,* Oct. 29, 1951, p. 88.

"Harking back": HYDE, p. 188.

"We ought to die", "I'll read it later": Waller, Douglas. *Wild Bill Donovan: The Spymaster Who Created the OSS and Modern American Espionage.* Free Press, 2011, p. 239.

"You understand, David": Ibid., p. 245.

"But suppose": Bruce, David K. E., and Nelson D. Lankford. *OSS Against the Reich: The World War II Diaries of Colonel David K. E. Bruce,* Kent State University Press, 1991, p. 220.

"This was an arrangement": HYDE, p. 225.

"In the field": *Life,* Nov. 19, 1945, Vol. 19, No. 21, p. 122.

"Having just returned", "All these various": Dunlop, Richard. *Donovan: America's Master Spy.* Rand McNally, 1982, p. 440.

"As usual": Churchill Archives, Char 20/141a/69, image 2.

"I have always been": "Military Intelligence." U.S. Army Intelligence Center & School, 1984, p. 13.

CHAPTER 29

On October 19, 1944: Details of presidential diary records from "Day by Day" project of the Pare Lorentz Center at the FDR Presidential Library.

"I entered the Oval Room": ECM, p. 29.

"He reminded me", "As I glimpsed" and other details of Oval Office exchange: FDR, Stephenson British Intelligence file, pp. 26–30.

PART IV

"I am afraid": Conrad, Joseph. *Collected Works of Joseph Conrad, Volume 9.* Doubleday, 1925, p. 146.

"Among the increasingly intricate arsenals": Lathrop, Charles E. *The Literary Spy.* Yale University Press, 2008, p. 205.

CHAPTER 30

"I found myself", "I realized": Bentley, Elizabeth. *Out of Bondage.* Devin-Adair Company, 1951, p. 287.

"With the advent": Houghton, Vince. *The Nuclear Spies: America's Atomic Intelligence Operation against Hitler and Stalin.* Cornell University Press, 2019, p .7

"Float away into an ecstasy": Bentley, Elizabeth. *Out of Bondage.* Devin-Adair Company, 1951, p. 101.

"She may damage us": Olmsted, Kathryn S. *Red Spy Queen: A Biography of Elizabeth Bentley.* University of North Carolina Press, 2003, p. 94.

"For some time, Cedric": Bentley, Elizabeth. *Out of Bondage.* Devin-Adair Company, 1951, p. 202.

"Given the unprecedented": Andrew, Christopher, and Vasili Mitrokhin. *The Mitrokhin Archive: The KGB in Europe and the West.* Allen Lane, 1999, p. 146.

"Certain things": West, Nigel. *Cold War Spymaster: The Legacy of Guy Liddell, Deputy Director of MI5.* Frontline Books, 2018; quoted in Corera, Gordon. "Cedric Belfrage, the WW2 spy Britain was embarrassed to pursue." *BBC News*, Aug. 21, 2015, *https://www.bbc.com/news/uk-34012395*, which included Philby's quote about Belfrage's career.

"I sensed an end run", "I asked him": FDR, Against OSS and BSC file, p. 31.

"I wrote the appraisal": FDR, Stephenson British Intelligence file, p. 22; FDR, Crusader to Intrepid file, p. 92.

"You have put": Letter Sept. 28, 1945, from William Donovan to Duncan Lee, approved by CIA for release June 8, 2011, *https://www.cia.gov/readingroom/docs/DOC_0005657670.pdf.*

"Never divulged": Lee testimony in Hearings Regarding Communist Espionage in the U.S. Government: 80th Congress, Jul. 31–Sept. 9, 1948, p. 723.

"All of the agent information": Persico, Joseph E. *Roosevelt's Secret War: FDR and World War II Espionage.* Random House, 2002, p. 294.

"Something very secret": Elizabeth Bentley testimony in Hearings Regarding Communist Espionage in the U.S. Government: 80th Congress, Jul. 31–Sept. 9, 1948, p. 728.

"American Gestapo": Troy, Thomas F. "Donovan and the CIA: A History of the Establishment of the Central Intelligence Agency." Approved for release April 2000 by the CIA, p. 280.

"A few youthful": Gentry, Curt. *J. Edgar Hoover: The Man and the Secrets.* W. W. Norton & Company, 2001, p. 265.

"Russia will emerge": McCullough, David. *Truman.* Simon & Schuster, 2003, p. 456.

"I am afraid": Treglown, Jeremy. *Roald Dahl: A Biography.* Harvest, 1995, p. 318.

CHAPTER 31

"Through the keyhole": Gouzenko, Igor. *This Was My Choice.* Eyre & Spottiswoode, 1948, p. 318.

"Any criticism": Ibid., p. 221.

"He left some documents": Ibid., p. 319.

"Heaven sent opportunity": Molinaro, Dennis. "How the Cold War Began…with British Help: The Gouzenko Affair Revisited." *Labour/Le Travail*, Spring 2017, Printemps, Vol. 79, pp. 143–155.

"Even as we dismantled": Cuneo, Ernest. "The Russian Anaconda." *American Legion Magazine*, April 1980, p. 12.

"The Gouzenko revelations": Molinaro, Dennis. "How the Cold War Began…with British Help: The Gouzenko Affair Revisited." *Labour/Le Travail*, Spring 2017, Printemps, Vol. 79, pp. 143–155.

"Stephenson immediately realized": HYDE, p. 230.

"It must not be written": Gilbert, Martin. *Churchill and America.* Simon & Schuster, 2005, p. 362.

"The story of what": Carleton University. Centre for Research on Canadian-Russian Relations. *The Gouzenko Affair: Canada and the Beginnings of Cold War Counter-Espionage.* Penumbra Press, 2006, p. 139.

"It marks": FDR, Stephenson British Intelligence file, p. 24.

"After consultation": Whitaker, Reg, and Gary Marcuse. *Cold War Canada: The Making of a National Insecurity State, 1945–1957.* University of Toronto Press, 1994, p. 60.

"I did not give it": FDR, OSS and Stephenson file, p. 14.

"The biggest story": Ritchie, Donald A. *The Columnist.* Oxford University Press, 2021, p. 83.

"The Soviet penetration": Whitaker, Reg, and Gary Marcuse. *Cold War Canada: The Making of a National Insecurity State, 1945–1957.* University of Toronto Press, 1994, p. 60.

"Bill Stephenson worked himself": HYDE, preface by Ian Fleming, p. xi.

"Mr. President, there is": Gentry, Curt. *J. Edgar Hoover: The Man and the Secrets.* W. W. Norton & Company, 2001, p. 344.

"There is no explaining away": Craig, R. Bruce. *Treasonable Doubt: The Harry Dexter White Spy Case.* University Press of Kansas, 2004, p. 261.

"It is not so generally known": HYDE, p. 235.

"I wrote a little bit of crap": Sturrock, Donald. *Storyteller: The Authorized Biography of Roald Dahl.* Simon & Schuster, 2011, p. 244.

"We had to improvise": Report on Interviews with Sir William S. Stephenson, in Paget, Bermuda, Feb. 11–15, 1969, released by CIA May 1, 2002, *https://www.cia.gov/readingroom/docs/CIA-RDP78-03087A000100030069-6.pdf.*

"When the full story": HYDE, p. 1.

"This one is dear": Lovell, Mary S. *Cast No Shadow: The Life of the American Spy Who Changed the Course of World War II.* Pantheon Books, 1992, p. 344.

"Before leaving New York", "If Mr. Churchill should wish": Churchill Archives, CHUR 2/230A-B, 03 Oct 1945–07 Aug 1946.

CHAPTER 32

"Tim was not sure": Vidal, Gore. *The Golden Age*. Doubleday, 2000, p. 41.

"Insisted on a second front": FDR, Against OSS and BSC file, p. 5.

"Stalin was looking": Cuneo, Ernest. "The Russian Anaconda." *American Legion Magazine*, April 1980, p. 12.

"Gave him very rough": FDR, Against OSS and BSC file, p. 32.

"Drew Pearson's article is a specimen": Churchill Archives, Char 20/170/77-78.

"We became": Conant, Jennet. *The Irregulars: Roald Dahl and the British Spy Ring in Wartime Washington*. Simon & Schuster, 2008, p. 146.

"On this critical point": ECM, Part 1–3, p. 1129.

"The Commies": FDR, Crusader to Intrepid file, p. 109.

"This is the truth": Gabler, Neal. *Winchell: Gossip, Power and the Culture of Celebrity*. Alfred A. Knopf, 1994, p. 378.

"He was a Broadway": FDR, Against OSS and BSC file, p. 7.

"Did not conceive": Ibid., pp. 53–56.

"This impending war": Ibid., pp. 70–71.

"Outright", "Drew just couldn't": FDR, Crusader to Intrepid file, p. 97.

"Impersonation investigation", "He liked David Karr personally": FBI Vault File, Henry Wallace, Part 04 of 05, *https://vault.fbi.gov*.

"In a last desperate", "I never hated to fight": FDR, Crusader to Intrepid file, pp. 98–99.

"He's like a man": Pearson, Drew. "Washington Merry-Go-Round," syndicated column, Dec. 11, 1948.

"Cuneo is frank", "I think the real reason": Pearson, Drew. "Washington Merry-Go-Round," syndicated column, Feb. 19, 1974.

CHAPTER 33

"We almost suffered emotional", "Bill Stephenson was gone", "No, Ernie", "It's a ballet": Fleming, Fergus, ed. *The Man with the Golden Typewriter: Ian Fleming's James Bond Letters*. Bloomsbury Publishing USA, 2015, pp. 76–89.

"He took elaborate steps", **"I couldn't bear"**: Pearson, John. *The Life of Ian Fleming.* Bantam, 1967, p. 84.

"War has been", **"You say this is the best horse"**: FDR, Ian Fleming file, (Folder 2 of 2), pp. 13–20.

"Dear Walter": Cuneo, Ernest 1939–1968, Walter Winchell Papers, Briscoe Center for American History, University of Texas at Austin.

"I thought you might": Benson, Raymond. *The James Bond Bedside Companion.* Dodd, Mead & Co., 1984, p. 42.

"I thought it would": Pearson, John. *The Life of Ian Fleming.* Bantam, 1967, p. 186.

"She [West] sees a Communist", **"Turkish sandwich"**, **"As [Alfred] Kinsey could"**: Fleming, Fergus, ed. *The Man with the Golden Typewriter: Ian Fleming's James Bond Letters.* Bloomsbury Publishing USA, 2015, pp. 78–81.

"When we have won", **"The clues"**: Macintyre, Ben. *For Your Eyes Only: Ian Fleming and James Bond.* Bloomsbury, 2008. pp. 147, 89.

"A Japanese cipher expert cracking", **"James Bond is"**: HYDE, preface by Ian Fleming, pp. x–xi.

"They have tough windows": Fleming, Ian. *Casino Royale.* Penguin Books, 1953, p. 134.

"Dreadful oafish opus", **"If you get a chance"**: Pearson, John. *The Life of Ian Fleming.* Bantam, 1967, pp. 206, 223.

CHAPTER 34

"Fleming was at this time": Fleming, Fergus, ed. *The Man with the Golden Typewriter: Ian Fleming's James Bond Letters.* Bloomsbury Publishing USA, 2015, pp. 76–89.

"We were halfway": Benson, Raymond. *The James Bond Bedside Companion.* Dodd, Mead & Company, 1984, p. 10.

"I would love to see Las Vegas": Ibid., p. 82.

"Off we go", **"Fleming was entranced"**: Fleming, Fergus, ed. *The Man with the Golden Typewriter: Ian Fleming's James Bond Letters.* Bloomsbury Publishing USA, 2015, pp. 54, 84.

"After being a bachelor for 44 years": Ibid., p. 9.

"By almost any count": Benson, Raymond. *The James Bond Bedside Companion*. Dodd, Mead & Company, 1984, p. xii.

"What came to Bond's mind": Fleming, Fergus, ed. *The Man with the Golden Typewriter: Ian Fleming's James Bond Letters*. Bloomsbury Publishing USA, 2015, pp. 76–89.

"Fleming never killed", **"Knocked unconscious"**: FDR, Ian Fleming file, (Folder 2 of 2), pp. 59–60.

"You missed the point": Fleming, Fergus, ed. *The Man with the Golden Typewriter: Ian Fleming's James Bond Letters*. Bloomsbury Publishing USA, 2015, p. 85.

"And a damned nuisance": Lycett, Andrew. *Ian Fleming*. St. Martin's Press, 2013, p. 263.

"We send a car": FDR, Ian Fleming file, (Folder 2 of 2), p. 34.

"Captain, Mr. Fleming": Lycett, Andrew. *Ian Fleming*. St. Martin's Press, 2013, p. 265.

"Have you ever": FDR, Ian Fleming file, (Folder 2 of 2), p. 32.

"Ian used a lot", **"Figure it out"**, **"To Ernie"**: Fleming, Fergus, ed. *The Man with the Golden Typewriter: Ian Fleming's James Bond Letters*. Bloomsbury Publishing USA, 2015, p. 84.

CHAPTER 35

"You must know": Amis, Kingsley. *The James Bond Dossier*. New American Library, 1965, p. 9.

"He sent me": Fleming, Fergus, ed. *The Man with the Golden Typewriter: Ian Fleming's James Bond Letters*. Bloomsbury Publishing USA, 2015, p. 87.

"Here's the Sands": Fleming, Ian. *Diamonds Are Forever*. Penguin, 2002, p. 131.

"We've got": Ibid., p. 120.

"He enjoyed using the names": Bryce, Ivar. *You Only Live Once: Memories of Ian Fleming*. Orion Publishing, 1975, p. 94.

"Like all writers": Ibid., p. 93.

"If the quality": Buckton, Oliver S. *Espionage in British Fiction and Film since 1900: The Changing Enemy*. Lexington Books, 2015, p. 18.

"Were able to take a man's", "I think it is very friendly": FDR, Ian Fleming file, pp. 73–75.

"The war just": Macintyre, Ben. *For Your Eyes Only: Ian Fleming and James Bond.* Bloomsbury, 2008, p. 89.

"Scribbled off": Benson, Raymond. *The James Bond Bedside Companion.* Dodd, Mead & Company, 1984, p. 25.

"Just the right degree": Lycett, Andrew. *Ian Fleming.* St. Martin's Press, 2013, p. 350.

"Ernest Cuneo is mentioned": FDR, Ian Fleming file, (Folder 1 of 2), p. 101.

"As you know producers": Fleming, Fergus, ed. *The Man with the Golden Typewriter: Ian Fleming's James Bond Letters.* Bloomsbury Publishing USA, 2015, p. 289.

"The man they have chosen": Ibid., p. 257.

"This is all true": Macintyre, Ben. *For Your Eyes Only: Ian Fleming and James Bond.* Bloomsbury, 2008, p. 93.

CHAPTER 36

"I wish to note": Memo dated Jun. 27, 1954, from Allen Dulles to Inspector General, CIA approved release on Mar. 11, 2004, *https://www.cia.gov/readingroom/.*

"McCarthy, a psychopathic alcoholic": FDR, Against OSS and BSC file, pp. 64–65.

"You did a wonderful": Treglown, Jeremy. *Roald Dahl: A Biography.* Harvest, 1995, p. 418.

"I consider him": FDR, OSS and Stephenson file, p. 71.

"Presentations": Senate testimony of Carl Marzani, Interlocking Subversion in Government Departments: Hearing Before the Subcommittee to Investigate the Administration of the Internal Security Act and Other Internal Security Laws, 83:1-2, Apr. 10, 1953 through 1954, p. 895.

"Ridicule, chiefly": Pearson, John. "Rough Rise of a Dream Hero." *Life,* Oct. 14, 1966, p. 124.

"Here is a book": Dulles, Allen. "Our spy-boss who loved Bond." *Life,* Aug. 28, 1964, p. 19.

"Jack Kennedy, professing": Benson, Raymond. *The James Bond Bedside Companion*. Dodd, Mead & Company, 1984, p. xii.

"Kennedy gave", "An experiment", "Ludicrous depictions": Klady, Leonard. "007: Bonding Fact and Fiction." *Los Angeles Times*, Jul. 26, 1987.

"The expert on Joe Kennedy", "I was closer": Pearson, Drew. *Washington Merry-Go-Round: The Drew Pearson Diaries, 1960–1969*. University of Nebraska Press, 2015, p. 609.

"We spent most": Ibid., p. 66.

"Sorry about old Trujillo": FDR, Ian Fleming file, (Folder 1 of 2), p. 93.

"Nonpartisan", "the growing Castro-Communist": Kihss, Peter. "44 in U.S. Establish Committee to Fight Communism in Cuba." *New York Times*, May 6, 1963, p. 1.

"There was never a Bond": FDR, Ian Fleming file, (Folder 2 of 2), pp. 70–71.

"I'll keep this entirely quiet": LBJ Library, Telephone conversation #155, sound recording, LBJ and Allen Dulles, 11/29/1963.

"A lengthy article", "He stated that Allen Dulles": FBI memo from C. D. DeLoach, Jun. 23, 1964, Weisberg Archive, Hood College.

"Assassination of the President": FBI memo from C. D. DeLoach, Dec. 2, 1963, Weisberg Archive, Hood College.

"Book of the week type", "Judge Tamm stated", "Cuneo has interviewed": FBI memo from J. Edgar Hoover, Jun. 22, 1964, Weisberg Archive, Hood College.

"Ludicrous health", "These are now": FDR, Ian Fleming file (Folder 1 of 2), p. 93.

"Suffered a great deal", "Most of all": FDR, Ian Fleming file, (Folder 2 of 2), p. 108.

"Of course, he loved": Int. with Ivar Bryce, John Pearson Papers, Indiana University, p. 21.

"A knight out of phase": O'Keefe, David. *One Day in August: Ian Fleming, Enigma, and the Deadly Raid on Dieppe*. Icon Books, 2020, p. 28.

CHAPTER 37

"It would be absolutely intolerable": Churchill, Winston S., and Robert Rhodes James. *Winston S. Churchill: His Complete Speeches, 1897–1963: 1908–1913.* Chelsea House Publishers, 1974, p. 1562.

"It is obvious": Atkinson, Brooks. "Theatre: Little Flower Blooms Again; 'Fiorello!' Begins Run at the Broadhurst." *New York Times,* Nov. 24, 1959, p. 45.

"I did give him": Nichols, Lewis. "Musical Biography." *New York Times* (Drama section), Nov. 22, 1959, p. 3.

"When people think of Italians": Lambert, Philip. *To Broadway, To Life!: The Musical Theater of Bock and Harnick.* Oxford University Press, 2010, p. 67.

"My only aim": Cuneo, Ernest. *Life with Fiorello.* Macmillan, 1955, p. xiv.

"The manuscript as it stands": FDR, Ian Fleming file, p. 26.

"Fiorello really was": Cuneo, Ernest. *Life with Fiorello.* Macmillan, 1955, p. 201.

"I actually think": Cuneo, Ernest 1939–1968, Walter Winchell Papers, Briscoe Center for American History, University of Texas at Austin.

"The only man": Winchell, Walter, with introduction by Ernest Cuneo. *Winchell Exclusive.* Prentice-Hall, 1975, p. xv.

"The beginning of the end", "The silence of the phones": Gabler, Neal. *Winchell: Gossip, Power and the Culture of Celebrity.* Alfred A. Knopf, 1994, pp. 412, 525.

"Historians will": Kaufman, Marjorie. "Seeking the Roots of a Celebrity Society." *New York Times,* Dec. 11, 1994, p. 41.

"Winchell became the firepoint": Gabler, Neal. *Winchell: Gossip, Power and the Culture of Celebrity.* Alfred A. Knopf, 1994, p. 291.

"For a year or so": HYDE, p. 238.

"Put his files", "His experience and knowledge": Ibid., p. xiii.

"If it had not", "Dynamic link": Ibid., p. 244.

"Only the removal": HYDE, foreword by Ian Fleming, p. x.

"But it did accomplish": BSC, p. xvi.

"For some men": le Carre, John. "England's Spy in America." *New York Times,* Feb. 29, 1976, p. 215.

"Sir William", "There can be no doubt": Naftali, Timothy J. "Intrepid's Last Deception: Documenting the Career of Sir William Stephenson" inside *Espionage: Past, Present, Future?* edited by Wesley K. Wark, Cass Series: Studies in Intelligence, Frank Cass & Company Ltd., 1994, pp. 72–99.

"I did not read": FDR, OSS and Stephenson file.

"My war record is obscure": Macdonald, Bill. *The True Intrepid: Sir William Stephenson and the Unknown Agents.* Timberholme Books, 1998, p. 393.

CHAPTER 38

"We all think our own secrets": Fleming, Ian. *Goldfinger.* Macmillan, 1959, p. 46.

"Stoicism does not": Int. with Sandra Cuneo.

"My mother did not keep a diary": Int. with Jonathan Cuneo.

"First met her husband": Margaret Watson Cuneo obituary. *New York Times*, Aug. 17, 1976, p. 34.

"Margaret always loved you": 1976 letter from Ernest Cuneo.

"It is considered a great disgrace": Thomas Corcoran Papers, Library of Congress, Box 123, Folder 7, p. 65.

"He was just fantastic": Field, Matthew. "Bond Bibles—Raymond Benson," Nov. 23, 2021, *https://www.mi6-hq.com.*

"The warmest kind", "I thought I knew": Benson, Raymond. *The James Bond Bedside Companion.* Dodd, Mead & Company, 1984, pp. xi–xiii.

"Without whose assistance": Troy, Thomas F. "Donovan and the CIA: A History of the Establishment of the Central Intelligence Agency." Approved for release April 2000 by the CIA, p. 83.

"Hell, you shouldn't have told them [the FBI] that": Batvinis, Raymond J. *Hoover's Secret War against Axis Spies.* University Press of Kansas, 2014, p. 299.

"My first assignment": FDR, OSS and Stephenson file, p. 51.

"A man named Ellis": West, Nigel. *Historical Dictionary of International Intelligence.* Rowman & Littlefield, 2015, p. 111.

"Vast quantities": Dalrymple, James. "Newly published SS handbook gives blueprint for Nazi Britain." *The Independent*, Mar. 3, 2000.

"Philby's name is synonymous with treachery": "'A Spy Among Friends' dramatises the treachery of Kim Philby." *The Economist*, Dec. 14, 2022.

"Ellis denied everything", **"Ellis was a venal, sly man"**: Wright, Peter. *Spycatcher: The Candid Autobiography of a Senior Intelligence Officer.* Viking, 1987, p. 329.

"Ellis had spied": Pincher, Harry Chapman. *Their Trade is Treachery: The full, unexpurgated truth about the Russian penetration of the world's secret defences.* Biteback Publishing, 2014, p. 203.

"As a spy for the Germans": West, Nigel. *At Her Majesty's Secret Service: The Chiefs of Britain's Intelligence Service, MI6.* Frontline Books, 2016, p. 69.

"If the charge": Cuneo quoted in Mahl, Thomas E. *Desperate Deception: British Covert Operations in the United States, 1939–44.* Brassey's, 1998, p. 19.

"Scorn the idea", **"In this vale of tears"**: FDR, Dick Ellis file; pp. 1–5.

"Animator": Fowle, Farnsworth. "Medical Group From Italy Opens Meeting Here." *New York Times*, Sept. 24, 1963.

"Ernie's Gang", **"Vowed to correct"**: Hart, M. Cordell. "A Patriot: Ernest L. Cuneo." Association of Former Intelligence Officers website.

"Truly a modern": Schaer, Sidney C. "E.L. Cuneo, 82, Roosevelt Adviser." *Newsday*, Mar. 4, 1988, p. 37.

"His line was always": Personal letter written by executive assistant in the Henry M. Jackson Foundation, FDR, Condolences Letters file, Box 163, p. 21.

"The largest, most intricate": Vidal, Gore. *The Last Empire: Essays 1992–2000.* Knopf Doubleday Publishing, 2002, p. 131.

"Ernest L. Cuneo, 82; Owned News Service": *New York Times*, Mar. 5, 1988, p. 33.

"It's one of the most amazing": Int. with Jonathan Cuneo.

"She looked me up out of the blue", **"Beats the hell out of me"**: Int. with Sandra Cuneo and Eliza Nascarella.

INDEX